World Economics Association

Book Series

Volume 12

Capital and Justice

Titles produced by the World Economics Association & College Publications

Volume 2:
Finance as Warfare. Michael Hudson
Volume 3:
Developing an Economics for the Post-crisis World. Steve Keen
Volume 4:
On the Use and Misuse of Theories and Models in Mainstream Economics. Lars Pålsson Syll
Volume 5:
Green Capitalism. The God that Failed. Richard Smith
Volume 6:
40 Critical Pointers for Students of Economics. Stuart Birks
Volume 7:
The European Crisis. Victor Beker and Beniamino Moro, eds.
Volume 8:
A Philosophical Framework for Rethinking Theoretical Economics and Philosophy of Economics. Gustavo Marqués
Volume 9:
Narrative Fixation in Economics. Edward Fullbrook
Volume 10:
Ideas Towards a New International Financial Architecture. Oscar Ugarteche, Alicia Payana and Maria Alejandra Madi, eds
Volume 11:
Trumponomics. Causes and Consequences. Edward Fullbrook and Jamie Morgan, eds.
Volume 1:2
Capital and Justice. Gerson P. Lima and Maria Alejandra Madi, eds

The **World Economics Association (WEA)** was launched on May 16, 2011. Already over 13,000 economists and related scholars have joined. This phenomenal success has come about because the WEA fills a huge gap in the international community of economists – the absence of a professional organization which is truly international and pluralist.

The World Economics Association seeks to increase the relevance, breadth and depth of economic thought. Its key qualities are worldwide membership and governance, and inclusiveness with respect to: (a) the variety of theoretical perspectives; (b) the range of human activities and issues which fall within the broad domain of economics; and (c) the study of the world's diverse economies.

The Association's activities centre on the development, promotion and diffusion of economic research and knowledge and on illuminating their social character.

The WEA publishes 20+ books a year, three open-access journals *(Economic Thought, World Economic Review* and *Real-World Economics Review)*, a bi-monthly newsletter, blogs, holds global online conferences, runs a textbook commentaries project and an eBook library.

www.worldeconomicassociation.org

Capital and Justice

Edited by
Gerson P. Lima
and
Maria Alejandra Madi

ISBN 978-1-84890-247-3 print
ISBN 978-1-911156-36-9 eBook-PDF

Published by College Publications (London) on behalf of the World Economics Association (Bristol)

http://www.worldeconomicsassociation.org
http://www.collegepublications.co.uk

Cover design by Laraine Welch
Printed by Lightning Source, Milton Keynes, UK

Acknowledgements

We are grateful to the World Economics Association for giving us the opportunity to lead an online conference on *Capital Accumulation, Production and Employment: Can we bend the arc of capitalism toward justice?* (http://capital2016.weaconferences.net/) and to develop this book from it.

We benefitted from many of the open comments that the conference attracted and we would like to thank the following contributors to the debate: *John Vandenberg, Eugen Wagner, Richard Mochelle, Doug Carmichael, Stephen I. Ternyik, Paul Zarembka, Harish Yadav, Dominic Tweedie, Gerry Tone, Mohinder Kumar, Stefania Perna, Gentilucci Eleonora, Basudeb Sen, Adrian de Leon Arias, Jerome Joffe, Raymond Aitken, David Harold Chester, Marco Saba, Grazia Ietto-Gillies, John Vandenberg, Worku R. Urgaia, Deniz Kellecioglu, Rubens Sawaya and Fernando de Almeida Martins.*

A special thanks to Malgorzata Dereniowska and Jake McMurchie for all their support during the Conference organization and through the Discussion Forum.

Gerson P. Lima and Maria Alejandra Madi (Editors)

Contents

Preface

Peter Radford

The arc of capitalism begins, as does that of democracy, in the great upheaval of the hundred years or so either side of the mid 1700s. It was then that both our modern economy and our modern polity began to take shape.

That early search for liberty with its attendant overthrow of the old order comprising various combinations of monarchic, aristocratic and religious repression propelled society out of its long torpor and into what we now consider its perpetual change. Freedom to decide for ourselves, to determine our different trajectories through life, to escape the prior certitude of social station and aspire to being something else, and, ultimately, to embrace our own role in government, all contrived to produce the tumult we now experience.

Back then freedom was a multifaceted phenomenon. It was a complex of different and ultimately conflicting objectives. Looking at early protagonists of liberty we find that some called for freedom for commerce, for the protection of the rights of private property owners, and for the right to engage in trade unfettered by restrictions placed upon them in the name of the state. The motivation of profit ran strongly through this version of liberty. Others were focused more on ridding themselves of arbitrary rule by some traditionally privileged person or group. Their objective was the right of self-government and the right to play a role in the affairs of state. They sought to define citizenship and recognized that society ought to be an assemblage of equals.

Liberty was thus a conflation of assertions of individuality and a redefinition of the collective. The polity was to become "we the people" and the economy was to become the domain of individuals free to trade however they saw fit. The advocates of this primitive liberty, the founders of our modern social landscape, were intensely bourgeois. They saw no need to extend the franchise much beyond themselves, indeed they abhorred the notion of universal suffrage which they imagined would lead to instability and poor government. Yet they asserted, within their narrow confines, new ideas of citizenship, of responsibility, of egalitarian pride in self-government, and in the potential of great wealth hidden in the realm of more free markets.

All these things: the rights and responsibilities of citizenship, the egalitarian nature of self-government untainted by privilege, and the possibility of growing wealthy from trade, were tied together in that early call for liberty. Society was to be re-conceived and there was a sense of inherent justice in the new balance thus achieved.

Capitalism was born in this call, so too was democracy. In our more modern terms there was an equality between the free economy and the free polity. There was a basic sense of justice in the balance between the two. Neither was meant to dominate the other. Not one anticipated the consequences of freedom. On the contrary political freedom and economic freedom were thought to be indistinguishable. Being bourgeois was to be free.

Then came industrialization. Then came the satanic mills. Then came the great migration from agriculture. Then came urbanization. Then came the realization that the true polity ought extend beyond a narrowly defined limit, that suffrage ought be extended, and that we the people actually meant all, and not just a select few of the people. Modern democracy thus slowly emerged as a more true expression of the egalitarian ideal. Along the way it displaced more radical alternatives as the accepted way of assuring that the voices of all the people were heard when matters of state were discussed. There was a sense of justice in this evolution. That justice was in the preservation of an idea of equality of citizenship being integral to liberty.

Meanwhile capitalism surged forward and followed a different path. It was given intellectual protection by early advocates of liberty precisely because of their conflation of freedom of commerce with freedom of citizenship. They radically misunderstood, or simply failed to comprehend, the tension that capital accumulation could, and would, bring to bear on society. They willfully overlooked, as they do to this day, that liberty stands on more than

2

one leg, and that failing to recognize the legitimacy of equality of citizenship as a separate concept from that of freedom to trade, introduces the certainty that society is eventually stripped of justice.

Freedom of trade unconstrained by its companion equality of citizenship necessarily tends towards its own negation. It remains capitalism, but it is no longer free. It eventually simply substitutes a new aristocracy for the old, with the basis of privilege in the newer form being accumulation of capital rather than in the more abstract ancient beliefs in divine or heritably conferred power.

Since its beginnings, critics of capitalism have misunderstood its resiliency. They have predicted its demise many times and from many causes. We have been told variously that overproduction, under-consumption, the supposed tendency of profit to fall, the saturation of needs, the exhaustion of resources, a stagnation in technological innovation, the emergence of oligopoly control of markets, and a bureaucratic suppression of entrepreneurial spirit, would all eventually bend the arc of capitalism towards its doom. All these claims have elements of truth, none of the predictions have been correct. Instead capitalism has shown itself capable of adapting even in the midst of what looks like crisis. Indeed it seems that capitalism requires chaos in order to thrive.

In its latest incarnation, neoliberal capitalism, it has survived by drastically redefining citizenship, and by thus bringing into disrepute and decay our institutions of democracy. It has tried, and nearly succeeded, in claiming that the only social justice available to us is that inherent in the freedom to trade. Other forms, so goes the claim, are actually infringements on that freedom so great that we ought be vigilant and avoid them. Government, even by and for the people, can only do damage to the creation of collective wealth. So government is to be demeaned. It is to be slandered.

This disingenuous and perverse division of justice is designed simply to serve narrow interests: the oligopolists who now control our state. And it has brought us to this critical moment. We are living through not a crisis of capitalism, but through a crisis of democracy.

Capital and Justice

Somewhere in the debris of our current discontent sits the remnants of that democracy. Capitalism appears to have undermined it to the extent that it scarcely functions any longer. Our political discourse is monotonic, expressed as it is inside the framework of market based thought, shareholder value, and the perpetual pursuit of profit. There is no opposition along the corridors of power: our erstwhile parties of the left long ago were co-opted into the neoliberal enterprise. They nowadays are shadows of what was once a heartfelt alternative to the capitalist monolith. So talk of social justice, of the inequities of the distribution of our prosperity, and of decrying the steady ossification of the social structures that once provided opportunity for most of our fellow citizens is met with ribald criticism.

We are reminded of the great enrichment society has experienced these past hundred or more years, and that even our most poor are well off relative to their ancestors of only a few generations ago. We are scolded that to imagine a socially more just distribution of this cornucopia is simply to be envious. We are told that there are great and inevitable forces that produce our economic outcomes, and these forces are resisted at too great a cost to our overall welfare. We are lectured about the dangers of intrusion by governments into the pristine waters of the marketplace. We are reminded that redistribution is a form of "theft" of the "just" accumulation of wealth by those whose contributions to our collective welfare is, in the warped definition, more valuable than ours.

To sum up, we are led to understand that democracy itself is inseparable from the free operation of the marketplace, that it is best conflated within it, and that trying to resurrect other ideas of social justice is both wasteful and counterproductive. In this version of reality democracy is nested within capitalism and cannot, or ought not, stand alone. The freedom to trade has engulfed the freedom based upon equality of citizenship. Profit is privileged over work and capital over labor, thus bifurcating citizenship into those who are presumed to have "succeeded" and those who are presumed to have "failed".

This is a perversion of history. It defies any well-grounded understanding of freedom. It is an error of horrible consequence. And it deserves to be fought with all our energy.

Preface

The freedom to trade, which has inarguably brought us great wealth, is inseparable from an equality of citizenship, which is the right to determine how that wealth is distributed. Both legs of freedom must be strong for either to stand. Neither stands alone. But they cannot be confused. They act as constraints on each other. If one fails or is undermined, then both fall and all possibility of a long lasting social justice is swept away.

It is our current task to re-assert and re-build democracy, to bend the act of capitalism back towards justice and to bring society back from the brink where it sits so uncomfortably close to perpetual injustice. This task is urgent.

And so we must begin.

Peter Radford, Vermont, December 2016

Part I
Introduction

Setting the scene

Maria Alejandra Madi and Gerson P. Lima

In the new millennium, the proliferation of financial assets, with economic growth limited and sporadic, has given way to widespread unemployment, income gaps and weaker welfare programs. The same policies that have obliterated social services and kept labour cheap have supported the expansion of new global business models and financial deepening. Besides, the onset of the new millennium represents a new political age where the social, economic and political significantly violates democratic ideals of political equality and social peace. Indeed, *democracy has been allowing for election to office but not to power* (Madi, 2015). Politicians and policy makers have given priority to their sponsors instead of to society urgent challenges, and political decisions have been influenced by the top 1 percent who turned out to favour policies of increasing inequality.

Taking into account evidence from the USA, Fullbrook warns "American democracy has become a sham. It still maintains the trappings of democracy, but in reality it is a system of government controlled by the richest 1 percent of its citizens" (Fullbrook, 2011). Stiglitz elaborates the same; in his opinion, much of current inequality is due to the manipulation of rules in the financial industry: "The government lent money to financial institutions at close to 0 percent interest and provided generous bailouts on favorable terms when all else failed" (Stiglitz, 2011).

In truth, given that central banks' shareholders are in the top 1 percent, the global economy, or at least the world's number one economy, has been commanded by their specific interests. Page, Bartels and Seawright (2013) inform that the top 1 percent or so of US wealth-holders "... are extremely active politically and much more conservative than the American public as a whole with respect to important policies concerning taxation, economic regulation, and especially social welfare programs." Moreover, the top one-tenth of 1 percent of wealth holders may tend to hold still more conservative views. Their conclusion is that these contrasting views about the economic policy may explain why some public policies in the United States seem to contradict the expectations of the majority of US citizens. And, considering that policy makers may give priority to their sponsors instead of to the people, the resultant economic policy will significantly violate democratic ideals of political equality.

Considering the specific interests that command policymaking, Michael Hudson (2015) remembers that, "The financial sector has the same objective as military conquest: to gain control of land and basic infrastructure, and collect tribute. To update von Clausewitz, finance has become war by other means." Actually, public debt crises suggest the possibility that the objective of main creditors is to raise rent by forcing governments to borrow, and forcing them to pay by relinquishing public property or people's income. In Hudson's words, "debt-strapped nations permit bankers and bondholders to dictate their laws and control their planning and politics". Indeed, the power of wealth holders to drive the economy and to impose deleterious effects on the working conditions must be seriously considered.

Moreover, the impacts of globalization need to be re-conceptualized in the contours of the current global accumulation dynamics where the relationship among nation states and capital flows has created a new policy and business framework where profits derive from tight working conditions, low nominal wages and changing labor contracts. Indeed, within contemporary capitalist societies, the expansion of global finance has favoured the expansion of financial assets, capital mobility and short term investment decisions – increasingly subordinated to rules of portfolio risk management. In this scenario, changes in production have been based on competitiveness and corporate governance criteria.

The current trends in capital accumulation and production have shaped a scenario where unemployment job instability and fragile conditions of social protection increased (Stiglitz, 2011). First, labour-saving technologies have reduced the demand for many middle-class, blue-collar jobs. Second, globalization has created a global marketplace, confronting expensive unskilled workers with cheap unskilled workers overseas and implementing outsourcing practices. Third, social changes have also played a role in the labor market changes, such as the decline of unions. Four, political decisions are influenced by the top 1 percent who privileged policies that increase income inequality.

Piketty (2014) has also acknowledged the relevance of wealth and income inequality and highlighted that in the current economic scenario there is no general tendency towards greater economic equality and inequality within generations has remained vastly greater than it used to be. In truth, the relatively high degree of equality seen after the Second World War was partly a result of deliberate policy, especially progressive taxation, but even more a result of the destruction of inherited wealth, particularly within Europe, between 1914 and 1945. Nowadays, in Europe, a "patrimonial capitalism" – the world dominated by inherited wealth – of the late 19th century is being slowly re-created; while in the U.S, the rise of the "super-managers" could help to explain why the richest 1 percent appropriated 60 percent of the increase in US national income between 1977 and 2007.

As Ruccio (2015) points out, since the global crisis, the American recovery has been mainly related to corporate profits and incomes for the 1 percent. And in spite of the expansion of profits, they have not been invested. As a matter of fact, he says: "while profits (especially from domestic sources) continue to grow, corporations are using those profits not for investment, but for other uses, including stock buybacks, mergers and acquisitions, and CEO salaries".

Indeed, both business investment and consumer spending have slowed down and private investment remains lower than before the 2007/8 crisis. As Stiglitz (2011) highlighted, the current policy rules encourage "competition among countries for business". This competition drives down taxes on corporations and weakens environmental protections. In addition to the recent global changes in working conditions, the competition among nations undermines fundamental core labor rights, including the right to collective bargaining. In this setting, consumer spending has been mainly influenced by the stagnation of most people's incomes after the 2008 credit crisis.

Unfortunately, without changes in capital accumulation and production, automation and technological unemployment will also increase inequality. It is worth recalling Stephen Hawking's words: "If machines produce everything we need, the outcome will depend on how things are distributed." Indeed, given that the machine-produced wealth may be evenly shared, or concentrated in the machine-owners small group, the technological trend seems to drive an "ever-increasing inequality" (Ruccio, 2015a).

In truth, all these questions reflect issues of current power, politics and economics in a social context where democratic institutions are being threatened. Taking into account this reality, Peter Radford (2015) highlights that: "Unfortunately America has, for four decades or so, bent over backwards to privilege capitalism over democracy. The result is the ongoing economic crisis that we continue to live through." Therefore, considering the current social and economic challenges, it is required that the creation of wealth be democratically compelled to build the foundation for employment, income equality and social cohesion.

The book

This book is an outcome of the 2016 World Economics Association Online Conference *"Capital Accumulation, Production and Employment: Can We Bend the Arc of Global Capital?"* that called for a reflection on the increasing challenges to support an ethically defensible approach to working conditions and the organizers collected interesting contributions in this direction.

The selected papers have been organized in three parts. After the introduction, Part II, "Global economics dynamics", opens with the contribution of Richard C. Koo. His chapter elucidates what has been missing in economics in the last decades and what changes are needed to make the profession relevant for the society again. Recalling his own words: "The failure of the vast majority of economists in government, academia and markets to predict the post-2008 Great Recession and its severity is raising a serious credibility issue for the economics profession."

Setting the scene

Koo states that the discipline of macro-economics, which was started in the late 1940s, covered in its short history only half of the total phases an actual economy may encounter. The overlooked other-half, however, contained many key determinants of economic growth that have been either taken for granted or conveniently assumed away in traditional economics. Considering this background, the purpose of Koo's contribution is to elucidate what was missing in economics all along and what changes are needed to make the profession relevant for the society again. In order to understand how we got from the centuries of economic stagnation to where we are today where economic growth is taken for granted, Koo believes that we need to review certain basic facts about the economy and how it operates.

Chapter 2 presents Arturo Hermann's contribution to the analysis of tendency of effective demand to lag behind the supply of full employment in the context of financialization. In his view, the role of effective demand has been perhaps put a bit in the background in the explanation of current economic imbalances. He addresses the main aspects of Keynes's theory of effective demand and analyze more in detail the role of public spending and credit creation in sustaining effective demand and profits for the entrepreneurs. After emphasizing the negative role of income and wealth concentration on effective demand, Hermann develops the analysis of some structural features that may contribute to render more complexity to the dynamics of effective demand, such as labour productivity and environmental sustainability.

Taking into account that financialization enhances the redistribution and reallocation of power and wealth, Chapter 3, written by Maria Alejandra Madi, assesses, from a Keynesian approach, that the private equity funds' business model foster social vulnerabilities. After presenting a brief overview of global business environment and the post-crisis evolution of private equity funds, Madi discusses the factors that shape the microeconomic and macroeconomic effects of their typical investment strategies. In truth, the social impacts of the private equity business model based on "rationalization" have been less explored by academic researchers, while extensive studies have been developed by private sector companies and industry bodies that tend to report only stories of success. This chapter highlights that the private equity expansion involves *social* relations driven by profit and competition in a context characterized by increasing labour challenges. The financial practices of the private equity funds are, in truth, mechanisms that promote the expansion of the global financial markets with decisive effects on wealth, income growth and working conditions. Today, private equity funds express the power of centralized money to define not only investment flows but also working conditions. Private equity funds have been responsible for the employment standards of tens of millions of workers worldwide and the impacts of private equity investments on working conditions is raising growing concerns. Considering this scenario, analysis rethinks the relations between private equity funds and labour as involving new forms of production at the current frontier of global capital expansion.

Part III, "Globalization: winners and losers", opens with C.R. Yadu and B. Satheesha's contribution that aims to analyze the trends in wealth inequality in the state of Kerala, India and the policy alternative. The authors highlight the effects of financialization on living conditions where land is found to be the most important asset that determines the household's wealth status. The analysis focuses the social outcomes of current capital accumulation dynamics and reveals the economic, social and political tensions between privileged caste groups and historically deprived groups.

The contribution of Lyn Eynon, in Chapter 5, recalls for the need to re-think political strategies in order to face current social and economic challenges. Eynon reminds the British election in September 2015 of the socialist MP Jeremy Corbyn as leader of the Labour Party that came as a profound shock to the British political establishment. The author explains the background to Labour's electoral defeat and Corbyn's subsequent victory, then discusses economic policy before briefly considering what we should learn for campaigning and narratives. The author investigates the underpinnings of the emerging programme and its potential to "bend the arc of global capital towards justice" on issues such as investment, taxation or wages, discussing the UK in the international context of the aftermath of the financial crash. Central to that will be an alternative approach for managing public finances to the austerity of the Conservative government aiming at fiscal surpluses, but the discussion on the "New Economics" goes well beyond macroeconomic policy into questions such as innovation, inequality and the labour market. At issue, Eynon analyses the practical problem of defining a realistic programme offering genuine progress in contemporary Britain, with sufficient credibility to attract both electoral backing and active support against hostility from global elites. There are lessons and questions here that go beyond the British Labour Party.

Part IV, "Economic, justice and democracy", firstly presents John Komlos's contribution on unemployment and justice. The chapter is based on the ideas of political philosopher John Rawls and suggests that in a just economy full employment would have to go beyond the implications of NAIRU. Rawls argues that the just economy is one which would be created behind a veil of ignorance, that is to say, without knowing where we would end up in the society's distribution of talent and other attributes. After a reflection about the mistaken "nature" of the natural rate of unemployment and the current organization of the labor market, the author presents a proposal to restructure the labor market and reduce unemployment down to the minimum feasible rate – which in the U.S. is most likely around 1.2 percent, the rate which prevailed in 1944 and which probably represents the lower bound attainable. His point of departure is that the right to work needs to be recognized as a natural right, because the right to life depends upon it.

Also critical of mainstream economics, Gerson P. Lima, in Chapter 7, presents an attempt to build the foundations of a modern version of an old theory, with the aid of an experiment, aiming to suggest a starting point to the development of a real world economic theory reliable enough to replace the contemporaneous monetarist mainstream doctrine and to "Bend the Arc of Global Capital Toward Justice". Taking into account the current debates on democracy and economic policy, Lima assumes that the contemporaneous monetarist mainstream economics is not qualified to explain what is going on, to tame financial markets, to avoid crises and to provide a concrete solution to the poor and deteriorating situation of the largest portion of the world population. Many people are asking for and expecting a new economics, a real world economic science. These are the reasons for this essay to propose a new approach to economics. In Lima's view, democratization of the economic policy involves a political action, but this action requires a new economic theory that may replace the present monetarist mainstream autocratic economics. In short, the chapter aims at giving a potential first step in this direction presenting a new version of Marshall and Keynes's statements aiming at fixing the real world notion of demand and supply in order to especially demonstrate that the monetarist monetary policy harms society.

Expanding the monetary and financial challenge, the last chapter, written by Marc Morgan-Milá, investigates the link between capital, nationality and state sovereignty, both historically and in the context of our current globalized world. The author also challenges the conventional viewpoint that capital has no nationality, which implies limited state sovereignty with regards to fiscal policy and developmental strategies. The author argues that while capital does not properly ascribe to a de jure nationality, it has always had a de facto nationality that follows the nationality of the capitalist, as testified by the history of economic policy and decision-making. But the political-economy paradigms within which this nationality has been manifested have changed over time and so have the tools for states to preserve their sovereignty. In the current environment of advanced information technology, fiscal competition and an increasing presence of tax havens, the chapter aims to evaluate various proposals to give capital a *de jure* nationality for the benefit of state sovereignty in the 21st century.

In truth, the book called for a deep examination of current power, politics and economics in a social context where democratic institutions are being threatened. This attempt involved critical thinking of theories of justice in light of applied challenges: What kind of justice should we bend the arc of global capital to? What are justice conditions and criteria, given the concern about capital accumulation, employment, and production?

References

Fullbrook, E. (2011) Of the 1%, by the 1%, for the 1%. *RWER Blog*, April 13 Available at https://rwer.wordpress.com/2011/04/13/%E2%80%9Cof-the-1-by-the-1-for-the-1%E2%80%9D-joseph-e-stiglitz (Accessed on March 4, 2016) https://rwer.wordpress.com/2011/04/13/%E2%80%9Cof-the-1-by-the-1-for-the-1%E2%80%9D-joseph-e-stiglitz/

Hudson, M. (2015) *Finance as warfare*. UK: WEA Books.

Setting the scene

Madi, M. A. (2013) Ethics and Economics, *WEA Pedagogy Blog*, November 10. Available at https://weapedagogy.wordpress.com/2013/11/10/ethics-and-economics/ (Accessed on March 4, 2016)

Madi, M. A. (2015) 2016: Promises and Problems. *WEA Pedagogy Blog*, December 29. Available at: https://weapedagogy.wordpress.com/2015/12/29/2016-promises-and-problems/ (Accessed on March 4, 2016)

Page, B. I., Bartels, L. M. and Seawright, J. (2013) Democracy and the Policy Preferences of Wealthy Americans. *Perspectives on Politics*, 11 (01), March, pp. 51-73.

Piketty, T. (2014) *Capital in the 21ˢᵗ century*, Harvard University Press.

Radford, P. (2015) Quote: Capitalism. *RWER Blog*, September 28. Available at https://rwer.wordpress.com/2015/09/28/quote-capitalism (Accessed on March 4, 2016)

Ruccio, D. F. (2015) 6 and 1/2 years into the "recovery". *RWER Blog*, November 5. Available at https://rwer.wordpress.com/2015/12/05/6-and12-years-into-the-recovery-but-little-has-been-recovering-except-corporate-profits-and-incomes-for-the-1-percent/ (Accessed on March 4, 2016)

Ruccio, D. F. (2015a) Capitalism and technology and Stephen Hawking. *RWER Blog*, October 19. Available at: https://rwer.wordpress.com/2015/10/19/capitalism-and-technology-and-stephen-hawking (Accessed on March 4, 2016)

Stiglitz, J. (2011) Of the 1%, by the 1%, for the 1%. *Vanity Fair Magazine*, April 30. Available at: http://www.vanityfair.com/news/2011/05/top-one-percent-201105. (Accessed on March 4, 2016)

Part II
Global economic dynamics

Chapter 1

The other half of macroeconomics and three stages of economic development

Richard C. Koo

1. Introduction

The discipline of macroeconomics, which was started in the late 1940s and based on the assumption that private sector is maximizing profits, covered in its short history only half of the total phases an actual economy may encounter. The overlooked other half, where private sector may be minimizing debt, contained many factors that explain why economies stagnate, why much-touted policies of quantitative easing and zero or even negative interest rates failed to produce expected results. With the lack of economic growth and wage growth becoming a major issue in most advanced countries, it is time for the economics profession to leave its comfort zone and face the other half of macroeconomics head on.

The failure of the vast majority of economists in government, academia and the markets to predict either the post-2008 Great Recession or the degree of its severity is raising serious credibility issues for the economics profession. The widely varying opinions of these "experts" on how this recession should be overcome, together with the repeated failures of central banks and other policymakers to meet their inflation or growth targets, are making the public and political leaders rightfully suspicious of economists. This paper seeks to elucidate what was missing in economics all along and what changes are needed to make the profession relevant for economic challenges of today.

Human progress is said to have started when civilization sprung up in China, Egypt and Mesopotamia over 5,000 years ago. With the Renaissance, which began in Europe in the 13th century, people accelerated their search for both a better understanding of the physical world and better government. But for centuries that progress affected only those few who had enough to eat and time to think about worldly affairs. Life for the masses was not that much better in the 18th century than in the 13th century when the Renaissance began. Thomas Piketty (2014) in his well-known book *Capital in the 21st Century* indicated that economic growth in those centuries averaged only 0.1 percent per year – basically a standstill. In order to understand how we got from centuries of economic stagnation to where we are today, when economic growth is taken for granted, we need to review certain basic facts about the economy and how it operates.

Basic macroeconomics: someone's expenditure is someone else's income

One person's expenditure is someone else's income. It is this unalterable linkage between the expenditures and incomes of millions of thinking households and businesses that makes the study of economy both interesting and unique. More specifically, it means that at a national level, if someone is saving money, someone else must be borrowing and spending those funds to keep the economy running. If everybody tries to save and no one is borrowing, all of the saved funds will leak out of the economy's income stream, resulting in less and less income for everybody.

For example, if a person with an income of $1,000 decides to spend $900 and save $100, the $900 that is spent is already someone else's income, which means it is already circulating in the economy. Typically, the $100 that he saved would be deposited with a financial institution such as a bank, which would then lend it to someone else who could use the money. When that person borrows and spends the $100, the total expenditure in the economy equals $900 plus $100, which is the same as the original income of $1,000, and the economy moves forward.

In a normal economy, this function of matching savers and borrowers is performed by the financial sector, with interest rates moving higher or lower depending on whether there are too many or too few borrowers. If there are too many borrowers for the saved funds, interest rates will go up and some of those borrowers will drop out. If there are too few borrowers, interest rates will come down and prompt potential borrowers who stayed on the sidelines to step forward.

The government also has two types of policy, known as monetary and fiscal policy, to help stabilize the economy by matching private-sector savings and borrowings. Of the two, the most frequently mobilized is the central bank's monetary policy, which involves raising or lowering interest rates to reinforce the matching process. Since a state of too many borrowers is usually associated with a strong economy, a higher policy interest rate might be appropriate to prevent overheating and inflation. Similarly, a state of too few borrowers is usually associated with a weak economy, in which case a lower policy rate might be appropriate to avert a recession or deflation.

In fiscal policy, on the other hand, the government itself borrows and spends money to build infrastructure such as highways and airports. Compared with monetary policy, which can be decided very quickly by the central bank governor and his or her associates, fiscal policy tends to be very cumbersome in a democracy during peacetime because of the need for elected representatives to agree on how much to borrow and where to spend the money. Because of the political nature of these decisions and the time it takes to implement them, most recent economic fluctuations were dealt with using monetary policy.

The paradox of thrift as a macroeconomic phenomenon

Now that we have covered the basics, consider an economy in which everyone wants to save but no one wants to borrow even at near-zero interest rates. There are at least two major possibilities for such a situation to arise. The first possibility arises when private-sector businesses cannot find investment opportunities that would pay for themselves. After all, the private sector will not borrow unless it believes it can pay back the debt with interest. And there is no guarantee that such opportunity is always available.

In the second set of circumstances, private-sector borrowers sustain huge losses and are forced to rebuild savings or pay down debt to restore their financial health. Such a situation may arise following the bursting of a nationwide asset price bubble in which a large part of the private sector participated with borrowed funds. When the bubble bursts, such borrowers are left with huge liabilities but no assets to show for those debts. With a huge debt overhang, these borrowers have no choice but to pay down debt or increase savings regardless of the level of interest rates in order to restore their financial health.

If there are no borrowers for the saved $100 in the above example, the total expenditure of the economy drops to $900 while the saved $100 remains in financial institutions or under mattresses. This means the economy has shrunk 10 percent, from $1,000 to $900. That $900 is now someone else's income. If that person decides to save 10 percent and there are still no borrowers, only $810 would be spent, shrinking the economy even further to $810. The economy will then contract to $730 if borrowers continue to absent themselves. This is what is called a deflationary spiral.

The $100 that is left in the financial sector could still be shifted among various asset classes. It could even create mini-bubbles from time to time. But without real-economy borrowers, it will not be able to support transactions that add to GDP.

The contractionary process does not continue forever, since the savings-driven leakages from the income stream are eliminated once people become too poor to save. For example, if a person can no longer save any money at all from an income of $500, that person will spend the entire $500. If the person receiving that $500 in income is in the same situation, that person will also spend the entire $500. The result is that the economy stabilizes at $500 in what we call a depression.

Keynes called this state of affairs, in which everybody wants to save but is unable to do so because nobody is borrowing, the paradox of thrift. It is a paradox because if everybody tries to save, the net result is that no one is able to save.

Disappearance of borrowers finally recognized after 2008

Until 2008, the economics profession considered this kind of contractionary equilibrium (the world of $500) brought about by a lack of borrowers to be an exceptionally rare occurrence – the only recent example was the Great Depression, which was triggered by the stock market crash in October 1929 and during which the US lost 46 percent of nominal GNP in the process described above. Although Japan fell into a similar predicament when its real estate bubble burst in 1990, its lessons were almost completely ignored by the economics profession until the Lehman shock of 2008.[1]

Economists failed to consider the case of insufficient borrowers because when macroeconomics was developing as a separate academic discipline starting in the 1940s, investment opportunities for businesses were plentiful as new "must-have" household appliances ranging from washing machines to televisions were invented one after another. With businesses trying to start or expand production of these new products, there were plenty of borrowers in the private sector and interest rates were quite high, at least in comparison with the post-2008 world.

With borrowers never in short supply, economists' emphasis was very much on the availability of savings and the use of monetary policy to ensure that businesses got the funds they needed at interest rates low enough to enable them to continue investing. Economists also disparaged fiscal policy – i.e., government borrowing and spending – when inflation became a problem in the 70s because they were worried the public sector would squander the private sector's precious savings on largely inefficient pork-barrel projects.

During this period, economists also assumed the financial sector would make sure that all saved funds are borrowed and spent, with interest rates moving higher when there are too many borrowers relative to savers and adjusting lower when there are too few. This assumed automaticity is the

---

[1] One exception is the National Association of Business Economists in Washington, D.C., which awarded its Abramson Award to the author's paper, titled "The Japanese Economy in Balance Sheet Recession," which was published in its journal *Business Economics* in April 2001.

reason why most macroeconomic theories and models developed prior to 2008 contained no financial sector.

The advent of the Great Recession starting in 1990 for Japan and in 2008 for the West, demonstrated, however, that private-sector borrowers can disappear altogether in spite of zero or negative interest rates when faced with daunting financial problems following the bursting of a debt-financed bubble. In post-1990 Japan and the post-2008 Western economies borrowers disappeared completely due to the following sequence of events described below.

To begin with, people tend to leverage themselves up in an asset price bubble in the hope of getting rich quickly. But when the bubble bursts and asset prices collapse, these people are left with huge debts and no assets to show for them. With their balance sheets underwater, these people have no choice but to pay down debt or rebuild savings to restore their financial health.

For businesses, negative equity or insolvency implies the potential loss of access to all forms of financing, including trade credit. In the worst case, all transactions must be settled in cash, since no supplier or creditor wants to extend credit to an entity that may seek bankruptcy protection at any time. In order to safeguard depositors' money, many depository institutions such as banks are also prohibited by government regulations from extending or rolling over loans to insolvent borrowers. For households, negative equity means savings they thought they had for retirement or a rainy day are no longer there.

Since these conditions are very dangerous, both businesses and households will focus on restoring their financial health regardless of the level of interest rates until they feel safe again. With survival at stake, businesses and households are in no position to borrow even if interest rates are brought down to zero. There will not be many lenders either, especially when the lenders themselves have balance sheet problems. That means these households, businesses and financial institutions are effectively in debt minimization mode instead of the usual profit maximization mode.

The other half of macroeconomics

No name for recession driven by private sector minimizing debt

Although it may come as a huge shock to non-economist readers, the economics profession have never considered this type of recession driven by private-sector debt minimization until very recently. Economists simply ignored the whole concept of financial health or the need to restore it when building their macroeconomic theories and models because they assumed the private sector is always maximizing profits. But for the private sector to be maximizing profits, two conditions must be met. First, it has to have a clean balance sheet. Second, there must be attractive investment opportunities. By assuming that the private sector is always maximizing profits, economists assumed, mostly unconsciously, that both of the two conditions are met. And those two conditions were largely met for over 50 years – until bubbles burst in Japan in 1990 and in the West in 2008.

When that happened, a surplus of borrowers not only disappeared suddenly, but many of those borrowers started paying down debt even with record low interest rates. Flow-of-funds data show US private sector has been saving (which includes debt repayments), on average, 5.9% of GDP since the third quarter of 2008, Spain's private sector 7.3%, Ireland's 8.6%, and Portugal's 4.6%. In view of ultra-low interest rates businesses and households should be borrowing massively, but instead they have been saving massively to repair their balance sheets. And they will not start borrowing again until they feel comfortable with their financial health.

Yet economists continue to assume that there are many borrowers because that assumption is built into their models and theories. Because that assumption is no longer valid in the post-bubble world, their forecasts for growth and inflation based on those same models and theories have completely missed the mark. Moreover, because the assumption of a profit-maximizing private sector is so fundamental to their theories, most economists failed to suspect that their models are failing because this basic assumption about private-sector behavior is no longer warranted.

The economics profession not only neglected to consider the type of recession brought about by a debt-minimizing private sector, it never even had a name for the phenomenon. Indeed, the author had to come up with the name *balance sheet recession* in the late 1990s to describe this ailment, and the term is finally entering the lexicon of economics in the West in the wake of the 2008 collapse of Lehman Brothers and the subsequent global financial crisis. Economists' inability to understand that borrowers can actually disappear from the economy has already resulted in some very bad outcomes in modern history, including the Great Depression in the US and the rise of the National Socialists in Germany in the 1930s, as well as the emergence of similar groups in the Eurozone after 2008.

Paradox of thrift was the norm before industrial revolution

Looking further back in history, however, we can see that economic stagnation due to a lack of borrowers was much closer to the norm for thousands of years before the industrial revolution in the 1760s. As indicated in Figure1, economic growth had been negligible for centuries before that. There were probably many who were trying to save during this period of essentially zero growth, because human beings have always been worried about an uncertain future. Preparing for old age and the proverbial rainy day is an ingrained aspect of human nature. But if it is only human to save, the centuries-long economic stagnation prior to the industrial revolution must have been due to a lack of borrowers.

For the private sector to be maximizing profits, it has to have clean balance sheets and promising investment opportunities. After all private-sector businesses will not borrow unless they are sure they can pay back the debt with interest. But with near-zero technological innovation before the industrial revolution, which was a technological revolution, there were very few investment projects that would pay for themselves. Businesses also tend to minimize debt when they see no investment opportunities because the probability of facing bankruptcy is reduced drastically if the firm carried no debt. Given the dearth of investment opportunities in pre-industrial revolution world, it is easy to understand why there were so few willing borrowers.

Because of this absence of worthwhile investment opportunities, the more people tried to save, the more the economy shrank. The result was a permanent paradox of thrift in which people tried to save but their very actions and intentions kept the national economy in a depressed state. This state of affairs lasted for centuries in both the East and the West.

Figure 1 Economic growth became norm only after industrial revolution

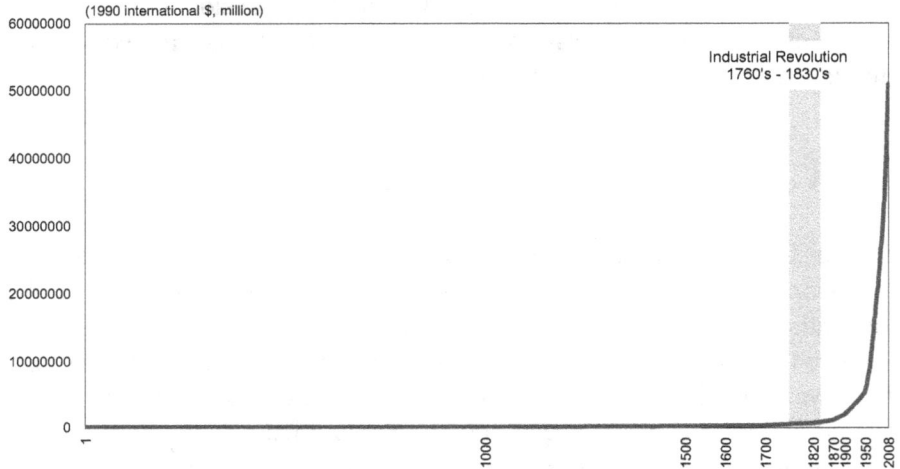

(1990 international $, million)

Source: Angus Maddison, "Historical Statistics of the World Economy: 1-2008 AD",
http://www.ggdc.net/maddison/Historical_Statistics/vertical-file_02-2010.xls

Powerful rulers sometimes borrowed the funds private sector saved and used them to build social infrastructure or monuments. On those occasions, the vicious cycle of the paradox of thrift was suspended because the government borrowed the saved funds (the initial savings of $100 in the above example) and re-injected them into the income stream, generating rapid economic growth. However, unless the project paid for itself, the government would at some point get cold feet in the face of a mounting debt load and discontinue its investment. The whole economy would then fall back into the paradox of thrift and stagnate. Consequently, those regimes often did not last as long as some of the monuments they created.

Countries also tried to achieve economic growth by expanding their territories, i.e., by acquiring more land, which was the key factor of production in pre-industrial agricultural societies. Indeed, people believed for centuries that territorial expansion was essential for economic growth. This drive for prosperity was the economic rationale for colonialism and imperialism. But both were basically a zero-sum proposition for the global economy as a whole and also resulted in countless wars and deaths.

Four possibilities of borrowers and lenders

The discussion above suggests that there are altogether four possibilities regarding the presence of lenders (savers) and borrowers (investors). They are as follows: (1) both lenders and borrowers are present in sufficient numbers, (2) there are borrowers but not enough lenders even at high interest rates, (3) there are lenders but not enough borrowers even at low interest rates, and (4) both lenders and borrowers are absent. These four states are illustrated in Figure 2.

Of the four, only Cases 1 and 2 are discussed in traditional economics, which implicitly assumes there are always borrowers as long as real interest rates can be brought low enough. Of these two, only Case 1 requires the minimum of policy intervention – such as slight adjustments to interest rates – to keep the economy going.

The causes of Case 2 (insufficient lenders), the causes may be found in both financial and non-financial factors. Non-financial factors might include a culture that does not encourage saving or a country that is simply too poor and underdeveloped to save. A restrictive monetary policy may also qualify as a non-financial factor that weighs on savers' ability to lend. (If the paradox of thrift leaves a country too poor to save, this would be classified as Case 3 or 4 because it is actually caused by a lack of borrowers.)

Financial factors weighing on lenders might include banks having too many non-performing loans (NPLs), which depress their capital ratios and prevent them from lending. This is what is usually called a credit crunch.

When many banks have NPL problems at the same time, mutual distrust among lenders may lead to a dysfunctional interbank market, a state of affairs typically known as a financial crisis. Over-regulation of financial institutions by the authorities can lead to a credit crunch as well. An underdeveloped financial system may also be a factor.

Figure 2 Borrowers and lenders: four possible states

		Borrowers (=investors)	
		Yes	No
Lenders (=savers)	Yes	1	3 ← world economy today
	No	2	4

↓ Textbook world (private sector maximizing profits)   ↓ Overlooked world (private sector minimizing debt)

1. Lenders and borrowers are present in sufficient numbers (textbook world) ⇨ **Ordinary interest rates**
2. Borrowers are present but not lenders due to the latter's bad loan problems (financial crisis, credit crunch) ⇨**Loan rates much higher than policy rate**
3. Lenders are present but not borrowers due the latter's balance sheet problems and /or lack of investment opportunities (balance sheet recession, "secular" stagnation) ⇨ **Ultra-low interest rates**
4. Borrowers and lenders both absent due to balance sheet problems for the former and bad loan problems for the latter (aftermath of bubble burst) ⇨ **Ultra-low interest rates. but only got highly rated borrowers**

Non-developmental causes of a shortage of lenders, however, all have well-known remedies in the literature. For example, the government can inject capital into the banks to restore their ability to lend, or it can relax regulations preventing financial institutions from performing their role as financial intermediaries. In the case of a dysfunctional interbank market, the central bank can act as lender of last resort to ensure the clearing system continues to operate. It can also relax monetary policy.

The conventional emphasis on monetary policy and concerns over the crowding-out effect of fiscal policy are justified in Cases 1 and 2, where there are borrowers but (for a variety of reasons in Case 2) not enough lenders.

A lack of borrowers and the other half of macroeconomics

The problem is with Cases 3 and 4, where the bottleneck is a lack of *borrowers*. This is the other half of macroeconomics that has been totally overlooked by traditional economists.

As noted above, there are two main reasons for an absence of private-sector borrowers. The first is that they cannot find attractive investment opportunities that will pay for themselves, and the second is that their financial health has deteriorated to the point where they are unable to borrow until they repair their balance sheets. An example of the first case would be the world that existed before the industrial revolution, while examples of the second case can be found following the collapse of debt-financed asset price bubbles.

Borrowers who have absented themselves because their balance sheets are underwater will not return until their negative equity problems are resolved. Depending on the size of the bubble, this can take many years even under the best of circumstances. Furthermore, the economy will enter the $1,000-$900-$810-$730 deflationary scenario mentioned earlier if the private sector as a whole is saving money (or paying down debt) in spite of zero interest rates.

When borrowers disappear, there is very little that monetary policy, the favorite of traditional economists, can do to prop up the real economy. Figure 3 shows that the close relationship between central-bank-supplied liquidity, known as the monetary base, and growth in private sector credit seen prior to 2008 broke down completely after the bubble burst and the private sector began minimizing debt. This Figure makes it clear that the monetary base and credit to the private sector were closely correlated prior to 2008, just as economics textbooks teach. In other words, the private sector was utilizing all the funds supplied by the central bank, and economies were in Case 1 of Figure 2.

The other half of macroeconomics

Figure 3 Massive liquidity supply and record low interest rates after 2008 failed to increase credit to private sector

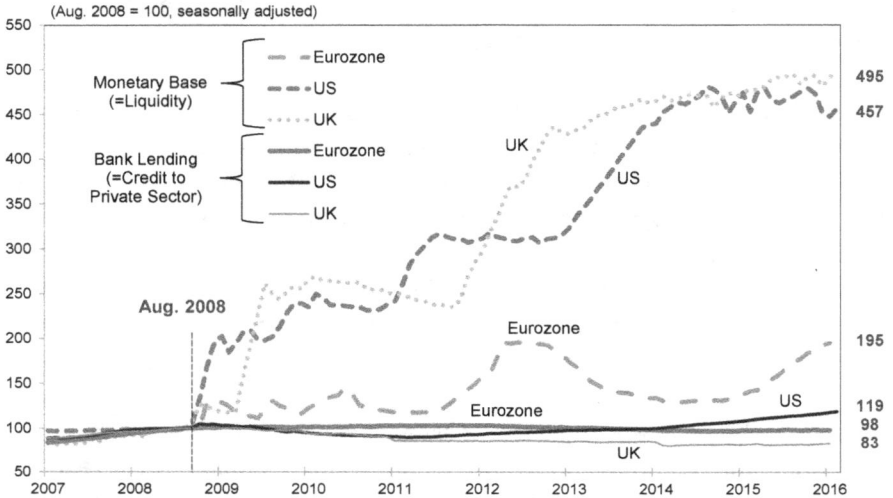

Notes: 1. US monetary base and UK's reserve balances data are seasonally unadjusted.
2. UK's bank lending data exclude intermmediate financial institutions.
3. Base money's figures of Eurozone are seasonally adjusted by Nomura Research Institute.
Source: Nomura Research Institute, based on FRB, ECB and Bank of England data.

But after the bubble burst, forcing the private sector to repair its balance sheet by minimizing debt, no amount of monetary easing by the central bank was able to increase borrowings by the private sector. The US Federal Reserve, for example, expanded the monetary base by 357 percent from the time Lehman went under. In an ordinary (i.e., textbook) world, this should have led to similar increases in the money supply and credit, driving corresponding increases in inflation.

Instead, credit to the private sector increased only 19 percent over seven and a half years. A central bank can always add liquidity to the banking system by purchasing assets from financial institutions. But for that liquidity to enter the real economy, banks must lend out those funds: they cannot give them away because the funds are ultimately owned by depositors. A mere 19 percent increase in lending means new money entering the real economy from the financial sector has grown only 19 percent since 2008. Similar patterns have been observed in the Eurozone and the UK. This explains why inflation and growth rates in the advanced economies have all failed to respond to zero interest rates or astronomical injections of central bank liquidity since 2008.

Unsurprisingly, the same decoupling of monetary aggregates was observed in the US during the Great Depression and in Japan after 1990. Figure 4 shows the monetary base, the money supply, and credit to the private sector before and after the October 1929 stock market crash. It shows that the three were moving together until the crash, just as textbooks teach, but diverged sharply afterwards as the US private sector sought to repair its battered balance sheet by minimizing debt. This can be seen from the fact that loans to the private sector fell the farthest, by as much as 54.7 percent from the 1929 peak, a phenomenon that was also observed in the post-2008 recessions.

Believers in monetary policy might argue that in the 1930s the Fed did not expand the monetary base as quickly as it did post-Lehman, and that this lack of early action contributed to the severity of the subsequent depression in the 1930s. A close look at the reserve data, however, indicates that American banks were actually paying borrowed reserves back to the Fed at a rapid pace immediately after the stock market crash, as shown in the bottom of Figure 4. Between June 1929 and March 1930, bank borrowings from the Fed fell 95 percent, from $801 million to just $43 million. This was probably because the collapse in loan demand left banks with no reason to hold borrowed reserves. And with lenders so eager to return reserves back to the Fed, there was no reason for the Fed to increase reserves.

Figure 4 Decoupling of monetary aggregates observed in 1930s US

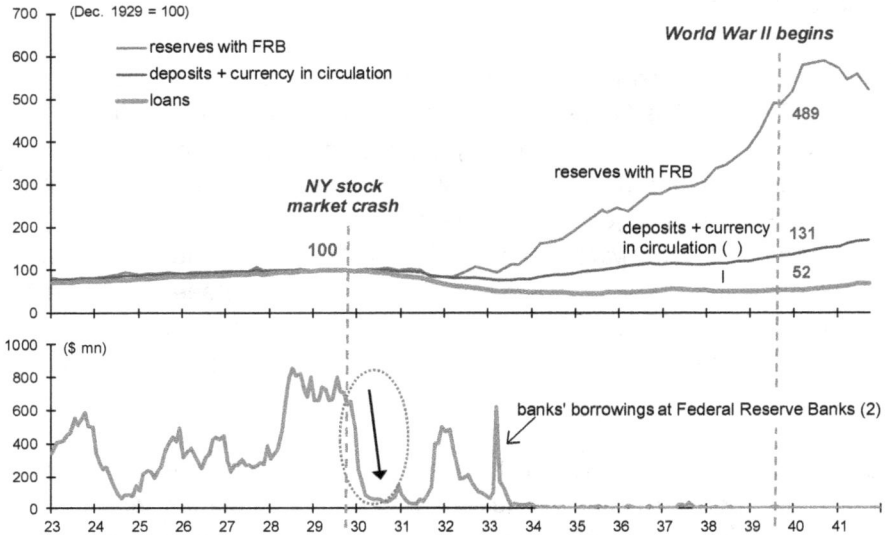

Notes: 1. deposits = demand deposits adjusted + other time deposits
2. Only this data series is based on member banks in 101 leading cities. All other data series are for all membr banks.
Source: Nomura Research Institute, based on the data from Board of Governors of the Federal Reserve System (1976),
Banking and Monetary Statistics 1914-1941, pp.72-75 pp.138-163 and pp.409-413

The same decoupling of monetary aggregates was also observed in Japan after its bubble burst in 1990, as shown in Figure 5. Here, too, the Bank of Japan's massive injections of reserves to the banking system failed to increase lending to the private sector or boost inflation (shown at the bottom of Figure 5).

The behavior of monetary aggregates following a bubble collapse suggests that monetary policy loses its effectiveness when the private sector is minimizing debt, i.e., when the economy is in Cases 3 and 4 in Figure 2. Central banks have continued to miss their inflation targets since 2008 because private sectors are all minimizing debt. And they are doing so because their balance sheets are impaired. The fact that a number of central bank governors continue to insist that further monetary easing will enable them to meet their inflation targets suggests they still do not understand why their models are not working, a disturbing thought indeed.

35

Figure 5 Decoupling of monetary aggregates observed in post-1990 Japan

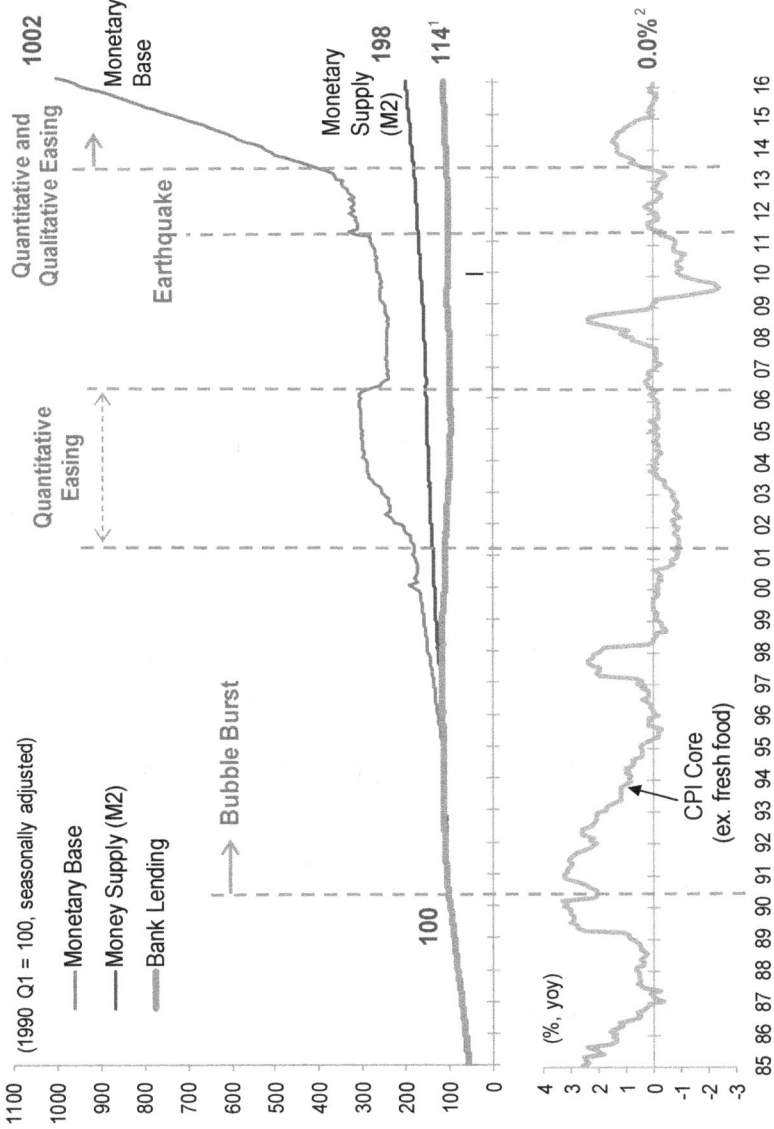

Notes: 1. Figures for bank lending are seasonally adjusted by Nomura Research Institute.
2. Excluding the impact of consumption tax.

Source: Bank of Japan

Once the bubble bursts and investors are left facing debt overhangs, no amount of monetary easing by the central bank will persuade them to borrow money. These businesses and households will not resume borrowing until their balance sheets are fully repaired. Some may never borrow again – even after their balance sheets are repaired – if they were badly traumatized by the painful deleveraging experience. When the private sector as a whole is not borrowing money even at zero interest rates because it has to repair its balance sheet, the economy will fall into the deflationary spiral described above because the lack of borrowers prevents saved funds from re-entering the economy's income stream.

Self-corrective mechanism of economies in balance sheet recessions

When private-sector borrowers disappear and monetary policy stops working, the correct way to prevent a deflationary spiral is for the government to borrow and spend the excess savings in the private sector ($100 in the example above). In other words, the government should mobilize fiscal policy and serve as *borrower of last resort*. If the government borrows and spends the $100 left unborrowed by the private sector, total expenditures will amount to $900 plus $100, or $1,000, and the economy will move on. This way, the private sector also has the income to pay down debt or rebuild savings. The government should attempt fiscal consolidation only after the private sector is ready to borrow again. Otherwise, it risks restarting the deflationary spiral.

The bond market will also encourage the government to act as borrower of last resort during this type of recession by keeping government bond yields very low. This happens because the government is the only remaining borrower in a balance sheet recession. Fund managers at life insurers and pension funds who must earn an investment return but are not allowed to take on too much foreign exchange risk or principal risk (i.e., they cannot invest all their money in stocks) have little choice but to buy government bonds. Their rush into government debt pushes yields to exceptionally low levels and encourages the government to act as borrower of last resort in what may be called the self-corrective mechanism of economies in balance sheet recessions.

It is a self-corrective mechanism because the government should be able to find projects that can earn enough to pay those exceptionally low yields. To the extent that those projects are self-sustaining, additional borrowing by the government will not burden taxpayers. And the government's fiscal action will support the economy and provide the private sector with income to repair its balance sheet.

Exceptionally low government bond yields were first observed in post-1990 Japan and since 2008 can be seen in Western economies as well. It is also hoped that modern governments will be better than the emperors and kings of the past at selecting projects that will ultimately pay for themselves.

Borrowers may remain traumatized by the long and painful experience of deleveraging even after they have repaired their balance sheets. Under such conditions, which were observed in the US for decades after the Great Depression and in Japan more recently, the authorities may need to provide incentives to borrow and invest, such as accelerated depreciation allowances.

Economies do not stay in Case 4 for long

When a bubble bursts, the economy typically finds itself facing an absence of both lenders and borrowers (Case 4). Lenders disappear from the scene because during the bubble they lent money to now-insolvent speculators, and the resulting non-performing loans have eroded their capital. In fact, many lenders may be effectively bankrupt themselves.

The whole society suffers when impaired balance sheets leave banks unable to function. That is why the government and the central bank respond to banking sector problems with the kinds of policies described in the discussion of Case 2 on page 7. Even though some of these policies, such as capital injections to the banks, are not always popular, the necessary remedies are well known and, once implemented, will usually resolve lenders' problems within two years. Once banks are functioning again, the economy moves from Case 4 to Case 3.

In contrast to lender-side problems, there are no quick fixes for problems at borrowers, whether they are due to balance sheet difficulties or a lack of technological innovation. An economy in Case 3 can therefore remain there for years if not decades.

It should be noted that if the debt overhang at borrowers is small enough for the rest of the society to absorb, debt forgiveness, debt-for-equity swaps, and similar measures can be used to address the problem. But if a large part of the society is facing the same overhang problem, which is usually the case when a nationwide asset price bubble bursts, such measures merely transfer the problem from one part of society to another without solving it. When the problems are broad-based, therefore, measures to help all borrowers rebuild their balance sheets are needed, and this process takes time.

When a lack of investment opportunities deters borrowers

If borrowers are absent because businesses cannot find attractive investment opportunities, which was the cause of economic stagnation that lasted for centuries before the industrial revolution, a very different mind-set is needed to solve the problem. To begin with, there are many different potential causes for this problem, depending on the stage of economic development, each requiring a different policy response.

Today's developed economies all started out as agrarian societies, and the centuries-long paradox of thrift finally ended with the arrival of the industrial revolution. The invention of new products and the machines to make them produced a huge number of investment opportunities for the first time in history. Private-sector businesses that would not borrow money unless they were sure they could pay it back found many promising projects and started borrowing. The financial sector also developed to meet the strong demand for funds. This process could continue as long as the debt-financed projects were sound enough to pay for themselves.

Thus began a virtuous cycle in which investments created more jobs and income, which in turn created more savings to finance more investments.

Unlike the government-financed investments in earlier centuries that eventually ran into financing difficulties, private-sector-led investments could sustain themselves as long as attractive new products were continuously brought to the market. The end result was the rapid economic growth observed since the industrial revolution.

At the beginning of the industrial revolution, constraints to growth included a lack of social infrastructure (e.g., transportation networks), insufficient savings to fund investments, an illiterate work force, and the slow pace of technological innovation. But some of these constraints were soon transformed into investment opportunities in the form of railways and other utilities. The urbanization of the population alone created massive investment opportunities as rural workers moved to the cities to work in factories. As new household appliances, cars, cameras and airplanes were invented and developed in rapid succession, a lack of investment opportunities was seldom a constraint to growth during this period.

Household savings also became a virtue instead of a vice from a macroeconomic perspective, and economies where people felt responsible for their own future and saved more tended to grow more rapidly than those where people saved less.

Borrower availability and the three stages of economic development

The availability of investment opportunities, however, is never guaranteed. It depends on a myriad of factors, including the stage of economic development, the pace of technological innovation and scientific breakthroughs, the ability of businesspeople to uncover such opportunities and their willingness to borrow, the availability of financing at a reasonable interest rate, the protection of intellectual property rights, and the state of the economy and world trade.

The importance of these factors also depends on a nation's stage of economic development. The pace of innovation and breakthroughs is probably more important for countries already at the forefront of technology, while those in emerging economies might find the availability of financing and the protection of intellectual property rights just as important.

When Germany was emerging as an industrial power, for instance, the UK accused the Germans of copying its products and demanded "Made in Germany" labels to distinguish them from the British originals. Japan faced similar accusations from Western countries, as did China from both the West and Japan. Today, many Chinese businesses are demanding the Beijing government to implement stronger intellectual property rules because they worry that any new product they develop will be copied by domestic competitors in no time, rendering their research and development efforts worthless. Thus the ability to copy, which is a huge positive at one stage of economic development, becomes a major negative later on.

In terms of the availability of investment opportunities, it may be useful to divide the industrialization process into three stages: urbanizing economies, which have yet to reach the Lewis Turning Point (LTP), maturing economies, which have already passed the LTP, and pursued economies, which are in the final stage. The LTP refers to the point at which urban factories have finally absorbed all the surplus rural labor. (In this paper, LTP is used only because it is a well-known term for a point in a nation's economic development and does not refer to the economic growth model proposed by Sir Arthur Lewis.)

At the beginning of industrialization, most people are living in rural areas. Those with technical knowledge of how to produce goods and where to sell them are limited to the educated elite, who are very few in number. Those whose families have lived on depressed farms for centuries have no such knowledge. Most of the gains from the initial stage of industrialization therefore go to the educated few, while most of the population simply provides labor for the industrialists.

The pre-LTP urbanizing economy is extremely lucrative for those few business owners, since they can secure a boundless supply of labor from rural districts simply by paying the going wage. In this world, capitalists need not worry about a shortage of labor and can expand their businesses essentially without limit as long as they have the necessary production facilities and a market for their products. Capitalists who grasp such investment opportunities before the LTP is reached can earn huge profits, further increasing their incentive to expand.

Figure 6 Three phases of industrialization/globalization

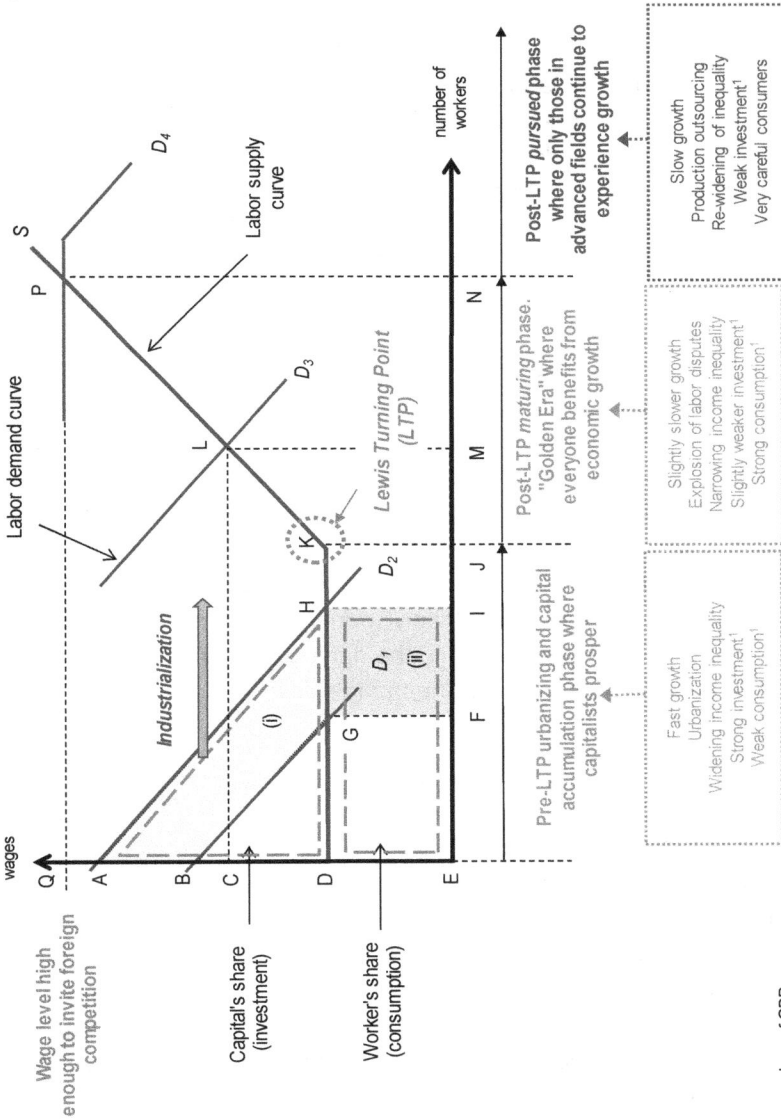

wages

Wage level high enough to invite foreign competition

Capital's share (investment)

Worker's share (consumption)

Labor demand curve

Industrialization

Labor supply curve

Lewis Turning Point (LTP)

number of workers

D_4

D_3

D_2

D_1

S, P, L, K, H, G, A, B, C, D, E, Q, F, I, J, M, N

(i) (ii)

Pre-LTP urbanizing and capital accumulation phase where capitalists prosper

Fast growth
Urbanization
Widening income inequality[1]
Strong investment[1]
Weak consumption[1]

Post-LTP maturing phase. "Golden Era" where everyone benefits from economic growth

Slightly slower growth
Explosion of labor disputes
Narrowing income inequality[1]
Slightly weaker investment[1]
Strong consumption[1]

Post-LTP pursued phase where only those in advanced fields continue to experience growth

Slow growth
Production outsourcing
Re-widening of inequality[1]
Weak investment[1]
Very careful consumers

1. as a share of GDP
Source: Nomura Research Institute

Figure 6 illustrates this from the perspective of labor supply and demand. The labor supply curve is almost horizontal (DHK) until the Lewis turning point (K) is reached because there is an essentially unlimited supply of rural laborers seeking to work in the cities. Any number of such laborers can be assembled simply by paying the going wage (DE).

In this graph, capital's share is represented by the area of the triangle formed by the left axis, the labor demand curve, and the labor supply curve, while labor's share is represented by the rectangle below the labor supply curve. At the time of labor demand curve D1, capital's share is the triangle BDG, and labor's share is the rectangle DEFG. During this phase of industrialization, the capital share BDG may be shared by a few persons or families, whereas the labor share DEFG may be shared by millions of workers.

Successful businesses in this world will continue to invest in an attempt to make even more money. That raises the demand for labor, causing the labor demand curve to shift steadily to the right (from D_1 to D_2) even as the labor supply curve remains flat. As the labor demand curve shifts to the right, total wages received by labor increase from the area of the rectangle DEFG at time D_1 to the area of rectangle DEIH at time D_2 as the length of the rectangle below the labor supply curve grows. However, the growth is linear. The share of capital, meanwhile, is likely to increase at more than a linear rate as the labor demand curve shifts to the right, expanding from the area of the triangle BDG at D_1 to the area of the triangle ADH at D_2.

Growth exacerbates inequality during pre-LTP stage

Until the LTP is reached, GDP growth is likely to increase the portion of GDP that accrues to the capitalists, exacerbating inequalities. A key reason why a handful of families and business groups in Europe a century ago and the zaibatsu in Japan prior to World War II were able to accumulate such massive wealth is that they faced an essentially flat labor supply curve (wealth accumulation in North America and Oceania was not quite as extreme because these economies were characterized by a shortage of labor). Some in post-1979 China became extremely rich for the same reason.

43

During this phase, income inequality, symbolized by the gap between rich and poor, widens sharply as capitalists' share of income (the triangle) often increases faster than labor's share (the rectangle). Because capitalists are profiting handsomely, they will continue to borrow and re-invest profits in a bid to make even more money. Sustained high investment rates mean domestic capital accumulation and urbanization also proceed rapidly. This is the takeoff period for a nation's economic growth.

Until the economy reaches the Lewis turning point, however, low wages mean most people will still lead hard lives, even though the move from the countryside to the cities may improve their situations modestly. For typical workers this was no easy transition, with 14-hour workdays not at all uncommon until the end of the 19th century. According to the OECD, annual working time in the West in 1870 was around 2,950 hours, or double the current level of 1,450 hours (Maddison, 2006: 347). Business owners, however, were able to accumulate tremendous amount of wealth during this period.

Stage II of industrialization: the post-LTP maturing economy

As business owners continue to generate profits and expand investment, the economy eventually reaches its LTP. Once that happens, urbanization is largely finished and the total wages of labor – which had grown only linearly until then – start to increase rapidly since there is no more surplus labor in the rural areas and wages start to rise with any additional demand for labor. In other words, the labor supply curve will have a significant positive slope after the LTP. For example, even if labor demand increases just a little, from J to M in Figure 6, total wages accruing to labor will rise dramatically, from the area of rectangle DEJK to the area of rectangle CEML.

Once the LTP is reached, labor has the bargaining power to demand higher wages for the first time in history, which reduces the profit share of business owners. But businesses will continue to invest as long as they are achieving good returns, leading to further tightness in the labor market. It is at this point that the inequality problem begins to correct itself.

Figure 7 Western urbanization* continued until the 1960s

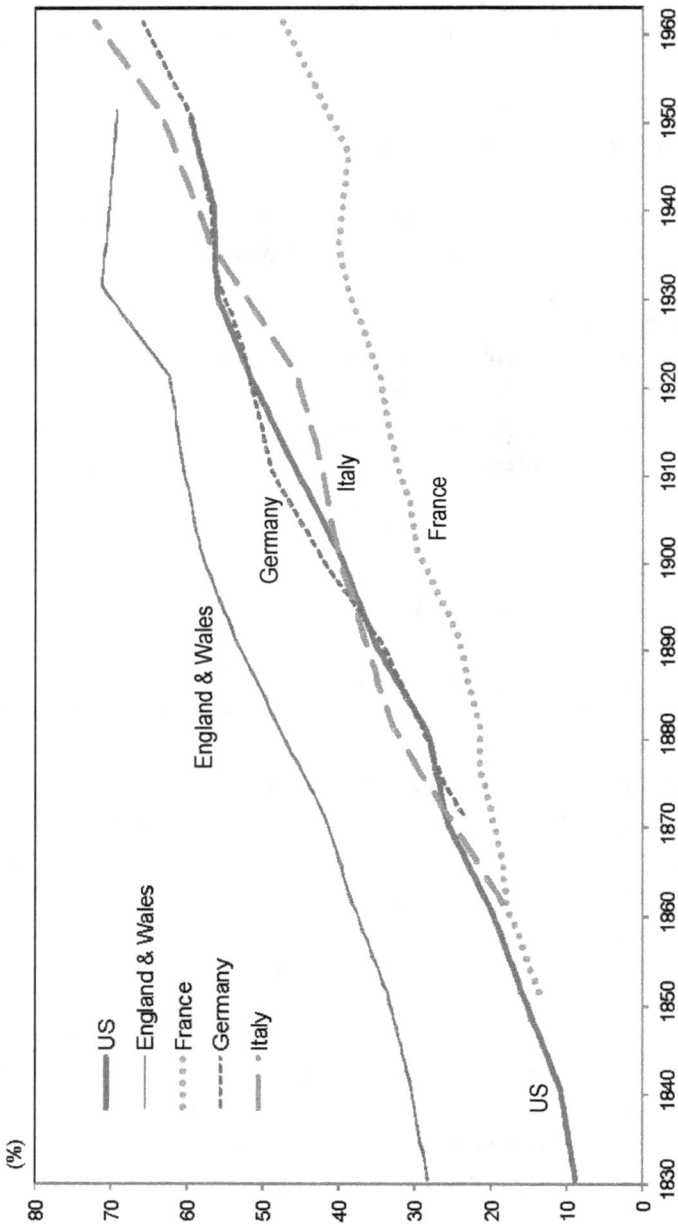

* Percentage of population living in urban areas with 20,000 people or more in England & Wales, 10,000 or more in Italy and France, 5,000 or more in Germany and 2,500 or more in the US.
Sources: U.S. Census Bureau (2012), *2010 Census*, Peter Flora, Franz Kraus and Winfried Pfenning ed., (1987), *State, Economy and Society in Western Europe 1815-1975*

A significant portion of the US and European populations still lived in rural areas until World War I, as shown in Figure 7. Even in the US, where – unlike in Europe – workers were always in short supply, nearly half the population was living on farms as late as the 1930s. The mobilizations for two world wars then pushed these economies beyond the LTP, and standards of living for average workers began to improve dramatically. With workers' share of output increasing relative to that of capital, inequality diminished as well, ushering in the so called Golden Sixties in the US. With incomes rising and inequality falling, this post-LTP maturing phase may be called the golden era of economic growth.

As labor's share increases, consumption's share of GDP will increase at the expense of investment, and with reduced capital accumulation, growth will slow as well. At the same time, the explosive increase in the purchasing power of ordinary citizens means most businesses are able to increase profits simply by expanding existing productive capacity. From that point onward the economy begins to "normalize" in the sense in which we use that term today.

Once the economy reaches its LTP and wages start growing rapidly, the workers begin to utilize their newfound bargaining power. The huge number of strikes many countries in the West experienced from the 1950s to the 1970s reflects this development.

Capitalists initially resist labor movements with union busters and strike busters. But as workers grow increasingly scarce and expensive, the capitalists must back down and start accepting some of labor's demands if they want to keep their factories running. After about 20 years of such struggles, both employers and employees begin to understand what can be reasonably expected from each other, and a new political order is established. The political order dominated by center-left and center-right political parties now in place in the West and Japan reflects this learning process.

Figure 8 Western urbanization slowed in the 1970s

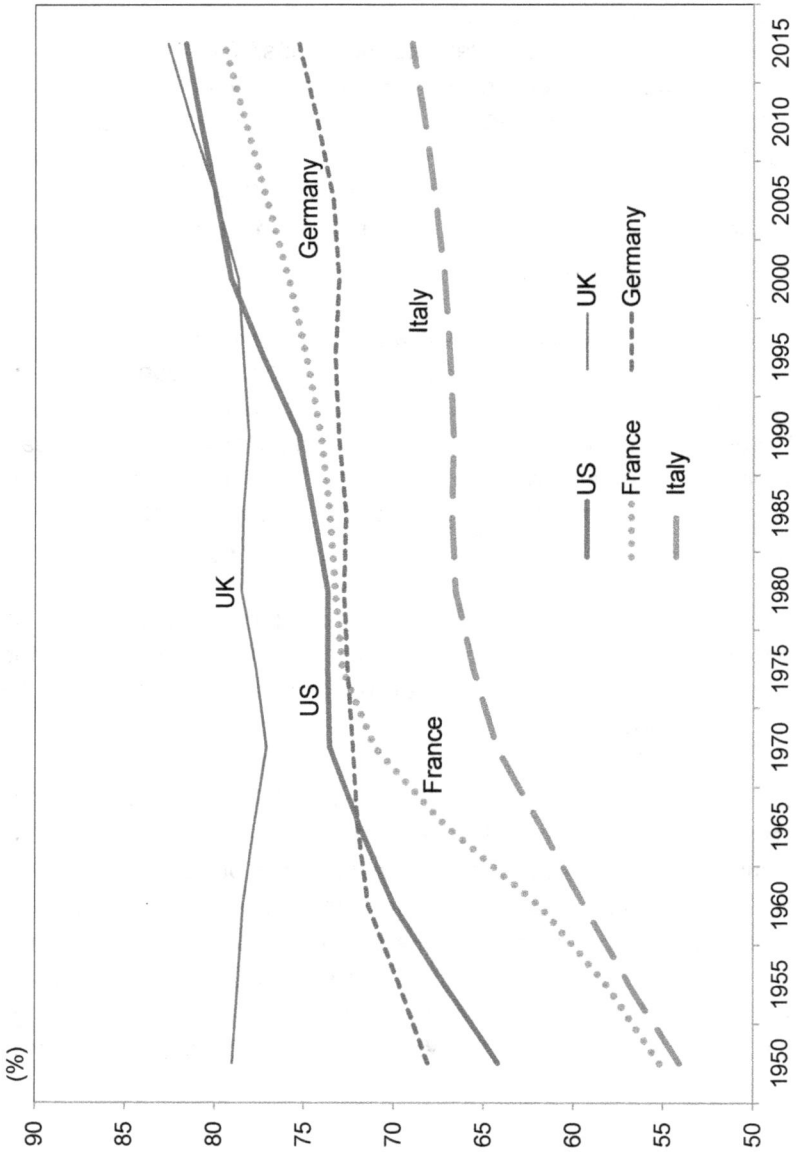

Source: United Nations, Department of Economic and Social Affairs, Population Division (2014). World Urbanization Prospects: The 2014 Revision, custom data acquired via website.

With rapid improvements in the living standards of most workers, the post-LTP maturing phase is where everyone in the economy benefits from economic growth. Even those with limited skills can make a good living, especially if they belong to a strong union.

Higher wages force businesses to look harder for profitable investment opportunities. On the other hand, the explosive increase in the purchasing power of ordinary workers who are paid ever-higher wages creates major investment opportunities. Businesses invest heavily in productivity-enhancing equipment to meet this demand from increasingly rich consumers at a time of rising wages. Even if workers' skill level remains unchanged, their productivity increases during this period because of such investment made by businesses, which is necessary for them to remain competitive.

Government tax receipts also increase rapidly during this period, allowing the government to offer an ever-expanding range of public services. That, in turn, reduces the sense of inequality among the population. In the West this golden era lasted until around 1970.

Stage III of industrialization: post-LTP pursued economy

This golden age does not last forever. The first signs of a serious threat to Western economic growth appeared when businesses in the US and Europe faced Japanese competition in the 1970s. Initially this was blamed on the wage gap between the US/Europe and Japan. But the wage gap had always existed. The real reason was that Japanese businesses were approaching and in some cases, surpassing the technological and marketing sophistication of the West while benefiting from lower wage costs.

Many in the West were shocked to find that Japanese cars required so little maintenance and repair after purchase. The Germans may have invented the automobile, and the Americans may have established the process to make cars cheaply, but it was the Japanese who created cars that do not break down. The arrival of Nikon F cameras from Japan in the 1960s also came as a huge shock to the German camera industry because it was so much more rugged, adaptable, easy to use and serviceable than German

48

Leicas and Exaktas, prompting professional photographers around the world to switch to the Japanese brand. For the first time since the industrial revolution, the West found it was being pursued by a formidable competitor from the East.

Once the country finds itself being chased by a technologically savvy competitor, often with a younger and less expensive labor force, it becomes far more challenging for businesses in the pursued country to find attractive investment opportunities at home. This is because it often makes more sense for businesses to buy directly from the chasing country or to invest in the chaser themselves. Indeed, many US and European companies happily bought Japanese products to add to their product lines or sell through their dealerships. Those products carried proud American or European brands but were actually made in Japan. By the mid-1970s, for example, General Motors was buying cars from Toyota, Ford from Mazda, and Chrysler from Mitsubishi. In the "German" camera industry, Leicas were increasingly made with Minolta components – if not produced entirely by the Japanese company – and cameras with such venerable names such as Exakta and Contax were made entirely in Japan.

Businesses in the pursued country no longer have the same incentive to invest in productivity-enhancing equipment at home because there is now the viable alternative of investing in or purchasing from lower-cost production facilities abroad. In other words, capital invested abroad often earns higher returns than when it is invested at home. As a result, productivity gains made possible by investments in productivity-enhancing equipment at home slow down significantly.

According to US Bureau of Labor Statistics data compiled by Stanley Fisher (2016) at the Fed, productivity growth in the non-farm business sector averaged 3.0 percent from 1952 to 1973. Average productivity growth then fell to 2.1 percent for the 1974 to 2007 period, and to 1.2 percent for the 2008 to 2015 period. These numbers not only confirm the trend mentioned above, but also suggest that worker productivity in the future will depend increasingly on the efforts of individual workers to improve their skills, instead of on corporate investment in productivity-enhancing equipment.

In terms of Figure 6, labor demand curve D4 in a post-LTP pursued economy becomes largely horizontal at wage level EQ, where outsourcing to foreign production sites becomes a viable alternative. This means real wage growth will be minimal from this point onward except for those with abilities that are not easily replicated abroad.

With domestic investment opportunities shrinking, economic growth also slows in the pursued countries. This is very much the reality of Western economies today, with a steadily increasing number of emerging countries joining the chasers.

Japan's ascent forced changes in the West

The Japanese ascent disturbed the US and European industrial establishments in no small way. As many workers lost their jobs, ugly trade frictions ensued between the US/Europe and Japan. This was the first case of Western countries that had passed their LTPs being chased by a country with much lower wages.

Many well-known US companies such as Zenith and Magnavox disappeared altogether under the assault from Japanese competition, and the West German camera industry, the world's undisputed leader until around 1965, had all but disappeared by 1975. While those at the forefront of technology in the West continued to do well, the disappearance of many well-paying manufacturing jobs led to worsening income inequality in these countries.

There was initially tremendous confusion in the West over what to do about the Japanese threat. As the Japanese took over one industry after another, many industry and labor leaders sought protection via higher tariffs and non-tariff barriers. France, for example, ruled that all Japanese video recorders must clear customs in the remote countryside village of Poitiers, which had few customs officers, to discourage their entry into the country. This was done even though France had no local manufacturers of video recorders. Others argued for exchange rate realignments that were realized in the Plaza Accord of 1985, which halved the dollar's value against the yen.

Still others said the West should study Japan's success and learn from it, which resulted in a Western infatuation with so-called "Japanese management." At the time, many well-known business schools in the US actively recruited Japanese students so they could discuss Japanese management practices in the classroom. Some even argued that eating fish – and sushi in particular – would make them as smart as the Japanese. All in all, Western nations' confidence in being the most technically advanced economies in the world was shattered.

Some of the pain Western workers felt was naturally offset by the fact that, as consumers, they benefited from cheaper imports from Japan. And businesses that were at the forefront of technology were still doing well. But it was no longer the case that everybody in society was benefiting from growth. Those whose jobs could be transferred to lower-cost locations abroad saw their living standards stagnate or actually fall.

Inequality worsens in post-LTP pursued stage

Figure 9 shows the real income of the lowest quintile of US families from 1947 to 2014. It shows that even for this group, incomes grew rapidly in the post-LTP maturing stage lasting until around 1970. Since then, their income growth has stagnated as the country entered the post-LTP pursed phase.

Figure 10, which shows the income growth of other quintiles relative to the lowest 20 percent, demonstrates that ratios remain remarkably stable until 1970 but diverge thereafter.

Figure 9 Incomes of lowest 20% of us families shot up until 1970 but stagnated thereafter

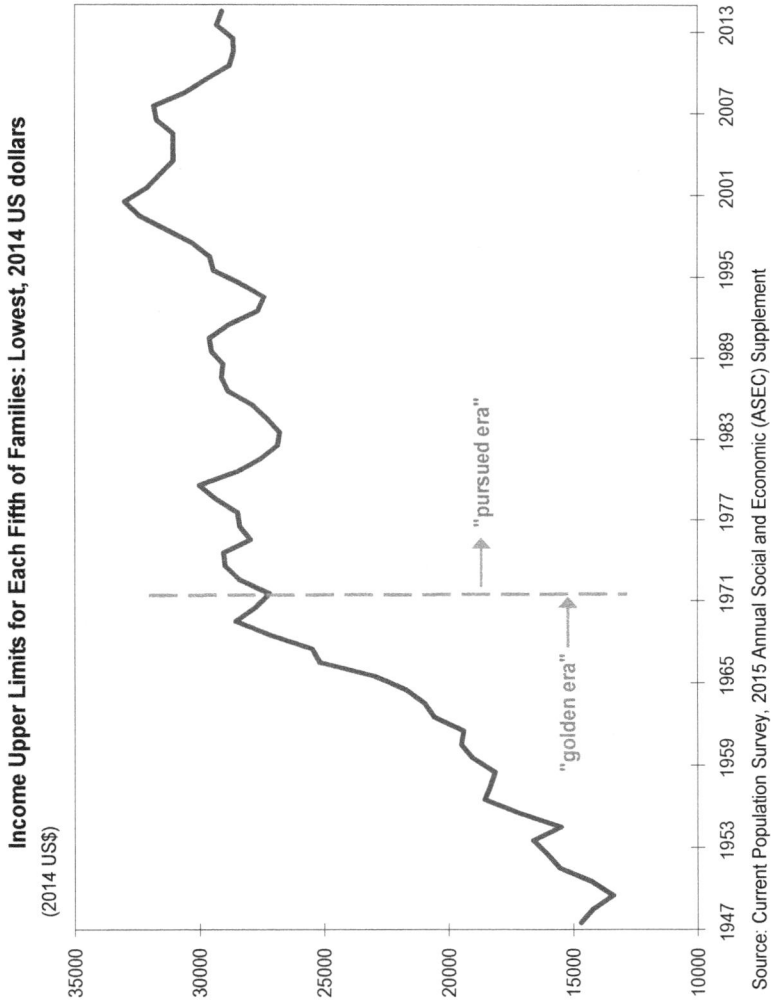

Figure 10 US income inequality began to worsen after 1970

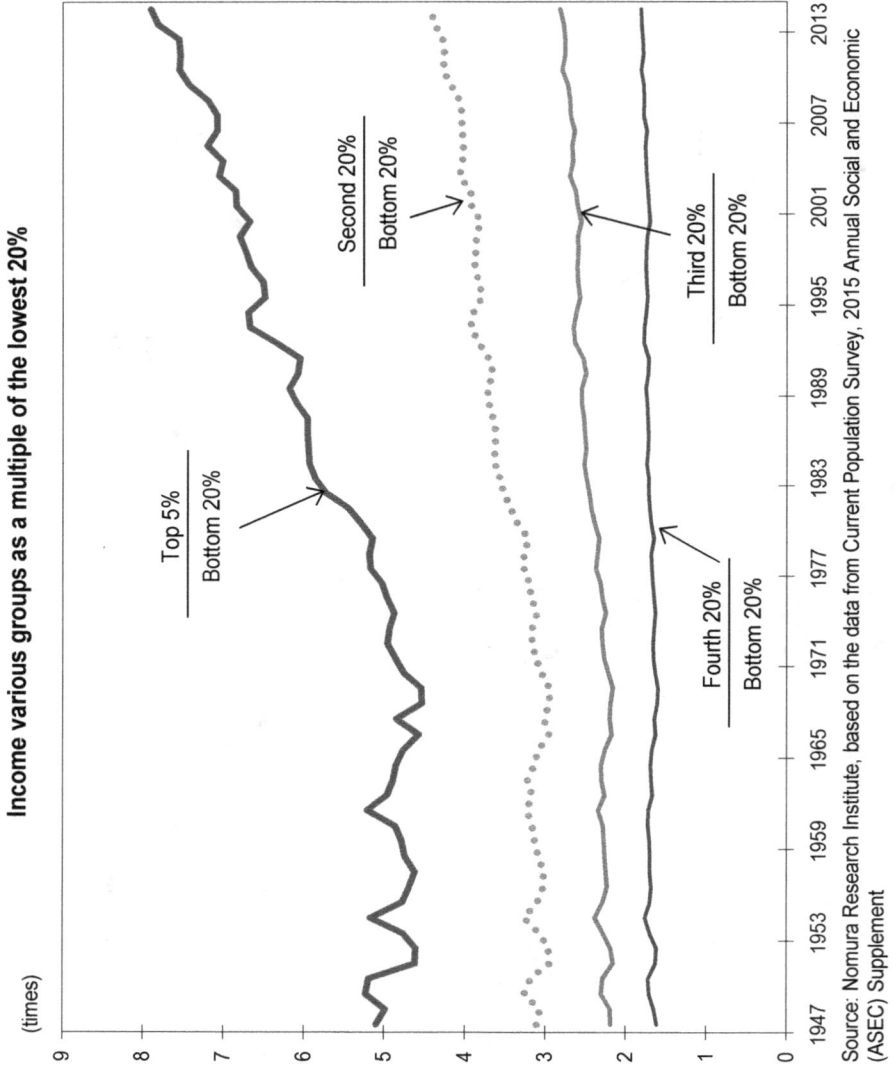

Income various groups as a multiple of the lowest 20%

Source: Nomura Research Institute, based on the data from Current Population Survey, 2015 Annual Social and Economic (ASEC) Supplement

Table 11 Annualized growth rates of US family income by income quintile

(annualized %)

	lowest 20%	second 20%	third 20%	fourth 20%	top 5 %
Post-LTP maturing phase 1947-1970	2.805	2.854	2.861	2.719	2.496
Post-LTP pursued phase 1970-2014	0.107	0.345	0.657	0.965	1.270

Source: Nomura Research Institute, based on the data from the Current Population Survey, 2015 Annual Social and Economic (ASEC) Supplement

Table 11 shows annualized income growth for income quintiles in the post LTP maturing phase from 1947 to 1970 and the post-LTP pursued phase from 1970 to 2014. It shows that the lowest 60 percent actually enjoyed slightly faster income growth than those at the top before 1970, meaning there was a decrease in income inequality during this period. This was indeed a golden era for the US economy, where everybody was becoming richer and enjoying the fruits of economic growth.

The situation changed drastically, however, once Japan started chasing the US. Figure 9 shows that the income growth of the lowest quintile stagnated from that point forward, all the way to the present. Figure 10 and Table 11 show that the income growth of other groups was only slightly better – except for the top 5 percent, which continued to experience significant income gains even after 1970. This group probably includes those who were at the forefront of innovation as well as those who were able to take advantage of Japan's emergence.

Table 11 demonstrates that income growth for different income quintiles was quite similar during the golden era but began to diverse significantly once the country became a chased economy. Income growth for the top 5 percent group drops from 2.49 percent per year during the maturing stage to just 1.27 percent during the pursued stage, but that is still 12 times higher than the growth rate for the lowest 20 percent.

Figure 12 Real wages in six European countries after WWII

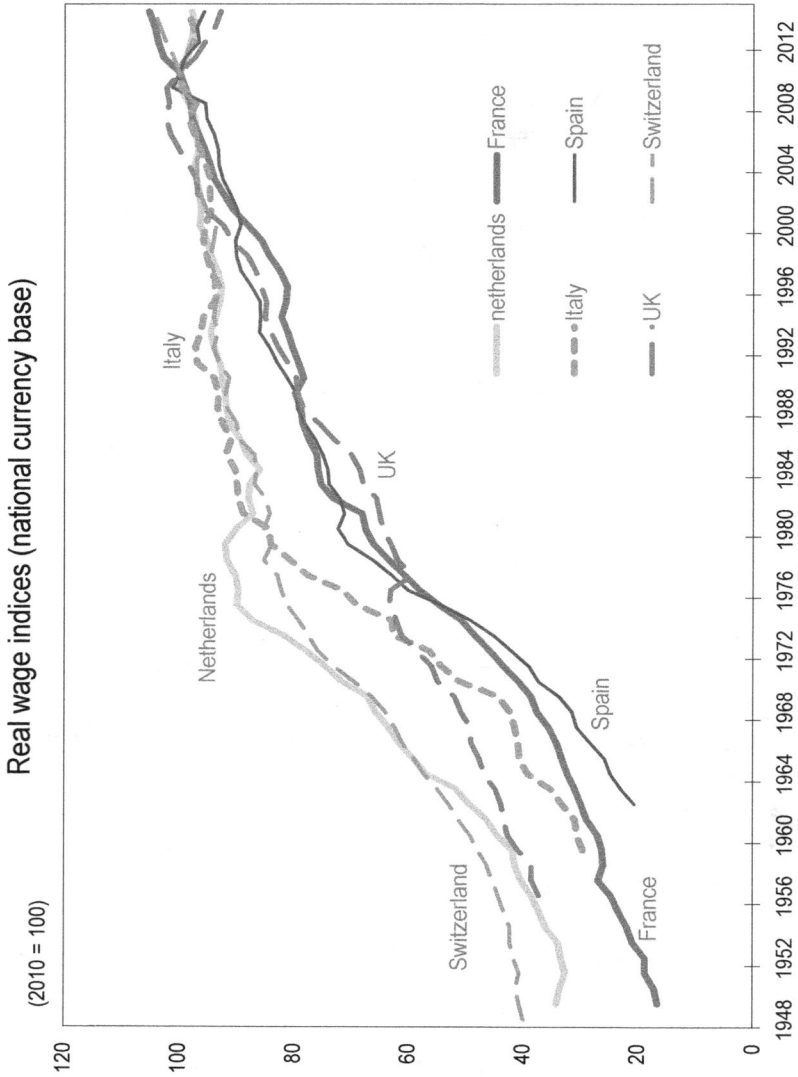

Real wage indices (national currency base)
(2010 = 100)

Source: Nomura Research Institute, based on the data from IMF, *International Financial Statistics* and Swiss Federal Statistical Office, *Swiss Wage Index*

The three stages of Japanese industrialization

Japan reached its LTP in the mid-1960s, when the mass migration of rural graduates to urban factories and offices, known in Japanese as *shudan shushoku,* finally came to an end. During this period, investment opportunities in Japan were plentiful because the hard work needed to develop new products and processes was done in the West. All Japan needed to do was make those products better and less expensive, a task the Japanese system was well suited for. Rapid urbanization and the need to rebuild cities devastated by US bombing during the war also offered plenty of "low-hanging" investment opportunities.

Indeed, the main constraint on the Japanese growth at that time was on the savings side, i.e., there was not enough savings to meet the investment demand from Japanese businesses. Japan found itself in an extreme variant of Case 1 where the number of borrowers completely overwhelmed the number of lenders. Japanese interest rates in those years were therefore quite high, leading the government to channel savings to high-priority industries. The government and the Bank of Japan also implemented numerous measures to encourage savings by Japanese households.

Once Japan reached its LTP in the mid-1960s, the number of labor disputes began to skyrocket, as shown in Figure 13, and Japanese wages began to increase sharply (Figure 14). Thus Japan was entering the post-LTP maturing phase that the West had experienced 40 years earlier.

Japan was fortunate in that it was not being chased at the time, enabling it to focus on catching up with the West. Wages were increasing rapidly, but Japanese companies invested heavily at home to improve the productivity of the work force. As long as productivity rose faster than wages, Japan's golden era of strong growth and prosperity could continue.

Figure 13 Labor demand skyrockets after passing Lewis Turning Point (1): Japan

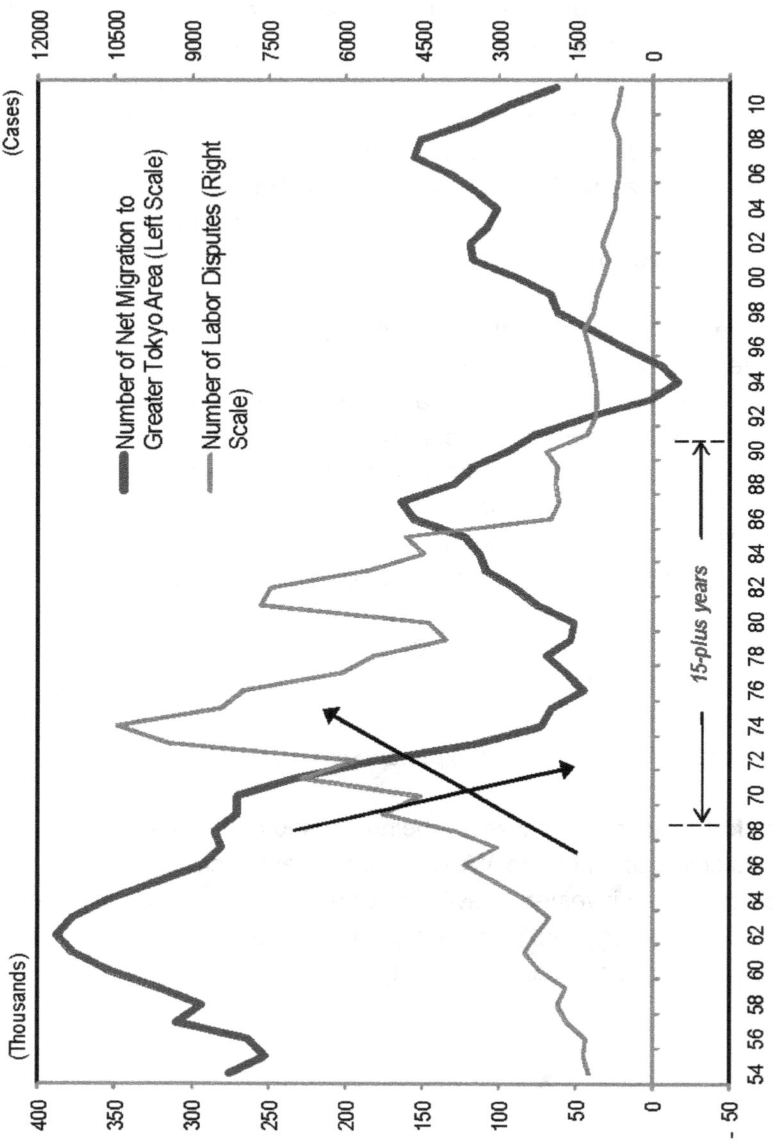

Note: Greater Tokyo Area consists of Tokyo Metropolis, Kanagawa prefecture, Saitama prefecture and Chiba prefecture.
Sources: Ministry of Internal Affairs and Communications, *Report on Internal Migration in Japan*, and Ministry of Health, Labour and Welfare, *Survey on Labour Disputes*

Figure 14 Japanese wages peaked in 1997 when country entered post-LTP pursued stage

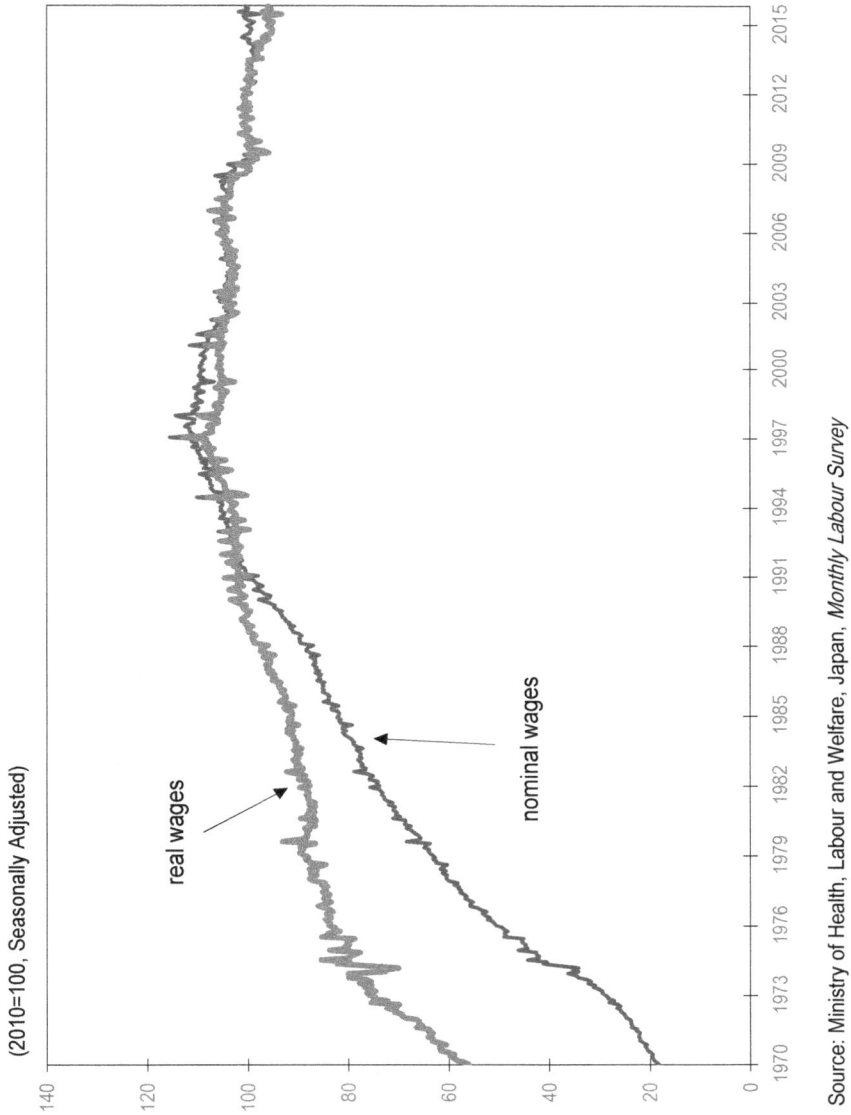

Labor's share of profits rose along with wages, and Japan came to be known as the country of the middle class, with more than 90 percent of the population identifying itself as such. The Japanese were proud of the fact that their country had virtually no inequality. Some even quipped in those days that Japan was how Communism was *supposed* to work.

The happy days for Japan lasted until the mid-1990s, when Taiwan, South Korea and China emerged as serious competitors. By then, Japanese wages were high enough to attract chasers, and the country entered its post-LTP pursued stage. As Figure 14 shows, Japanese wages stopped growing in 1997 and started stagnating or falling thereafter.

Although these three Asian countries were also chasing the West, the shock to Japan was larger because it was the first time the country had been chased from behind. That had never happened since the 1868 Meiji Restoration opened Japan up to the world, and all of Japan's institutions, ranging from education to employment, were optimized for catching up with the West, not fending off competitors from behind. In contrast, the Europeans and Americans who had experienced the Japanese onslaught 25 years earlier and had adjusted their economies accordingly were less disturbed by the emergence of China.

Today the Japanese are worried about the problem of income inequality as well-paying manufacturing jobs have migrated to lower cost countries. They are also concerned about the appearance of the so-called working poor who used to work in manufacturing but are now forced to take low-end service jobs. Some estimate that as many as 20 million out of a total population of 130 million are now living in poverty (Nikkei Business, 2015). In other words, the country is experiencing what the West went through when it was being chased by Japan.

Figure 15 Labor demand skyrockets after passing the Lewis Turning Point (2): South Korea

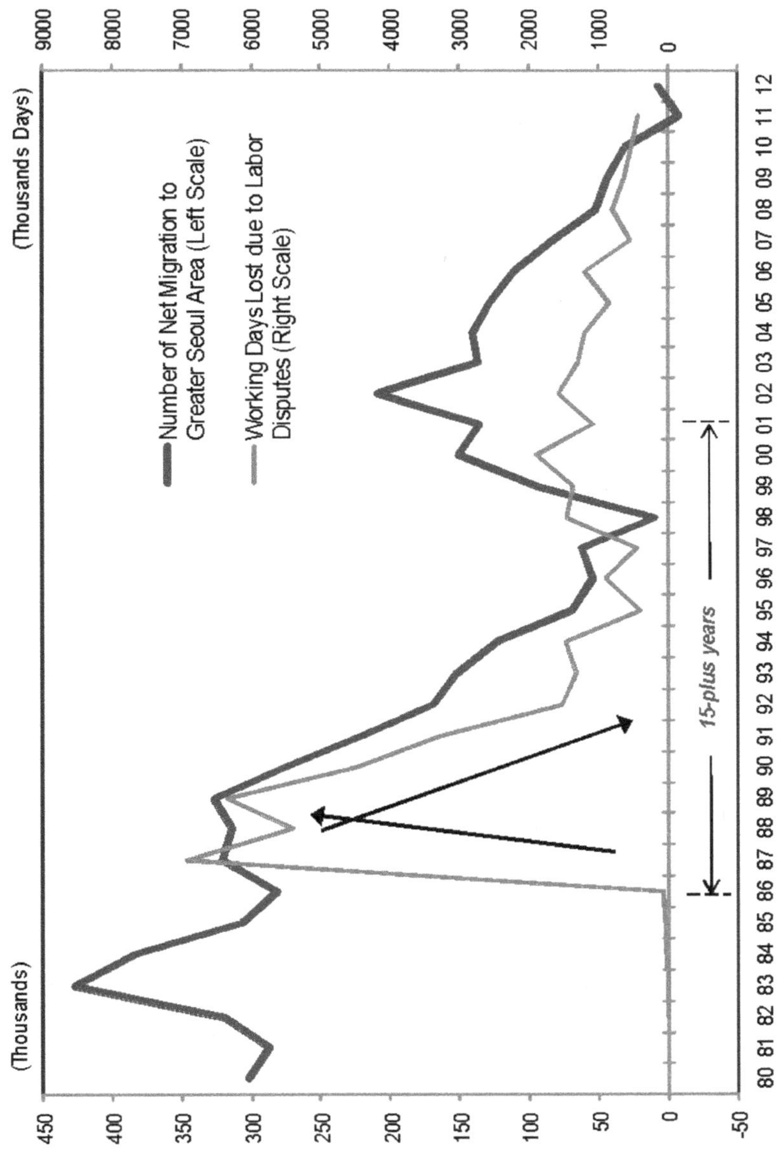

Note: Greater Seoul Area consists of Seoul city, Incheon city and Gyeonggi-do.
Sources: Statistics Korea, *Internal Migration Statistics* and *Korea Statistical Year Book*

Figure 16 Taiwanese wages peaked around 2005 when country entered
Post-LTP pursued stage

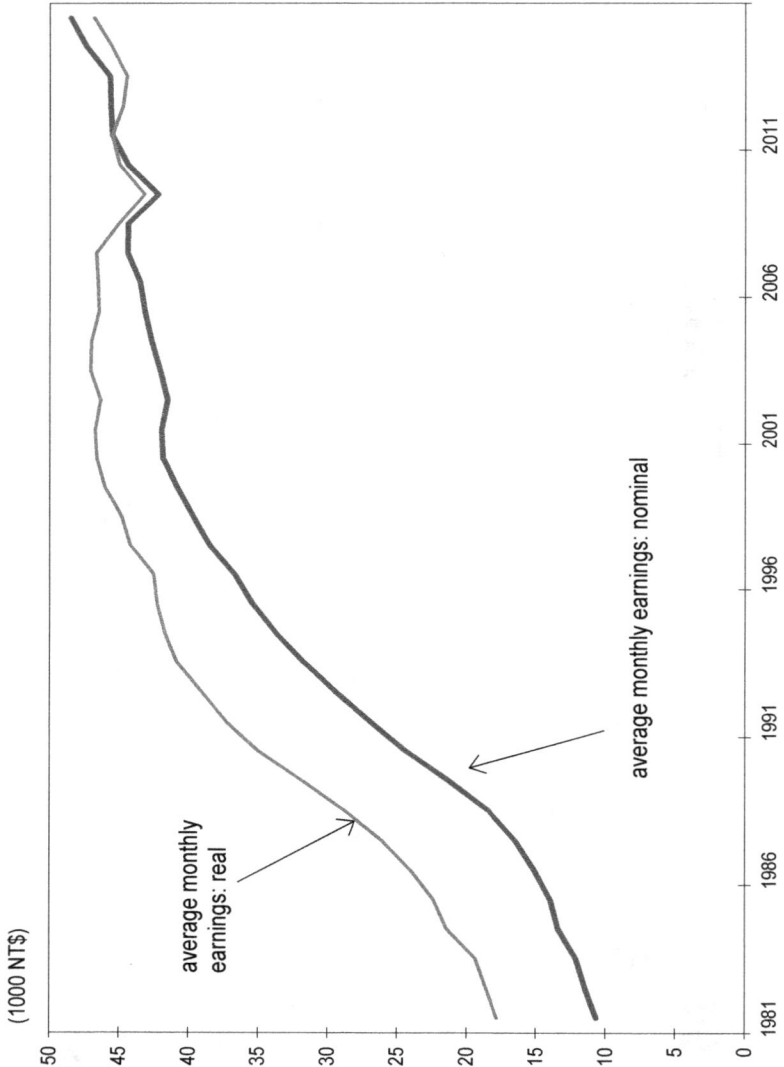

average monthly earnings: nominal

average monthly
earnings: real

(1000 NT$)

Source: Nomura Research Institute, based on the data from Directorate General of Budget, Accounting and Statistics (DGBAS),
the Executive Yuan, Taiwan, *Consumer Price Indices* and *Average Monthly Earnings*

Similar concerns are being voiced in Taiwan and South Korea as they experience the same migration of factories to China and other even lower-cost locations in Southeast Asia. These two countries passed their LTPs around 1985 and entered a golden age that lasted perhaps until 2005. The frequency of Korean labor disputes also shot up during this period, as shown in Figure 15, as workers gained bargaining power for the first time and won large wage concessions. In Taiwan, wages grew rapidly during the post-LTP golden period but peaked around 2005 and stagnated thereafter, as shown in Figure 16. Now both countries are feeling the pinch as China steadily takes over the industries that generated so much growth for these two countries in the past.

Free trade has rendered war obsolete

To understand the emergence of Asia and where globalization is headed, we need to understand how the free-trade regime introduced by the US transformed the world economy after 1945. Before 1945, there were many constraints to trade that slowed down industrialization as described above – namely, a shortage of aggregate demand and the difficulty of accessing markets. In those days, most countries imposed high tariffs on imported products both to raise revenues and to protect domestic industries. If the workers constituted the main source of consumption demand in the pre-LTP urbanizing world, they could not have provided enough demand for all the goods produced because their share of income was so low, while capitalists typically had a higher marginal propensity to save. Consequently, aggregate supply often exceeded aggregate demand.

To overcome this constraint, European powers turned to colonization and imperialism in a bid to acquire sources of raw materials and captive markets where they could sell the goods they produced. It was indeed believed for centuries that national economies could not grow without territorial expansion. That led to countless wars and killings until 1945.

When World War II ended, the victorious Americans introduced a free-trade regime known as the General Agreement on Tariff and Trade (GATT) that allowed any country with competitive products to sell to anyone else.

The other half of macroeconomics

Although the concept and practice of free trade were not new, the US took the giant lead by opening its vast domestic market to the world. With the US economy accounting for nearly 30 percent of global GDP at the end of World War II, the impact of this game-changing move was absolutely massive.

The US was partly motivated by the need to fend off the Soviet threat by rebuilding Western Europe and Japan quickly, but the free-trade regime allowed not only Japan and Germany but also many other countries to prosper *without* the need to expand their territories. Indeed, it is difficult to find a country that grew rapidly in the post-1945 world that did *not* utilize the US market.

The advent of free trade made obsolete the whole notion of territorial expansion as a necessary condition for economic growth. While victorious allies after World War II were busy fighting indigenous independence movements in their colonies at enormous expense, Japan and Germany – which had lost all of their overseas and some of their domestic territories – quickly grew to become the second and third largest economies in the world. In other words, post-war Japan and Germany have proven that what is really needed for economic growth is markets and investment opportunities, not territories. Economic growth will accelerate if markets can be accessed without the expense of acquiring overseas territories.

The relative infrequency of wars after 1945 is often attributed to the Cold War and the deterrent of Mutually Assured Destruction (MAD), but the drastic reduction in conflicts between countries that had been fighting since history began may also be due to the fact that territorial expansion was no longer a necessary or sufficient condition for economic prosperity in the free trade era. Indeed, after the free-trade regime took hold, colonies became more of a liability than an asset as far as economic growth was concerned. Today, almost no one talks about the need for territorial expansion as a pre-requisite to economic prosperity.

In Asia, it was the Japanese who discovered in the 1950s that their economy could still grow and prosper by producing quality products for the US market. They then put their best and brightest to the task while leaving all complicated diplomatic and national security issues to be decided by the

Americans. The spectacular success of Japan then prompted Taiwan, South Korea and eventually the rest of Asia to follow the same export-oriented growth formula in a process dubbed the "flying geese" pattern of industrialization.

China is in a post-LTP maturing stage of industrialization

The biggest beneficiary of the US-led free trade movement, of course, was China, which was able to transform a desperately poor agrarian society of 1.3 billion people into the world's second-largest economy in just 30 years. The 30 years following Deng Xiaoping's opening of the Chinese economy in 1979 probably qualify as the fastest and greatest economic growth story in history as the per capita GDP of over one billion people grew from just over $300 to   nearly $8,000. China wasted no time in integrating itself with the global economy, which enabled it to attract an astronomical amount of foreign direct investment, not just from the West and Japan, but also from the Asian tigers including Taiwan, Hong Kong, Singapore and South Korea.

More precisely, China's fantastic economic growth was made possible by the US-led free-trade system, which allowed Chinese and foreign companies producing in China to sell their products anywhere in the world. It was that access to the global market that prompted so many businesses from around the world to build factories in China. Were it not for the markets provided by the US-led free-trade regime, it could have taken China far longer to achieve the growth it did.

Businesses in the West and elsewhere that were able to take advantage of China found almost unlimited investment opportunities there and operated like the capitalists in their own countries' pre-LTP eras. Those investments added massively to China's economic growth and turned the country into "the world's factory".

But those in Asia and the West who have to compete with Chinese workers are experiencing zero or even negative income growth. Foreign businesses expanding rapidly in China are also likely to be investing less at home, which has a depressing effect on growth in their home countries' economies and productivity. Indeed, the slow productivity growth in advanced countries is the flip side of the massive productivity growth in China and other emerging markets that was made possible by investments by firms in advanced countries.

Figure 17 China may grow old before it grows rich: working age population* has started to contract

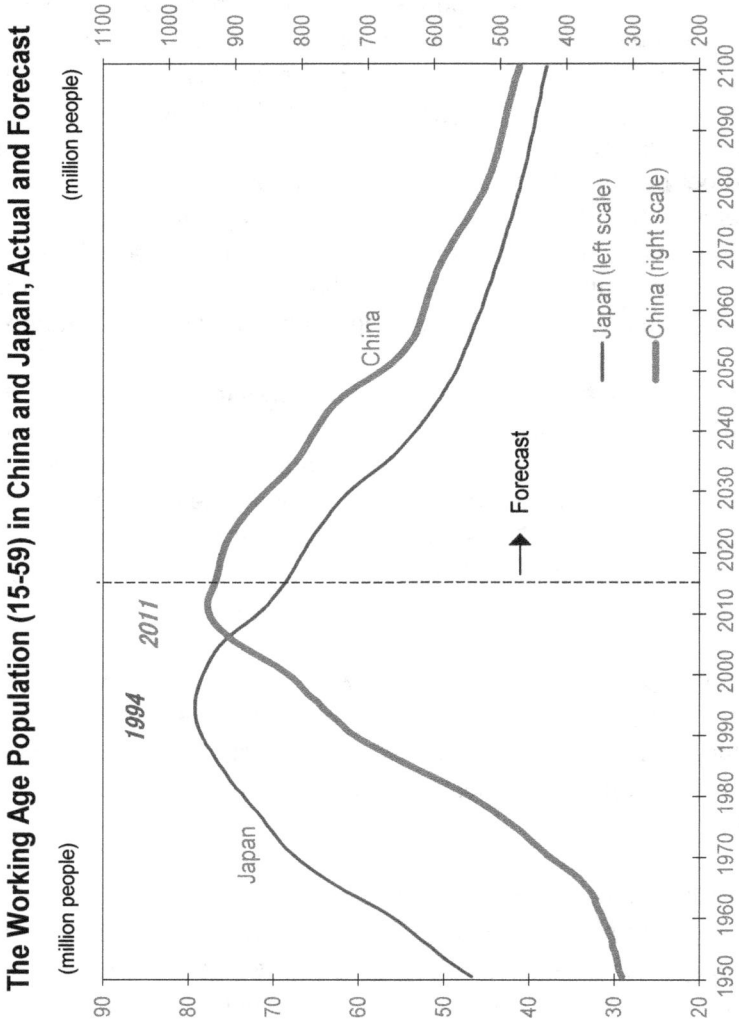

The Working Age Population (15-59) in China and Japan, Actual and Forecast

Note: The Chinese National Statistical Office defines the working age population as the people from 15 to 59.
Source: United Nations, Department of Economic and Social Affairs, Population Division (2015). World Population Prospects: The 2015 Revision, custom data acquired via website.

Those in the advanced economies who are still wondering what has happened to all the enthusiasm for fixed capital investment, all they have to do is get a window seat on a flight from Hong Kong to Beijing (or vice versa) on a nice day. They will see below an endless landscape of factories after factories stretching in all directions that were started mostly by foreign capital. They were started with foreign capital because when Deng Xiaoping opened up the Chinese economy in 1979, there were no capitalists left in China: they had all either been killed or driven out of the country by the Communist revolution in 1949 and by Mao's Cultural Revolution in the 1960s. The point is that businesses in advanced countries are still investing, but not necessarily in their home countries.

Post-LTP China faces "middle income trap"

China is also subject to the same laws of industrialization, urbanization and globalization as other countries. China actually passed its LTP around 2012 and is now experiencing sharp increases in wages. This means the country is now in its golden era or post-LTP maturing phase. Because the Chinese government is wary of public disturbances of any kind, including strikes and other labor disputes, it is trying to pre-empt such disputes by delivering significant wage increases on an annual basis. Businesses are therefore required to raise wages under directives issued by local governments. In some regions, these administered wages have been increased at double-digit rates in order to prevent labor disputes. It remains to be seen whether such pre-emptive actions by the government can substitute for a process in which employers and employees learn through confrontation what can reasonably expected from the other party.

At the same time, the working age population in China actually started shrinking in 2012. This is a highly unusual combination of demographics in that the whole labor supply curve began shifting to the left just as the country reached its LTP. The huge demographic bonus the country enjoyed up to 2012 is not only gone, but has now reversed, as shown in Figure 17. This means China will not be able to maintain the rapid pace of economic growth seen in the past, and in fact its growth rate has slowed sharply.

Higher wages in China are now prompting both Chinese and foreign businesses to move factories to lower-wage countries such as Vietnam and Bangladesh. This move is prompting fears that China will get stuck in the so-called "middle-income trap." This trap arises from the fact that once a country loses its distinction as the lowest-cost producer, many factories may leave for other lower-cost destinations, resulting in less investment and less growth. This means the laws of globalization and free trade that benefitted China when it was the lowest-cost producer are now posing real challenges for the country.

The easy part of China's economic growth story is over. The challenge now is how to raise the productivity of each and every Chinese worker to offset higher wages when there are easier ways for businesses to make money by simply moving factories to lower-cost locations. That is precisely the challenge advanced countries faced when they were chased by emerging economies, including China, some decades earlier.

Growth, happiness and maturity of nations

The discussion above regarding the stages of economic growth is summarized in Figure 18. Here, "Industrialization with Urbanization" refers to the pre-LTP urbanization phase, "Golden Era" to the post-LTP maturing phase, and "Pursued by ..." to the post-LTP pursued phase. The bold arrows point in the direction of pursuit.

It appears that countries are reaching their "Golden Eras" sooner with the accelerated globalization made possible by free trade and rapid developments in information technology, but the eras themselves are becoming shorter as more countries join the globalization bandwagon. For example, the golden era for the US and Western Europe lasted for about 40 years until the mid-1970s, while Japan's lasted around 30 years until the mid-1990s. For Asian NICs like Taiwan and Korea, the golden era probably lasted about 20 years through 2005 or so. It will be interesting to see how long this era lasts for China, where policymakers are already worried about the middle-income trap.

67

Figure 18 Growth, happiness and maturing of nations

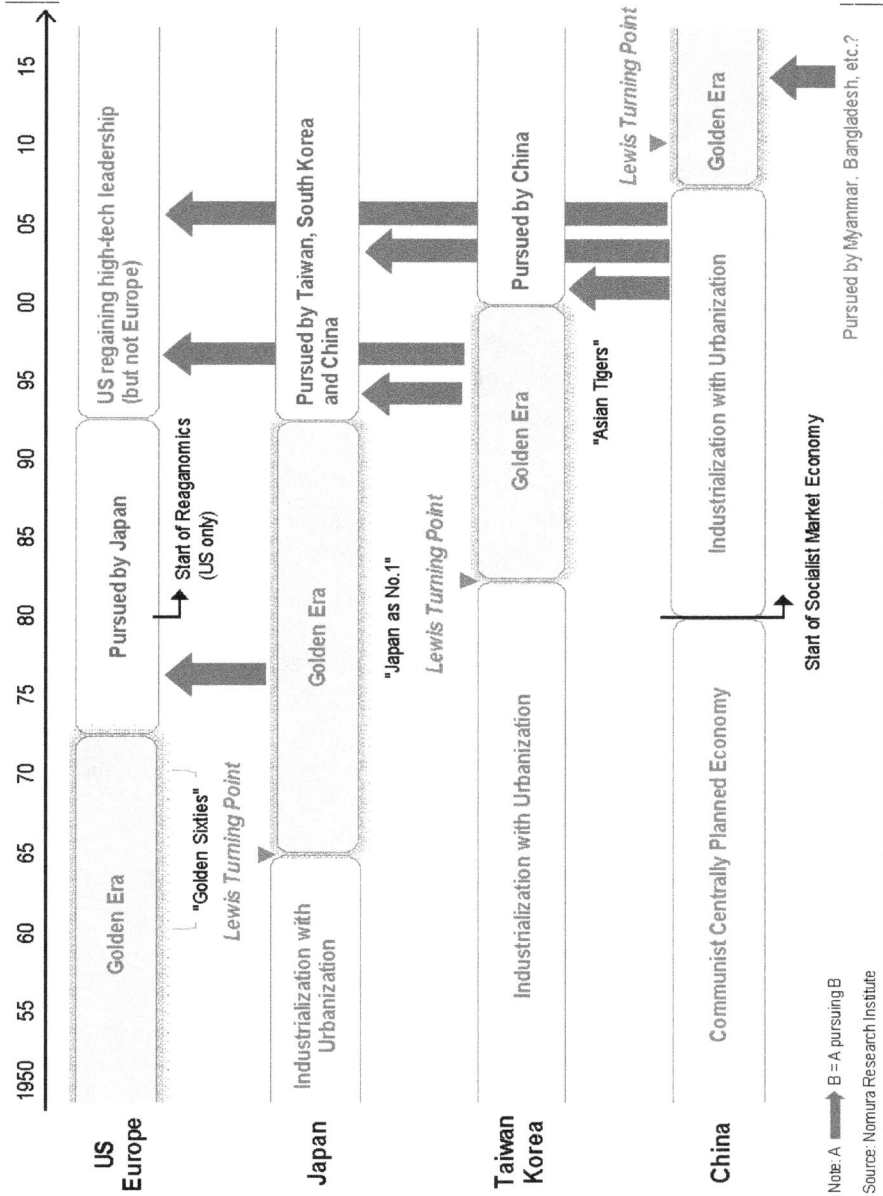

The other half of macroeconomics

If the happiness of nations can be measured by (1) how fast inequality is disappearing and (2) how fast the economy is growing, then the post-LTP maturing period would qualify as the period when a nation is at its happiest. During this phase, strong demand for workers from a rapidly expanding industrial sector forces the service sector to offer comparable wages to retain workers. As a result, almost all members of society benefit from economic growth because wages are rising for everybody. Hence this is a Golden Era in which everybody is hopeful for the future and inequality is shrinking rapidly.

From a global perspective, this implies that nations are at their happiest – i.e., inequality is disappearing and people are enjoying the fruits of their labor – when they are either well ahead of other nations or are chasing other economies but are not being pursued themselves.

The West was at its happiest until Japan started chasing it in the 1970s because it was ahead of everybody else. It was a French person who said before the Berlin Wall came down that the world would be a much nicer place if there were no Japan and no Soviet Union.

The Japanese were at their happiest when they were chasing the West but nobody was chasing them. The nation's happy days were over when the Asian Tigers and China began pursuing Japan in the mid-1990s. The Asian Tigers then enjoyed their own golden era for about 20 years until China started pursuing them.

The key issue in most advanced countries now that they are in the post-LTP pursued phase is how a society at this stage of development should re-organize itself. Unfortunately, the policy debate is seldom coached in such terms. Instead, the slogans used by many presidential and prime ministerial hopefuls in these countries suggest that many still long for the return of the golden era they remember from the pre-pursued days. But until they fully appreciate their economic reality in a global context, they are unlikely to do much to improve the lives of ordinary people.

Capital and Justice

The rise and fall of Communism

The preceding description of how inequality increases and decreases before and after the LTP also explains why so many found Communism appealing at a certain juncture in history. Marx and Engels, who lived in pre-LTP industrializing Europe, were appalled and outraged by the horrendous inequality they observed around them and the miserable working and living conditions for ordinary people. As indicated earlier, it was not uncommon then for people to work 16 hours day in a dirty, dangerous industrial environment while capitalists rapidly accumulated wealth. Any intellectual with a heart would have been hard-pressed to stand quietly in the face of the social and economic inequality of the time.

Marx responded to this inequality with the concept of Communism, which called for capital to be owned and shared by the laborers. He argued that if capital is owned by the workers, the exploitation of workers would end and workers would enjoy a greater share of the output. For "exploited" workers forced to work long hours in dreadful conditions, Communism appeared to offer a hope for a better life with little to lose, and many embraced it enthusiastically. In that sense, the birth of Communism itself may have been a historical imperative of sorts.

Marx and Engels' greatest mistake, however, was to assume the extreme inequality they witnessed (points G and H in Figure 6) would continue forever. In reality, it was just one inevitable step on the path towards industrialization. If the capitalists were earning large profits in the period before LTP, they will probably continue to invest in the hope of making even more money. It is that drive for more profits that eventually pushes the economy to reach and pass the LTP, when a totally different labor market dynamics kicks in.

As soon as the economy reaches its LTP and wages start increasing rapidly, the appeal of Communism quickly wanes as workers begin to realize that they can get what they want within the existing framework. Such a period is characterized by frequent strikes and labor disputes of all kinds as workers start to utilize their newfound bargaining power for the first time ever. After 15 or 20 years of such struggles, employers and employees alike begin to understand what can be reasonably expected from the other side, and a new political order based on that understanding is put in place.

Although the resultant center-left and center-right political parties served advanced countries well in their post-LTP maturing stage, it remains to be seen whether they are the most appropriate arrangements in the post-LTP pursued stage, which is characterized by a very different labor dynamic.

Ironically, those countries that adopted Communism before reaching their LTPs, such as pre-1979 China and pre-1986 Vietnam, ended up stagnating because the profit motive needed to promote investment and push the economy beyond its LTP was lost.

Interestingly, when labor becomes too powerful and expensive *before* the country reaches its LTP, the economy also ends up stagnating, for both economic and political reasons. First, because the protected workers are too expensive for capitalists to expand production, the economy stops growing and gets stuck in the pre-LTP phase. Second, those unionized and privileged workers end up creating a two-tier labor market with a permanent underclass that is denied meaningful jobs because the economy is not expanding (or not expanding fast enough). This two-tier labor market then creates massive political problems that slow down the economy even further, as seen in some Latin American countries since the 1950s.

The discussion above suggests that many if not most inclusive social and political reforms are possible only after a country passes its LTP. Even in advanced countries, most inclusive reforms took place after they passed their LTPs. This suggests that sequencing matters and that there are certain laws of economic growth that must be observed in addition to the laws of physics and chemistry. People in emerging countries who want more inclusive reforms might first need to grow their economies beyond the LTP.

Real driver behind Thomas Piketty's inequality

Income inequality has recently become one of the hottest and most controversial issues in economics, not just in the developed world but also in

China and elsewhere. Many people are becoming increasingly uncomfortable with the divide between the haves and the have nots, especially after Thomas Piketty's *Capital in the 21st Century* opened up a fresh debate on the optimal distribution of wealth, an issue that had been largely overlooked by the economics profession.

Although the author cannot claim to have understood all the implications of Piketty's enormous contributions, the analysis presented here contradicts one of the key historical points he makes. Namely, he claims that the extreme inequality that existed prior to World War I was corrected by the wealth destruction of two world wars and the Great Depression. He then goes on to argue that the retreat of progressive taxation in the developed world starting in the late 1970s ended up creating a level of inequality that approaches that which existed prior to World War I.

In spite of having ample data to back his assertions, the pre-World War I results he obtained may be due to the fact that those countries were all in the pre-LTP industrialization stage, where inequality grows rapidly. The post-World War I results he obtained may also be due to the West entering the post-LTP maturing phase or "golden era" of industrialization where everybody enjoyed the fruits of economic growth. Although Piketty attributes this to the destruction of wealth brought by two world wars and the introduction of progressive income taxes, this was also a period in which urbanization came to an end in most of these countries. The four decades to 1970 were a golden era for Western economies in which they were ahead of everyone else and were being chased by no one.

Finally, Piketty's post-1970 results may be attributable to the fact that Western economies entered their post-LTP pursued phase when Japan and others began chasing them. For Western capitalists able to utilize Asian resources, it was a golden opportunity to make money. But this was not a welcome development for manufacturing workers in the West who had to compete with cheaper imports from Asia.

This also suggests that the favorable income distributions observed by Piketty in the West before 1970 and in Japan until 1990 were also *transitory* phenomena. These countries enjoyed a golden era of growing income and shrinking inequality not because they had the right kind of tax regime but because the global economic environment was such that nobody was chasing them.

Just because such a desirable world was observed once does not mean it can be preserved or replicated. Any attempt to preserve that equality in the face of fierce international competition would have required massive and continuous investments in human and physical capital, something that most countries are not ready to implement. It is not even certain whether such investments constitute the best use of resources, since businesses would still be under pressure from shareholders to invest in countries producing higher returns.

It will also be difficult for governments to force businesses to invest at home when the return on capital is much higher elsewhere. This means a much greater degree of protectionism may be needed to keep cheaper foreign goods out and force businesses to invest at home.

The US experience in fending off Japan

Instead of trying to return to a lost golden era, advanced nations that are chased from behind should implement policies that allow them to fend off the pursuers. Assuming that free trade is here to stay, the primary concern of policymakers in most of the developed world today should be how to increase investment opportunities when the economy is in the post-LTP pursued phase. On this point, the US experience in fending off Japan is instructive.

When the US began losing industries left and right to Japanese competition starting in the mid-1970s, it pursued a two-pronged approach to counter the Japanese threat. This involved keeping Japanese imports from coming in too fast while simultaneously trying to make domestic industries more competitive.

The US utilized every means available to prevent Japanese imports from flooding its market. Those measures included dumping accusations, Super

301 clauses, gentlemen's agreements of all sorts, and exchange rate depreciation via the Plaza Accord of 1985.

At the same time, so-called "Japanese management" was all the rage at US business schools in the 1980s and 1990s, as mentioned earlier. Many of those schools eagerly recruited Japanese students so they could discuss Japanese management techniques in their classes. Ezra Vogel's *Japan as Number One: Lessons for America*, published in 1979, was widely read by people on both sides of the Pacific. The challenge from Japan, coupled with the aftermath of the Vietnam War, sent the confidence of Americans to an all-time low, while their consumption of sushi went up sharply.

As a resident of Japan who had worked for the Federal Reserve as an economist and also held American citizenship, the author was frequently asked by the US Embassy in Tokyo to explain the US trade position to Japanese TV audiences, as the author was a frequent guest on those programs. Although the author tried his best to explain to the Japanese public why it was in their own interest to find compromises with the US, he will never forget the intense mutual hostility that characterized the US-Japan trade relationship from the mid-1980s to the mid-1990s. The author not only received his share of death-threats, but trade frictions were so bad that it began to resemble a racial confrontation.

After trying everything else, however, the US seems to have concluded that when a country is being pursued from behind the only real solution is to run faster – i.e., to stay ahead of the competition by continuously generating new ideas, products and designs. In this regard the US has been fortunate that the supply-side reforms of President Ronald Reagan – which cut taxes and deregulated the economy drastically starting in the early 1980s – had the effect of encouraging innovators and entrepreneurs to come up with new ideas and products.

Reaganomics itself was a response to the so-called stagflation of the 1970s, which was accompanied by frequent strikes, poor quality of products coming out of US factories, and mediocrity all around. It was a reaction against labor, which was still trying to extend gains made during the post-LTP maturing stage without realizing that the US had already entered the post-

The other half of macroeconomics

LTP pursued stage in the 1970s with the arrival of Japanese competition. The fact that the US was losing so many industries and good jobs to Japan also created a sense of urgency that it was necessary to break from the past.

When President Reagan lowered tax rates and deregulated the economy, people with ideas and drive began to take notice. These people then began pushing the technological frontier of the IT industry, eventually enabling the US to regain the lead it lost to the Japanese in many high-tech areas. In other words, the US learned how to run faster.

More precisely, deregulation and lower taxes improved the allocation of resources, especially of human capital, within the US economy. With both money and the best minds flowing toward promising high-tech areas, the US was able to acquire a new growth engine.

Although the US success in regaining the high-tech lead from Japan was a spectacular achievement, the process took nearly 15 years. It was in the early 1980s that Reagan's ideas were implemented, but it was not until Bill Clinton became president that those ideas actually bore fruit. The US economy continued to struggle during Reagan's two terms and the single term of George H.W. Bush, who served as Vice President under Reagan.

The senior Bush achieved monumental diplomatic successes that included the end of the Cold War, the collapse of the Soviet Union, and victory in the first Gulf War. Yet he lost his re-election campaign to a young Governor from Arkansas by the name of Bill Clinton who had only one campaign line. And that line was "It's the economy, stupid!" The fact that Bush lost the election to Clinton suggests the economy was still far from satisfactory in the eyes of most Americans 12 years Reaganomics was launched.

Once Clinton took over, however, the US economy began to pick up even though few can remember his administration's economic policies. The economy was doing so well that the Federal government was running budget surpluses by Clinton's second term. The conclusion to be drawn here is that while supply-side reform is essential in encouraging innovation, it will take many years for such measures to produce macroeconomic results that average people can recognize and appreciate. The fact that structural reforms take so long to bear fruit also means they are no substitute for fiscal stimulus if the economy is in a balance sheet recession.

The challenge of finding and encouraging innovators

The problem is that not everyone in a society is capable of coming up with new ideas or products. And it is not always the same group that generates new ideas. It also takes an enormous amount of effort and perseverance to bring new products to market. But without innovators willing to persevere to create new products and industries, the economy will be relegated to stagnation or worse.

The most important consideration for countries being pursued from behind, therefore, should be how to maximize the number of people capable of coming up with new ideas and products and how to give them the right set of incentives to maximize their creative efforts.

On the first point, the number of people who can come up with new ideas is limited in any society. Often they are not in the mainstream, because those in the mainstream are not incentivized to think differently from the rest. Some may also show little interest in educational achievement in the ordinary sense of the word. Indeed, many successful start-ups have been created by college dropouts. Many innovators may actually infuriate and alienate the establishment with their "crazy" ideas. If they are sufficiently discouraged by the orthodoxy, they may withdraw altogether from their creative activities. That means finding these people and encouraging them to continue on their creative pursuit is no easy task.

In this regard, the so-called liberal arts education served the West well. In particular, the notion that students must think with their own minds and substantiate their thinking with logic and evidence instead of just absorbing and regurgitating what they have been taught is crucial in training people who can think differently and independently. In some top universities in the US, students who simply reproduce what the professor said may only get a B; an A requires that they go beyond the professor. Thus, they are encouraged to challenge the status quo, which is the only way to come up with new ideas and products.

This Western liberal arts education has a long tradition starting with the Renaissance and Enlightenment, where the value of the human intellect was finally recognized after being suppressed for centuries by the Catholic Church. This long struggle to free the intellect from church authorities was no easy battle – many brilliant thinkers were burned at the stake. The implication here is that citizens' creativity may not be fully utilized in societies where the authorities, including educational establishments, continue to act like the Catholic Inquisitors of the past.

The problem, however, is that a true liberal arts education is expensive. It requires first-rate teachers to guide the students, and teachers with such capabilities are usually in strong demand elsewhere. Indeed, tuition at some of the top US universities has reached almost obscene levels. Furthermore, the ability to think independently does not guarantee that students will immediately find work upon graduation. As such, this type of education is usually accorded to a limited few who can afford it, which exacerbates the already widening income gap in post-LTP pursued economies

The need to have the right kind of education

In contrast, the cookbook approach to education where students simply learn what the teachers tell them is cheaper and more practical in the sense that students at least leave school knowing how to cook. The vast majority of the population is therefore exposed only to this type of education, where there is limited room to express creative ideas. This means many creative minds could be buried in such educational establishments.

The US always had an excellent liberal arts education system that encouraged students to challenge the status quo. As such, it was able to maintain the lead in scientific breakthroughs and new product development even as it fell behind the Japanese and others in manufacturing those new products at competitive prices.

Capital and Justice

In contrast, many countries in catch-up mode adopted the cookbook-style education system where the maximum number of people can be readied for employment in an industrial setting in the shortest possible time. When a country is in catch-up mode, this type of education system is often sufficient and more practical because the hard work of inventing and developing something new is already being done by someone else in the developed world.

However, these countries will have to come up with new products and services themselves once they exhaust the low-hanging investment opportunities from industrialization and urbanization. The question then is whether those countries can adjust their educational systems so as to produce a sufficient number of independent, innovative thinkers to sustain growth in their economies. This can be a major challenge if the society has discouraged people from thinking outside of the box for too long, since both teachers and students may be unable to cope with the new task of producing more independent thinkers.

One way to overcome or sidestep this problem is to import creative thinkers and innovators from abroad. The immigration-friendly US is full of born-abroad innovators competing with each other as well as with native innovators in universities and in the business world. Singapore is also pushing hard to attract foreign talent by inviting not just the well-known names, but also their entire teams and families to do research in Singapore. Many pursued countries should seriously consider implementing and augmenting similar programs to acquire and retain those who can come up with new ideas and products.

For many traditional societies in Europe and Japan, some sort of shake-up may also be needed to open fields to new outside-the-box thinkers. In Japan, long years of economic stagnation and the diminished appeal of established companies are prompting some college graduates to consider starting businesses for the first time in many decades. This is a welcome development in a country where tradition and authority still carry a great deal of weight. Some younger engineers in Japan, for example, find it difficult to challenge the achievements of older engineers in the same company because such actions can be viewed as a sign of disrespect. Such seniority-based rigidity has discouraged innovation in no small way. Some European designers are also migrating to the US and Australia to free themselves from traditional constraints on how and where they can express their creative talents. Tradition-bound societies therefore have a desperate need for new businesses that are open to new ideas and innovations.

Importance of having the right tax and regulatory environment

Regarding the second point – the need for appropriate financial and tax regimes to encourage creative activity – it must be stressed that to create something out of nothing and actually bring it to market often requires insane amount of effort that "any rational person will give up," *Real-World Economics Review*, issue no. 75 subscribe for free 39 in the words of Steve Jobs. In a similar vein, Thomas Edison famously claimed a new invention is 1 percent inspiration and 99 percent perspiration.

Although some individuals are so driven that they require no external support, most mortals find outside encouragement important in the long, risky and difficult journey to produce something that no one has seen before. This means financial, regulatory and tax regimes should do everything possible to encourage such individuals and businesses to continue with their pioneering efforts.

Piketty cited the retreat of progressive tax rates as the cause of widening inequality in the post-1970 developed world. But the US, which led the reduction in tax rates, has regained its high-tech leadership while Europe and Japan, which shied away from similar cuts in tax rates, have stagnated. This outcome suggests a tax regime that was reasonable when no one was chasing the country may no longer be appropriate when the country is being pursued.

An advanced economy that is pursued from behind must run faster to remain an advanced country. And it is the outside-the-box thinkers that create the innovations and breakthroughs that allow these countries to stay ahead by providing new investment opportunities for businesses. Although sustained and substantial fiscal stimulus is absolutely necessary during a balance sheet recession, at all other times the policy priority for any country in the post-LTP pursued phase should be tax incentives and other measures to maximize innovation and investment opportunities.

The difficulty of achieving public consensus

Unfortunately for many countries, these sorts of measures are often decried as "favoring the rich" and are therefore rejected. For emerging economies with plenty of low-hanging investment opportunities, such opposition may not lead to a noticeable economic slowdown. But for mature economies that are being chased from behind and must therefore run faster, an inability to fully utilize the creative and innovative potential of their people could have highly detrimental consequences for everyone. For those countries in the developed world now facing this challenge from the emerging world, future growth may well depend on how quickly they can achieve a social consensus and develop the necessary infrastructure, such as true liberal arts education and an innovator-friendly corporate culture and tax system, to maximize their innovative capacity.

This may require the creation of a new consensus where those who are not blessed with the ability to think outside the box understand and appreciate the fact that their wellbeing is dependent on those who can. Indeed, the whole of society must understand that such thinkers are essential in generating new investment opportunities to keep the economy out of prolonged stagnation.

This is far from easy, however. As Thomas Piketty noted, inequality in the West began increasing in the 1970s and is reaching "alarming" levels in some countries. This increasingly unequal income distribution is prompting many developed countries to raise taxes on the rich. But such actions, which represent the opposite of supply-side reforms, could easily backfire by discouraging innovation and risk-taking, the most important drivers of economic growth in a pursued country.

To make matters worse, most Western countries were engulfed in balance sheet recessions when their housing bubbles burst in 2008. This development accelerated the disappearance of borrowers that started in the 1970s when these countries entered their post-LTP pursued phases.

Moreover, when these countries finally come out of their balance sheet recessions, they will be saddled with huge public debt because they implemented fiscal stimulus to fight the recession. The natural tendency of orthodox economists and policymakers faced with a large public debt is to raise taxes wherever possible. But such wonton tax hikes may discourage businesses from investing aggressively in new innovation, thus prolonging sub-par economic growth.

In other words, the economies currently emerging from balance sheet recessions need to resist the temptation to raise taxes that may thwart innovation. Only in this way can they gain the escape velocity necessary to fend off competitors from behind. This is particularly important in Japan, where debt levels are truly onerous.

Of all the post-LTP pursued economies, the US probably comes closest to having achieved this sort of consensus on a growth-friendly tax regime, which is why it is attracting innovators from around the world. But with the rich getting ever richer while the remaining 80 percent of the population have seen little income growth for the last 20 years, the temptation to raise taxes on the rich is getting stronger even in the US. The real challenge for countries being chased from behind is how to persuade voters to maintain innovator-friendly tax regimes when the public debt is so large and the vast majority of the population has experienced no income growth for many years.

Labor's role in three stages of economic development

If incentives are needed for innovators in the pursued economies to maximize their output, what is in store for ordinary workers? It was already mentioned that when the economy is in the pre-LTP urbanizing phase, capitalists can take advantage of workers because there are so many of the latter in rural areas who are willing to work in urban factories at the going wage. Workers really have no bargaining power until the country reaches its

LTP. During this stage, many if not most workers are not particularly well educated or skilled because of limited opportunities for education and vocational training in the rural areas where they spent most of their lives prior to migrating to the cities. With so many of them competing for a limited number of jobs in the cities, there is not much job security, either.

Once the economy passes the LTP, however, the table is turned completely in favor of the workers. The supply of surplus workers in the rural areas is exhausted and the labor supply curve takes on a significant positive slope. As long as some businesses are trying to expand their workforce, all businesses will be forced to pay ever-higher wages. At this stage, businesses also have plenty of reasons to expand because workers' purchasing power is increasing rapidly.

And at this stage, expansion means domestic expansion: firms have little experience producing abroad, and domestic wages, while rising, are still competitive.

To satisfy demand while paying ever-higher wages, businesses invest in labor-saving equipment to keep costs down. Domestic demand for cost-saving and productivity-enhancing machinery is therefore very strong during this period, and this demand manifests itself in the form of large capital investment. With strong demand for funds to finance capital investments, the economy is firmly in Case 1 of Figure 2. The new equipment effectively raises the productivity of employees even if the workers themselves are no more skilled or educated than before the country reached its LTP.

With wages rising rapidly, job security for workers also improves significantly as companies try to hold on to their employees. Lifetime employment and seniority-based remuneration systems also become more common. The emerging power of unions also forces employers to improve the job security of workers. Working conditions improve as businesses offer safer, cleaner working environments to attract and retain workers.

During this post-LTP maturing period, therefore, businesses are investing to keep labor costs down, which in turn allows them to pay the higher wages dictated by the labor market. In contrast to the pre-LTP period when businesses were effectively "exploiting" workers because there were so many of them, businesses in the post-LTP maturing period were "pampering" workers with productivity-enhancing equipment so they can afford to pay them more.

At some point, however, wages reach point EQ in Figure 6 where businesses are forced to look for alternative production sites abroad because domestic production is no longer competitive. Businesses may find domestic production uncompetitive for two reasons. One is that domestic wages have gone up too far relative to overseas wages. The other is that, even if domestic wages have not increased, foreign producers may have picked up sufficient technical know-how and marketing savvy to challenge domestic producers. The two could also happen at the same time. Although different industries may reach this point at different times, a country can be said to have entered its post-LTP pursued stage if a meaningful number of industries have reached this point.

The way businesses perceive workers then changes again because they now have the option of using overseas labor resources. Many businesses are likely to find that a unit of capital invested abroad goes much further than if it is invested at home in labor-saving equipment. This means they have fewer incentives to invest at home, and fixed-capital investment, which was such a major driver of economic growth during the post-LTP maturing phase, begins to slow down. As investment slows, growth in labor productivity, which shot up during the post-LTP maturing phase, also starts to decelerate. Wages, too, begin to stagnate.

It is at this point that the ability of individual workers begins to matter for the first time because only those who can do something that people abroad cannot do will continue to prosper. This is in contrast to the previous two stages, where wages were determined largely by macro factors such as labor supply and institutional factors such as union membership, both of which had little to do with the skills of individual workers. Once the supply constraint is removed by the possibility of producing abroad or outright outsourcing, the only reason a firm will pay a high wage at home is because that particular worker can do something that cannot be easily done abroad.

If workers were "exploited" during the pre-LTP urbanization stage and "pampered" during the post-LTP maturing stage, they are "entirely on their own" in the post-LTP pursued stage. This is because businesses are much less willing to invest in labor-saving equipment to increase the productivity of their workers at home. The workers must invest in *themselves* to enhance their productivity and marketability.

Indeed, job security and the seniority-based wage system become increasingly rare in industries forced to become more agile and flexible to fend off pursuers from behind. It is no accident that lifetime employment and seniority-based wages, which were common in the US until the 1970s, disappeared once Japanese competition appeared. The same has happened to Japanese labor relations since China emerged in the mid-1990s.

Those who take the time and effort to acquire skills that are in demand will continue to do well, while those without such skills will be earning close to a minimum wage. Those who benefited from union membership during the post-LTP maturing phase will find the benefits of membership in the new pursued era are not what they used to be. This means inequality will increase again even though *when adjusted for skill levels* it may not change all that much.

Workers in post-LTP pursued economies must therefore think hard about their individual prospects and what skills they should acquire in the new environment if they want to maintain or improve their living standards. The answer to this question will differ depending on the individual, and in that sense they are truly on their own. The "good old days," when businesses invested to increase workers' productivity so they could pay them more money, are gone for good.

Summers' secular stagflation thesis

When Larry Summers first mentioned secular stagnation in 2013, the US was in a midst of balance sheet recession where the private sector was saving over 7 percent of GDP at zero interest rates. He then added in a private conference in Paris on June 4, 2015 that the return on capital was already falling in the West in the 1970s, long before the advent of the global financial crisis in 2008.[2]

The sudden loss of momentum in Western economies after 2008 is obviously due to the fact that they are all suffering from serious balance sheet recessions. Similarly, when Alvin Hansen coined the term "secular stagnation" in 1938, the US was in the midst of the greatest balance sheet recession of all, the Great Depression, and its unemployment rate was 19 percent.

In contrast, in Germany, where sustained and substantial fiscal stimulus needed to fight balance sheet recession was implemented starting in 1933, unemployment rate fell from 28 percent in that year to only 2 percent in 1938, and no-one was talking about secular stagnation.

The fact that both Hansen and Summers mentioned secular stagnation during balance sheet recessions and the fact that Germany which overcame balance sheet recession by 1938 was not suffering from stagnation suggest that the main driver of "secular stagnation" is actually balance sheet recession.

The pre-2008 decline in return on capital, however, may be due to the fact that Western countries reached their post-LTP pursued phase when an increasing number of businesses in these countries found it more attractive to invest in emerging economies.

Rethinking macroeconomics

Macroeconomics is still a very young science. It really started when Keynes started talking about the concept of aggregate demand in the 1930s. With only 85 years of history, it is like a toddler when compared to such disciplines as physics and chemistry. As a young science, it has achieved

[22] Lawrence H. Summers's webpage on secular stagnation; http://larrysummers.com/category/secular-stagnation/

only limited coverage of the broad range of economic phenomena and remains prone to fads and influences.

The profession's immaturity was amply demonstrated by the fact that only a handful of economists saw the Great Recession coming, and even fewer predicted the time it would take to recover from it. This is because most macroeconomic theories and models developed during the last 85 years assumed that private-sector agents are always willing to borrow if only the central bank lowers real interest rates far enough. This kind of thinking led Nobel laureate Paul Krugman to argue that if an inflation target of 2 percent is not enough to bring expectations of real interest rates down far enough, central banks should shoot for a 4 percent target. The assumption here, of course, is that the economy is in Case 2 in Figure 2.

This way of thinking implicitly assumes (1) that there are always investment opportunities worth borrowing for and (2) that borrowers always have clean balance sheets. But by presuming that there are always willing borrowers, economists have assumed away the two most critical challenges to economic growth, i.e., the questions of whether there are sufficient investment opportunities worth borrowing for and whether there are enough businesspeople who are able and willing to shoulder the risks entailed by those investments.

Moreover, most economists simply *assumed* a rate of long-term potential growth based on the trend growth of capital, labor and productivity and argued that policymakers should strive to bring the economy back to that growth path. But such "potential growth rates" mean absolutely nothing when businesspeople on the ground are either unable (because of balance sheet concerns) or unwilling (because of a lack of investment opportunities) to borrow money and invest it. This also suggests that conventional economics has no meaningful theory of economic growth.

When macroeconomics was in its formative years in the 1940s and 1950s, most advanced economies had passed their LTPs and were experiencing a golden age with no one chasing them. New products were being invented one after the other and people were optimistic about the future. Their balance sheets were also strong thanks to the astronomical government spending during World War II that repaired the balance sheet damage wrought by the Great Depression.

Even though the extraordinary effectiveness of fiscal policy in lifting the developed economies out of the Great Depression during World War II was obvious for everyone to see, Keynes, who argued for such policies, never realized that fiscal stimulus should be used *only* when the private sector is minimizing debt. Because of this critical omission by him and his followers, the Keynesians, the post-war fad among economists was to believe that fiscal policy could solve all problems. But with private sector balance sheets already repaired, the government's attempt to fine-tune the economy with fiscal policy in the 1950s and 1960s only resulted in more inflation, higher interest rates, and a general misallocation of resources.

When inflation became a problem in the 1970s, the fad shifted to the opposite extreme, with people like Milton Friedman arguing that monetary policy and smaller government were the answer to most problems. Some even tried to rewrite history by arguing that the Great Depression could have been avoided with better use of monetary policy by the Fed (Koo, 2008: 109-120).

When the private sector lost its head in a bubble and sustained massive balance sheet damage first in Japan in 1990 and then in the West in 2008, the economics profession was still beholden to monetary policy fads, and many economists argued for more monetary easing even though fiscal policy is the only tool that can address balance sheet recessions. Although fiscal policy was mobilized immediately after the Lehman collapse, by 2010 the orthodoxy had regained their grip on power and forced countries to cut their fiscal deficits at the G20 summit in Toronto, effectively throwing the world economy into reverse.

Policymakers who realized soon afterwards that the Toronto agreement had been a mistake, such as former Fed Chair Ben Bernanke and current Chair Janet Yellen, issued strong warnings about the fiscal cliff to ensure that the government continued to serve as borrower of last resort. That helped keep the US economy from shrinking. Japanese Finance Minister Taro Aso also recognized this danger and made fiscal stimulus the second "arrow" of

Abenomics. Their actions went a long way towards supporting the Japanese and US economies where unemployment rates now stand at fully-employed levels of 3.2 percent and 5.0 percent, respectively.

In the Eurozone, however, no such understanding emerged in policy circles, and millions are suffering from unemployment and deprivation because the Maastricht Treaty, which created the Euro, requires member governments to reduce the deficit to 3 percent of GDP regardless of the size of private sector savings. In other words, the Treaty makes no provision whatsoever for balance sheet recessions, where the private sector may be saving far in excess of 3 percent of GDP in spite of zero or negative interest rates. In view of the fact that Spain's private sector has been saving on average 7.3 percent of GDP since the third quarter of 2008, Ireland's 8.6 percent and Portugal's 4.6 percent, it is no surprise that these economies are suffering badly from the limitations imposed by the Treaty.

If the private sector is saving 7 percent of GDP but the government is allowed to borrow only 3 percent, the remaining 4 percent will leak out of the economy's income stream and become a deflationary gap. As a result, one Eurozone country after another fell off the fiscal cliff, with devastating human consequences. Moreover, this balance-sheet-driven deflationary gap cannot be addressed with structural reforms or ECB monetary easing, the two measures employed by the Eurozone authorities to fight the recession. As a result, there are still 5 million more unemployed workers in the Eurozone today than when Lehman Brothers collapsed in 2008.

It is truly ironic that it is the Germans who are imposing this fiscal straitjacket on every country in the Eurozone even though they were the first victims of a similar fiscal orthodoxy back in 1929 when Allied governments imposed austerity on the Brüning administration. That devastated the German economy and pushed its unemployment rate up to 28 percent as mentioned earlier. But with established center-right and center-left political parties largely beholden to orthodox economics and insisting on a balanced budget, the only choice left for the German people after four years of suffering was to vote for the National Socialists, who argued against both austerity and reparation payments. People voted for the Nazis because the established parties, the Allied governments, and the economists were totally incapable of rescuing them from the four years of deflationary spiral and resultant poverty that followed the crash of 1929.

For better or for worse, Adolf Hitler quickly implemented the kind of fiscal stimulus needed to overcome a balance sheet recession – public works projects undertaken by the Nazis included construction of the nation's autobahn expressway system. By 1938, just five years later, the nation's unemployment rate had fallen to 2%. That prompted Joan Robinson, a famous British economist and a contemporary of Keynes, to say,

> "I do not regard the Keynesian revolution as a great intellectual triumph. On the contrary, it was a tragedy because it came so late. Hitler had already found how to cure unemployment before Keynes had finished explaining why it occurred" (Robinson, 1972: 8).

Germany's spectacular economic success also led Hitler to think he could win a war this time because the German economy was in a virtuous cycle and generating plenty of taxes to support re-armament efforts. In contrast, the US, UK and French economies, still beholden to fiscal orthodoxy, were in a vicious cycle of unattended balance sheet recessions with ever-dwindling tax receipts and military budgets.

That led to the tragedy of the Second World War. Once the war began, however, the democracies were able to carry out the same sorts of policies that Hitler had implemented six years earlier. Allied governments started acting as borrower and spender of last resort to procure tanks and fighter planes, and the US and UK economies jumped back to life, just as the German economy had done six years earlier. The combined productive capacity of the Allies soon overwhelmed that of the Third Reich, but not before millions had perished in the hostilities.

Perhaps the Germans today are so appalled by the utter brutality of the Nazi regime that everything Hitler did is now automatically rejected. This kind of total repudiation of a person or an era can be extremely dangerous because people will be totally naïve and unprepared when the next Hitler comes, since they were never taught all the right things that Hitler did to win the hearts of the German people.

With so many Nazi-like political parties gaining ground in countries suffering from balance sheet recessions but unable to do anything about them because of the ill-designed Maastricht Treaty, it is urgent that the people of Europe be made aware of this economic disease as quickly as possible.

More generally, economists must wake up to the fact that the world they have been analyzing, where monetary policy is effective because there are ample investment opportunities and the private sector has a clean balance sheet and is maximizing profits, describes only one half of the macroeconomic picture (Cases 1 and 2 in Figure 2). In the other half, the private sector is minimizing debt because of either balance sheet problems or a dearth of investment opportunities (Cases 3 and 4 in Figure 2). The economy can also shift from Case 1 to Case 3 or 4 very quickly after a bubble burst. Even though government and central bank have the tools to move the economy from Case 4 to Case 3, it may take years if not decades for the economy in Case 3 to return to Case 1.

Only fiscal policy can support an economy in this second half in the short to medium run, while measures to encourage innovation become absolutely essential in the long run. But until universities start explicitly teaching students about the second half, policy makers and public in general are likely to make mistakes or zigzag through when the economy is in the second half. Some may even backtrack on human rights progress if they feel a Nazi-like government is the only way to break through a policy orthodoxy that makes sense only when the economy is in Case 1 or 2.

The experiences of Japan since 1990 and of the West since 2008 have demonstrated that if balance sheet problems leave borrowers missing in action, the government must serve as borrower of last resort via fiscal policy. If the absence of borrowers is due to a lack of worthwhile investment opportunities, the government must consciously implement supply-side reforms to taxes and regulation to maximize the output of private-sector innovators and entrepreneurs.

In the latter case, policymakers should also recognize that tax and regulatory regimes that were appropriate in earlier years when there were numerous low-hanging investment opportunities and nobody was chasing them may no longer be optimal when those opportunities are exhausted and the country must come up with new products and services to stay ahead of pursuing countries. In some cases, the government may also have to direct fiscal spending toward the development of cutting-edge technology – in effect serving as innovator of last resort. And the need for these actions is growing larger every day in countries that are in the post-LTP pursued phase.

At the most fundamental level, the economics profession must realize that, apart from the early stages of industrialization, which are characterized by a surplus of easy investment opportunities, shortages of borrowers have always been a bigger problem for growth than shortages of lenders. Economists need to confront this problem head-on instead of making facile assumptions about "trend growth rates" and ever-present borrowers. The existence of investment opportunities and willing borrowers should never be taken for granted, especially in countries that are in balance sheet recessions or are being pursued from behind, a group that includes every advanced country in the world today.

References

Banca d' Italia. *Financial Accounts*, Rome. Available at http://www.bancaditalia.it/statistiche/tematiche/conti-patrimoniali/conti-finanza/index.html (Accessed on 15 August 2016)

Banco de España. *Financial Accounts of the Spanish Economy,* Madrid. Availabe at http://www.bde.es/webbde/en/estadis/ccff/ccff.html (Accessed on 15 August 2016)

Banco de Portugal. *National Financial Accounts,* Lisbon. Available at https://www.bportugal.pt/enUS/Estatisticas/Dominios%20Estatisticos/Pages/ContasN acionaisFinanceiras.aspx (Accessed on 15 August 2016)

Bank for International Settlements. *Residential Property Price Statistics*, Basel. Available at http://www.bis.org/statistics/pp.htm (Accessed on 15 August 2016)

Bank of England. *Bankstats (Monetary & Financial Statistics),* London. Available at http://www.bankofengland.co.uk/statistics/Pages/bankstats/default.aspx (Accessed on 15 August 2016)

Bank of Japan. *Loans and Bills Discounted by Sector*, Tokyo. Available at http://www.boj.or.jp/en/statistics/dl/loan/ldo/index.htm/ (Accessed 1 April 2016)

Bank of Japan. *Monetary Base,* Tokyo. Available at http://www.boj.or.jp/en/statistics/boj/other/mb/index.htm/ (Accessed 1 April 2016)

Bank of Japan. *Money Stock*, Tokyo. Available at http://www.boj.or.jp/en/statistics/money/ms/index.htm/ (Accessed 1 April 2016)

Board of Governors of the Federal Reserve System. *Banking & Monetary Statistics, 1914-1970*, 2 vols. Washington D.C.

Board of Governors of the Federal Reserve System. *Aggregate Reserves of Depository Institutions and the Monetary Base*, Washington D.C. Available at http://www.federalreserve.gov/releases/h3/current/ (Accessed 4 April 2016)

Board of Governors of the Federal Reserve System. *Assets and Liabilities of Commercial Banks in the United States*, Washington D.C. Available at http://www.federalreserve.gov/releases/h8/current/default.htm (Accessed 4 April 2016)

Board of Governors of the Federal Reserve System. *Financial Accounts of the Unites States*, Washington D.C. Available at http://www.federalreserve.gov/releases/z1/ (Acccessed on 15 August 2016)

Board of Governors of the Federal Reserve System (date?) *Money Stock Measures*, Washington D.C. Available at http://www.federalreserve.gov/releases/h6/current/default.htm (Acccessed on 15 August 2016)

Central Bank of Ireland. *Quarterly Financial Accounts*, Dublin. Available at http://www.centralbank.ie/polstats/stats/qfaccounts/Pages/releases.aspx (Accessed on 15 August 2016)

Central Statistics Office, Ireland. *National Accounts*, Cork. Available at http://www.cso.ie/en/statistics/nationalaccounts/ (Accessed on 15 August 2016)

Directorate General of Budget, Accounting and Statistics (DGBAS), the Executive Yuan, Statistics Bureau, Taiwan. *Consumer Price Indices,* Taipei. Available at http://eng.stat.gov.tw/ct.asp?xItem=12092&ctNode=1558&mp=5 (Accessed on 28 April 2016)

Directorate General of Budget, Accounting and Statistics (DGBAS), the Executive Yuan, Statistics Bureau, Taiwan. *Earnings and Productivity,* Taipei. Available at http://eng.stat.gov.tw/np.asp?ctNode=1544 (Accessed 28 April 2016)

European Central Bank. *Minimum Reserves and Liquidity,* Frankfurt am Main. Available at http://www.ecb.europa.eu/stats/monetary/res/html/index.en.html (Accessed on 4 April 2016)

European Central Bank. *Monetary aggregates,* Frankfurt am Main. Available at https://www.ecb.europa.eu/stats/money/aggregates/aggr/html/index.en.html (Accessed 4 April 2016)

Eurostat, *Quarterly National Accounts,* Luxembourg; Available at http://ec.europa.eu/eurostat/web/main/home (Accessed on 15 August 2016)

Fisher, S. (2016) "Reflections on Macroeconomics Then and Now," remarks at "Policy Challenges in an Interconnected World" 32nd Annual National Association for Business Economics Economic Policy Conference, Washington D.C., 7 March. Available at https://www.federalreserve.gov/newsevents/speech/fischer20160307a.htm

Flora, P., Kraus, F., Pfenning, W. (Ed.) (1987) *State, Economy and Society in Western Europe 1815-1975. Volume II. The Growth of Industrial Societies and Capitalist Economies.* Frankfurt am Main: Campus Verlag.

International Monetary Fund. *International Financial Statistics,* Washington D.C. Available at http://data.imf.org/?sk=388DFA60-1D26-4ADE-B505-A05A558D9A42 (Accessed on 15 August 2016)

Italian National Institute of Statistics, *Quarterly National Accounts*, Rome. Available at http://www.istat.it/en/ (Accessed on 15 August 2016)

Japan Real Estate Institute. *Urban Land Price Index*, Tokyo, Available at http://www.reinet.or.jp/en/index.html (Accessed on 15 August 2016)

Koo, R. (2001) The Japanese Economy in Balance Sheet Recession. *Business Economics,* National Association of Business Economists, Washington, D.C., April.

Koo, R. (2003) *Balance Sheet Recession: Japan's Struggle with Uncharted Economics and its Global Implications,* Singapore: John Wiley & Sons,.

Koo, R. (2008) *The Holy Grail of Macro Economics: Lessons from Japan's Great Recession,* Singapore: John Wiley & Sons,.

Koo, R. (2014) *The Escape from Balance Sheet Recession and the QE Trap: A Hazardous Road for the World Economy,* John Wiley & Sons, Singapore.

Koo, R. (2015) China and the US-led International Order, in *How Do Asians See their Future?* edited by François Godement, London: European Council on Foreign Relations. Available at http://www.ecfr.eu/page/-/ECFR130_CHINA_ASIA_REPORT_pdf.pdf (Accessed on 15 August 2016)

Maddison, A. (2006) *The World Economy. A Millennial Perspective (Vol. 1). Historical Statistics (Vol. 2),* Paris: OECD.

Maddison, A. *Historical Statistics of the World Economy: 1-2008 AD.* Available at http://www.ggdc.net/maddison/Historical_Statistics/vertical-file_02-2010.xls (Accessed 28 July 2015)

Ministry of Health, Labour and Welfare, Japan. *Monthly Labour Survey,* Tokyo. Available at http://www.mhlw.go.jp/english/database/db-l/monthly-labour.html (Accessed on 15 December 2015)

Ministry of Health, Labour and Welfare, Japan. *Survey on Labour Disputes,* Tokyo. Available at http://www.mhlw.go.jp/english/database/db-l/labour_disputes.html (Accessed on 11 July 2013)

Ministry of Internal Affairs and Communications, Japan. *Consumer Price Index,* Tokyo. Available at http://www.stat.go.jp/data/cpi/ in Japanese (Accessed 1 April 2016)

Ministry of Internal Affairs and Communications, Japan. *Report on Internal Migration in Japan,* Tokyo. Available http://www.stat.go.jp/english/data/idou/index.htm in Japanese (Accessed on 11 July 2013)

National Statistics Institute, Spain. *Quarterly Spanish National Accounts,* Madrid. Available at
http://www.ine.es/jaxi/menu.do?type=pcaxis&path=%2Ft35%2Fp009&file=inebase&L =1 (Accessed on 15 August 2016)

Nikkei Business (2015) Tokushu: Nisen Mannin-no Hinkon (20 Million Japanese in Poverty), in Japanese, *Nikkei BP,* Tokyo, 23 March, pp. 24-43.

Piketty, T. (2014) *Capital in the Twenty-First Century.* Belknap Press

Real Estate Economic Institute, Japan. *Manshon Tateuri Shijo Doko (Reports on the sales of the condominiums and built-for sale houses),* Tokyo. Available at https://www.fudousankeizai.co.jp/mansion (Accessed on 15 August 2016)

Robinson, J. (1972) The Second Crisis of Economic Theory, *American Economic Review* 62(1/2), pp.1-10.

Statistics Korea. *Internal Migration Statistics,* Seoul. Available at
http://kosis.kr/eng/statisticsList/statisticsList_01List.jsp?vwcd=MT_ETITLE&parmTabl d=M_01_01 (Accessed 11 July 2013)

Statistics Korea. *Internal Migration Statistics,* Seoul. *(2008) Korea Statistical Year Book 2008,* Statistics Korea, Seoul.

Statistics Korea. *Internal Migration Statistics*, Seoul. *(2013) Korea Statistical Year Book 2012,* Statistics Korea, Seoul.

Statistics Portugal. *Portuguese National Accounts,* Lisbon. Available at https://www.ine.pt/xportal/xmain?xpid=INE&xpgid=ine_cnacionais (Accessed on 15 August 2016)

Summers, L. H. (2009) *Rescuing and Rebuilding the US Economy: A Progress Report* Speech at the Peterson Institute for International Economics, Washington D.C., 17 July.

Summers, L.H. (2015 and 2016) *Secular Stagnation,* several articles. Available at http://larrysummers.com/category/secular-stagnation/ (Accessed on 15 August 2016)

Swiss Federal Statistical Office. *Swiss Wage Index,* Neuchâtel, Switzerland. http://www.bfs.admin.ch/bfs/portal/en/index/themen/03/04/blank/data/02.html (Accessed on 15 August 2016)

Swiss Federal Statistical Office. *Consumer Prices Index,* Neuchâtel, Switzerland. http://www.bfs.admin.ch/bfs/portal/en/index/themen/05/02/blank/key/basis_aktuell.ht ml (Accessed on 15 August 2016)

S&P Dow Jones Indices. *S&P CoreLogic Case-Shiller Home Price Indices,* New York, NY. Available at http://us.spindices.com/index-family/real-estate/sp-corelogic-case-shiller (Accessed on 15 August 2016)

Uchihashi, K. (2009) *Shinpan Akumu-no Saikuru: Neo-riberarizumu Junkan (The cycle of nightmares: the recurrence of neoliberalism),* updated version, in Japanese, Tokyo: Bunshun Bunko.

United Nations, Department of Economic and Social Affairs, Population Division (2014). *World Urbanization Prospects: The 2014 Revision (ST/ESA/SER.A/366),* United Nations, New York, NY. https://esa.un.org/unpd/wup/https://esa.un.org/unpd/wup/ (Accessed 15 April 2016)

United Nations, Department of Economic and Social Affairs, Population Division (2015) *World Population Prospects,* New York, NY. Available at https://esa.un.org/unpd/wpp/ (Accessed on 11 September 2015).

US Department of Commerce. *Gross Domestic Product (GDP),* Washington D.C. Available at http://www.bea.gov/national/index.htm#gdp (Accessed 15 August 2016)

US Department of Commerce. Census Bureau (2012), *2010 Census,* Washington D.C. Available at http://www.census.gov/2010census/ (Accessed 15 August 2016)

US Department of Commerce. Census Bureau. *Current Population Survey,* Washington D.C. Available at http://www.census.gov/programs-surveys/cps.html (Accessed 15 December 2015)

Chapter 2

The tendency of effective demand to lag behind the supply of full employment

Arturo Hermann

Introduction

Following our long-standing interest for the analysis of economic imbalances, this chapter focuses on the tendency of effective demand to lag behind the supply of full employment. As a matter of fact, in the post Keynesian oriented analysis[1] of the economic imbalances, much attention has been paid to the destabilizing role of the "financialisation" of the economy and to the inadequacy of neoclassical theories[2] in addressing these phenomena. Along these lines, a number of important issues were investigated, from labour market to banking policy, from market imperfections to international relations.

Among them, an aspect which has received a good deal of attention has been the redistribution of income in favour of the wealthier classes that has occurred in the last decade. This phenomenon has had an adverse effect on

---

[1] There are many contributions that address these aspects, so we are at loss to fairly select among them. Refer, among many others, to Arestis and Sawyer (2010), Davidson (2009 and 2011), Harcourt and Kriesler (2013), Jespersen (2013), Keen (2011), King (2002 and 2015), Lee (2009), Lee and Lavoie (2012), Minsky (2008), Nell (1988), Stiglitz (2009).
[2] The main aspect of these theories is to place an unconditioned emphasis on the rationality of economic man and on the maximizing virtues of free markets. The chief drawback of this account lies in its excessive simplification of economic phenomena which prevented these economists from detecting the complexity and imperfections of the markets and of human behaviour. Reality, in fact, has proved to be much different from these simplified pictures. It became apparent that, in particular but not only, in the financial sector, economic behaviour was often driven by irrational or non-rational elements and that, relatedly, markets not only did not adequately signalled the risk of certain ventures but in some cases provided perverse incentives to go on with these initiatives.

the effective demand because, as is known, the marginal propensity to consume tends to be higher with lower incomes. Furthermore, as this redistribution has been accompanied by a growing economic precariousness and insecurity of work and life conditions, the overall effects of this trend have been much worse, as this redistribution has affected the (relative) stability of the economic and social fabric.

In these contributions, the role of effective demand in the explanation of economic imbalances has been perhaps put a bit on the background. In fact, the overall impression is that the emphasis has been more on the effects of financialisation on the system than on the effects of the chronic insufficiency of the effective demand of full employment (however defined) on the emergence of financial-led economy.

We think a more comprehensive analysis appropriate also on account of the paramount role that, along other systemic factors, the lack of effective demand has played in the emergence of the recent economic crisis; and, in turn, in the effects of the economic crisis in reinforcing societies based on intolerance, authoritarian relations and armed conflicts.

This also happens because, as witnessed by many historical events, public spending on military objectives constitutes, at least in the short run, a powerful way to create effective demand. In fact, for this kind of public spending there is no need to embark on the arduous task of convincing consumers to buy products, because the demand is created directly by the public sector in a virtually unlimited way.

We have organized the work as follows. In the first section, we make a reappraisal of the most important theories of effective demand, with particular attention to the aspects of divergence and reciprocal influence. We begin by analysing the theories of underconsumption, with particular attention to the *Physiology of Industry* of J.A. Hobson and F.A. Mummery. In the second section we will address the main aspects of Keynes's theory of effective demand. We try to show its revolutionary import, together with some aspects of weakness which, in our view, are caused by some adherence of such theory to neoclassical economics, in particular with regard to the relations between wages and employment. In the third section we will outline a broad theory of effective demand by considering more in detail a number of aspects of Keynes's theory which, in our opinion, are not sufficiently clarified. In particular, the possible divergences between expected demand and effective demand, and the role of public spending and credit creation as fundamental drivers of effective demand, and profits for the entrepreneurs.

Then, in the fourth section we consider a number of structural factors that may contribute to render more complex and slow the dynamics of effective demand. We conclude the work by pointing out the relevance and complementarity of these contributions to the analysis of current imbalances and for devising, on this ground, a course of policy action able to consider in an integrated way macroeconomic and structural policies.

1. The Issue of underconsumption

Underconsumption: a neglected issue

When dealing with the issue of underconsumption, a twofold reality emerges: **(i)** the relevance of the phenomenon in real economies, which finds expression in several ways; from the advertising strategies of producers, to the chronic excess of production and/or productive capacity, to the multiplication of firms, to the deflation stage of more overt economic crisis. **(ii)** Despite this overwhelming evidence, economic theory has always shown a notable reluctance to comprehensively address this phenomenon. As a matter of fact, classic and neoclassic theory, by accepting the so-called "Say's law", have totally overlooked the issue. Also Marx's economics, although providing significant insights into the dynamics of economic crisis, does not adopt an "underconsumption" or demand side approach. This happens because Marx's economics partly rests, although in a critical and dialectic way, on Ricardian economics.[3] The same can be said for neo-Ricardian contributions. Also the various strands of neo-Schumpeterian and Austrian theories, while providing interesting contributions to the evolutionary and dynamic aspect of economic systems, are not much concerned on how

---

[3] We have treated in more detail these aspects in Hermann (2014).

the level of consumption necessary to ensure this trend is attained. The only exceptions are represented by a number of contributions of the "old" institutional economics and of Keynesian perspective.

But what are the distinctive aspects of underconsumption theorists? They underscore, although with various differences between their analyses, that the crucial feature of capitalistic economies is a structural tendency towards underconsumption in respect to the level of full employment (however defined). To any level of underconsumption corresponds an over-saving in respect to the level of investment into which the latter can be channeled. There are a number of reasons for these phenomena: **(i)** the lower propensity to consume of the richer people which, especially in presence of an unequal distribution of income, tends to reduce the amount of aggregate consumption; **(ii)** if this takes place, an increased amount of investment cannot make up for less consumption; in fact, since investment expenses are instrumental to consumption, they must bear a well-defined relation with the production of consumption goods; **(iii)** these aspects are reinforced by the tendency, especially in times of boom, towards over investment and multiplication of firms,[4] with consequent excess of productive capacity.

The Physiology of Industry of Mummery and Hobson

These are in extreme synthesis the key-points addressed by this "school". Considering that, for space reasons, we cannot address all the contributions,[5] we concentrate our attention on a significant book: namely, The Physiology of Industry of J.A. Hobson and A.F. Mummery.

This book can be considered as a central contribution on the subject. It sets as its main objective to lay out a perspective of the economic theory alternative to classic economics. The latter, by chiefly resting on the

[4] The phenomenon of waste arising from an excessive competition leading to a multiplication of firms was highlighted by many contributions of the original institutional economics (see for more detail Rutherford, 2011 and Tugwell, 1924).
[5] See, in particular, Foster and Catchings (1926), Mummery and Hobson (1889). Also the work of Henry A. Abbati (see for more detail the book edited by Di Gaspare, 2011) and Hansen's theory (1939) of secular stagnation, have significant complementarities with the theories of underconsumption.

acceptance of the so-called Say's law and on the idea that "the love of money is the root to all economic good", is considered inadequate for explaining the reality of modern economies. In this regard, the authors' purpose is

> "(..) to show that these [orthodox] conclusions are not tenable, that an undue exercise of the habit of saving is possible, and that such undue exercise impoverishes the community, throw labourers out of work, drives down wages, and spreads that gloom and prostration around through the commercial world which is known as depression in trade; that, in short, the love of money is the root of all economic evil" (Mummery and Hobson, 2015 [1889]: iv).

The key to understand why this happen is that aggregate demand and aggregate supply[6] tend to be structurally divergent, with the tendency of the latter to structurally exceed the former. When this comes about, the market adjusts itself chiefly through reducing quantity, and the result is an equilibrium of underemployment. The central reason explaining this outcome (see also later) is that the price mechanism is considered unable to reach an "equilibrium" of full employment (however defined). Before addressing this aspect, let us see why over-saving will lead to an economic depression. The following passage synthesizes the core of the argument,

> "The object of production is to provide 'utilities and conveniences' for consumers... The only use of Capital being to aid the production of these utilities and conveniences, the total used will necessarily vary with the total or utilities and conveniences daily or weekly consumed. Now saving, while increasing the existent aggregate of capital, simultaneously reduces the quantity of utilities and conveniences consumed; any undue exercise of this habit must therefore, cause an accumulation of capital in excess of that which is required for use, and this excess will exist in

---

[6] We employ these terms to indicate the whole programmed demand and supply as distinguished from effective demand and supply, which relate to the real quantities exchanged in the market.

the form of a general over-production...[hence]...in the normal state of modern industrial Communities, consumption limits production and not production consumption" (ibidem: v, vi).

The previous passage raises four relevant questions, which reflect the unfolding of the book: **(i)** Can an excess of investment "financed" by saving make up for less consumption? **(ii)** Why there tends to be an excess of production and productive capacity? **(iii)** Can price mechanism equilibrate the market at full employment level? **(iv)** What are the characteristics of sticky prices and their consequences on the economic system?

(i) As for the first question, the obvious answer should be in the negative, but it is astonishing to note how this concept has been overlooked by the most important economic theories. They tend to consider, more or less explicitly, investment as independent of consumption, as if there would not be a functional and binding relation between the two.

In this regard, *The Physiology of Industry* provides, also through suitable examples, a detailed reconstruction of the links between the various stages of the production process. In their words,

"At each step in the process [of production] there will be a portion of the raw material on its way to become a commodity, a portion of natural agents in the shape of land, a portion of plant in the shape of factories, storehouses, and machinery, and a portion of human labour...[hence]...the amount of capital required at each stage [of production] bears an exact and fixed relation to the amount of consumption of commodities, and any excess or deficiency throws out of gear the whole machinery of production....[in fact]...if the raw material does not regularly passes through all stages until it becomes a commodity, it must accumulate somewhere, and such accumulation will tend to decay, or at any rate to stand useless...in a word, the quantity of wealth in existence and functioning as a wealth cannot increase or diminish except in relation with immediate or future consumption" (ibidem: 23, 25, 28, 29).

These passages indicate that saving can be useful only as long as it is channelled into investment leading to a present or near future consumption. Every saving in excess of the amount of consumption absorbable by the market is bound to destroy itself in the aggregate.

Another relevant aspect is the complexity and interconnection between the various stages of production. In particular, what emerges from this account is that an appropriate level of consumption constitutes the necessary fuel and incentive for the continual reconstitution of capital. It is then put forward the important identity between effective demand and effective income. In fact,

> "(..) the actual money paid by consumers is the ultimate source[7] of all income.", and therefore, "the aggregate demand, or prices paid, for the use of requisites of production is the aggregate money income of all the individuals composing the community" (ibidem: 88, 89).

(ii) This leads us to the second question, "Why there tends to be an excess of production and productive capacity?"

According to the authors, a depression in trade consists in a general reduction in the rate of incomes. This can be traced to a reduction of effective demand which, in turn, is a consequence of a too high rate of saving. Hence, "depression in trade and excessive thrift are terms describing different phases of the same phenomenon" (ibidem: 98).

However, this process demands an explanation of why firms are unable to predict and manage such event and go on producing more than the market can absorb. The process leading to this result is located in the spirit of competition. In fact, whereas the aggregate saving is necessarily bound by the aggregate income, an individual is always free to save more in order to

---

[7] This can be true only if we do not consider the role of public consumption and investment.

invest more. But, if the consumption needed to embody the new investment is insufficient, the result is a general over-production. These effects are reinforced by the improvements of the productive system, whose consequence is to diminish the needed capital for unit of production.

In order to illustrate how this process works, the authors make the example of a competitive examination for a dozen posts for which the passing mark is 60(%) points. In these conditions, the sufficient requirement for covering the posts is that twelve candidates participate with a mark of 60 for a total score of 720. Normally, however, many more candidates participate, and often get a score higher than a simple pass. If, for instance, 50 candidates get an average score of 80, the total score will be 4.000. In this case, all the extra work of the candidates, which is equal to 3.280 (4.000 − 720) will be "overproduction", namely a result totally useless for the examination[8] purposes. In this respect, "each candidate has, or thinks he has, a chance of success, and this chance stimulates him to work" (ibidem: 115). This incentive will be reinforced, up to a certain point, when the chances of success are smaller.

This example vividly describes the same kind of phenomenon that comes about in the marketplace: also here the normal condition is a general over-production and/or excess of productive capacity. We can note this phenomenon virtually everywhere: for instance, in shops, restaurants, hotels, we almost invariably find that the offer of goods and services far exceed what is demanded by consumers. We can find the same tendency in the industrial and agricultural production, where in the former predominates an excess of productive capacity whereas in the latter, an excess of production.

This phenomenon is particularly relevant in theory and policy action, and was underscored also by many contributions of original institutional economics and Keynesian theories. In fact, by providing a much more realistic picture of how the market economy works in practice, these contributions allow to realize that the market is not an abstract and

---

[8] We do not consider the learning effect of the competitive examination and the circumstance that having passed the examination with good marks is a qualification for future applications.

optimizing mechanism but an institution created and maintained by public intervention.

(iii) This leads us to the third question, "can price mechanism equilibrate the market at full employment level"?

This question lies at the crux of economic theory: in fact, if we suppose that price mechanism can equilibrate the market at an optimal level, this implies that neoclassical economics substantially holds true and that, hence, the sound policy prescription is one of *laissez faire*.

In this regard, the authors thoroughly criticize the neoclassical account by basing their analysis on the observation of real economies. They note that, in presence of an over-supply, a corresponding reduction of prices would not solve the problem. The reason for this is that a reduction of prices will also bring down the sellers' income, and so the net effect on demand tends to vanish. This effect is supposed to hold true even if additional demand will perfectly make up for price reduction – namely, if the elasticity of demand is equal to one. This would happen because this effect will unfold only in the long run and hence will not impinge on the reduction of income in the short run. Furthermore, a reduction of prices, if stimulates additional demand, is also likely to bring prices again at the former level. For similar reasons, also a reduction in the rate of profit, owing to the negative effects on the expectations, is considered ineffectual to increase effective demand. It is on account of these phenomena, then, that prices are more likely to be sticky or, even if flexible, are unable to equilibrate demand and supply at full employment level.

This analysis, however interesting, is a bit confused. As a matter of fact, there is no notion of the elasticity of demand to price, and hence no identification of the income effect and substitution effect in the composition of effective demand. Consequently, considering the temporary reduction of income as the only cause of the ineffectuality of price reduction seems very unconvincing. This is because, as widely analysed, **(a)** firms base their action upon a middle-long term strategy where expectations play a relevant role, and that **(b)** a significant part of firms' activities is financed by credit creation, which means that future incomes tend to be "anticipated" to them by banking system in the forms of bank deposits.

For all these reasons, we can well suspect that a central reason for the inability of prices to equalize supply and demand at the full employment resides in the tendential satiation of consumers for many products. The effect of these tendencies is that demand is rather inelastic at price reduction. If so, then, one reason why firms are reluctant to reduce prices is simply that this would entail a reduction of their current revenues, let apart any future effect on income. Another related reason for sticky prices can be found in market imperfections,[9] in particular market power most often based on asymmetric information.

(iv) These aspects are more acknowledged by the authors in chapter 5, where they address the issue of the characteristics of sticky prices and their consequences on the economic system. They highlight the presence of a notable asymmetry between the two classes of producers, the makers (producers) and the traders. When demand is brisk and approaches the supply of full employment, the makers have the better part of the stake. In fact, under such circumstances they become the limiting factor whereas traders tend to outbid one another in order to get more goods to sell. As a result, there tends to be a shift of activity from the traders towards the production sector. The reverse comes about when demand is sluggish. As a result of the overproduction and/or the excess of productive capacity, producers are in a much weaker position. Hence, they tend to undersell as much goods as they can to traders, who then get the best part of the profit.

As can be noted, the crucial factor that allows such dynamics is that retail prices tend to be sticky (in particular downward), and in a far larger degree than wholesale prices. Why? The authors pinpoint two notable factors: **(a)** the greater flexibility of the trading sector in respect to production sector. In fact, where in the latter technical requirement put a tight bound on the limit of the employable persons and/or on dividing production in smaller units, no such thing takes place in the trading sector. Here, there is much more room for, say, employing more people in a shop and/or for opening up new ones.

---

[9] As shown in section 4, sticky prices can also convey the corresponding complexity of the economic and social structure.

Tendency of effective demand to lag behind the supply of full employment

In these conditions retail prices tend to be sticky (or to follow very imperfectly the fall of wholesale prices). The result is that the same amount of business is shared among a larger number of sellers. All the people engaged are then very busy in trying to get the better slice of the cake in a situation where the average slice tends to shrink.

At this stage, **(b)** one can look in more detail why retail prices are so sticky. As already noted, one reason is simply the fact that in most cases their reduction is not remunerative. But why can this happen? Here the authors put forward an interesting and psychologically oriented analysis of the reasons why retailers tend to have a striking advantage over consumers. In their words,

> "The reasons for this comparative want of flexibility of retail prices resides in the detailed conditions of retail trade. If the average consumer had as intimate a knowledge of all the details affecting the prices of every kind of commodity he buys, as the traders has of the special goods he buys from makers; if he were as keen in ascertaining and taking full advantage of the slightest fall of price; if he were absolutely independent of locality; and, most important of all, if he were able to fully seize the opportunity of a fall in prices to lay in a large stock of commodities, we might have the same and rapid fluctuations in retail prices as in wholesale....in short, the trader is a specialist with regard to prices and qualities of the things he buys from the makers; the consumer, who buys not one but every kind of thing from traders, is not a specialist, and suffers accordingly" (ibidem: 147, 148).

In consequence of these economic and psychological features of the retail trade — note the author — the average consumer is largely unable to effectively detect[10] the quality, "value for money", and sometimes even the right way to quantify and measure the products. This is effectively expressed in the following passages,

---

[10] The only exception to this situation — note the authors — is represented by a price increase, that are normally promptly identified and reacted to by consumers.

"(The) purchasers, even when poor, and with every inducement to see that they get 'their money's worth', are not merely unable to judge the quality, but even of so simple a matter as quantity...[and, as a consequence]... against fraudulent descriptions of goods we have a list of enactments dealing with such articles like milk, butter, meat, fish, vegetables, and the like, the *raison d'être* of these Acts being that the purchaser is not mere unable to judge whether the article supplied to him is what it professes to be, but even whether it is fit for human food...[hence, in these circumstances]...the law of competition does not apply. The purchaser can only estimate the quality of goods by the price, and if a retailer lowers his prices, the customers assume immediately that the quality is proportionately lower. In small grocers' shops it is habitual to get two or three qualities of butter out of a single tub, and the purchasers of the higher-priced butter never for a moment suspect that the lower-priced is identical in every respect" (ibidem: 149, 150).

Critical aspects and policy implications

As appears from the foregoing account, *The Physiology of Industry* provides a very innovative and heterodox account of the reasons underlying underconsumption – namely, the incapacity of the effective demand to absorb the supply of full employment. Particularly relevant in this respect are the identification of the factors through which these maladjustments take place: the tendency to overinvest, the relations between consumption and investment, and the asymmetric information between buyers and sellers.

Along this positive trend, there are also in the book a number of underdeveloped and more critical aspects that make this contribution a kind of half-finished edifice. In particular, there is a certain lack of theoretical foundations for many relevant issues. For instance, the idea that a reduction in the rate of profit is negative for investment is wholly ungrounded. In fact, there is no explanation of the relation between profit and investment decisions, and why and to what extent the former should influence the latter. Hence, there is no clue as how to identify an "adequate or optimal" rate of profit, and then an "adequate or optimal" rate of wage and an "adequate or optimal" mechanism of price determination. In the same line, there is little awareness of the role of time, expectations and firms' strategies in influencing their investment decisions.

The only clue is that (in particular in the chapter 6) income distribution between labour, capital and land depend on the relative scarcity of these factors. However, this notion resonates with neoclassical economics and, moreover, does not answer the questions as to whether **(1)** there are structural reasons that make, for instance, capital have a better stake over labour, and **(2)** whether the market structure and the related income distribution so arising are "right or optimal".

Another weak aspect is the too "orthodox" notion that saving "finances" investment, which makes them adhere to the classical notion of interest rate as a reward for "abstinence". This is coupled by a parallel unawareness of the role credit creation in increasing effective demand, and by a like overlooking of the role of public spending in sustaining effective demand. There is only an interesting reference to such theme in chapter 5, when he remarks that in a healthy economy military spending is useless (or even harmful) for sustaining effective demand. Hence, only in times of depression military spending can act as an imperfect surrogate of the insufficient demand. They note, however, that the same result can be much better achieved by increasing the consumption of luxuries, raising the income of the working classes and improving the conditions of the towns.

Coming to the analysis of the relations between makers and traders, the authors' conclusions are interesting but not totally grounded. There is in fact no clear account of the influence of market power on price determination. For instance, if makers are more monopolistically organized than traders, it is less sure that even in periods of slump the best part of the profit will go to traders. Besides, there is no analysis of the role of the cost structure on these dynamics: for instance, the role played by scale economies to push firms to produce in excess and to (relatively) undersell the stocks to traders; and how this production in excess will negatively affect traders' profit. Also the analysis of structural factors – such as the role of institutions, culture and technology in economic development – is scantly addressed in the work.

As regards policy implications, they center on the way to remedy underconsumption, which is (rightly) seen not as "a momentary and occasional crisis...[but as]...a commercial malady which is chronic in the industrial life of modern European nations" (ibidem: 205).

Hence, the authors would welcome a taxation system able to disincentive saving and incentive consumption. Also, they would endorse a better remuneration of work and/or a reduction of the working time, but they warn that, in order not (in their view) to discourage investment, these provisions should be applied symmetrically by all Countries. However, apart from these measures, what seems lacking is a more comprehensive course of policy action for addressing these problems. In this regard, it is important to note that Hobson has written several books after *The Physiology of Industry*.

We can mention, in particular, *The Industrial System* (1910), where he more precisely identifies the sources of insufficient demand in the excess of economic surplus, in particular of the *entrepreneurs*, and in the market power associated with it. Hence, in order to reduce unemployment he proposes to regulate to some extent monopolistic sectors, to tax excessive saving (in particular in times of depression) for financing public works and to get better education and training for the workers. However, he does not seem much sympathetic with the action of the labour movement, which he considers chiefly driven by the individualistic attempt to get a part of the industrial surplus.

In conclusion, *The Physiology of Industry* contains very interesting insights, along with weaker aspects. These aspects, of course, do not diminish the validity and topicality of the authors' findings. It is easy to note that these dynamics constitute an original anticipation of the circumstance that consumption decisions and investment decisions are independent and uncoordinated.

The same can be said for the other theories of under-consumption (or related to it). They, along with a fairly similar theoretical framework, present also a number of differences that increase their degree of complementarity. For instance, in the work Abbati it is paid some more attention to the role of public spending and credit creation in sustaining effective demand. And, in

Foster and Catchings' contribution, there is a very interesting analysis of the role of corporate saving in causing under-consumption. This is especially so when such saving is directed not to productive investment but to financial speculation.

At this stage, we can wonder why the theories of under-consumption were rather downplayed by Keynes and also by other economists. As for Keynes, in his opinion these theories did not stress enough the role of the Marginal Efficiency of Capital (MEC) in promoting investment. This can be true up to a point, but it is also true that Keynes tended to overlook the reasons for under-consumption elaborated by these authors.

As for other economists, the reasons for this neglect can be twofold: **(i)** On the one side, there was a general reluctance to accept a theory which overtly questions the "Say's law", one of the central tenet of classical and neoclassical economics.

Furthermore – and unlike Keynes who was more introduced within the economics profession – the under-consumption economists were in the main outsiders of the profession and with little political influence. **(ii)** On the other side, there are also more "endogenous" reasons for this neglect. These can be traced back to the circumstance that, as already noted, these theories remained underdeveloped for several aspects. For instance, there is no clear analysis – let apart a number of interesting insights – of the role of public spending and credit creation in sustaining effective demand. Also, the reasons for under-consumption remain a bit in the shadow: in particular, it is not much clear whether these reasons relate to micro and macro market imperfections or to other structural features of the system.

Owing to these shortcomings, the policy implications of these analyses are interesting but rather piecemeal, and then unable to acquire a more comprehensive perspective. What they chiefly suggest — as in the case of the *Physiology of Industry* — is a policy action aimed at reducing unnecessary saving and promoting consumption. This can be attained through an appropriate system of taxation and by realizing (whenever possible) a general betterment of labour conditions. This is fine, of course,

111

but in order to render these proposals workable, there is a need of having a more complete macro and micro economic picture of their overall effects.

For instance, if we, in times of depression, tax idle incomes in order to finance public works, what should we do when the depression is over, reduce, maintain stable, or increase the level of taxation and public spending? It is difficult to answer, of course, if we do not have a well-crafted theory regarding whether or not public spending "crowds out" private spending.

For these reasons, a better collaboration between under-consumption, Keynesian and structuralist theories seem particularly appropriate.

2. Keynes's theory of effective demand

In addressing Keynes's theory of effective demand as laid out in *The General Theory of Employment, Interest and Money* (GT), one remains astonished at noting its simple, and at the same time revolutionary, character. In order to convey the principal aspects of such theory, the best thing is to let Keynes speak about it,

> "It follows that in a given situation of technique, resources and factor cost per unit of employment, the amount of employment, both in each individual firm and industry and in the aggregate, depends on the amount of the proceeds which the entrepreneurs expect to receive from the corresponding output. For entrepreneurs will endeavour to fix the amount of employment at the level which they expect to maximise the excess of the proceeds over the factor cost. Let **Z** be the aggregate supply price of the output for employing N men, the relationship between **Z** and **N** being written as **Z = φ(N)**, which can be called the *aggregate supply function*. Similarly, let D be the proceeds which the entrepreneurs expect to receive from the employment of N men, the relationship between **D** and **N** being written **D = f(N)**, which can be called the aggregate demand

> function...The value of **D** at the point of aggregate demand
> function, where it is intersected by the aggregate supply
> function, will be called *the effective demand"* (Keynes, 2013
> [1936]: 18).

The simple and revolutionary aspect of this theory is that marks a neat departure from the so-called Say's law, according to which effective supply always creates an equal amount of effective demand. As Keynes notes, this implies that $Z = \varphi(N)$ is always equal to $D = f(N)$ for every value of **N**. In his words,

> (according to Say's law) "...Effective demand, instead of
> having a unique equilibrium value, is an infinite range of
> values all equally admissible; and the amount of
> employment is indeterminate except in so far as the disutility
> of labour sets up an upper limit. If this were true, competition
> between entrepreneurs would always lead to an expansion
> of employment up to the point at which the supply of output
> as a whole ceases to be elastic... evidently this amounts to
> the same thing as full employment" (ibidem: 19).

Before addressing these aspects, and in particular the circumstance that he remained partly attached to the neoclassical theory of employment, let us complete our sketch of Keynes's theory of effective demand by quoting the following passage,

> "The outline of our theory can be expressed as follows.
> When employment increases, aggregate real income is
> increased. The psychology of community is such that when
> aggregate real income is increased aggregate consumption
> is increased, but not by so much as income. Hence
> employers would make a loss if the whole of the increased
> employment would be devoted to satisfying the increased
> demand for immediate consumption. Thus, to justify any
> given amount of employment there must be an amount of
> current investment sufficient to absorb the excess of total

output over what the community chooses to consume when employment is at the given level...The amount of current investment will depend, in turn, on what we shall call the inducement to invest; and the inducement to invest will be found to depend on the relation between the schedule of the marginal efficiency of capital and the complex of rates of interest on loans on various maturities and risks" (ibidem: 19).

This is the gist of Keynes's theory of effective demand as laid out in the GT. In this regard he clarified that the book has the goal of developing in detail the core concepts of such theory. It constitutes a path-breaking innovation in respect to the classical and neoclassical world dominated by "Say's law". However, Keynes was by no means alone in elaborating such theory. We should mention, at least, **(i)** the contributions of various authors who were in closer contact with Keynes, such as R.F. Kahn and D.H. Robertson. **(ii)** The various theories of under-consumption (addressed before).

In this regard, Keynes's great contribution lies in having organized these insights into "a general theory" of the functioning of economic system largely innovative in respect to the traditional theory. There are, however, at least in our view, some aspects of this theory that appear weak and/or demand a better clarification.

2.1 Wages and employment

In chapter 2 of GT, Keynes critically addresses "the classical theory", in which he includes both classical and neoclassical economics. He considers the postulates of the neoclassical theory of employment — in particular in Marshall's and Pigou's versions — which are: **(a)** "the wage should be equal to the marginal product of labour"; **(b)** "the utility of the wage when a given volume of labour is employed is equal to the marginal disutility of that amount of employment."

While Keynes finds himself substantially in agreement, except for some minor qualifications, with the first postulate, he is more critical of the second one. He notes that the supposed rigidity of real wages is more apparent than real. This happens because what are really more sticky are nominal wages, because, normally, workers try to resist their reduction. And this also on account of the circumstance that such reduction, as it is likely to be more pronounced in the weaker economic sectors, is tantamount to a redistribution of income and power among sectors.

Hence, notes Keynes, workers, when contracting a certain level of money-wages, can only imperfectly forecast the future variations of prices. More in general, workers tend to resist much less an increase in the cost of living than a reduction in the nominal wages. If things stand like this, the second postulate does not hold, because workers are willing to accept lower real wages. Hence, a moderate process of inflation, by reducing real wages (and real interest rates), would be able to increase the level of employment.

This theory, however interesting in several respects, presents various aspects of weakness, which find their common origin in Keynes's attitude towards the classical theory of employment. In our view, he remained too much attached to such theory[11] as he seemed to agree with the neoclassical view that more flexible real wages would entail more employment. In this respect, Keynes remains highly sceptical about the positive effects of a reduction in nominal wages on employment (see also below), and to the real

---

[11] This appears in particular from the following passage,
"In emphasizing our point of departure from the classical system, we must not overlook an important point of agreement. For we shall maintain the first postulate as heretofore, subject only to the same qualifications as in the classical theory; and we must pause, for a moment, to consider what this involves.
It means that with a given organisation, equipment and technique, real wages and the volume of output (and hence of employment) are uniquely correlated, so that, in general, an increase of employment can only occur to the accompaniment of a decline in the rate of real wages...thus, *if* employment increases, then, in the short period, the reward per unit of labour in terms of wage-goods must, in general, decline and profit increases...[hence, his critique the classical theory concerns its second postulate]...But when we have thrown over the second postulate, a decline in employment, although necessarily associated with labour receiving a wage equal in value to a larger quantity of wage-goods, is not necessarily due to labour's demanding a larger quantity of wage-goods; and a willingness on the part of labour to accept lower money-wages is not necessarily a remedy for unemployment. The theories of wages in relation to unemployment, to which we are leading up, cannot be fully elucidated, however, until chapter 19 and the related Appendix has been reached.", [Keynes, *The General Theory*, 2013 (1936): 15].

possibility of workers to fix real-wages but this does not really shake the neoclassical core of the reasoning.

First, the emphasis put by Keynes on the incapacity of workers (and their unions) to fix real wages seems utterly exaggerated. Of course, the fact that money-wages are more sticky than real wages is indicative of an imperfect adjustment between the two. But not completely, however. As a matter of fact, the factual analysis shows that workers and unions consider – although with varying degrees of accuracy – in their bargaining of the money-wages, both the increase of the level of prices intervened in the period prior to the contract renewal and the expectations about their future increase.

Moreover, what seems really unconvincing is the core reasoning of neoclassical (and also of Keynes[12] in this respect) analysis: namely, that it is chiefly on account of a social and institutional convention that money-wages are rigid and workers can only imperfectly fix their real wages. Hence, should real-wages become more flexible, this would eliminate unemployment (however defined).

Indeed, Keynes made various qualifications to this statement. In particular, his acceptance of the first postulate of the classical theory hardly squares with his theory of effective demand. He notes that a reduction in nominal wages, in order to have a positive effect on employment, requires that effective demand remains unaffected by such reduction. In order to attain this result, it becomes necessary that a reduction in nominal wage be

---

[12] One can wonder what are the reasons underlying this attitude. There could be the objective difficulty in devising a new theoretical paradigm. But there are also the psychological conflicts (and the related feeling of guilt) in overcoming ingrained habits of thought. In all his writings one can perceive this tension between the old and the new by his continual reassurances that his theory, however innovative, continues to have a significant adherence which the neoclassical theory. It is perhaps for this reason that, even when he declares to adhere to neoclassical principles, he seems not very convinced about the realism of these hypotheses.

Another related explanation for this attitude can be found in a kind of "diplomatic reason": namely, the attempt, in order to gain a wide political acceptance, to hide as much as possible the innovative aspects of his theory. This hypothesis seems plausible also on account of other aspects. For instance, the interesting analysis contained in the last part of the "Essays in Persuasion" on the structural transformations of the system towards a "society of free time" is barely alluded to in the GT.

Tendency of effective demand to lag behind the supply of full employment

accompanied by an increase of the investment led by a parallel increase of MEC.

But, notes Keynes, the fulfilment of these conditions in response to a diminution of nominal wages is highly uncertain and problematic. In particular, there **(i)** is no guarantee that to such reduction will follow an increase of investment sufficient to make up for the reduction of consumption due to the diminution of wages. In particular, if prices tend to follow the reduction of nominal wages, there is likely to arise a harder burden of real debt for firms.

Furthermore, notes Keynes in chapters 19 and 21 of the GT, **(ii)** a situation of wild flexibility of nominal wages (in response to a reduction of the employment) would not warrant any stable equilibrium until an (unlikely) situation of full employment (possibly with wages equal to zero) is attained in this way.

Hence, some form of sticky wages and prices is necessary for ensuring the stability of the system. And finally, **(iii)** a reduction of nominal wages, especially if carried out imperfectly according to the different contractual powers of the various economic sectors, is likely to trigger unwelcome social conflicts and to undermine the relative stability of social fabric.

Then, for all these reasons, says Keynes, it seems more expedient to achieve a reduction of real wages through a moderate process of inflation. These are in the main valid arguments, but not strong enough to effectively withstand the neoclassical attempt to dismiss Keynes's theory by considering it just as a special instance of unemployment caused by market rigidities. In particular, his acceptance of the first postulate risks to be a Trojan horse able to weaken and confuse the whole Keynesian edifice. And this is much more so, on the ground of the "fiscal crisis of the state" and the supposed urgency of dismantling public sector and render productive factors "more flexible".

In fact, despite all these qualifications, Keynes's analysis of the labour market still rests in a good degree on the neoclassical idea that, in a situation of deflation, unemployment is due (besides the role of the MEC) to the incapacity of workers – owing to an institutional set up that makes it inexpedient to reduce nominal wages and prices – to oppose the increase of their real wages.

2.1.1. Further remarks on the inadequacy of neoclassical theory of wage determination

As just seen, Keynes assumes that, in a situation of unemployment and other factor remaining stable, a decrease of real wages – better if realized, as just seen, through a moderate process of inflation – would bring a better MEC, and then more investment, product and employment. This conclusion appears weak also for these reasons:

(I) It is unrealistic, as noted before, to consider investment as an independent variable in relation to consumption, as the former is instrumental to the latter;

(II) Another aspect where such neoclassical-driven reasoning is intrinsically flawed is the following: one cannot suppose — without running into a severe contradiction — at the same that MEC increases (with beneficial effects on investment and aggregate income) whereas, at the same time, wages should comply all the time with the first neoclassical postulate, which, as we know, implies the hypothesis of perfect competition. As a matter of fact, a higher MEC implies that firms expect to get a better mark up over their sales. Hence, in order to realize this, they need to move away as much as they can from perfect competition, where the mark-up should be equal to zero.

This being so, it is utterly unrealistic (and also a bit unfair) to suppose that the neoclassical framework should apply with its strict rules only to workers.

(III) In our view, what is needed for overcoming these shortcomings is a sharp departure from the neoclassical theory of employment. In particular, both hypotheses **(a)** and **(b)** of such theory seem very unrealistic. As for the hypothesis **(a)** – "the wage is equal to the marginal product of labour" – this seems to be, at the best, only a kind of lower bound of a much wider range of choices. As a matter of fact, we should also consider the following aspects:

118

Tendency of effective demand to lag behind the supply of full employment

(1) As just noted, in modern economies, market imperfections are the rule rather than the exception. In these systems, economic actors try to get a differential advantage – based on various degrees of monopoly – from their activities. For this reason, firms do not try to equalize mechanically marginal costs to prices but to realize a certain mark-up over their costs. But, even more significant, firms do not try to realize such mark-up in a *vacuum* but in accordance with a certain strategy (which can be, of course, more or less accurate). This implies that decisions about employment and other matters are likely to be oriented in a "holistic way" by firms' strategies.

For instance, supposing that hiring an additional worker would involve the same prospective gain for two firms, this would not warrant that their choices would be the same. As a matter of the fact, these choices are likely to vary according to the objective of firms in terms of long-term growth, product and market strategies, relations with workers, innovation strategies, and many other factors.

This reminds of the circumstance that markets, market imperfections and firms' strategies are closely interlinked[13] and are heavily embedded within the social and institutional framework.

(2) Also the workers would try to get a differential advantage out of their expertise, but it is likely that their bargaining power is, at least in the average, much less than that of firms. Hence, a notable difference in bargaining power between workers and entrepreneurs tends to be the rule rather than the exception; but, this being the case, it is very unrealistic to stick to the hypothesis of perfect markets in determining labour remuneration.

Relatedly, the hypothesis **(b)** – "the utility of the wage when a given volume of labour is employed is equal to the marginal disutility of that amount of employment" – is unrealistic for most workers. In fact, for many of them the

---

[13] In order to better analyse these manifold relations, we believe much useful to realize a closer collaboration between Keynesian theories and other fields of economics: we can mention institutional economics, especially in its "old" tradition, Marx's and other theories of socialism and social justice, also in their relations with social and psychological sciences.

wage constitutes the only and vital source of income. Hence, there is little room for a precise balance of the utility/disutility of work, because in most cases workers need a job even in presence of a high disutility of work.

Furthermore, this argument implicitly rests on the assumption that firms are moving along a neoclassical production function, namely, with decreasing returns beyond the minimum average cost (and no technological innovation for the time being). Hence, according to such hypothesis, workers can always get a job by accepting a lower real wage corresponding to a lower marginal productivity. If they do not work, then, it depends on their "free choice" – on the fact that their disutility of work is higher than the real wage.

It is easy to note the inconsistency of this idea. In fact, by following the "logic" of this reasoning, it follows that the only actual equilibrium will be reached at zero real wage. In fact, before that level, however infinitesimal, there could always be, according to the "disutility" argument", a lower and lower level of real wage compatible with a lower and lower marginal productivity of labour. But when zero real wage is reached, for obvious reasons no labour supply (in economic terms) would be available in the aggregate.

But we need not follow in detail this exercise, since real firms' behaviour is governed by very different principles. First, production functions rarely display the characteristics of a typical Cobb-Douglas form. Rather, they tend to be characterised by a range of production possibilities where marginal costs are rather sticky, and, beyond that range, they rapidly increase.

In this instance, then, increasing employment by indefinitely moving up along the curve of marginal cost becomes uneconomical, and hence unfeasible, for firms. More realistically, when firms intend to increase production in a more permanent way, they do so by adding new plants and/or by technological innovation.

Finally, the hypothesis of "disutility" is also inadequate for "intrinsic" reasons. As a matter of fact, in many instances it is likely that workers obtain an intrinsic utility from working, and it is then useful for individual and collective progress to constantly improve job satisfaction.

(3) In addition and in complement to the foregoing aspects, the idea that real wages should be equal to the marginal product in value raises another relevant problem. As we know, this prescription rests on the hypothesis of a Cobb-Douglas type function characterized by an increasing marginal productivity followed by a decreasing marginal productivity beyond a certain "optimum" point.

If things stand like this, the marginal product beyond such point will quickly become lower than the average product. If all wages are fixed at that point, the result will be an increase of mark-ups. In order to see these aspects, let us suppose the simplest example: a discreet production function, based only on labour, whose values for the marginal product are perfectly symmetrical:

Number of workers	1	2	3	4	5	6	7	8	9
Real Product	8	16	26	38	52	68	82	94	104
Marginal Product (for an increase of labour unit)	8	10	12	14	16	14	12	10	8

In this case it is plain that, for instance, the marginal product (MP) of the 9th worker (8), is lower than the average product (AP, 11.55), even if the difference is not so large.

However, it is possible to conceive of situations in which the difference between AP and MP is very marked. For instance, a continuous[14] growing function with decreasing returns can assume the form,

1. $Y = f(X)^{0.8}$

---

[14] As noted before, the hypothesis of continuity for the production function is rather unrealistic, and every simplification in this regard can be highly misleading. Only a careful analysis of the real productions can indicate the related "production functions".

Where X stands for labour, and the first derivative is,

$$2. \quad \frac{d}{dx} = \frac{0.8}{x^{0.2}}$$

We obtain the following absolute and relative marginal values:

Number of workers	1	2	3	4	5	6	7	8	9
Real Product	1.0	1.74	2.4	3.03	3.62	4.19	4.74	5.27	5.8
Marginal Product (for an increase of labour unit)	0.80	0.69	0.64	0.60	0.57	0.55	0.54	0.52	0.51

In this case, the average real product, 3.53, is almost six fold the average marginal product, 0.6. In this respect, the crucial point is whether it is fair or expedient that a decrease of marginal productivity should affect the wages of all the workers.

After all, one can well claim, marginal means marginal and hence should affect only the marginal unit. Of course, some people can say, the reduction of marginal productivity should apply to all the workers, but it is also true that the choice of moving along a less productive path was taken by the firm by hiring the marginal worker.

Hence, when a worker is hired the wage should be fixed (according to such theory) in line with his/her marginal productivity. For instance, for the 5th worker of the two functions the wages should be 16 and 0.57. Now, if a firm chooses – and most likely without asking the opinion of the infra-marginal workers – to hire the 9th worker at the wages of 8 or 0.51, why this should impinge on the wages of infra-marginal workers? By pushing the example to the extreme (but not totally unrealistic) case, if a firm chooses to hire a worker at the marginal product of 1 penny per day, is it fair or reasonable to reduce accordingly the wages of all the workers?

In this regard, we think it much fairer and expedient that workers should retain their original wages, especially in situations of decrease of labour productivity for which no responsibility can be attributed to workers.

However, and besides our opinion, we think it important to stress that, beyond a number of technical and more "objective" parameters, there are no necessary and efficient laws of wage determination. All these matters find their settlement in the institutional, cultural and psychological dimensions of socioeconomic relations.

2.2. Public spending, credit creation and the relation between consumption and investment

In Keynes's foregoing account there is another aspect which deserves more clarification. As we have seen, in Keynes's analysis a moderate process of inflation, by reducing real wages (and real interest rates), would bring about more employment. We can wonder how the additional production would create (or find ready at hand) an equal amount of additional demand. Keynes's answer is that — although he does not seem himself much convinced of its real viability — a parallel increase of investment would absorb the additional demand. We believe this conclusion rather weak for two reasons:

(I) it is unrealistic to think of investment as a kind of "independent variable" in relation to consumption. As we have seen, such expenses are instrumental to produce a programmed vent of consumption goods. Hence, in a given state of technique and organization, investment expenses are checked by the programmed amount of consumption goods. Furthermore, if we consider technological (and organizational) progress, we can note that the ratio of strictly productive investment – fixed and circulating capital related to production process – on consumption sector has steadily diminished over time across the most industrialized Countries. To these elements we should add the circumstance, which we shall address in the next section, that for the firms as a whole, their investment expenses cannot constitute a source of profit. As a matter of fact, to the gain for the investment sector would correspond an equal loss for the consumption sector, and hence the aggregate profit would remain unaffected.

(II) Considering these aspects, a solution for increasing effective demand would be a parallel expansion of public spending and credit creation. How did Keynes deal with these aspects? As for public spending, it can be noted that the idea of its necessity for addressing situations of crisis and unemployment constitutes, however in an implicit[15] way, a *leit-motif* of the GT.

However, it remains unclear whether, and to what degree, public spending can be replaced by private action. This is due to his rather substantial adherence to the neoclassical theory of employment. As we have just seen, his account seems to imply that, were workers more willing or able to accept lower real wages, this would bring about more employment.

This analysis brings a degree of ambiguity and indeterminacy to his analysis of public spending. As a matter of fact, it seems that public spending becomes necessary only in so far as **(a)** real wages are imperfectly flexible, and **(b)** it is not fair or expedient to try to lower them through a reduction of money-wages.

Of course, Keynes made important qualifications to this conclusion and seemed never really convinced about its real viability. On that account, especially in chapter 19, he strongly opposes the hypothesis of a money-wage reduction. In his view, as just noted, a moderate process of inflation, coupled when necessary with an increase in public spending, could work much better towards the end of full employment.

---

[15] In fact, as unbelievable it may appear on account of the widespread interpretation of Keynes's theory as a quest for the necessity of public spending (possibly in deficit) for ensuring full employment, in the GT public spending is barely mentioned, and even less analysed. Its necessity for overcoming situations of equilibrium of unemployment (and when, as just noted, real wages are not flexible enough) is only alluded to throughout the book. Only in the final chapter there is a somewhat more precise (but still vague) reference to the necessity of a certain socialization of investment, but it is not clear how this should be realized. In this respect, it should also be stressed that Keynes had never been a blind advocate of public spending as such. Even in the works – in particular the *Essays in Persuasion* – where he more openly proposes public works as a way to increase demand and employment, he considered these measures useful only as long as they minimize their impact on the level of taxation on productive activities.

Tendency of effective demand to lag behind the supply of full employment

In this regard, he was aware that markets are structurally imperfect (in particular at the macro level) and that, for this reason, "a certain socialization of investment" is necessary for ensuring the working of the market system. However, notwithstanding these qualifications, Keynes's theory of effective demand remains slippery with respect to the neoclassical theory of employment. These feeble aspects have been readily caught up by the "neoclassical synthesis" to dismiss all the innovative aspects of Keynes's theory. In the last decades, as a result of the increase of public spending and the "fiscal crisis of the state", these criticisms appeared more convincing and ended up in a strong neo-liberalistic orientation.

The main aspect of this tendency – which has gained acceptance not only in conservative quarters but also in more progressive fields – is an uncritical exaltation of the virtues of free markets, which is coupled with a systematic dismissing of public intervention. In the next paragraph we will show that the increase in public spending of the last decades is not due to the failure of "Keynesian policies", but to its irreplaceable role in performing many relevant functions, and, not least, in sustaining effective demand, and hence profits for private sector.

As regards credit creation, Keynes's analysis of its role in increasing effective demand is little developed. True, there is in GT a very acute and detailed analysis of the supply and demand of money, with particular attention to their implications on the real interest rate and their negative effects on the MEC. This is linked to his bright analysis of long-term expectations and the role of "animal spirits" in economic development. However, in all this account the role of money and of the banking system in creating new credit for firms and families, and hence additional demand in the economic system, is left in the background.

This was partly different in the *Treatise on Money* (TM) (1930), where he more explicitly addresses the role of the banking system in creating new money (and hence new additional purchasing power) for the firms. The stress is put on the effect on economic cycles of the divergences between saving and investment, which are also related to the latter being partly financed by credit creation. However, it can safely be stated that the crucial role of credit creation in creating new demand is left a bit in the shadow.

Furthermore, these early insights were rather dropped in GT, where the demand for money is chiefly treated in its relation to its effect on the real interest rate. This, of course, is a central issue, but by no means the sole one in monetary issues.

All this, of course, does not diminish the relevance of the TM as a comprehensive "non-orthodox" attempt to consider the role of money and banking system in the development of capitalistic institutions.

In the next section we will address the role of public spending and credit creation in sustaining effective demand. Here we can note that a more comprehensive account of these aspects would allow a better appraisal of the divergences between effective supply and effective demand, with the structural tendency of the latter to lag behind the supply of full employment (however defined).

As we know, Keynes located the eruption of a crisis in a sudden diminution of investment, caused by a decline of the (actual and expected) MEC, in relations to saving. The reduction of investment, if severe, is likely to trigger a vicious circle of further diminution of demand and employment.

This analysis catches a relevant aspect of the underemployment of resources. However, a more detailed appraisal of these aspects would reveal that the reduction of investment is not the sole cause for the reduction of demand. As we shall presently see, a reduction of the effective demand may also be due to a decrease in consumption and/or investment, chiefly stemming from a diminution of public spending and credit creation.

In concluding this section, we can note that a better collaboration of Keynesian economics with the theories of under-consumption would help shape a more complete and powerful interpretative framework of the macroeconomic imbalances.

3. The role of public spending and credit creation in sustaining effective demand

As noted by several authors and witnessed by historical events, modern economic systems are increasingly moving away from a pure capitalistic system – composed of private agents acting within a self-sustaining mechanism, the market, with the state playing only the external role of controller.

To be sure, this system existed only in "mainstream" oriented textbooks even in the heyday of the "laissez-faire capitalism" of the 19th century. However, as this system seemed to approach that ideal in various respects, the theoretical foundations of these theories were little questioned. Needless to say, even in that period public intervention had played a relevant role in promoting and maintaining the institutions of capitalism. However, as the emphasis centered on the changes brought about by the industrial revolution, and as such revolution had its most apparent driving engine in the activities of private firms, the role of public sector was easily downplayed. Other circumstances that reinforced this tendency are: **(i)** public sector tended (and tends) to be perceived as the locus of corporatist interests, as contrasted with the dynamic forces of modern industry; **(ii)** public policies and public spending, however important, had not yet reached the overwhelming importance of today. As we know, in the past two centuries the role of public sector has steadily – with various "cyclical" ups and downs – grown in importance both from quantitative side, through a long-term increase of the share of public spending on GDP; and from a qualitative side, through a continual enlargement and diversification of its functions.

There are many reasons for this phenomenon, a noteworthy group of them referring to the role of public sector in managing the complexity and contradictions of the "mixed economies" of our days. Public action, among other things, performs an irreplaceable role in providing public goods, including the legal and institutional framework; in managing and/or regulating important economic sectors; in redistributing resources; and in promoting research and innovation.

3.1 The impressive increase of public spending and credit creation

Among its many functions, the public sector plays a relevant role – directly through public spending and more indirectly through credit creation – in the formation of effective demand. Now we focus[16] attention on a number of macroeconomic implications of this aspect. We can start by noting the impressive increase of public spending (PS), not only in absolute, but also in relative terms, as shown by the ratio of public spending on GDP. The available data clearly make evident this trend. The values of the ratio have shifted, for the most important OECD Countries, from 20-30% of 1970s to 40-50% of recent years. In the latest 15 years, also as a result of the "austerity policies", the ratio PS/GDP has diminished in some Countries, and remained stable or slightly increased in others. However, and very interestingly for our theme, there has occurred in the same period a parallel and notable increase of the ratios of public debt/GDP and private debt/GDP for virtually all Countries, with values particularly impressive for the latter. This can be a good indication of the circumstance that the reduction in public spending, in order not to negatively influence effective demand, needs to be accompanied by a parallel process of credit creation. In the following tables we report the data for the years 2000 and 2014. A more complete illustration of the data can be found in the links at the bottom of the tables.

---

[16] The present and the following section expand on some sections of chapters 12 and 14 of the book *The Systemic Nature of the Economic Crisis: The Perspectives of Heterodox Economics and Psychoanalysis*, Routledge, April 2015.

Tendency of effective demand to lag behind the supply of full employment

Table 1 General government spending as a percentage of GDP selected countries

Countries	Year 2000	Year 2014	Countries	Year 2000	Year 2014
Australia	35.3	36.2	Luxembourg	36.9	42.4
Austria	50.3	52.5	Netherlands	41.8	46.2
Belgium	49.1	55.1	Norway	42.0	45.6
Czech Republic	40.4	42.0	Poland	45.3*	42.1
Denmark	52.7	56.0	Portugal	42.6	51.7
Estonia	36.4	38.0	Slovak Republic	52.0	41.6
Finland	48.0	58.1	Slovenia	46.1	49.8
France	51.1	57.3	Spain	39.1	44.5
Germany	44.7	44.3	Sweden	53.6	51.8
Greece	Na	49.9	Switzerland	Na	33.7
Hungary	47.2	49.9	United Kingdom	37.8	43.9
Iceland	Na	45.7	United States	33.7	38.1
Ireland	30.8	38.3	Italy	45.5	51.3
Israel	48.2	41.2	Japan	Na	42.1
Latvia	37.3	37.3			

Note: * 2002
Source: OECD (2016), General government spending (indicator).
Doi: 101787/a31cbf4d-en

What are the structural reasons for such an impressive increase in public spending and credit creation? As regards public spending, this phenomenon has been first underscored by Adolph Wagner, who remarked that economic and social development carries with it an enlargement and diversification of the functions of the public sector. With regard to credit creation, Keynes and other authors pointed out the role of public sector (meant in a broad sense, and then also including Central Banks) in guaranteeing the value of money and in orienting the banks in their policies of credit creation.

Table 2 Private sector debt as a percentage of GDP, selected countries

Nations	Year 2000	Year 2014	Nations	Year 2000	Year 2014
Australia	156.5	214.4	Japan	259.3	243.1
Austria	143.9	169.2	Korea	Na	253.5
Belgium	185.9	255.5	Luxembourg	297.8**	461.1
Canada	185.3	241.9	Netherlands	264.2	269.37
Chile	167.6**	191.0	Norway	226.7	268.5
Czech Republic	142.0	146.2	Poland	88.8***	120.0
Denmark	201.5	273.2	Portugal	208.3	288.6
Estonia	117.5	188.6	Slovak Republic	101.3	115.7
Finland	148.0	209.1	Slovenia	111.4*	154.3
France	177.0	223.2	Spain	181.1	229.3
Germany	171.2	150.1	Sweden	232.5	271.2
Greece	67.3	142.6	Switzerland	186.2	207.9****
Hungary	105.6	165.4	United Kingdom	194.3	239.0
Ireland	197.0*	373.3	United States	180.8	197.3
Israel	123.4*	124.2	Italy	131.1	177.2

Notes * 2001, ** 2002, *** 2003, ****2013
Source: "Financial Indicators – Stocks"
http://stats.oecd.org/Index.aspx?DataSetCode=FIN_IND_FBS in OECD.StatExtracts
http://stats.oecd.org/

The reason why we accept banknotes of intrinsic minimal value is that we are fairly confident that their real purchasing power is monitored and guaranteed (up to a certain degree, of course) by public action. In this sense, as highlighted by many authors, money is a highly institutional phenomenon.

These insights have evolved into three lines of research, which often tend to be blurred: **(i)** public choice, chiefly belonging to mainstream domain, which investigates the role of interest groups in lobbying the political system for obtaining more public resources in their favour. The limitations of these studies lie in the circumstance that they tend to consider public spending only as a negative phenomenon – a kind of unwelcome departure from the perfect world of mainstream hypotheses; **(ii)** a number of theories belonging to the fields of institutional and evolutionary economics, which point out the potential of the institutional framework for the unfolding of the national system of science and innovation, and of the related framework of human

Tendency of effective demand to lag behind the supply of full employment

and social capital; **(iii)** Keynesian oriented theories, which investigate the role of public spending and credit creation in ensuring macroeconomic stability and the full employment of the labour force.

Table 3 General government debt as a percentage of GDP, selected countries

Countries	Year 2000	Year 2014	Countries	Year 2000	Year 2014
Australia	40.9	64.2	Japan	144.5	246.6
Austria	70.5	101.8	Latvia	Na	45.9
Belgium	120.4	129.5	Luxembourg	12.3**	33.7
Canada	102.2	107.7	Mexico	Na	44.9
Chile	Na	22.6	Netherlands	60.5	81.2
Czech Republic	24.0	57.4	Norway	32.2	32.7
Denmark	60.5	60.0	Poland	54.8***	66.2
Estonia	6.8	13.6	Portugal	62.0	150.6
Finland	51.0	70.8	Slovak Republic	57.9	60.1
France	71.9	118.8	Slovenia	33.0*	97.2
Germany	59.4	82.3	Spain	65.2	117.9
Greece	111.4	178.8	Sweden	62.7	62.5
Hungary	61.0	99.4	Switzerland	52.7	45.5****
Ireland	38.7	125.4	Turkey	Na	39.0
Israel	91.2*	79.1	United Kingdom	51.3	113.6
Italy	119.0	156.4	United States	61.5	123.2

Notes * 2001, ** 2002, *** 2003, ****2013
Source: OECD (2016), General Government (indicator). Doi: 10.1787/a0528cc2-en

Especially in the last three decades, the strands **(i)** and **(ii)** have received surely more attention than the point **(iii)**. In particular, both critics and advocates of public spending often implicitly agree that today's level of public spending is "too high" and should be abated in one way or another. And this opinion has gained some ground even among Keynesian economists, chiefly as a result of the supposed "failure" of the "Keynesian" oriented policies of the post-WWII period.

However, since the data indicate that such massive increase of PS/GDP ratio has been fully compatible with the development of capitalistic system (in reality, "mixed economies"), a macroeconomic explanation along Keynes's insights is highly needed for casting more light on the profound reasons for such increase.

Public spending is important for private sector not only as a component of the effective demand but also because such component is paramount (along with credit creation) for forming the profit of firms. Since this aspect, as we have seen, remains largely implicit in Keynes's analysis, in the next paragraph, we try to "disentangle" the macroeconomic components of effective demand.

3.2 A Keynesian inspired interpretative framework

In this simple interpretative framework that we develop, we do not assume specific hypotheses regarding its microfoundations and/or the effects on growth, income distribution, quality of life. We assume only that profits, in the meaning given below, imply a certain degree of market power and hence of market imperfections. On that account, we tend to consider markets as social and institutional phenomena characterized by many "imperfections". The latter does not necessarily represent negative phenomena because they can play the role – as shown, for instance in the theory of "small menu costs" (see, in particular, Mankiw, 1985) – of stabilizing the economic and social relations underlying market transactions. In the same spirit, we do not assume any particular hypotheses as regards the links between profits and the rate of accumulation. This happens also because we believe much more important the qualitative transformations of the system, which can be compatible with a steady state.

Let us consider some macroeconomic effects of public spending and credit creation. On that account, it is interesting to note that, in the absence of such factors, no significant aggregate profit[17] would be possible for firms. As a matter of fact, labour cost constitutes an aggregate cost to the system of firms. This cost can be brought to zero if employees spend all their earnings, but can never become a source of profit. But, very interestingly, not even the entrepreneurs' investment expenses can constitute an aggregate profit for the firms as a whole. In such case, in fact, to the profit of an entrepreneur must correspond the expense of another, so that the net result for the firms would be zero.

As a consequence, aggregate profit[18] must derive from sources "external" to the system of firms: these sources − not considering, for the sake of simplicity, international trade whose balance[19] is zero at world-level − take

---

[17] By the expression aggregate profit we mean an amount of profit which exceeds the "normal" incomes of all the workers engaged in the private sector, including the so-called executive-salaries. Needless to say, a kind of aggregate profit can be present also in a hypothetical pure private economy, but in this case it is difficult that it acquires the nature of the extra-profits typical of expansionary period driven by public spending and credit creation. As a matter of fact, in a "pure private economy", the income differences between persons and classes find a limit in the principle of the effective demand. For instance, if the entrepreneurs want to increase their profits by reducing real wages, they must also make up for the reduction in the effective demand caused by wages reduction. In a private economy, as investment goods are intrinsically related to consumption goods, the only available way for increasing the effective demand is to attain a higher level of the entrepreneurs' consumption. However, this process finds many limits, especially in the presence of scale-economies associated with mass consumption (the entrepreneur can buy himself a yacht, but for the class of entrepreneurs buying, say, one thousand iPads each in order to sustain effective demand is likely to be a bit less practical). This aspect can help explain why the marginal propensity to consume tends to be lower for the richest sections of populations. For these reasons, we consider the consumption of entrepreneurs in the formation of aggregate profit as a relatively unimportant phenomenon.
It is important to underscore that all these economic relations embody, at the same time, also a social, cultural and psychological aspect, the study of which becomes paramount for a full understanding of the real features and problems of the examined contexts.
[18] Another condition for the existence of profits as defined above is the presence of some kind of market power on the part of entrepreneurs. This can arise in the labour market, where normally entrepreneurs have strong contractual powers over the workers, and in the market for goods, when firms hold various forms of monopoly power.
[19] Needless to say, this is a gross simplification. In fact, as well underscored by the theories of unequal exchange, the total effects of international trade tend to adversely affect the weaker countries.

two interrelated forms: public spending and net credit[20] creation. We can express these relations in the following way:

1. $$P + L \equiv Y = C + I + G \equiv amG + bmCD + bmID +$$
    $$+ (1- a)mG + (1 - b)mCD + (1 - b)mID + C_p + I_p$$

where **P** denotes the aggregate profit for the system of private[21] firms, **L** the sum of "labour" incomes, including the "executive salaries", **G** public spending and **CD** the amount of aggregate consumption generated by credit creation, **ID** the amount of investment generated by credit creation, **m** the value of multiplier, **a** and **b,** and **(1- a)** and **(1 – b)** the ratios of the effective demand generated by public spending and credit creation accruing to private profits and to labour incomes, **C$_p$ + I$_p$** the sum of consumption and investment originated[22] in the private sector. **CD** and **ID** indicate that, in a monetary economy, purchasing power is created through a process of credit creation (both short and long term based) made available to borrowers. In this context, **P** constitutes a fraction of the aggregate income and is equal to:

2. $$P \equiv amG + bmCD$$

---

[20] In order to calculate the effects of credit creation on the effective demand (and hence on profits), we should detract, for any time span, from the total credit creation the amount of "credit destruction", which is equal to the amount of credit repayments. As highlighted by the available data, the amount of net credit creation tends to be far superior to the amount of credit destruction. The reason why this becomes possible resides in the circumstance that, as we know, money can be created *ex-nihilo* from the banking system, provided that the State (including the Central Bank) provide an "institutional guarantee" for such creation. If things stand like this, it is easy to see that the real issue does not lie in debt repayments – as debt can be consolidated over longer periods, and when repaid, is likely to be soon employed in new loans – but in the sums received by the creditors in the forms of interest payments.

[21] Also in this case, the multifarious aspects of the growing complexity of the system comport with a parallel articulation of the structure of ownership of the firms, with the presence of many "mixed" forms. It is interesting to note that this analysis will apply also to the case of state-owned enterprises, provided be they organized as administratively independent bodies.

[22] We are aware of the difficulty of "disentangling" the various components of effective demand in real economies. Besides, in our complex credit-based economies, it seems really arduous to find significant instances of a pure private economy: namely, an economy in which credit creation and public spending play a minor role in creating aggregate demand. Such realities can perhaps be found in simple economic arrangements, like local markets based on craftsmanship and typical products.

Now, considering a "pure system" of private agents, we obtain that:

3. $P + L \equiv C_p + I_p \equiv C + I$

such identity implies that in a private system, without public spending and credit creation, the sum of consumption and investment tends to be equal to wages and salaries and, therefore, there is little room for aggregate profit, in the meaning described above.

This analysis is geared to the following central question, namely, whether in the familiar identity,

4. $Y \equiv C + I + G$

the terms **I** and **G** are mutually replaceable. As a matter of fact, it is on this (more or less explicit) assumption that the neoclassical economists anchor their reasoning—namely, that the economic space now "ineffectively occupied" by the public sector can easily be replaced by private investment. But to what degree is this alternative feasible (and advisable)? We have two main hypotheses:

Let us assume that we have, at the time zero, with an income multiplier equal to 1,66, and supposing that the volume of credit creation would remain the same :

5. $Y_0 \equiv C + I + G \equiv 400 + 100 + 500 \equiv 1000$

In this case, neoclassical oriented theories tend to posit that a diminution, say, by 100 in public spending would entail a parallel increase in private investment.

In the opinion of many, if 1000 is an equilibrium of underemployment, the reduction in public spending would generate an increase in **I** even higher than the corresponding reduction in public spending. In this way, the new level of Y_1 would be higher than Y_0. By assuming that the decrease in public spending by 100 is accompanied by an increase of I equal to 150, we obtain:

6. $Y_1 \equiv 429 + 250 + 400 \equiv 1079$

which corresponds to the neoclassical hypothesis.

In the Keynesian case, if the reduction in public spending is not accompanied by a parallel increase in private investment, and supposing that the volume of credit creation would remain the same, the result of the cut is, with the same multiplier equal to 1,66, a diminution of GDP equal to:

7. $Y_0 \equiv 400 + 100 + 500 \equiv 1000$

8 $Y_1 \equiv 330 + 100 + 400 \equiv 830$

In this case, even the gain for public budget will be scant. In fact, if we assume, as a reasonable hypothesis, that the total taxation (direct + indirect) is approximately equal to 50%, the reduction of public spending will cause a reduction of fiscal revenue equal to 170*0,5 = 85. The net balance of this operation for public finance is then only + 100 - 85 = 15 and is only the role of the "social absorbers" that can mitigate these negative effects.

Which hypothesis is closer to reality?

For the reasons we have tried to set forth, and also on account of actual economic trends, the Keynesian hypothesis seems much closer to reality. This is of course compatible, and requires indeed, an increase of the efficiency of public spending. In this regard, the real issue is to focus public spending less on the agenda of the various interest groups and more on proactive policies for economic and social development. Besides, the crowding out effect of mainstream economics does not take place since the hypothesis of perfect substitutability between I and G is very far from reality. In fact, as we have seen, public spending and credit creation are the main drivers of aggregate profit. Furthermore, a perfect substitutability[23] between I

---

[23] As noted in the previous part, the notions of public and private action, markets, competition and efficiency are determined by the complex and evolutionary systems

Tendency of effective demand to lag behind the supply of full employment

and **G** finds a limit in the circumstance that the amount of investment goods needs be related to the amount of consumption goods that firms plan to produce which, in turn, depend on the available income of the labour force. We can represent this situation with the general equation:

9. $C = f(I)$

we define this equation general to imply that, in order to produce a given amount of consumption goods, many productive ways are possible. However, the possibility of choosing different productive techniques does not imply the perfect flexibility of productive factors postulated by neoclassical economics.

Quite the contrary, this formulation takes into account that any kind of productive process – with their present and prospective techniques – is highly evolutionary and path-dependent as it is fully ingrained in the complexity of the social and cultural context.

An implication of this analysis is that a "perfect" private economy is unlikely to be attained in the modern world. Such an economy, in allowing little growth, little innovation and little change, can have as its correlate only very simple economic systems, based on vicinity and direct personal relations. But, as soon as these systems start growing, the role of public sector (and of credit creation) becomes paramount, paradoxically enough, for ensuring the profit associated with modern capitalistic institutions (in reality, mixed economies). Both public spending and credit creation originate from public intervention. This is evident for public spending, but also for credit creation the role of the public sector is no less important. In fact, as just noted, public sector (meant in a broad sense and then including also the Central Bank) plays a pivotal role in creating and guaranteeing the value of money.

---

of norms, institutions, policies in their relation with the cultural and psychological orientations at the individual and collective level. In this respect, one noteworthy phenomenon is the growing importance of the "mixed forms" of economic activities. They are characterized by an articulated presence of "stakeholders" carrying different objectives and systems of value.
Also for this reason, it becomes more and more necessary an adequate level of coordination between institutions and policies in order to take in due account the multifariousness of these issues.

Public spending and credit creation can accrue to the effective demand in numerous ways: as for public spending, in particular, **(i)** classic multiplier effects related to public consumption, public investment and civil servants' incomes; **(ii)** subsidies and incentives to firms, which can accrue to both firms' consumption and investment expenses. And, **(iii)** as for credit creation, the various types of consumer credit and investment credit, which also combine to shape the level and forms of public spending.

For these reasons, it appears clearly that the neoclassical idea of a *crowding out* effect of public spending[24] on private sector can display, if any, only a limited effect in our economies. As we have tried to show, in a "pure private economy" aggregate profit is unlikely to be very high. Public spending and credit creation play the fundamental role of pushing the growth of the system, also because they contribute to create an important part of the effective demand, which accrues to the private sector.

It can also be interesting to note that these conclusions hold true whatever be the elasticity to prices of the aggregate supply function. As a general

---

[24] In this sense, a psychoanalytic perspective can also be employed for the study of this and other economic and social issues. On that account, it can be very interesting to analyse how people perceive and interpret their economic and social realities and the reasons that can hinder the attainment of a more equitable and sustainable society (see also Hermann 2015). We can observe these aspects by investigating how people tend to perceive and interpret the increase in public spending of the past decades. Most often, a vicious circle tends to arise: as a result of the structural tendency towards increase in public spending, it is gained ground the opinion, even across various sectors of the progressive domain, that the only remedy to the present crisis consists in a progressive reduction of public spending.
In these situations, in which the only faith in economic progress rests on a kind of a wild and unregulated competition, the market tends to be psychologically perceived as an inflexible and punitive *superego*. In that vision, the only possible thing we should do is to comply with the "needs of the market", without any further enquiry on the adequacy of the system to respond to the profound needs of economy and society. Similar remarks can be made for the psychology of debt and credit creation.
In this regard, the *superego* can constitute an important explanation of the difficulty to move towards a society of "free time". The *superego* represents the psychological instance through which cultural values are internalized by the child. For this reason, it constitutes a fundamental nexus between individual and collective psychology. The *superego* can be considered as the heir of the *Oedipus* complex, since it arises from the internalization of the prohibitions and of the moral and cultural values – as perceived by the child – of the child's parents and also of later institutional figures such as teachers and other opinion leaders.

remark, we believe that the aggregate supply function is in most cases elastic enough in the short run, and even more in the medium and long run, due to the effects of technological progress.

4. The role of the structural factors

As we have seen, a central trait of the modern "mixed economies" lies in a chronic tendency of effective demand to lag behind the supply of full employment (however defined). In this respect, we have tried to identify a number of theories and factors that can explain in the short run these dynamics. However, there are also a number of structural (and complementary) reasons for this tendency: we can mention, first of all, the central problem of rendering compatible the objectives of full employment and environmental sustainability. Although, for space reasons, we do not address this issue here, we are fully aware of its utmost significance for our theme. We will now turn attention to other structural factors: in particular both the growing productivity of labour and the satiation for certain categories of goods combine to render the objective of full employment more difficult to achieve.

In the former case, this happens because the increase in productivity signifies that, for a given level of production, fewer jobs are required; and that, in order to keep up with the same level of employment, more goods should be produced and sold in the market. In the latter case, this comes about because, since the needs of consumers are becoming increasingly tied to the immaterial and the intellectual side[25] of consumption, their fulfillment tend to depend less and less on the "material and quantitative" aspects of consumption. In fact, we do not buy books by kilos and cultural activities by mere numbers. Also, if we buy a high-tech product, we are likely to be more interested in learning well how to use it, than in changing it with every new model.

These aspects constitute a significant explanation of the tendency of the socio-economic systems to move from work activities resting on "the

---

[25] See, for instance, R. Skidelsky and E. Skidelsky (2012) and J.K. Galbraith's (1958) *The Affluent Society.*

economic motive" to activities – social, cultural, scientific, artistic – more based on the expression of the real needs and inclinations of persons. In this regard, what are the effects of technological progress on job creation? The increase in productivity requires a growing amount of goods for guaranteeing the same level of employment. Of course, firms can introduce new products on the market, but this would not solve that structural issue. In fact, even if new jobs are created in these fields, the increase in productivity extends also, and perhaps even more, to the new products. This could contribute to explain that every innovative wave tends to create fewer and fewer jobs. For instance, it is easily observable that, whereas the durable goods typical of 1960s and 1970s involved hundred thousand workers, innovative cycles of today high-tech products would employ no more than some thousands workers. All this suggests that a kind of "forced" over-consumption is the only and very imperfect way, in our present economies, for attaining some kind of full employment level.

How many high-tech items, cars, clothes, etc., should we buy to sustain the effective demand? For a host of economic, social and environmental reasons, this system is untenable in the long run. In this respect, the problem becomes to identify the set of institutional and policy arrangements for moving along a new avenue of economic and social progress.

4.1 The nature of the problem in a nutshell

We can delineate some aspects of these problems by developing a very simple scheme which, of course, needs become far more complex in the analysis of specific issues.

Let us denote with **N** the number of workers – who are supposed to work approximately for the same time and with the same productivity π – the average labour productivity and **Y** the aggregate product. Supposing that, for the sake of simplicity, the product is homogenous, consists of additive units and is sold at the unit price, we obtain:

$$N^{\pi} = Y$$

Tendency of effective demand to lag behind the supply of full employment

Supposing **N** = 1000 be the level of full employment (however defined), and $\pi = 5$, the corresponding value of **Y** for a given time span will be equal to:

$1000*5 = 5000$

Now, if, for instance, the productivity increases by 20% the potential product will be equal to:

$1000*6 = 6000$

As it can be easily seen, in order to maintain the same level of employment, it is necessary that the new product of 6000 will be produced and sold in the market.

Conversely, if, with the new level of productivity, the product sold would remain at 5000, the productive capacity could not run at full blast. As a result, the new level of employment will be equal to,

$$N = \frac{Y}{\pi} = \frac{5000}{6} = 833.3$$

with a corresponding drop of 166.6 units (1000 – 833.3).

In this way, 166-167 labour units will be made redundant. Thus, in order to secure full employment, it is necessary to sell on the market 6000 units. How can this be accomplished? There are two main ways, with all the degrees of intermediate cases: **(a)** a corresponding reduction of prices, in which case the benefit of the productivity increase will be transferred on consumers; **(b)** the invariance of prices, which implies that the benefits of the productivity increase will not change the level of mark-up.

As for the case **(a),** which more closely corresponds to neoclassical economics, the required flexibility of the factors of production rarely occurs in practice. As also noted before, for a number of reasons prices, wages and mark-ups tend to be rather sticky, also because these "prices" tend to reflect the social and institutional arrangements upon which economic activity is framed.

But also supposing a sudden realization of that condition, the problems of satiation pointed out before would still remain, and even getting worse over time. As a matter of fact, the increased vent of product, by compelling us to buy a growing quantity of goods, would rapidly induce satiation for many of them. This being the case, the elasticity of the demand would be in most cases inferior to the unity, which implies that it is not convenient for firms to reduce prices.

As for the case **(b)**, its realization demands — not considering the phenomenon of satiation — nothing less than a parallel increase of the demand in the form of disposable income of the consumers. As we have seen, the main channels for attaining such increase are a continual expansion of the share of public spending and credit creation on GDP.

4.2 Can prices and wages flexibility help to achieve full employment?

From the previous account it appears that the prevailing productive paradigm, based on ever-growing consumption and on unlimitedness of natural resources, is becoming more and more unfit for ensuring a sustainable and equitable development of economic systems.

For this reason, measures aimed only at increasing effective demand are important, but not sufficient for thoroughly addressing these problems.

As for the neoclassical oriented policies of reducing public spending and taxation, we have seen that – although it can be possible and advisable to realize a better rationalization and accountability of public sector – it is utterly unrealistic to believe that public spending can be easily and massively replaced by private spending.

For these reasons, policies based on these premises are unlikely to be effective in sustaining the effective demand.

Tendency of effective demand to lag behind the supply of full employment

At this stage, it can be interesting to wonder if the other central prescription of neoclassical economics can work in our economies. As we know, such prescription relates to the importance of realizing a high level of "flexibility"[26] of productive factors, and in particular of prices and wages.

We have just seen that, in presence of an increase in productivity, a corresponding reduction of prices is in many cases unlikely, owing to a low level of the elasticity of demand, to absorb the corresponding demand.

Now we can wonder what happens in the hypothesis of a money-wages reduction – which we need not suppose, for our reasoning, substantially different from a real-wages reduction – with an unchanged level of labour productivity.

For instance – and even letting apart the circumstance that sticky prices also reflect the complexity of socio-economic relations and hence cannot be properly explained through the lens of a simple framework of market imperfections – in presence of a rate of unemployment (however defined) of 20%, can a corresponding reduction of labour cost restore full employment?

Our impression is that measure can possibly have some positive effect on employment in the short run. Such effect, however, tends to vanish in a longer while. Why? First, even in the short run, there is no guarantee that a reduction of wages of, say, 20% would entail a corresponding increase of employment. In fact, if the entrepreneurs perceive that this reduction is due to the weakening of workers' contractual power, they would be induced to increase the intensity and duration of the workday. These measures can be accompanied by the attempt of further reducing the wages, which can be made more effective by prospecting a delocalization of production in lower labour cost Countries.

---

[26] In this discussion, of course, we do not refer to the desirability that "productive factors" should possess a degree of flexibility but to the simplistic idea (see also the previous paragraph on the complex reasons underlying the phenomenon of sticky prices) that un unlimited flexibility can easily be realized and that, once realized, would be able to realize an economic growth of full employment.

But even supposing that such reduction can work in the short period, in the long run the effects are likely to disappear because the factors just depicted – also in conjunction with the increasing difficulty of effective demand to reach the full employment level discussed before – tend to grow stronger over time.

In fact, as observed in the previous sections, in the capitalistic, or "mixed", systems of today, the "natural" tendency of entrepreneurs is to reduce as much as possible labour cost in order to try to acquire price competitiveness and accrue their profits.

In this regard, we can also note that, as underscored by many studies on technological accumulation, a policy action based only on the reduction of labour cost will contribute – by disregarding the need of a proper development of human and social capital for upgrading the capacity of a Country to compete in the higher levels of the value chain – to marginalize and impoverish that Country.

4.3 Towards an alternative paradigm

A central aspect of a novel economic system relates to the building a society less based on the "economic motive" and more on the unfolding of the true inclinations and potentialities of persons.

This comports that this system will be fully compatible with limited growth, steady state, or de-growth. The objective of our work is not that of indicating what option is preferable but how to facilitate the move towards this path of progress.

It can be interesting to note that this more "qualitative" tendency was noted by important economists, and now we mention some significant examples. The first one can be found in the most "heterodox" classical economist, John Stuart Mill. In his appraisal of the long term economic evolution, he remarks that the structural tendency towards the stationary state does not imply a static way of living but, on the contrary, constitutes the necessary condition for the full expression of the more advanced aspects of personality. The central element for attaining such a state is the control of population. In his words,

> "There is room in the world, no doubt, and even in the old countries, for a great increase of population, supposing the arts of life to go on improving, and capital to increase. But even if innocuous, I confess I see very little reason for desiring it....I sincerely hope, for the sake of posterity, that they....[the future generations].....will be content to be stationary, long before necessity compels them to it.

> It is scarcely necessary to remark that a stationary condition of capital and population implies no stationary state of human improvement. There would be as much scope as ever for all kinds of mental culture, and moral and social progress; as much room for improving the Art of Living and much more likelihood of its being improved, when minds ceased to be engrossed by the art of getting on. Even the industrial arts might be as earnestly and as successfully cultivated, with this sole difference, that instead of serving no purpose but the increase of wealth, industrial improvements would produce their legitimate effect, that of abridging labour. Hitherto it is questionable if all the mechanical inventions yet made have lightened the day's toil of any human being....Only when, in addition to just institutions, the increase of mankind shall be under the deliberate guidance of judicious foresight, can the conquests made from the powers of nature by the intellect and energy of scientific discoverers, become the common property of the species, and the means of improving and elevating the universal lot" (Mill, 1994 [1871]: 128, 129, 130).

Another relevant contribution[27] to these issues has been provided by J.M. Keynes, in particular in the final part of the *Essays in Persuasion.*

---

[27] For more detail refer also to Hermann (2014a).

This can appear a bit surprising because Keynes, owing to his proposals for recovering from economic depression, is often depicted as the theorist of the short period. This opinion tends to be reinforced by his famous expression "in the long run we will be all dead". However, from the reading of the *Essays* we discover that the long-term perspectives of economy and society play a central role in his analysis.

For Keynes, focusing attention on short-term problems constitutes only a part of a more profound awareness of the structural transformations of society. The pith of these changes will centre on a substantial shortening of the working time, made possible by the increase of productivity. The main obstacle to the attainment of this potential rests not in a technical but in a psychological difficulty, which can be related to an unconscious feeling of guilt related to the presence of *superego*. He pinpoints, with great psychological intuition, the difficulty of people to employ leisure time for a better realization of their personalities. In his words,

> "We are being afflicted with a new disease of which some readers may not yet have heard the name, but of which they will hear a great deal in the years to come – namely, *technological unemployment*. This means unemployment due to our discovery of means of economising the use of labour outrunning the pace at which we can find new uses for labour.... But this is only a temporary stage of maladjustment. All this means in the long run *that mankind is solving its economic problem*... [but, despite this opportunity]...Yet there is no country and no people, I think, who can look forward to the age of leisure and of abundance without a dread. For we have been trained too long to strive and not to enjoy... [hence, in this perspective, economics] ...should be a matter for specialists – like dentistry. If economists could manage to get themselves thought of as humble, competent people, on a level with dentists, that would be splendid!" (Keynes, 1963 [1931]: 364, 368, 373).

Also J.K. Galbraith's *The Affluent Society* complements in interesting ways with this analysis. In his words,

"To furnish a barren room is one thing. To continue to crowd in furniture until the foundation buckles is quite another. To have failed to solve the problem of producing goods would have been to continue man in his oldest and most grievous misfortune. But to fail to see that we have solved it, and to fail to proceed thence to the next tasks, would be fully as tragic" (Galbraith, 1998 [1958]: 260).

In order to solve these problems, it becomes central to reduce the all-important role of production. In order to attain this objective, Galbraith observes, there is no other way that to loosen the dependence of the income on production. This can be achieved, firstly, by increasing the duration and the amount of unemployment benefits and other forms of support for people who cannot carry out work activities. And, secondly, by increasing public spending on essential public goods, in order to achieve a better "social balance" between public and private property, and thus abate the phenomena of social and environmental decay.

But how can these measures be financed? In this regard, an increase in taxation, both direct and indirect, is the only way to attain a better balanced economic and social system. There is, however, a general reluctance to tax increase, both in progressive and conservative domains. In fact, any change in the tax regime will trigger the debate on equality, with the likely result that the reciprocal vetoes will render arduous to attain significant changes.

Furthermore, the conventional wisdom is prone to cut taxation in any case, even if this involves a reduction of essential public services. Therefore, a tax cut for the poor, although it may seem more equitable, threatens to undermine the central goal of the elimination of the causes of poverty and degradation. In this sense, Galbraith complains, "The modern liberal rallies to protect the poor from the taxes which in the next generation, as the result of a higher investment in their children, would help eliminate poverty" (ibidem: 230).

To eradicate poverty, in fact, not only a higher income is needed, but also a thorough understanding of the social causes that determine such plague.

These negative factors, such as, for example, insufficient resources for primary and secondary education, can be eliminated mainly through higher public investment. In this sense, "Poverty is self-perpetuating partly because the poorest communities are the poorest in the services which would eliminate it" (ibidem: 240).

Conclusions

As we have tried to show, we believe that much more than a simple *laissez faire*[28] option is needed for realizing full employment, and economic and social progress. The theories that we have addressed provide important elements for a more realistic account of the actual working of economic systems. In this respect, a more far-reaching theoretical background would foster a better coordination of many relevant dimensions of policy action. We can mention, among others:

(I) Macroeconomic policies targeted at driving effective demand to the level of supply of full employment; this requires, within a principle of subsidiarity, an adequate and efficient level of public spending; progressive taxation; a permanent low level of interest rate; a reform of the banking system aimed at discouraging speculative ventures and promoting productive activities.

(II) In following these policies, we should not forget the structural transformations of the system. As we have seen, they have as their correlate the tendency towards a progressive shrinking of the "economic motive" and the working time related to it. In order to orient these processes towards individual and social progress, a provision of a citizen's income seems particularly appropriate. However, in order to avoid the risk that these measures would induce laziness and marginalization, it is expedient to gear these provisions to social and educational activities.

(III) In pursuing these activities it would be preferable to follow a policy of a tendentially balanced public budget. As a matter of fact, a policy of deficit

---

[28] Interestingly enough, the inadequacy of *laissez-faire* and the corresponding importance of public policies for the functioning of a market economy was stressed by Léon Walras in particular in his *Studies in Social Economics*. We have addressed these aspects in Hermann (2016).

Tendency of effective demand to lag behind the supply of full employment

spending, although far more advisable than a policy of "austerity", has the serious drawback of increasing the burden of interest payments. In this way, an increasing share of public spending is diverted from objectives of public utility to rent. We think that this aspect plays a two-fold role in depressing the economic system, because: **(a)** the multiplier effects of rent-based incomes are likely to be lower than that of public spending; **(b)** public spending directed to public purposes is likely to be more useful than rent for economic and social progress.

In order to overcome these drawbacks, it is pertinent to note that, as highlighted by the "Haavelmo's theorem" (1945), public spending has an expansionary effect even if it is accompanied by an equal amount of taxation.

(IV) Policies for promoting human capital in the workplace, in particular through an on-going upgrading of the workers' competencies coupled with the improvement of their motivation and participation.

(V) Policies aimed at fostering scientific, cultural and technological development in public and private institutions, and in the society at large; and other structural policies directed at the building a more equitable and sustainable society.

This process can greatly benefit by a joint use of the theories addressed in the work. In fact, as we have tried to show, these contributions, however different in many respects, present notable complementarities, in the sense that the aspects more overlooked by one are more completely addressed by the others. Hence these theories, by helping identify the manifold aspects of economic system, can make headways towards a more effective policy action.

References

Arestis, P. and Sawyer, M. (eds.) (2010) *21st Century Keynesian Economics*, Annual Edition of International Papers in Political Economy, Houndmills, Basingstoke: Palgrave Macmillan.

Capital and Justice

Commons, J.R. (1995) *Legal Foundations of Capitalism*. New Jersey, US.: Transaction Publishers. Originally published by Macmillan in 1924.

Commons, J.R. (1990) *Institutional Economics: Its Place in Political Economy*. New Brunswick, New Jersey, US.: Transaction Publishers. Originally published by Macmillan in 1934.

Davidson, P. (2009) *The Keynes Solution: The Path to Global Economic Prosperity*. Basingstoke: Palgrave Macmillan.

Di Gaspare, S. (2011) *Henry A.Abbati: Keynes' Forgotten Precursor*. London and New York: Routledge.

Foster, W.T., Catchings, W. (1926) *The Dilemma of Thrift*. Pollak Foundation for Economic Research.

Galbraith, J.K. (1958) *The Affluent Society*. New York: Mariner Books, second edition 1998.

Haavelmo, T. (1945) Multiplier Effects of a Balanced Budget. *Econometrica*, vol.13, n.4, pp. 311-318.

Hansen, Alvin H. (1939) Economic Progress and Declining Population Growth. *American Economic Review*, 29(1), pp.1-15.

Harcourt, G., Kriesler, P. (eds.) (2013) *The Oxford Handbook of Post Keynesian Economics*. Oxford: Oxford University Press.

Hermann, A. (2014a) The Essays in Persuasion of John Maynard Keynes and Their Relevance for the Economic Problems of Toda". In Hölscher, J., Klaes, M. (eds.) *Keynes's Economic Consequences of the Peace: A Reappraisal*. London: Pickering and Chatto.

Hermann, A. (2014b) Market, Socialism and Democracy in an Interdisciplinary Perspective. *International Journal of Pluralism and Economics Education*. 5 (4), pp.327-353.

Hermann, A. (2015) *The Systemic Nature of the Economic Crisis: The Perspectives of Heterodox Economics and Psychoanalysis*. London and New York: Routledge.

Hermann, A. (2016) The Studies in Social Economics of Léon Walras and His Far-Reaching Critique of Laissez Faire. *International Journal of Pluralism and Economics Education*. 7(1), pp. 59-76

Hobson, J.A. (2013) *The Industrial System: An Inquiry into Earned and Unearned Income*. HardPress Publishing, originally published by Longmans, Green & Co. in 1910.

Jespersen, J. (ed.) (2013) *Teaching Post Keynesian Economics*. Cheltenham (UK): Elgar.

Keen, S. (2011) *Debunking Economics - Revised and Expanded Edition: The Naked Emperor Dethroned?* London: Zed Books.

Keynes, J.M. (1963) *Essays in Persuasion*. New York: Norton. Originally published by Macmillan in 1931.

Keynes, J.M. (1930) *A Treatise on Money*. London: Macmillan.

Keynes, J.M. (1936) *The General Theory of Employment, Interest and Money*. London: Macmillan. Quotations taken from Edison Martin Imprint 2013.

King, E. (2002) *A History of Post Keynesian Economics since 1936*. Cheltenham, UK: Elgar.

King, E. (2015) *Post Keynesian Economics*. Cheltenham, UK: Elgar.

Lee, F.S. (2009) *A History of Heterodox Economics: Challenging the Mainstream in the Twentieth Century*. London and New York: Routledge.

Lee, F.S.,Lavoie, M. (eds.) (2012) *In Defense of Post-Keynesian and Heterodox Economics: Responses to their Critics*. London and New York: Routledge.

Mankiw, G. (1985) Small Menu Costs and Large Business Cycles: A Macroeconomic Model of Monopoly. *The Quarterly Journal of Economics*. 100 (2), pp. 529-538.

Mill, John Stuart (1994) *Principles of Political Economy*. New York: Oxford University Press. Originally published by Longmans in 1871.

Minsky, H. (2008) *Stabilizing an Unstable Economy*. New York: McGraw Hill.

Mummery, F.A., Hobson, J.A. (1889) *The Physiology of Industry*. London: John Murray. Reprinted by Leopold Classic Library in 2015.

Nell. E. (1988) *Prosperity and Public Spending*. London and New York: Routledge.

Rutherford, M. (2011) *The Institutionalist Movement in American Economics, 1918-1947*. Cambridge: Cambridge University Press.

Skidelsky, R. and Skidelsky, E. (2012) *How Much Is Enough? Money and the Good Life*. New York: Other Press.

Slichter, S.H. The Organization and Control of Economic Activity, in R.G.Tugwell (ed.) (1924) *The Trend of Economics*. New York: A.Knopf.

Stiglitz, J.E. (2009) The Current Economic Crisis and Lessons for Economic Theory. *Eastern Economic Journal*. 35, pp.281-296.

Stiglitz, J.E. (2013) *Selected Works of Joseph E. Stiglitz: Volume II: Information and Economic Analysis: Applications to Capital, Labor, and Product Markets*. Oxford: Oxford University Press.

Chapter 3

Global business models and labour challenges

Maria Alejandra Caporale Madi

Introduction

Private equity (PE) firms have been key actors in the increasing financialization of the economy with deep effects on labour challenges (Roberston, 2015). Lying at the juncture of the real economy and the financial economy, private equity funds draw upon capital and debt in the financial markets to acquire stakes in companies that are intended to be sold for profit after a number of years.

Institutional investors have assumed a key role in the diversification of investments, based on expectations of high returns and liquidity. In the context of the current global crisis, new strategies have been adopted to guarantee high returns. Soon after the global crisis, large private equity deals have revealed the growing difficulties to secure the required levels of debt for deals as a result of the credit squeeze, the volatility in the valuation of assets and the recessive global trends. Alternatively, investors' liquidity preference have increased and put pressure on the consolidation of the private equity institutional set up toward greater global concentration.

Private equity is now globally significant with firms in these funds holding assets under management valued at $ 3.8 trillion in 2014 (Prequin, 2015). Although US private equity firms are still dominant, private equity has moved towards Europe, Asia and Latin America. An increasing number of private equity firms are now headquartered in Asia than Europe and China, Japan and India have been dominant in the rapid growth scenario. In China, private equity firms have grown from only 10 in 1995 to more than 6,000 in recent years.

The American model of private equity turns out to be the Western business model and Europe has largely followed its practices (Robertson, 2015). In this scenario, the financialization of management practices has been linked to the continuous growth of private equity funds that have assumed an active role in the selection of investments of high profit potential and in the creation of new business structures. The leveraged buyout business model of the private equity funds, as the main agent for mergers and acquisitions, has both evolved from and fed a broader process of increased financialization of corporate behaviour and economic activity while private equity funds emerged as major transnational employers. Workers are confronted with over US $ 1 trillion in concentrated buyout power (IUF, 2007). The British Venture Capital Association, for example, calculated that in Great Britain, 1 of every 5 employees was working for a company owned by private equity at the end of 2005 (BVCA, 2006).

The term "private equity" encompasses financial techniques aimed to finance investment in companies that do not involve the use of public tradable assets. In particular, private equity funds centralize endowments from banks, institutional investors – also pension funds – and high net worth individuals, in order to assume a key – role in the dynamic of investment buyouts of high profit potential. The shift in corporate ownership, trough waves of mergers and acquisitions, has created new business structures where companies are considered bundles of assets and liabilities to be traded in order to get short-term returns.

These new investment and portfolio management practices have been overwhelmed by the financialisation of wealth that has reinforced "short-termism" in American and European business, among others. In this setting, increasing income inequality has been related to business-friendly policies. In early 2006, Kevin Phillips warned that the financial services sector had overtaken the production sector in the United States.[1] Loosening monetary

---

[1] Like Great Britain in the 19th, the United States shifted from manufacturing and the production of goods and services to finance and speculation, "as the imperial apogees approached, the potential return from investing money domestically came to

and lending conditions have benefited wealth and income concentration in the financial and banking sector, since "finance distributes its concentrated profits to a much smaller slice of the population" (Phillips, 2006: 281).

According Appelbaum and Batt (2014), private equity firms control more than 17,000 companies and employ more than 7.5 million workers in the U.S. They buy and sell companies in virtually every industry. Indeed, in many countries, the equity funds' expansion has been highly leveraged and this process fostered market consolidation and capital concentration in different kinds of business. Consequently, private equity funds have been responsible for the employment standards of tens of millions of workers worldwide and the impacts of private equity investments on working conditions is raising growing concerns. Beyond the "rationalization" strategies, the social conflicts and tensions are strengthened as the flexibilization of labour relations need to be adjusted to the private equity investor needs: capital mobility and short-run returns. Indeed, employment trends have been subordinated to ownership changes and financial restructuring. Working conditions have been constantly reorganized and reconfigured after the buyouts and takeovers. Jacoby (2008) argued that in spite of the enormous literature on financial development and inequality, few studies consider the intersection between financial markets and the labour markets. This chapter aims to fill the gap in the existing literature and foster a greater understanding of the social and economic challenges as a result of the financial engineering management model of private equity firms.

Taking into account that financialization enhances the redistribution and reallocation of power and wealth, this paper assesses, from a Keynesian approach, that private equity funds foster social vulnerabilities. After presenting a brief overview of the global business environment and the post-crisis evolution of private equity funds, this chapter discusses the factors that shape the microeconomic and macroeconomic effects of their typical investment strategies. Rather than treating private equity funds as a financial phenomenon, the analysis rethinks the relations between private equity funds and labour as involving forms of production at the current frontier of capital.

---

seem inadequate, and... creditors and financial classes began to move more and more funds into overseas investments" (Phillips, 2006: 306).

1. The global business environment

The evolution of the current global business environment has been attached to the new financial dynamics where private-equity funds are new relevant institutional investors (Gonçalves and Madi, 2011). In a private-equity funds' portfolio structure, a company acquisition is equivalent to an addition to a stock of financial assets (Cullen and James, 2007). The funds' investments are generated by expectations about short-run cash flows, mainly anticipated dividends and non-equity based fees. Thus, the selection of the portfolio companies has been influenced by the potential market growth and profits, besides legal and incentive structures, among other factors. This investment is generated by expectations about short-run cash flows, mainly anticipated dividends and non-equity based fees. Exit conditions become crucial in the investment decision-making process because capital mobility shortens the maturation of investments.

The typical categories of private equity or "alternative investment" funds in the U.S. include: venture capital funds; leveraged buyout funds; hedge funds; fund-to-funds; and captive funds (Tannon and Johnson, 2005). The share of private equity investments in the total volume of mergers and acquisitions exceeds 20% in some OECD economies (Tate, 2007). In spite of the potential relevance of the private equity buyouts, there is a limited understanding of their impact on labour conditions. The growth of the private equity firms has been quickly becoming global voracious acquirers of assets (Dixon et al., 2007). Indeed, private equity buyouts have not only defined new parameters to attractive investment decisions, but also fostered the credit and capital market's expansion.

What the private equity leveraged buyout model has introduced is a high risk combination of leveraged debt financing with a short-term intent to resell the business in order to extract extraordinary returns (Klier et al., 2009). The planning horizon is becoming shorter and the returns on investments are prioritized above real economic performance. The change in the way investments is made, in how companies operate and in what kind of strategic planning is predominant in large parts of the business is intimately linked to the continuous growth of private equity and hedge funds – also called the new drivers of globalization (ITUC, 2007).

Global business models and labour challenges

Private equity funds have grown from a small participation in the financial market in the early 1980s to an important driver of financial globalization today. In 2005, for the first time, more money was invested into private equity than into stock mutual firms. At 2007, Morgan Stanley estimated that 2,700 private equity funds represented 25% of global mergers and acquisition activity and 50% of loan volumes (Jensen, 2007). Workers are confronted with over US $ 1 trillion in concentrated buyout power (IUF, 2007). Of the top 50 private equity firms, accounting for US 1,2 trillion of the U S $1,6 trillion in deals since 2002 up to 2007. In 2007, Great Britain accounted for 40 % of all European private equity deals, and is second only to the United States. They expanded their share in the global M&A market to 25% before the crisis and have remained a huge force to foster market concentration after 2008.

Considering this business scenario, new perspectives on working conditions have been driven by cost-reduction strategies in a context of high leverage, short-term profits and high competition. This business model has relevant impacts on the business environment, taxation system, social security and employment conditions (Tate, 2007).

In the first stage, a private equity firm creates a private equity fund and obtains commitments from investors (limited partners) to provide capital to its fund. Later, when the firm undertakes buyouts, it calls on the investors to provide the capital.

In particular, private equity fund centralize endowments from public and corporate pension plans, foundations, insurance companies, and wealthy individuals in order to assume a key – role in investment buyouts. In the second stage, the private equity firm identifies potential companies for its fund to acquire. In the third stage, the private equity firm obtains a loan commitment, typically from commercial or investment banks, that it then uses to help finance its fund's acquisition of the target company.

A loan commitment is a promise from the lender to make available in the future a specified amount of credit under specified terms and conditions. Loans are an essential component of an LBO (leveraged buyout) because private equity firms typically contribute through their funds only a fraction of the capital needed to complete the deal.

In the fourth stage, after the buyout of the target company, the private equity firm seeks to increase the value of the company, so that the private equity firm can sell the company (fifth stage) at a profit and earn a return for its fund investors.

A leveraged buyout differs fundamentally from a traditional merger or acquisition in two important ways. First, the acquired company pays the cost of its own acquisition through debt and fees. Secondly, the private equity investor is necessarily aggressive in pursuit of such profits. These two elements are central to the leveraged buyout process and pose particular challenges to unions when engaging and bargaining collectively with private equity portfolio companies. Generally, the potentially adverse restructuring impacts of leveraged buyouts on workers tend to increase the higher the targeted return on investment, the more leveraged the deal, the faster the withdrawal of equity and the shorter the period before exiting the investment (IUF, 2007).

Private equity funds typically hold an acquired company from 3 to 5 years before trying to realize their return. A private equity fund typically has a fixed life of 10 years, generally giving the private equity firm 5 years to invest the capital raised in its fund and 5 years to return the capital and expected profits to its fund investors.

As a matter of fact, private equity funds turned out to operate as holding companies in a setting of mergers and acquisitions where they articulate business in different markets on behalf of financial engineering practices. The concentration and diversification of investment, inherent strategies in holding companies, characterized the private equity funds' expansion. Private equity funds have come to view their portfolio companies as a set of assets where operation divisions and product lines may be sold in order to pursue short-term profits.

Private equity managers are spreading, in truth, a business model where the target is to sell small firms years later in a process called disinvestment

(Wheatley, 2010). In this scenario, the advancement of concentration and centralization of capital favoured the reordering of financial and productive structures where private equity investors aim to maximize their short-term returns rather building long term sustainable small business. The consequence is an uncertain future for workers. The adjustment of the labour force is described by Fligsten (2004: 182) "Workers are fired to improve next quarter's profits, and those who are left are supposed to carry the burden by increasing productivity."

At the heart of our argument is that the capital accumulation process involves social relations driven by profit and competition. As the private equity investors' motive is not growth *per se*, but value extraction, the social losses in terms of unemployment, working conditions, workers' rights and income distribution could be relevant: "*Short-termism is institutionalized at the workplace and in society*" (IUF, 2007: 24).

2. Private equity funds in the post-crisis scenario: investment and labour

In the aftermath of the global crisis, it is undoubtedly that the crucial factor that avoided the private equity institutions' default was the evolution of monetary policy. However, quantitative easing has failed to restore job creation since 2008 (Rochon and Rossi, 2013: 211).

Private equity's (PE) rebound from the downturn subsequent to the 2008 global financial crisis has been a manifestation of the enormous expansion of financial assets that have been building up in the global economy for more than 25 years.[2] Global liquidity played a lead role in private equity firms' ability to mobilize large pools of capital, fueling the buyout boom years between 2005 and 2007. As it approached a cyclical peak, global buyout deal value spiked from $293 billion in 2005 to $687 billion and $673 billion in 2006 and 2007, respectively. Private equity buyers were willing to pay high

---

[2] As highlighted in the Bain & Company's *Global Private Equity Report 2015,* the current capital superabundance is the product of financial engineering, high-speed computing and a loosening of financial services regulations. The resulting growth of financial assets has been prodigious and relentless: Global financial capital increased 53% from 2000 to 2010, reaching some $600 trillion.

prices to win intensely competitive auctions, as average deal multiples climbed to 9.7 times EBITDA on US and European leveraged buyouts in 2007. In the context of the crisis, mega-buyout funds (those greater than $4.5 billion) were the hardest hit by massive write-downs mandated by country regulations, barriers to exit channels and refinancing requirements to avoid default. After the global market crisis, three factors shape the private equity funds' performance, mainly the performance of big funds: massive asset write-downs mandated by mark-to-market accounting regulations, difficulties to accomplish exit strategies and increasing portfolio company debt refinancing needs. Thanks to global liquidity, the rate of default amounted to 6% among private equity firms between 2008 and 2013.

Indeed, central banks' policy based on quantitative easing has been decisive to favour debt refinancing and up to 2014, the PE sector has displayed resilience in a time characterized by torpid global growth. After the 2008 financial crisis, many institutional investors revealed a growing interest in investing in liquid assets. Therefore, institutional investors increased the levels of direct investing in a variety of ways, depending on the type of institution and its size, goals and comparative advantage as an investor. In mid-year 2014, the return for global buyout funds over a 10-year time horizon stands at 14.4%. As a result, the near-term returns on investment have been expected to be higher than the benchmark – the public equity markets.[3]

Quantitative easing favoured the expansion of liquidity that turned out to bring rates on high-yield bonds and leveraged loans back to pre-recession levels. The new, near-zero interest rate environment has been decisive in refinancing private equity borrowers, inflating asset valuations and influencing the investment and exit strategies of private equity funds (Bain & Company, 2014: 2).

Although the expansion of liquidity has played a key role in private equity funds' ability to promote investment diversification, the current financial market scenario suggests key-drivers and barriers to private equity investment. What determines the level of investment – addition to the

---

[3] There is an index public market equivalent to compare private equity and public equity returns (Bain & Company, 2015).

quantity of physical/capital assets? When entrepreneurs decide to increase their production capacities, how do they choose between buying new capital assets (investment) or existing capital assets (mergers, acquisitions)?

In conformity with the ideas of Keynes, Minsky highlighted that the level of investment depends on the relationship between the demand price and the supply price of capital assets.[4] The demand price of capital assets (P_d) is the price that entrepreneurs are willing to pay for acquiring *new or existing* (old) capital assets. The supply price of capital assets (P_s) is the replacement cost of *new* capital assets. The demand price of investment could be defined as the maximum price that the entrepreneur will pay for an additional unit of new or existing (old) capital assets. This price refers to the present value of the flow of expected returns, discounted at the appropriate interest rate, which is strongly influenced by expectations about the future central banks' actions. Expectations about the costs and revenues determine a flow of net expected returns during the maturation of capital assets. Given this set of expectations, P_d is the maximum price that the capitalist may pay for an additional unit of capital assets – new or existing (old). On the other hand, the supply price of investment, P_s, is related to the production of *new* capital assets. Given a set of expectations, P_s represents the minimum price that would lead to produce a *new* additional unit of capital assets.

Evidences from the current private equity investment scenario show that the demand price of capital assets is gradually being eroded while the limited supply of profitable assets put pressure on the price of old capital (P_k) as indirectly valued by financial markets, mergers and acquisitions:

a) The demand price of investment is gradually being eroded

Among the key-drivers to promote private equity investment, recent evidences from the private equity investment scenario show some relevant features such as:

- Low-interest-rates and cheap debt foster the availability of money to invest.

---

[4] This analysis is based on Tymoigne (2010).

- There are positive expectations that private equity markets will continue to outperformance other markets in the future, such as public equity, real estate investments and fixed income;
- As organic companies' growth is hard to achieve in a low-inflation economy, mergers and acquisitions turn out to be an attractive path forward;
- The recycling of capital of mature investments is one important pillar for private equity fund-raising. For instance, in the United States and Europe, private equity distributions have exceeded new cash calls since 2011;
- There are high levels of liquidity in the assets of institutional investors looking to be invested or re-invested in private equity funds. Indeed, institutional investors have been participating in private equity deals beyond the conventional constraints of being passive partners. Worldwide, public pension systems and sovereign wealth funds have stepped up their private equity holdings as a percentage of total assets under management, from 6% in 2006 to 12% more recently.
- The rising stock prices have inflated the overall portfolio holdings of institutional investors, such as pension funds, and could boost new commitments to private equity.
- Institutions that belong to the shadow banking sector are injecting even more money into the already saturated deal market. Accordingly the Bain & Company report (2015), this "shadow capital" is looking to private equity firms to invest as co-sponsors and occasionally investing independently of and potentially in competition with them. Today, these co-investments frequently amount 10% of the private equity assets under management.

The very forces that have been supporting the performance of private equity investments – record low interest rates and liquidity – are currently magnifying two trends that put downward pressure on profits from current and future investments. First, asset prices are and will remain high as low-cost debt merely adds upward pressure on asset prices. Second, as a result of assets' higher prices, longer holding periods will be needed for exits that can command the profit target. While holding periods of three years or more look to be the new norm before the crisis; in the current scenario, it will take at least ten years to achieve the profit target. Third, as a result of the longer holding period, the current deals could certainly experience a turn in the business cycle during their holding period. And fourth, the legal, tax, regulatory and political environment could limit the deals and dampen profitability.

In short, today, the private equity returns have become more compressed and the private equity fund's ability to outplace public market gains over the long-run cannot longer be taken for granted. Taking into account this scenario, the private equity returns will decisively depend on the implementation of operational improvements that would certainly impact on labour.

b) The supply of profitable assets is limited and the price of old capital is increasing

The private equity investment decisions revealed the arbitrage between new and existing capital assets in the private equity investment scenario. The price of existing capital assets and the price of newly produced investment goods, P_k and P_s, come from two different sets of prices and behave very differently:

- The price of existing capital assets (P_k) is determined indirectly by the market quotation of shares and bonds of the owning firms, and by the price at which mergers and acquisitions are settled (Wray and Tymoigne, 2008). Therefore, P_k is influenced by: expectation of future profits, liquidity preference and return of liquid assets relative to illiquid assets. P_k decreases because of market saturation, that is to say, when expected monetary profits go down.
- The price of newly produced investment goods (P_s) is influenced by production costs and the level of mark-up: P_s increases because of upward pressures on unit cost as more investment occurs.
- When $P_k = P_s$, entrepreneurs are indifferent between buying new or old capital assets.
- By taking the price of old capital assets (P_k) as a point of reference, the quantity of investment goods purchased is determined where $P_d = P_s$. Investment can proceed only if the demand price (adjusted for borrower's risk) exceeds the supply price (adjusted for lender's risk) of

capital assets. Any factor that reduces expected future profitability can push the current demand price of capital below the supply price. Consequently, investment and current profits would be reduced below the level necessary to validate past expectations when previous investment projects were undertaken (Wray and Tymoigne, 2008).

By linking the goods market and the financial market in the "two-price" approach described above, Minsky addressed that asset prices play a crucial role in the determination of the investment level because this level depends on an arbitrage. Following the ideas of Keynes's *General Theory*, chapter 17, there is an arbitrage between old capital assets (existing capital equipment) and new capital assets (investment goods to be newly produced).[5] Considering this framework, low prices for existing assets could depress the production of new assets.

However, the current competition between private equity buyers has been pushing up the prices of the buyout deals since profitable assets are in limited supply. Indeed, the investment scenario is characterized by one of "hunt for deals" or "hunt for acquisitions" and private equity deals – mainly mergers and acquisitions – overwhelm the investment scenario. Besides, the availability of a greater amount of external funds boosts low-debt contracts and the reduction of the "borrowers' risk" puts further pressure on the prices of existing capital assets.

As a result, through the middle of 2014, purchase-price multiples for leveraged buyouts in the United Sates averaged 9.6 times EBITDA and 10 times in Europe, these records had not been seen since the peak of the cycle (2006-2008). Taking into account the increased prices of old capital, private equity funds are looking to acquire sufficiently large stakes in the companies in order to gain board representation and decision rights to hire or fire the key managers and to influence the company's investment decisions and profit targets. Among other efficiency strategies, private equity

---

[5] In *General Theory*, chapter 17, Keynes assumed that investors make arbitrages among all types of assets (financial and capital assets) in order to get what is expected to be the greatest monetary return, given the liquidity and maturity of the assets – among other factors.

funds plan to invest in complementary investments in the set of portfolio companies.

3. The private equity business model: redefinition of the labour relations

Rather than treating the private equity expansion as simply a financial phenomenon, our analysis rethinks the challenges to labour as involving forms of production at the financial frontier of capital. Today, there is a controversial understanding of the role of private equity funds in labour conditions.[6] Private equity associations' and consultants' recent studies claim positive effects of private equity funds on employment. By contrast, trade unions' reports have claimed that the private equity industry has enhanced deleterious effects on employment and working conditions: job losses, reductions in payments and retirement incomes. In fact, the social impacts of the private equity business model based on "rationalization" have been less explored by academic researchers, while extensive studies have been developed by private sector companies and industry bodies that tend to report only stories of success (Cressy et al., 2007). These reports of cases of success show private equity buyouts as revolutionizing corporate ownership by creating new funding options and corporate governance structures, as well as by providing investors with attractive, long term investment opportunities.

Under other perspective, Appelbaum and Batt (2014) address that this business model has led to fewer jobs, lower wages and pensions, rising inequality and a huge increase in "moral hazard". Indeed, these authors note that favourable employment and working conditions are the exception, rather than the rule.[7] What private equity firms more often do is asset stripping and

---

[6] About the positive effects 1990-2011, see the research paper written by Aldatmaz, Brown (2013).

[7] Appelbaum and Batt (2014) note that in some cases, particularly with smaller and medium-sized companies, private equity firms can provide needed investment and management expertise to turn companies around, or to help them grow. Besides, while noting there were job losses, they point favorably to Wilbur Ross's investments to turn around several steel companies, and his negotiations with the United Steelworkers in order to keep the plants open. They also highlight the USW's and

financial engineering with harmful results in terms of job and working conditions. As the private equity investors' motive is not growth *per se*, but value extraction, the vulnerability in social relations tends to increase within this accumulation pattern.

Labour unions criticize private equity buyouts for harming workers, such as through job losses and lower benefits; providing private equity fund managers with, in effect, tax subsidies and other fiscal benefits.[8] Many global trade unions' reports have claimed that the private equity "secretive industry" has promoted deleterious effects on employment and working conditions (IUF, 2007). Indeed, the activist approach toward value creation has been reported by global unions since private equity firms have been responsible for the employment standards of tens of millions of workers worldwide (MacDonald, 2007).

Indeed, the growth of these new financial actors has contributed to the redefinition of labour relations because managers favour "downsizing". As labour costs are frequently considered large expense items, the reorganization of production aimed to reshape tasks and the control of workers in a context characterized by the absence of commitment to disclose information about the business practices. As a result, the portfolio companies could foster turnover, outsourcing and casual work. Montgomerie (2008) gives outstanding examples of the changing working conditions in Germany and the UK. The author found that labour is the main focus of cost saving measures, first through longer working hours, then the abolition of holiday pay and finally through the reduction in the workforce and worker displacement.

The generation of cash flows to pay non-equity based fees, dividends and debts usually requires deep cost reductions with decisive effects on labour

---

United Auto Workers' negotiations with the private equity owner of auto-parts supplier Dana Corporation as relatively positive examples.

[8] Public attention has also been increasingly focused on taxation practices as fund managers pay far lower taxes by having the gains after the deals treated as regular income. Besides, the benefits to buyout firms are amplified as, for example, tax deductibility applies to interest on debt borrowed to fund the leveraged buyout acquisition (Blum, 2008).

relations, employment trends, social benefits and unions' actions. These changing working conditions result from:

> (...) "continuous restructuring to generate cash outflow, falling levels of productive investment. Institutionalized short-termism, increased outsourcing & casualization to cut costs, sell-offs & closures regardless of productivity & profitability; deteriorating working conditions; diminished employment security, invisible employers" (IUF, 2007:17).

As a matter of fact, the level of productive capacity and the working conditions in a variety of industries, have been constantly reorganized and reconfigured after the private equity deals. The managers' commitment – related to the payment of debt and the portfolio company – turns out to be subordinated to efficiency targets that include longer working hours, job destruction, turnover and outsourcing. Workforce displacement and loss of rights are also part of the spectrum of management alternatives aimed to cost reduction. In many cases, low operational results have stimulated new waves of buyouts. In fact, private equity deals have been mostly aimed to increase short-term performance. In this scenario, workers have no defence since the managers' practices limit the possibilities of trade unions' actions toward negotiation. One of the paradoxes of the global current investment scenario is that pension funds – the deferred wages of workers – provide money that private equity puts up to buy companies and introduce "rationalization" strategies.

In the near-future, slow economic growth would certainly constrain the generation of the outsized returns achieved in the recent past. Indeed, to increase future returns, private equity funds need to sustain an active management approach within portfolio companies so as to shape active operational strategies. In other words, engagement with the management of the portfolio companies dedicating more time and resources to identify potential sources of value and refining the value-creation models to help to extract it.

The current "key elements" in the analysis of production and employment trends are the extension of the holding period and the expected exit conditions. Uncertainty about the exit conditions could extend the holding period and put higher pressure on the levels of employment. In other words, the PE business model, fund managers acting as entrepreneurs may feel more or less confident with regard to their exit conditions and, therefore, put pressure on employment conditions throughout the holding period. The consequences of the activist approach might be:

- Development of strategies to an increasingly expensive workforce by substituting capital for labour, particularly as sophisticated robotic penetrates traditional services business like food, hospitality and healthcare.
- Utilization of advanced telecommunications and information technology to sleep services out of the Eurozone, presents opportunities to invest in business that specialize in, for example, remotely performed diagnosis or web based training.
- Strategies of outsourcing and crowdsourcing;
- Accelerated cost cutting through layoffs, closures, outsourcing;
- Further reductions in productive investment and in expenditures with Research & Development;
- Increased pressure on collective bargaining power, besides capping or closing pensions (IUF, 2007).

Final considerations

In the current global investment scenario, the apprehension of the meaning and dynamics of the recent spread of private equity finance is crucial to the understanding of the social impacts of the evolution of contemporary capitalism. Our argument highlights that the private equity expansion involves *social* relations driven by profit and competition in a context characterized by increasing labour challenges. The financial practices of the private equity funds are, in truth, mechanisms that promote the expansion of the global financial markets with decisive effects on wealth, income growth and working conditions.

While private equity firms have searched for liquidity and capital mobility, decisions taken by investors – strongly influenced by short-term returns and the legal and incentive structures – have turned out to challenge social sustainability. The analysis of the strategies and practices of the private equity firms has revealed the current challenges on behalf of the increasing social vulnerability favoured by institutionalized short-termism in the workplace and in society (IUF, 2008). Under the euphemism of "rationalization strategies", the private equity business model aims to increase short-term profits. As a result, the effects of the financial strategies at the core of workplace have added deep pressures on workers and trade unions. In fact, changing working conditions have become a constant feature of today's global business restructuring.

As the private equity investors' motive is not growth *per se,* but value extraction, the social losses in terms of unemployment, working conditions, workers´ rights and income distribution are deep. The employability perspectives are conditioned to private strategies that aim efficient targets, cost reductions and labour flexibility. Longer working hours, job destruction, turnover, outsourcing, workforce displacement and loss of rights could also be part of the spectrum of management alternatives. The current investment scenario, characterized by precarious jobs, has enhanced the vulnerability of workers, mainly young people. As Bauman warned, the clear cut between investors and managers favours the redefinition of the labour relations:

> "Flexibility is the slogan of the day, and when applied to the labour market it augurs an end to the 'job as we know it', announcing instead the advent of work on short-term contracts, rolling contracts or no contracts, positions with no in-built security but the 'until further notice' clause. Working life is saturated with uncertainty" (Bauman, 2000:147).

In the near future, the operational efficiency and the working conditions will certainly be affected by the expansion of the *Internet of Things* infrastructure (Rifkin, 2011). This expansion will further transform the production and labour scenario as the result of the diffusion of new practices at the micro-level, such as the convergence of automation, new software and real time networks that aims to increase productivity with cost reduction. As technology evolves, big data will accelerate a number of important trends in private equity business. On behalf of this high-technology revolution, the number of people underemployed or without work will rise sharply since computers, robotics, telecommunications, and other cutting-edge technologies are replacing human beings in manufacturing, retail, and financial services, transportation and agriculture.

Considering the current investment and technological scenario and its outcomes in terms of labour challenges, we can conclude that, in the near future, workers will be increasingly polarized into two forces: on one side, an elite that controls and manages the high-tech and financial global economy; and on the other side, a growing number of displaced workers who have few prospects for meaningful job opportunities.

References

Aldatmaz, S., Brown, G. W. (2013) Does Private Equity Hurt or Help the Economy?, *Research Paper, Private equity research Consortium*, Kenan-Flagler Business School, The University of North Carolina at Chapel Hill, March.

Appelbaum, E., Batt, R. (2014) *Private Equity at Work: When Wall Street Manages Main Street*, United States: Russell Sage Foundation.

Bauman, Z. (2000) *Liquid Modernity*. USA: Polity Press.

Bain & Company (2015) *Global Private Equity Report 2015*. U.S.A: Bain &Company, Inc.

Blum, R. (2008) *Leveraged buyouts, private equity and restructuring in the metal sector*. Special Report. Metal World, Available at http://www.imfmetal.org/files/08090411533679/special_report.pdf (Accessed on 10 October 2015)

Bogle, J. (2012) *The Clash of the Cultures: Investment vs. Speculation*. United States: Wiley.

Bryan, D., Rafferty, M.,and Jefferis, C. (2015) Risk and Value: Finance, Labor, and Production, *South Atlantic Quarterly*, 114:2, April.

BVCA (2005) *The economic impact of Private Equity in the UK 2005*. British Venture Capital Association Report, London.

Cressy, R., Munari, F., and Malipiero, A. (2007) Creative destruction? UK Evidence that buyouts cut jobs to raise returns. *Working Paper Series.* Available at SSRN: https://papers.ssrn.com/sol3/papers2.cfm?abstract_id=1030830 (Accessed on 10 October 2015)

Crotty, J. (2002) The effects of increased product market competition and changes in financial markets on the performance of nonfinancial corporations in the neoliberal era,. *Working Paper Series*, n. 44. University of Massachusetts Amherst, Political Economy Research Institute.

Cullen, A., James, S. (2007) Private equity and Business Information. Part 3: Business Information Services and Private equity: North American Involvement. *Business Information Alert.* Nov/Dec, Vol. 19, issue 10, pp.1-4.

Çelik, S., Isaksson, M. (2013) Institutional Investors as Owners: Who Are They and What Do They Do?, *OECD Corporate Governance Working Papers*, No. 11, France: OECD Publishing. Available at http://www.oecd-ilibrary.org/governance/institutional-investors-as-owners_5k3v1dvmfk42-en (Accessed on 10 October 2015)

Dixon, H., Cox, R., Chancellor, E. (2007) Conglomerate Comparisons – Will Private-Equity Empires Parallel Predecessors of 1960s and Fall Out of Fashion Too?, *Wall St. Journal,* January 2, p. C12.

Fligstein, N. (2001) *The architecture of markets,* New Jersey: Princeton Universit Press.

Froud, J., Haslam, C., Johal, S, Williams, K. (2000) Restructuring for shareholder value and its implications for labor, *Cambridge Journal of Economics,* v.24, 6, pp.771-797.

Froud, J., Sukhdev, J., Leaver, A., Williams, K. (2006) *Financialization and Strategy. Narrative and Numbers.* London: Routledge.

Gnos, C. (2006) French Circuit Theory, in P. Arestis and M. Sawyer (Eds.) *A Handbook of Alternative Monetary Economics*, Cheltenahm, UK and Northampton, MA, USA: Edward Elgar Publishing, pp. 87-104.

Gonçalves, J. R. B., Madi, M. A. C. (2011) Private equity investment and labor: faceless capital and the challenges to trade unions in Brazil. In: M. Serrano et al. (Eds.), 2011, *Trade unions and the global crisis: Labour´s visions, strategies and responses.* Geneve: International Labour Office.

Hill, J. M., Gambaccini, J.S. (2003) The Private Equity Paradox: When Is Too Much Control a Bad Thing?. *Journal of Private Equity.* Summer, 6 (3), p.37.

Hobsbawm, E. (1995) *The Age of Extremes: a History of the World, 1914-1991*, New York: Pantheon Books.

International Union of Food, Agricultural, Hotel, Restaurant, Catering, Tobacco and Allied Workers' Association –IUF (2007) *A Workers' Guide to private Equity Buyouts.* Geneve.

International Union of Food, Agricultural, Hotel, Restaurant, Catering, Tobacco and Allied Workers' Association – IUF (2008) *Private Equity Buyouts: A Trade Union View.* Public Hearing on Hedge Funds and Private Equity - Committee on Economic and Monetary Affairs of the European Parliament. Brussels.

ITUC- CSI (2007) *Labour and the Shifting Power Equation: Statement of Labour Leaders to the World Economic Forum Annual Meeting Davos,* 24-28, January. http://www.ituc-csi.org/IMG/pdf/WEF_Statement_-_Labour_and_the_Shifting_Power_Equation_-_Rev_EN.pdf (Accessed on 10 October 2015)

Jacoby, S. (2008) Finance and Labor: Perspectives on Risk, Inequality and Democracy, *Working Paper,* Institute for Research on Labor and Employment, USA, California Digital Library.

Jensen, M. (1989) The eclipse of public corporation. *Harvard Business Review.* Sept.-Oct., revised 1997.

Jensen, M. (2007) The Economic Case for Private Equity (and Some Concerns) -- pdf of Keynote Slides (November 27th). *Harvard NOM Working Paper* No. 07-02; Swedish Institute for Financial Research Conference on The Economics of the Private Equity Market. Available at SSRN: http://ssrn.com/abstract=963530 (Accessed on 10 October 2015)

Keynes, J. M. (1964 [1936]) *The General Theory of Employment, Interest, and Money.* New York: Harcourt Brace.

Keynes, J. M. (1973) *The General Theory and After: Preparation.* Vol. 8 of *The Collected Writings of John Maynard Keynes.* London: Macmillan.

Klier, D., Welge, M., and Harrigan, K. (2009) The Changing Face of Private Equity: How Modern Private Equity Firms Manage Investment Portfolios. *Journal of Private Equity,* 12 (4), Fall.

Lazonick, W., O'Sullivan, M. (2000) Maximizing shareholder value: a new ideology for corporate governance, *Economy and Society,* 29 (1). pp. 13-35,

Madi, M. A. C. (2014) *Global Finance and Development,* India: Sanbun Publishers.

Metrick, A., Yasuda, A. (2007) *The Economics of Private Equity Funds,* Wharton School: University of Pennsylvania.

Minsky, H.P. (1975) *John Maynard Keynes.* London: Macmillan.

172

Minsky, H.P. (1986) *Stabilizing an unstable economy*. New Haven: Yale University Press.

Pilkington, M. (2009) The financialization of modern economies in monetary circuit theory, in: J. F. Ponsot and S. Rossi (Eds.) *The Political Economy of Monetary Circuits. Tradition and Change in Post-Keynesian economics*. Basingstoke: Palgrave Macmillan, pp. 188- 216.

Philips, K. (2006) *American Theocracy: The Peril and Politics of Radical Religion, Oil, and Borrowed Money in the 21st Century*. New York: Viking.

Prequin (2015) *Prequin Private Equity & Venture Capital Report*. Available at https://www.preqin.com/docs/reports/2015-Preqin-Global-Private-Equity-and-Venture-Capital-Report-Sample-Pages.pdf (Accessed on 10 October 2015)

Rifkin, J. (2011) *The Third Industrial Revolution: How Lateral Power Is Transforming Energy, the Economy, and the World*. Palgrave Macmillan.

Rochon, L-P., Rossi, S. (2013) Endogenous Money: the Evolutionary Versus Revolutionary Views, *Review of Keynesian Economics*, 1 (2), pp. 210–229.

Rochon, L-P, Rossi, S. (Eds.) (2015) *The Encyclopedia of Central Banking*, Edward Elgar.

Roberston, J. (2015) *Localizing Global Finance: The Rise of Western-Style Private Equity in China*, United States: Palgrave Pivot.

Taymoigne, É. (2010) *Minsky's two-price theory of investment: uncertainty, financial structure, and arbitrage between new and existing capital assets*, Minsky's Summer School, Summer. Available at (and accessed on 20 November 2015) http://www.levyinstitute.org/pubs/conf_june10/Tymoigne_Two_Price.pdf.

Tannon, J. M., Johnson, R. (2005) Transatlantic Private Equity: Beyond a Trillion Dollar Force, *Journal of Private Equity*, 8 (3), pp. 77-80.

Tate, A. (2007) *The Effect of Private Equity Takeovers on Corporate Social Responsibility*. International Officer, Australian Council of Trade Unions.

Uni Global Union (2008). *Pension Fund Investment in Private Equity*. Report.

Wray, L. R., Tymoigne, É. (2008) Macroeconomics Meets Hyman P. Minsky: The Financial Theory of Investment, *Working Paper* No. 543, The Levy Economics Institute and University of Missouri–Kansas City. Available at http://core.ac.uk/download/pdf/6366463.pdf (Accessed on 25 November 2015),

Wheatley, J. (2010) *Capital markets: Private equity funds explore the market*. Available at https://www.ft.com/content/cbfe7ce6-571c-11df-aaff-00144feab49a (Accessed on 10 August 2011).

Part III
Globalisaton winners and losers

Chapter 4
Evolving wealth inequality in Kerala: mapping the winners and the losers
C.R. Yadu and B. Satheesha

Introduction[1]

Recent times have witnessed a mounting interest in studying economic inequality globally. Thomas Piketty's (2014) book *Capital in the Twenty-First Century* has captured global imagination and turned the debate towards wealth concentration and inequality under capitalist systems. His "grand theory on capital and inequality", as *The Economist* (2014) calls it, considers rate of return on wealth as an important variable in explaining economic inequality around the world. According to Piketty, wealth grows faster than output. Many other important studies also confirm the view that global inequality is on the rise (Ortiz and Cummins, 2011; Sala-i-martin, 2002) and it matters more in developing countries where the impact of inequality is much more pronounced (Boden, 2011; Wade, 2004; Zwan, 2014).

Inequality in the Indian context has been discussed in detail in literature though it is yet to capture serious policy attention. The available evidence suggests that the period of neo-liberal reforms was associated with the rise in income inequality in India (Subrmanian and Jayaraj, 2015; Deaton and Dreze, 2002; Pal and Ghosh, 2007; Himanshu, 2007). The divide between the rich and the poor has been growing over the years. Banerjee and Piketty (2005: 13) show that "the share of the very rich in Indian incomes is currently much higher than in Europe". From the early 1990s onwards, the number and the amount of wealth of India's billionaires have increased dramatically (Gandhi and Walton, 2012). "India", as Gandhi and Walton (2012) notes, "is

---
[1] Acknowledgment: thanks are due to the editors for their valuable comments and suggestions. The authors would like to thank M. Kabir, G. Pramod Kumar and Sreejith C.S. for their and support.

now an outlier with respect to the size of billionaire wealth relative to the size of her economy, especially for a relatively poor country".

This chapter is an attempt to understand the current wealth distribution in Kerala, the southern- most state in India. This is justified by two reasons. Firstly, most of the literature on inequality in India is based on income levels with consumption expenditure taken as the only proxy variable. This turns out to be limiting since income forms just one dimension of overall inequality. It should also be noted that studies on distribution with 'wealth' being taken as an indicator of inequality has been rare. Secondly, inequality in the sub national economies of India has, more or less, been overlooked in the whole discourse on the subject. With the given socio-historical and political contexts of the sub national economies, individual states may have a different picture of inequality than that for the whole of India. Therefore, Kerala, which has always stood on a divergent development path than the rest of India, becomes an interesting case for such a study.

The main of objectives of the paper are twofold, (1) to analyse the trends and pattern in wealth distribution in Kerala with the help of available secondary data (2) to discuss the possible reasons for the given distributional change. However, it must be remarked that the paper stops short of explaining the dynamics of the processes that drive inequality in the state in a complete and perfect manner, though some important hypotheses are put forward which need to be further studied empirically. The study opens up more questions than giving answers.

After the Introduction, the chapter is organized in four sections. The second section describes the socio-historical and political context where wealth inequality becomes important in Kerala. The following section discusses the data and methodology. Detailed analysis of the data and results are presented in the fourth section and fifth sections. The sixth section discusses the possible reasons for the rise in inequality in Kerala since the 1990s. Finally, we present the conclusion.

1. Setting the context

Kerala is a small state with a population over 33 million (as per 2011 census) that occupies 1.2 per cent of India's land area. The region has been known for its egalitarian development strategy, and for the public action-led progress model, for long under the banner "Kerala Model of Development" (Ramachandran, 1996). Reducing spatial and inter-group inequalities has been at the centre of Kerala's celebrated development experience with the state intervention playing a crucial role. In this way, Kerala could achieve higher social development comparable to the western countries even when its economic growth was low.[2]

However, in the last two decades, this development model seen to be losing its sheen owing to a multitude of problems which challenges the egalitarian ethos. Questions are being raised about the model with rising inequality being at the heart of the debate. It has been argued that Kerala, after a long period of economic stagnation, underwent a "turn around" in growth which is attributed to the economic reforms initiated at the national level from 1991 and to the large inflow of remittances on account of overseas migration (Shyjan, 2015: 11). But, the period of high growth rate in Kerala, starting from the end of the 1980s, also witnessed rising inequality (Subramanian and Prasad, 2008). The phenomenon of high economic growth and rising inequality clearly mark a departure from Kerala's celebrated development trajectory (Sreeraj and Vakulabharanam, 2015).

According to a recent study, Kerala has the highest income inequality in India (Satheesha, 2015). Though income inequality has been the subject of serious studies (Subramanian and Prasad, 2008; Sreeraj and Vakulabharanam, 2015; Satheesha, 2015), wealth inequality at the sub-national level has not been explored. However, a few studies at the national level shed some light on the wealth inequality in Kerala. Subramanian and

---

[2] Right from its formation as a state, Kerala's economic growth was on a slow pace. The period between 1971-72 and 1986-87 was viewed as one of "generalized stagnation" with an annual exponential growth rate of income just 1.88 per cent. However, the regional economy started showing signs of revival since 1987. After this "turn around" in growth, the economic performance of the state has been impressive. See Joseph and Harilal (2003) and Kannan (2005) for a detailed discussion on this.

Capital and Justice

Jayaraj (2006) bring out a discussion about the interesting pattern of wealth distribution in Kerala. They highlight the special case of the state for the pace at which asset accumulation has taken place over the years. In terms of wealth accumulation in urban areas, the authors find Kerala among the front-rankers. Another study written by Jayadev, Motiram and Vakulabharanam (2007) points out that the rate of wealth increase in Kerala has been the fastest compared with other major sub national regions in India. The indications from national level studies are not at all rosy and thus call for a deeper understanding of wealth inequality in the state.

The discussion of inequality in Kerala needs to be seen in its historical context. At an intuitive level, inequality in Kerala, over years, might have assumed a U-shaped transformation. Broadly speaking, there are three phases to the historical evolution of inequality in Kerala. The first phase spanning over a long period from the ninth century, the second commencing from the 1970s, following major land-reform measures, and the third from the 1990s coinciding with the period of nation-level economic reforms.

The first period was arguably associated with the caste based social hierarchy that evolved since the ninth century (Pillai, 1970). This social hierarchy was the determinant of the structure of inequality. Caste was the major determining factor of asset distribution where land was the major asset held by the people. Land ownership was completely dominated by the upper castes and the lower castes were denied of any land ownership rights (Varghese, 1970). This phase also witnessed other kinds of social and political inequalities, such as "unseeability", "untouchability", barring the low castes' entry into the public sphere (Bhaskaranuni, 1988). In this way, inequality in the society was fundamentally built into the system.

The period of high inequality continued, by and large, until land reforms on a significant scale was implemented in Kerala in the early 1970s. Through land reform, land ownership was transferred from the upper caste landlords to tenants and agricultural workers who belonged to lower gradations of the caste structure. This was a structural reform with far reaching impacts for the level of general inequality in the region. Studies show that both caste inequality and land inequality declined since the implementation of land reform (Radhakrishnan, 1981; Franke, 1992; Ramakumar, 2006). Indeed, land reform was a major blow to the caste based asset holding pattern, though it could not result in complete elimination of inequality in the caste-based asset holding. But, it had a major influence on the later development trajectory of Kerala, putting it at variance from the rest of India. Land reform was accompanied by other social welfare programmes that complemented this measure. Thus, public action which involved both state intervention and popular participation, led to the establishment and effective functioning of a system of public provisioning and support-led security (Oommen, 1993) which, in turn, ushered in an era where inequality was significantly reduced.

The third phase of inequality in the state starts from the early 1990's since the adoption of neo-liberal reforms at the national level. The domination of neoliberal ideology and the consequent withdrawal of Kerala's government from its "egalitarian developmentalist"[3] ideology is seen to have its ill effects on the level of inequality in the region. Subrahmanian and Prasad (2008) argue that adoption of unbridled market oriented policies were the major cause of rising inequality in the post-reform period. Almost in the same period, remittance flows from the Middle East to Kerala also began to increase (Kannan and Hari, 2002). Subramanian and Jayaraj (2006) observe the increased flows of remittances as an important factor that had affected the wealth distribution. The authors describe Kerala's upward mobility in wealth rankings as "an outcome greatly aided by repatriation of funds by migrants to the Gulf countries" (Subramanian and Jayaraj, 2006: 8). However, it might also be observed that the economic reforms have a role in the increasing role of remittances in the local economy. Devaluation of the Indian currency as part of the neo-liberal reforms raised the impact of remittances in the state economy further (Kannan, 2005).

2. The data: NSSO All India Debt and Investment Survey

National Sample Survey Office's (NSSO) All India Debt and Investment Survey (AIDIS) data is a grossly underutilized data by researchers despite being a rich source of information. Surveys from AIDIS are aimed at generating all India level data on value of assets and incidence of

---

[3] See Devika (2010) for a discussion on the topic.

indebtedness which can be disaggregated at the state level. NSSO first conducted this survey in 1971-72 (26th round). The 2013 latest round (70th) is the fifth in the series. In between, there are three rounds – those conducted in 1981-82, 1992 and 2003 respectively. However, we take into consideration the 48th (1992) and the 70th (2013) rounds for analyzing inter-household wealth distribution. Unfortunately, there is no disaggregated data at detailed caste levels in the NSSO Rounds prior to the 59th. Hence for analyzing social inequality in asset ownership, the data from the 59th round (2003) was compared to those from the 70th round. AIDIS data is generated by a stratified two stage sampling methodology devised by NSSO.

A good discussion of the limitations of AIDIS survey data can be found in Subramanian and Jayaraj (2006) and Jayadev et al. (2007). Jayadev et al. (2007: 3885) find three major shortcomings of the data. First, 'the sampling methodology' does not make an adequate attempt to oversample the wealthy'. This is a serious problem as there tends to be large concentrations of wealth at the top end of the population. Second, there is the tendency of households to under report wealth holdings. This seriously affects the quality of the data as people under report assets like land and gold. The problem of underreporting is more severe at the upper end of the wealth distribution where the wealthy households tend not to reveal the full extent of their assets. The third shortcoming relates to the evaluation of the reported assets. "Even if the reported prices are based on recent transactions, they tend to be underplayed so that the reported values turn out to be lower than the market values" (Jayadev et al., 2007: 3885). The absence of wealth deflators are also pointed out as a major problem when comparing multiple rounds of the survey. The data is also limited in scope for capturing the super-rich. As the survey does not capture wealth holdings of India's billionaires, a real picture of wealth distribution becomes elusive.

Total household assets, as NSSO defines it, comprise physical assets like land, buildings, livestock, agricultural machinery and implements, non-farm business equipment, all transport equipment and financial assets like dues receivable on loans advanced in cash or in kind, shares in companies and cooperative societies, banks, etc., national saving certificates and the like, deposits in companies, banks, post offices and with individuals. However, due to the change in the methodology of evaluation of assets, the results of the 70th round is not strictly comparable with the previous rounds and we should exercise caution while comparing the asset values in the latest round with that of previous rounds. As the NSS report says, "values of land & building as on 30.06.2012 were recorded in the 70th round as per their normative/guideline values, whereas in the 59th round they were recorded 'as reported by the informant'" (NSSO, 2014: 2). Secondly, in the previous rounds, household durables were taken into account while calculating the value of total assets whereas in the latest round household durables are excluded from the definition of total assets. This problem has been rectified by deducting the value of household durables from the value of total assets. Another concern lies in deflating the value of assets. As pointed out earlier, there is no wealth deflator available. Therefore, deflation has been done using the Consumer Price Index (CPI) using 1998-99 as the base year.

There are two things that need to be noted with the data presented in the article. Firstly, the data had been trimmed 0.05 per cent above and below to reduce the outlier effect. Secondly, to make the data internationally legible, the values in rupees have been converted into US dollar terms (after deflation using CPI, assuming exchange rate 1 US dollar = 65 Indian rupees).

3. Pattern of asset holding

(a) Gross assets

Table 1 shows the averages for gross assets and major individual items of assets for Kerala and their respective Compound Annual Growth Rates (CAGR) for the period. Taking cue from Deaton (2007), the averages are presented in per capita terms, as "welfare ultimately resides in individuals and not in households" (Deaton; Jayadev et al., 2007: 3853). Some caution is required while interpreting Table 1. As noted earlier, the method of assets' valuation in both the rounds is different. In the latest round, the assets' valuation was done on the basis of the normative or guideline values. In the previous round, the values were recorded as reported by the respondent.

Therefore, the asset values in the last round might be higher than when the earlier method was adopted[4].

Table 1 Mean and median values of assets at constant prices (in dollars)

Description	Mean			Median		
	1992	2013	Growth rates (%)	1992	2013	Growth rates (%)
Per capita assets	1188	6411	8.4	573	2931	8.1
Per capita value land	625	4341	9.7	229	1424	9.1
Per capita value building	369	1369	6.4	186	737	6.8

Source: Authors' calculations based on NSS AIDIS, respective rounds

The calculation of the median and the mean values for the values of gross assets in the two rounds, as the latter might have been influenced by the outlier values (Table 1). Medians for both the periods were substantially less than the corresponding mean values. In most cases, the median values are almost half the mean values. This shows that the outliers at the top end of the distribution are pulling up the average figures considerably. However, the growth rate of the median values is almost similar to that of the growth rate of the mean values with the growth rate of per capita land value outstripping the corresponding value for total assets, followed by the growth rate for per capita buildings, in that order. The high difference between the mean and median values indicates the highly skewed nature of the distribution of total assets in Kerala.

---

[4] This is partly shown by the higher annual growth rate of per capita land value than that of the Per capita assets. Further, the per capita value of buildings is less than that of the latter.

Table 2 Percentage distribution of major assets

Assets	1992	2013
Land	54.39	67.42
Building	31.43	21.68
Transport Equipments	1.27	1.88
Shares	0.21	0.17
Financial Assets	2.95	2.54
Bullion ornaments	8.59	5.84
Others	1.16	0.47
Total	100	100

Source: Authors' calculations based on NSS AIDIS, respective rounds

Table 2 presents the percentage distribution of major assets, at more disaggregated level in 1992 and 2013. In both the rounds, land constitutes more than half of the household wealth and the share of land in total assets sharply rises in between the two points. The share of land in total assets rose to 67.42 in 2013 from 54.39 % in 1992. The increasing share of land in total wealth might be a result of the land value appreciation in the state. Land, far from being a means of production, has transformed itself into a speculative asset. People found land as an attractive form of investment and the land market boom was further encouraged by the rapid expansion of the housing and real estate sector (Harilal, 2008).

Interestingly, the share of buildings in total assets declined to 21.68 in 2013 from 31.43 in 1992. While it might be a result of the possible undervaluation of buildings by the NSSO, it does in no way mean that the importance of buildings in total assets has declined in Kerala. The rate at which land value has risen in the state far outstripped the rate at which the value of buildings rose. At the same time, the share of financial assets and that of agricultural machinery and miscellaneous forms of other assets declined over the same period.

Table 3 shows the decile-wise distribution of assets and their respective mean values. It may be seen that the shares in all the decile groups except in the last, declined over the period. This makes clear the picture of a

185

"winner takes it all" situation whereby the richest class in the society has pocketed a significant part of the incremental wealth in the state.

Table 3 Percentage distribution of gross assets across decile classes

Decile	Assets	
	1992	2013
1	0.53	0.21
2	1.60	1.17
3	2.51	2.15
4	3.52	3.16
5	4.68	4.39
6	6.37	6.15
7	8.78	8.40
8	12.00	11.49
9	18.60	17.43
10	41.42	45.45

Source: Authors' calculations based on NSS AIDIS, respective rounds

Decile-wise distribution of assets in their various forms for the year 2013 and the respective change in the distribution from 1992 is shown in Table 4.[5] It may be seen that in the 20 year period, the share of land in total assets for the first decile went down by half. Deciles from the third witnessed significant increases in the share of land in their asset portfolio. Considering the fast pace of real estate growth in Kerala, this would imply that the poorest classes may be getting bypassed by the real estate boom. This is further corroborated by other studies which show that the richest classes are benefitting out of the land transactions in the state (Aravindan, 2006). If we compare the standard deviation of different assets across the ten deciles in the two points of time, it can be seen that the inequality in the distribution of landed wealth among different deciles has increased over time (Table 4).

---

[5] See Table Appendix Table 1 for the percentage distribution of different assets across deciles for the year 1992.

Table 4 Decile wise distribution of major assets in 2013 and changes therein from 1992 (in percentages)

Deciles	Land	Building	Financial assets	Bullion and ornaments	Other assets	Total
1	14.01 (-16.9)	12.95(-13.58)	10.90 (4.65)	54.15 (21.28)	7.99 (4.55)	100
2	33.77 (0.2)	34.73(2.39)	5.13 (1.41)	21.47(-7.05)	4.91 (2.99)	100
3	47.35 (6.08)	35.22(2.35)	3.49 (0.83)	10.83(-10.87)	3.10 (1.60)	100
4	50.27 (12.6)	34.76(13.36)	1.89 (-0.55)	10.42(-10.26)	2.66 (0.90)	100
5	51.84 (12.46)	33.43(-8.94)	2.53 (0.83)	9.37(-12.33)	2.83 (0.94)	100
6	55.34 (10.67)	33.22(-3.14)	1.71 (-14.51)	7.45(-7.92)	2.27 (0.73)	100
7	60.84 (13.2)	28.14(-7.7)	1.83 (5.85)	6.74(-5.94)	2.44 (0.21)	100
8	60.38 (15.6)	28.2(19.28)	2.52 (0.22)	6.22 (-3.99)	2.67 (1.06)	100
9	65.77 (10.93)	22.43(10.93)	2.78 (-0.44)	5.82(-1.2)	3.20 (0.81)	100
10	77.44 (12.56)	14.00(-10.7)	2.60 (-0.6)	3.85(-3.17)	2.10 (-1.43)	100
SD	17.63 (7.57)	8.51(2.87)	2.77 (-6.54)	15.04(5.73)	1.79 (0.74)	----

Note: Figures in parentheses indicate the changes from 1993
Source: Authors' calculations based on NSS AIDIS, respective rounds

It is worthy of note that the share of bullion and ornaments and of financial assets in the first decile registered considerable increase between the NSSO Rounds. However, this predominance of gold and financial assets in the poorer deciles might be because of the low overall asset holding by these classes. Moreover, it would be possible that the investible surplus of these groups might not be sufficient to buy land, given the high prices of the latter.

(b) Net assets

In order to get a real picture of wealth distribution in Kerala, the value of assets net of debts should be considered. The per capita mean and median values of assets net of debt in 1992 and 2013, would indicate that the distribution of net assets is almost similar to that of gross assets (Table 5).

The mean and the median values indicate the rise in the skewness in the distribution between the two points of time (Table 5).

Table 5 Decile-wise distribution and mean and median values of net assets

Decile	Net Assets	
	1992	2013
1	0.50	0.14
2	1.53	1.09
3	2.48	2.05
4	3.46	3.07
5	4.65	4.34
6	6.23	6.07
7	8.79	8.29
8	11.99	11.34
9	18.65	17.63
10	41.72	45.98
Per capita net asset (Mean)	75643	394416 (8.2)
Per capita net asset (Median)	36072	176460 (7.9)

Note: Figures in parentheses show the growth rate between 1992 and 2013
Source: Authors' calculations based on NSS AIDIS, respective rounds

The decile wise percentage shares show that the trend is the same as that for gross assets. Nevertheless, the decline in the share of net assets in the first decile is sharper than the corresponding decline in the share of gross assets.

The debt-asset ratio shows increase across decile classes. Interestingly, the ratio recorded a whopping increase for the first decile from 12 to 80 between the two rounds, indicating the deepening debt trap among the poorest in Kerala (Table 6).

Table 6 Debt-asset ratio across deciles

Decile	1992	2013
1	12	79.9
2	8.6	14.9
3	4.3	10
4	4.6	8.2
5	3.1	6.3
6	5	6.3
7	2.3	6.3
8	2.4	6.3
9	1.9	3.8
10	1.5	3.7

Source: Authors' calculations based on NSS AIDIS, respective rounds

4. Inequality in the distribution of assets

The previous discussion about the distribution of gross and net assets across decile groups shows up the growing inequality between decile classes in Kerala in the last two decades. In this section, the analysis aims to capture the extent of inequality and changes therein between the two NSSO Rounds. We consider two types of inequality which are relevant in the context of Kerala- overall inequality and social inequality.

(a) Overall Inequality

Overall inequality is the inter-household inequality that we calculate without considering the social identity of the households. Rather than relying entirely on commonly used relative Gini coefficient for estimating inequality, three alternative indices of inequality, *viz*, the absolute Gini coefficient, intermediate Gini coefficient and Palma ratio, are used here. This is necessitated by the recent debates around the measurement of inequality which criticize the relative Gini coefficient (Palma, 2011). Relative Gini is normally defined in a way which biases the measure in a *downward* direction, making inequality seem less large (Wade, 2013). The

189

problem with this measure is that if one scale up or down every household's wealth by the same factor, the value of it will remain unchanged. But, in absolute terms inequality might have risen up considerably.

For example, in an economy of two households – one having an income of $10 and other having an income of $100, if the income is scaled up by a factor of 2, the relative Gini will be the same as the proportion of the incomes of these two households remain unchanged. But, in the absolute level the inequality has actually increased from an absolute difference of 90 to 180. Therefore, it would be good to use an absolute measure also to check the robustness of relative Gini coefficient. In contrast to relative Gini, the absolute Gini's value will be unchanged if the same amount of wealth is added or subtracted from each household's wealth. Relative Gini is, thus, termed as a "rightist" measure and absolute Gini a "leftist" measure of inequality (Subramanian and Jayaraj, 2015: 42). But, this in no way suggests that absolute Gini coefficient is perfectly better than relative Gini coefficient as each measure has its own merits and demerits. Basole and Basu (2015: 46) suggest the use of an "intermediate Gini coefficient" which combine both the measures "which is sensitive to changes in both proportions and additions" of wealth "which it inherits from the two Gini coefficients".

Table 7 gives the trends in inequality of gross assets over the two rounds by using the three variants of the Gini coefficients as discussed above. It shows that the relative Gini coefficient for Gross assets and per capita asset went up between the two surveys. It also shows increase in the coefficient for per capita land and a decline in that for per capita buildings. On the contrary, absolute Gini coefficient went up not only for gross assets but also for all of its components. Intermediate Gini coefficient also shows similar results for gross and per capita assets, but the rise has been of a lower magnitude compared to that given by the Absolute Gini value. It may be noted that the trends in Gini coefficients for net assets also show the same trends (Table 8). Given this coincidence of the findings of the three variants of Gini, for both gross and net assets, one is on firmer grounds to believe the "significant" rise in the inequality of distribution of wealth in Kerala, between 1991 and 2013.

Table 7 Relative, absolute and intermediate Gini coefficients for gross and net assets

Relative Gini	1992	2013
Total assets	0.566	0.603
Per capita assets	0.592	0.643
Per capita land	0.692	0.721
Per capita building	0.621	0.613
Absolute Gini		
Total assets	188147	833829
Per capita assets	45680	267954
Per capita land	28138	203329
Per capita building	14911	54555
Intermediate Gini		
Total assets	106514	502821
Per capita assets	27021	172302
Per capita land	19474.5	146503
Per capita building	9267.01	33440.5

Source: Authors' calculations based on NSS AIDIS, respective rounds

Table 8 Relative, absolute and intermediate Gini coefficients for net asset

Relative Gini	1992	2013
Net asset	0.572	0.614
Per capita Net asset	0.598	0.656
Absolute Gini		
Net asset	186113	809245
Per capita Net worth	45239	258713
Intermediate Gini		
Net asset	106457	496876
Per capita Net asset	27053	169716

Source: Authors' calculations based on NSS AIDIS, respective rounds

While Gini coefficient gives equal weight to all observations, the "Palma ratio", capture the dynamics of the bottom and top deciles of the distribution more precisely. Palma ratio is defined as the share of richest 10 per cent to the share of the bottom 40 per cent. Hence, Palma measure can be regarded as a crude measure of class inequality – the inequality between the "richest" and the "poor". For example, if the Palma ratio is found to be 5, that means that the top 10 per cent of the population is grabbing five times more wealth than the bottom 40 per cent. Table 9 gives the Palma ratios for gross assets, net assets and the two major asset categories.

Table 9 Palma ratios

Item	1992	2013
Gross Assets	5.1	6.9
Net Assets	5.2	7.2
Land	8.73	11.62
Building	3.68	2.78

Source: Authors' calculations based on NSS AIDIS, respective rounds

While the ratios for gross and net assets increased between the two surveys, for land the rise has been of a higher magnitude than that for the other categories. This further gives credence to our earlier finding that land transactions in Kerala in recent times have largely been in favour of the rich.

(b) Social Inequality

Following Deshapande (2000), the pattern of wealth distribution across broad social groups in Kerala is examined in this section. Usually, NSSO gives data for social groups in three categories – Scheduled castes (SC), Scheduled Tribes and Other Backward Classes (OBC). Unfortunately, the 1992 AIDIS data does not provide data on OBC. Therefore, for the sake of analysis, data pertaining to an intermediate round (2003) is brought in for favour of comparison with the 2013 Round.

Evolving wealth inequality in Kerala

Table 10 Mean and median of per capita net assets at constant prices (in dollars)

Per Capita Net Assets	2003		2013	
	Mean	Median	Mean	Median
ST/SC	493	261	1904	1129
OBC	1383	694	5181	2515
Others	3601	1328	9579	4468

Source: Authors' calculations based on NSS AIDIS, respective rounds

Table 10 shows the mean and the median values of per capita net assets of different social groups in 2003 and 2013. It can be seen that between the two surveys, the mean and the median values of all social groups increased; but, the median value is almost half the mean across groups; the mean and the median values for the group "others" (excluding SC/ST and OBC) show the sharpest increase. Nevertheless, "others" have the highest absolute difference between the mean and the median, reflecting the sharp rise in the internal differentiation within the group.

Table 11 Debt-asset ratio of social groups

Debt-asset ratio	2003	2013
ST/SC	8.8	16.5
OBC	4.6	4.6
Others	3.3	3.6

Source: Authors' calculations based on NSS AIDIS, respective rounds

While the SCs and STs (combined) have the lowest per-capita net assets, they also have the highest debt-asset ratio among all the social groups (Table 11). Moreover, the debt asset ratio for ST/SC group increased by almost two times, to 16.5 percent in 2013 from 8.8 percent in 2003. During the same period the debt-asset ratio of OBCs remained unchanged and for "Others" it rose marginally.

Capital and Justice

To check whether the social gap is widening or narrowing over the period, "difference in differences" (D-I-D), following Deshpande (2013) can be used. Per capita wealth is taken as an indicator of social gap for the D-I-D[6] calculation. The D-I-D helps to understand the relative gains of different groups in terms of per capita assets. The results of the estimation, taking the median per capita net asset as the indicator, are given in Table 12.

Table 12 Relative gains of social groups over the period (in dollars)

	ST/SC	OBC	Others
Median per capita Asset in 2003	262	694	1328
Median per capita Asset in 2013	1129	2515	4468
D-I-D per capita assets	-953	-1318	2271

Note: a. D-I-D corresponding to the column ST/SC refers to the one calculated comparing SC/ST with respect to OBC, the D-I-D in column OBCs compares OBCs with respect to Others' and the D-I-D in column Others' compares Others with respect to ST/SC.
Source: Authors' calculations based on NSS AIDIS, respective rounds

The level of per capita assets of SC/STs has fallen behind that of the OBCs by $953 between the time points. The per capita asset gap between OBCs and others is to the tune of $-1318 which means that OBC group has fallen behind others in terms of per capita asset ownership by that amount. The group "Others" have a huge gain relative to SC/STs to the tune of $2271, showing the clear advantage gained by the group over other social groups in terms of wealth accumulation over the period. It becomes clear that though the OBCs have had relative gain over SCs and STs over the decade, the short-fall of the group "Others" is two times greater than their gain over SC/STs. It is important to note that the gains made by the three social groups are in order of their social rankings in the society which points fingers towards a "caste-wealth" nexus.

---

[6] D-I-D is estimated with the equation D-I-D$_{jk}$ = [(Indicator$_{ijs}$ − Indicator$_{iks}$) − (Indicator$_{ij(s-1)}$) − Indicator$_{ik(s-1)}$)], where j and k are the two social groups being compared, for the ith indicator between survey rounds s and s-1.

5. Explaining rising wealth inequality in Kerala: some speculations

Giving a comprehensive account of the reasons behind rising wealth inequality in Kerala based on the available evidences would be a difficult task. However, an attempt at is made to shed some light on the possible processes at work, in the form of some conjectures arising from empirical data and literature. We argue that wealth concentration is a vicious cycle; "who already hold wealth have the resources to invest or to leverage the accumulation of wealth, which creates new wealth" (Leung, 2015). As noted earlier, neo-liberal reforms and remittance inflows contributes to the worsening of inequality in the state. This section explores the effect of the two factors in the worsening of the inequality in the state.

As remittance income is pointed out to be an important determinant of inequality in Kerala, some inferences can be made by comparing the wealth status of remittance receiving households and non-remittance receiving households[7] (see Appendix Table A.2). The averages for per capita gross assets and net assets are very high for the remittance receiving households and are found significantly different from that of non-remittance receiving households (at 1 per cent level, $t=3.02$, $p=0.0013$). Zachariah and Rajan (2012) estimates that remittance from abroad forms 31.2 per cent of the State Domestic Product. Though not much can be said about the asset holding preferences of the migrants from AIDIS data, the field based results by Sreeraj and Vakulabharanam (2015) finds that there is a surge in investment in land, business concerns and residential construction in which the role of remittance income is significant. It has long been speculated that the real estate boom in the state is greatly aided by the huge remittance flows (Harilal, 2008; Oommen, 1993).

The argument behind the speculation is that, lacking avenues of investment in the productive sectors of the economy, the remittance income gets channeled towards the land market which in turn fuels the real estate. The investment of remittances in the land market has led to the shooting up in

---

[7] The schedule of the NSS 70th round, made specific enquiries whether any member of the surveyed household received any remittance during the 365 days preceding the survey, making it possible to have the data relating to asset held by the remittance receiving households *vis-à-vis* non-receiving ones.

land prices like never before (Joseph and Harilal, 2003). Land has increasingly become a speculative asset and the latest evidences reveal increasing land market activities in the state with its boom and bust cycles (Roy, 2013). The booming real estate sector in the state points towards the asset holding preferences. The share of 'real estate and ownership of dwellings' in Kerala's Net State Domestic Product (NSDP) has increased from 0.07 in 1992 to 13.58 in 2013-14 which is the sharpest of the increase among all sub sectors (see Appendix Table A.3).

Though remittance income is pointed out to be the important reason for Kerala's turn around in growth, the role of economic reforms in this cannot be ignored. The shift in policy paradigm that started in the early 1990s did not impact on Kerala in attracting private investment on any significant scale. Nevertheless, it made its influence felt in the regional economy through trade liberalization, tax cuts and reduction in government spending. The available literature show that neo-liberal policies had badly affected Kerala's agrarian population (Mohanakumar and Sharma 2006; Mohanakumar, 2008). The removal of quantitative restrictions, lowering of tariff levels on imports and Free Trade Agreements signed with other countries/regional blocks have worsened the financial condition of farmers (Jeromi, 2007) and has exposed the famers to unfair trade practices, global price volatility and recession-hit external markets (Banerjee-Guha, 2013). Combined with the other unfavourable conditions prevalent in the agricultural sector, the subsistence farmers along with small and marginal farmers were forced into debt traps.[8]

The rolling back of government spending especially subsidy cuts and the reduction in other supporting mechanisms resulted in 'decline in real earnings, food grain availability and consumption by the rural poor' (Banerjee-Guha, 2013). Empirical evidence suggests that the classes of middle farmers, small farmers, marginal farmers and agricultural workers are among the losers in terms of income in the high growth period in the state (Sreeraj and Vakulabharanam, 2015). On the other side, this period

---

[8] The incidence of indebtedness among farmer households is one of the highest in Kerala and so is the case of debt driven farmer suicides. According to a government report published in 2006, about 2000 farmers committed suicide in the state. Decline in the prices of farm products is pointed out to be one of the major factors that had increased farm debt in the state. See Jeromi (2007) for an elaborated discussion on this.

witnessed the booming of native and non-native retail giants in the services sector, which has lead to the dispossession of the petty traders and small shop owners (Navadanya, 2007; George, 2014) which might again force them to run on debts for their survival.

Faced with the stagnation in the creation of gainful employment in the economy, these people along with the "dispossessed" from the agricultural sector might have settled in the lower ranks of the service sector job where the conditions of employment are very poor and exploitative. Ostensibly, the only opportunity for these sections of people to gain some economic advantage was to take up the role of sellers in the already bouyant land market developed out of the remittance boom in the state.

The sale of the small parcels of land which these people own may be either "distress driven" or "opportunity driven". Some may sell their land to pay off debts. Others may sell their land seeing the high value it fetches. In any case, the speculative land market seemed an opportunity for both these sections to gain some economic mobility. The availability of more land for sale would have again fuelled the land market and the richest sections would have found no time to buy of these lands on sale. This may be one of the reasons for the sharp decline in the land shares of the first decile and an increase in the corresponding shares of the wealthiest class.

In the case of social inequality, it is difficult to ascertain whether inequality has increased over the period on the basis of the data presented in this article. However, it becomes clear from the analysis that the relative gains for the SC/ST is the lowest among all the social groups. The available studies also indicate that the gains of the real estate boom, which has come the major sector behind the fast economic growth in the state, is not equitably spread across different social groups and this would most probably bypass the SC/ST groups (Yadu, 2015; 2016).

The continuing lower status of these groups in terms of inherited wealth is a big question as inherited wealth is considered to be more important than earned wealth in determining inequality (Piketty, 2014). As Kanbur and Stiglitz (2015) notes "intergenerational transmission of inequality is more than simple inheritance of physical or financial wealth". Rather, the privileges that would accrue out of the inheritance of wealth should also be considered. Those who are wealthy or those who creates new wealth could convert their gains into human capital and other income generating forms in the next generation. As they attain more education, this would lead them to grab more gainful employment. This greatly explains the persistence of "wealth-caste" nexus and thus the dynamics of contemporary social inequality in Kerala.

Concluding observations

The foregoing discussion indicates the different magnitudes of wealth inequality in Kerala and indicates the increase in inequality over a period of two decades since 1991. The remarkable feature of the wealth inequality in the state is the role of landed wealth. The concentration of wealth in the hands of the richest is associated by an increase in the share of land in their asset portfolio and the decline in the share of the poorest class. Financialisation of land is the channel through which neo-liberalism and remittance inflows affected the wealth distribution in the state.

The pertinent question that emerges from the analysis is the social composition of the poorest who do not own asset to any significant level. Which are the classes and castes who are getting pauperized by this process? Though, this study gives some indications towards this, more investigation needs to be done. However, unless "redistribution" is brought back on the agenda, the current regime of accumulation will spell doom for Kerala's economically and socially marginalized. Apart from Piketty's (2014) suggestion for a global wealth tax, we would like to highlight the need for a second set of land reforms in Kerala, filling the gaps of the land reform of 1970. The need of the hour is a realization at the policy making level to bring about such a radical reform.

References

Aravindan, K.P. (2006) *Kerala Padanam.* Thiruvananthapuram: Kerala Shastra Sahitya Parishad.

Banerjee, A., Piketty, T. (2005) Top Indian Incomes. 1922-2000. *The World Bank Economic Review*, 19 (1), pp. 1-19.

Banjerjee-Guha, S. (2013) Accumulation and Dispossession: Contradictions of Growth and Development in Contemporary India. *South Asia: Journal of South Asian Studies*, 36 (2), pp. 165-179.

Basole, A and Basu, D. (2015) Non-Food Expenditures and Consumption Inequality in India. *Economic and Political Weekly*, 50 (36), pp. 43-53.

Bhaskaranunni, P. (1988) *Pathonpathaam Noottandile Keralam*. Thrissur: Kerala Sahitya Academy.

Boden, M. (2011) Neoliberalism and Counter-Hegemony in the Global South: Reimagining the State. In Motta, S., Nilsen, A.Gunvald (ed.) *Social Movements in the Global South: Dispossession, Development and Resistance*. UK: Palgrave Macmillan, pp. 83-103.

Deaton, A., Dreze, J. (2002) Poverty and Inequality in India. *Economic & Political Weekly,* 37 (36), pp. 3279-3748.

Deshpande, A. (2000) Does Caste Still Define Disparity? A Look at Inequality in Kerala, India. *The American Economic Review,* 90 (2), pp. 322-325.

Deshpande, A. (2013) How Backward are the Other Backward Classes? Changing Contours of Caste Disadvantage in India. *Working Paper* No. 233, Centre for Development Economics.

Devika, J. (2010) Egalitarian Developmentalism, Communist Mobilization, and the Question of Caste in Kerala State, India. *The Journal of Asian Studies,* 69(03), pp. 799-820.

Franke, R. (1992) Land Reform versus Inequality in Nadur Village, Kerala. *Journal of Anthropological Research*, 48 (2), pp.81-116.

George, S. (2014) New Forms of Retail Trade and Trajectories of Urban Exclusion in India: A Review. *Working Paper* 313, Institute for Social and Economic Change, Bangalore.

Ghandi, A., Walton, M. (2012) Where Do India's Billionaires Get Their Wealth? *Economic & Political Weekly,* 47 (40), pp. 10-14.

Ghosh, J. (2015) *Social Mobility in Latin America, Sub-Saharan Africa and Asia.* (Video). Available at: http://www.networkideas.org/vdo/jul2015/vdo21_JG_LA.htm (Accessed on 22 February 2015)

Harilal, K.N. (2008) Kerala Vikasanam: Bhuprashnam Muthal Bhuprashnam Vare. In Kunhikannan, T.P. (ed) *Keralam: Puthiya Anweshanangalku Oru Amukham.* Thrissur: Kerala Sasthra Sahitya Parishad.

Himanshu. (2007) Recent Trends in Poverty and Inequality: Some Preliminary Results. *Economic & Political Weekly,* 42(06), pp. 497-508.

Jayadev, A., Motiram, S., Vakulabharanam, V. (2007) Patterns of Wealth Disparities in India during the Liberalisation Era. *Economic & Political Weekly,* 12 (38), pp. 3853-3863.

Jeromi, P.D. (2007) Impact of Agricultural Trade Liberalisation: Farmers' Indebtedness and Suicides in Kerala. *Indian Journal of Agricultural Economics,* 62 (2), pp. 159-175.

Kanbur, R., Stiglitz, J. (2015) *Wealth and income distribution: New theories needed for a new era.* Centre for Economic Policy Research's Policy Portal. Available at http://voxeu.org/article/wealth-and-income-distribution-new-theories-needed-new-era (Accessed on 12 October 2015).

Kannan, K.P., Hari, K.S. (2002) Kerala's Gulf Connection: Emigration, Remittances and their Macroeconomic Impact 1972-2000. *Working Paper* No. 328, Centre for Development Studies, Thiruvananthapuram.

Kannan, K.P. (2005) Kerala's Turnaround in Growth: Role of Social Development, Remittances and Reform. *Economic and Political Weekly,* 40 (6), pp. 548-554.

Leung, May. (2015). *The Causes of Economic Inequality.* Seven Pillars Institute. Available at http://sevenpillarsinstitute.org/case-studies/causes-economic-inequality. (Accessed on 20 July 20 2016)

Mohanakumar, S.,Sharma, R.K. (2006) Analysis of Farmer Suicides in Kerala. *Economic and Political Weekly,* 41 (16), pp. 1553-1558.

Mohanakumar, S. (2008) Kerala's Agricultural Labourers: Victims of Crisis. *Economic and Political Weekly,* 43 (19), pp. 27-29.

Motiram, S., Vakulabhranam, V. (2013) Indian Inequality: Patterns and Changes, 1993-2010. In Mahedra Dev, S. (ed.), *India Development Report.* New Delhi: Oxford University Press, pp. 224-232.

National Sample Survey Office (2014) *Key Indicators of Debt and Investment in India.* New Delhi: Ministry of Statistics and Programme Implementation, Government of India.

Navadanya. (2007) *Corporate Hijack of Retail: Retail Dictatorship versus Retail Democracy.* New Delhi: Navadanya/Research for Science, Technology and Ecology.

Oommen, M.A. (1993) *Essays on Kerala Economy*. New Delhi: Oxford and India Book House.

Oommen, M.A. (2006) The Dreze-Sen Theory of Public Action and Kerala's Development Experience. In Tharamangalam, J.(ed.), *Kerala: The Paradoxes of Public Action and Development*. New Delhi: Orient Longman.

Ortiz, I., Cummins, M. (2011) Global Inequality: Beyond The Bottom Billion: A Rapid Review of Income Distribution in 141 Countries. *Social and Economic Policy Working Paper*, UNICEF.

Pal, P., Ghosh, J. (2007) Inequality in India: A survey of recent trends. *DESA Working Paper* No. 45. Available at http://www.un.org/esa/desa/papers/2007/wp45_2007.pdf (Accessed 2 Jan. 2015)

Palma, G. (2011) Homogeneous Middles vs. Heterogeneous Tails, and the End of the 'Inverted-U': It's All About the Share of the Rich. *Development and Change*, 42 (1), pp. 87-153.

Piketty, T. (2014) *Capital in the Twenty-First Century*. Cambridge: Harvard University Press.

Pillai, K. (1970) *Studies in Kerala History*. Trivandrum: National Book Stall.

Radhakrishnan, P. (1981) Land Reforms in Theory and Practice: The Kerala Experience. *Economic and Political Weekly*, 16 (52), pp. A129-135.

Ramachandran, V. K. (1996) On Kerala's development achievements. In Dreze, J. and Sen, A. (eds.), *Indian development: Selected regional perspectives*. New Delhi: Oxford University Press, pp. 205–356.

Ramakumar, R. (2006) Public Action, Agrarian Change and the Standard of Living of Agriculture Workers: A Study of a Village in Kerala. *Journal of Agrarian Change*, 6 (3), pp. 306-345.

Roy, V.P. (2013) *Financialisation and Land and Real Estate Markets in Kerala*, paper presented at "Kerala Vikasana Sangamam", IRTC, Palakkad.

Sala-i-Martin, X. (2002) The World Distribution of Income (Estimated From Individual Country Distributions). *Working Paper* No.8933, National Bureau of Economic Research. Available at http://www.nber.org/papers/w8933. (Accessed 14 Aug. 2015).

Satheesha, B. (2015) *Disparity in Land Holdings and Rising Income Inequality in Kerala*. MPhil Dissertation. Jawaharlal Nehru University, Centre for Development Studies.

Shyjan, D. (2014) *Services Sector Growth in Kerala: Character, Compostion and Implications.* PhD Dissertation. Jawaharlal Nehru University, Centre for Development Studies.

Sreeraj, A.P., Vakulabharanam, V. (2015) High Growth and Rising Inequality in Kerala Since 1980's. *Oxford Development Studies.* Available at http://www.tandfonline.com/doi/full/10.1080/13600818.2015.1111320 (Accessed 11 Dec. 2015)

Subrahmanian, K.K., Prasad, S. (2008) Rising Inequality with High Growth Isn't this Trend Worrisome? Analaysis of Kerala Experence. *Working Paper* No. 401, Center for Development Studies, Trivandrum.

Subramanian, S., Jayaraj, D. (2006) *The Distribution of Household Wealth in India,* Paper prepared for UNU-WIDER project meeting, May 4-6, WIDER, Helsinki.

Subramanian, S.,Jayaraj, D. (2015) Growth and Inequality in the Distribution of India's Consumption Expenditure: 1983 to 2009–10. *Economic & Political Weekly,* 50 (32), pp. 39-47.

The Economist (2014) Thomas Piketty's "capital" Summarised in Four Paragraphs, May 4. Available at http://www.economist.com/blogs/economist-explains/2014/05/economist-explains (Accessed 12 July, 2016)

Varghese, T.C. (1970) *Economic Consequences of Agrarian Change.* Bombay: Alliance Publishers.

Wade, R. (2004) Is Globalization Reducing Poverty and Inequality?. *World Development,* 32 (4), pp. 567-589.

Wade, R. (2013) Our Misleading Measure of Income and Wealth Inequality: The Standard Gini Coefficient. *Triple Crisis.* Available at http://triplecrisis.com/our-misleading-measure-of-income-and-wealth-inequality-the-standard-gini-coefficient/#more-8133 (Accessed 12 July 2016)

Wilkinson, R., Pickett, K. (2009) *The Spirit Level: Why More Equal Societies Almost Always Do Better,* London: Allen Lane.

Yadu, C R. (2015) Land Question and Mobility of the Marginalized: A Study of Land Inequality in Kerala. *Agrarian South: Journal of Political Economy,* 4 (3), pp. 327-370.

Zachariah, K.C., Rajan, S.I. (2012) Inflexion in Kerala's Gulf Connection Report on Kerala Migration Survey 2011. *Working Paper* No. 450, Center for Development Studies, Thiruvananthapuram.

Appendix

Table A.1 Decile wise composition of assets 1992 (in percentage)

Decile	Land	Building	Financial Assets	Bullion and ornaments	Total
1	30.91	26.53	6.25	32.87	100
2	33.50	32.34	3.72	28.52	100
3	41.27	32.87	2.66	21.70	100
4	38.21	36.91	2.44	20.68	100
5	39.38	42.37	1.70	14.66	100
6	44.67	36.35	1.21	16.22	100
7	47.64	35.84	1.60	12.68	100
8	44.78	41.10	2.30	10.21	100
9	54.84	32.53	3.22	7.02	100
10	64.88	24.70	3.69	3.20	100
SD	10.06	5.64	1.46	9.31	----

Source: Authors' calculations based on NSS AIDIS, respective rounds

Table A.2 Per capita Net and Gross Asset: Remittance Receiving and Non-receiving Households, 2013 (in dollars)

	Remittance receiving	Non-receiving
Mean per capita gross asset	7699	5814
Median per capita gross asset	3425	2663
Mean per capita net asset	7433	5436
Median per capita net asset	3287	2495

Source: Authors' calculations based on NSS AIDIS, respective rounds

Table A.3 Percentage share of different sectors in Kerala's NSDP

1	Agriculture	31.75	11.43
2	Forestry and logging	0.59	1.27
3	Fishing	1.59	1.05
4	Mining and quarrying	0.25	0.47
	Primary	**34.17**	**11.90**
5	Manufacturing	15.54	10.43
6	Electricity, gas, water supply & other utility services	1.41	0.95
7	Construction	7.64	14.66
	Secondary	**24.59**	**25.05**
8	Trade, repair, hotels and restaurants	13.84	18.82
9	Transport, storage, communication & services related to broadcasting	7.52	8.57
9.1	Railways	0.21	0.32
9.2	Transport by other means	6.23	6.77
9.3	Communication	1.08	1.48
10	Financial Services	7.01	4.81
11	Real estate and ownership of dwelling	0.07	13.58
12	Public administration	5.67	3.64
13	Other Services	7.13	12.62
	Tertiary	**41.23**	**62.05**
	Total	**100**	**100**

Source: Authors' calculation based on National Accounts Statistics, respective years.

Chapter 5

The British Labour Party and the "new economics"

Lyn Eynon

1. How did we get here?

From "New Jerusalem" to "New Labour"

Many issues facing the UK economy pre-date the financial crisis, even back to the late 19th-century transition from industrial pre-eminence towards managing global capital flows. The UK's post-war settlement has been challenged ever since the election of Margaret Thatcher in 1979. The domestic achievements of the 1945 Labour government were remarkable, including a National Health Service, enhanced social insurance, nationalisation of the Bank of England and core industries, and near-full employment after demobilisation. But despite steady improvement in living standards for a generation, UK growth was below other European countries (Crafts and Toniolo, 1995: 10), expressed, under Bretton Woods fixed rates, through balance of payments crises and sterling devaluations.

In the 1970s, the tensions within the post-war settlement exploded. Union power peaked under the Heath government of 1970-74: anti-union legislation was pushed back, shipbuilders occupied yards, and miners won historic victories. The British labour movement was strong enough to protect its gains but unable to impose an alternative vision. Labour would struggle in government from 1974-79 in a new world of floating currencies and commodity price rises, turning to the IMF for help. Union leaders cooperated but their members would not tolerate falling living standards as wages lagged inflation. Rising unemployment and a "winter of discontent" in public services opened the way for Thatcher.

Thatcher and her advisers had studied the experience of Heath and planned for confrontation (Ridley, 1977). Monetarism devastated British industry, reducing older cities to wastelands, tripling unemployment and weakening unions. Labour tore itself apart in recriminations and a split guaranteed Thatcher's re-election in 1983. The miners were defeated in an epic strike, utilities were privatised and the City of London freed from stabilising regulations to participate eagerly in the accelerating global circulation of capital. Inequality soared but fiscal and monetary loosening, lubricated by oil, allowed wages to rise, with discounted sales of council houses a seductive lure. Thatcher was re-elected in 1987 but removed in 1990 by MPs worried her opposition to further political integration would hinder open markets in Europe.

Thatcher's successor, John Major, won in 1992 but soon confronted the consequences of earlier policies. Thatcher had reluctantly conceded sterling should join the Exchange-Rate Mechanism to restrain resurgent inflation but German expenditure on reunification pushed the Deutschmark to an intolerable level for sterling, forcing withdrawal. Growth resumed but the Conservative reputation for economic competence had been destroyed and the party descended into sleaze and disputes over Europe.

New Labour from victory through crisis to defeat

Against the convictions of many members but desperate for government, the Labour Party had chosen Tony Blair, who duly delivered in 1997. Convincing marginal voters that he could soften Thatcher's legacy without threatening their personal gains, he won a landslide of seats. Blair had cajoled the party to drop its goal of "common ownership of the means of production, distribution and exchange", dating back to its 1918 constitution, although New Labour was not just Thatcherism in smarter clothes but hoped to use the prosperity of capitalism to fund a benevolent state. Gordon Brown as Chancellor set out to convince the City that Labour could be trusted. He proclaimed the Bank of England independent, granting its Monetary Policy Committee (MPC) control of interest rates. In his first budget, he declared a "golden rule" that over the economic cycle the government would borrow only to invest and meet current spending from taxation (Brown, 1997). Tight control of public finances followed, presented to Labour voters as "prudence for a purpose" (Brown, 1998) and reassuring markets. Labour easily won the 2001 election but the campaign exposed discontent over public services. In Labour's second term, Brown would use the fiscal space and credibility won through "prudence" to increase spending to the benefit of health, education and those on low incomes (Chote, et al., 2007: 12), and for a time providing macroeconomic succour after the dotcom bust. Enough was done to win again in 2005 and, with Blair damaged by Iraq, Brown became Prime Minister in June 2007.

As Chancellor, Brown had stressed stability but his hubristic claim (Brown, 1999) that "Britain will not return to the boom and bust of the past" would be shattered. Deregulating financial speculation and spurring property prices had not been prudent. London was again a serious competitor to Wall Street but exposed to global perils. As the financial crisis deepened from summer 2007, bank nationalisation became unavoidable even though anathema to the New Labour creed. In the deep 2009 recession Brown allowed the public deficit to rise and the Bank of England reduced interest rates to an unprecedented low of 0.5%. By 2010 the initial shock was passing but government debt became contentious, although Brown sought to resist spending cuts (Stratton, 2010). Defeat could not be averted and the Conservatives under David Cameron forged a coalition with the Liberal Democrats. Between its victory in 1997 and 2010 New Labour had lost 4.9 million votes (Audickas et al., 2016) and its years in office were over.

Tory austerity and Labour's response

Cameron and his Chancellor George Osborne had put deficit reduction at the centre of their manifesto, with a narrative blaming Labour spending. Now Britain would have to "live within its means" but would revive under the "long-term economic plan" (Osborne, 2016b). As most macroeconomists predicted, fiscal consolidation delayed recovery then, with Osborne easing austerity as the election approached, growth hesitantly returned. The recession had been difficult but by 2015 employment and median real wages were slowly rising, giving the Conservatives a healing narrative while still blaming Labour spending for the pain of debt.

Heavy electoral defeat came as a profound shock to Labour whose leader Ed Miliband immediately resigned. In Labour's internal election, prospects for the left looked hopeless and Jeremy Corbyn only just made it onto the ballot. Believing Labour had to rebuild trust with voters on debt, interim leader Harriett Harman provoked anger by not opposing a government proposal to cut tax credits (Wintour, 2015), introduced by Brown and providing vital income assistance to millions of working families. Of the candidates, only Corbyn voted against. In renouncing one of its own flagship policies, the leadership was confessing impotence but outside Westminster the party and its supporters would not accept this. Labour had undeniably lost but there was no endorsement of austerity. The Liberal Democrats had taken the full brunt of public anger, losing 4 million votes (Audickas et al., 2016), but the British first-past-the-post electoral system converted this into a Conservative Commons majority. Corbyn was decisively elected, but many MPs were unreconciled and the UK's Brexit vote would trigger a leadership challenge.

Corbyn's success rested on a desire for change and the confidence he inspired. He opposed austerity and inequality but what would that mean? Corbyn (2015a) accepted the current budget deficit should be closed but fairly and through growth rather than cuts. Among economists, his opposition to austerity was widely endorsed (Blanchflower et al., 2015) but other proposals were controversial (Levine et al., 2015), notably extending public ownership, tax justice and People's Quantitative Easing. At Labour's Conference, Shadow Chancellor John McDonnell (2015) criticised Osborne's Fiscal Charter legislating surpluses by 2020 but surprised by endorsing it, then reversed that prior to the Parliamentary vote, so that Labour opposed. Second term cuts threaten popular benefits and Cameron retreated on both tax credits and disability payments. Taxation is sensitive and both corporate deals and offshore accounts are unpopular. Labour has begun defining a programme, with McDonnell establishing an Economic Advisory Committee (EAC) of progressive economists[1] and opening up discussion.

---

[1] David Blanchflower, Mariana Mazzucato, Anastasia Nesvetailova, Ann Pettifor, Thomas Piketty, Joseph Stiglitz and Simon Wren-Lewis (Labour Press, 2015).

2. Fiscal and monetary policy

Crisis, recession and debt

The core Conservative narrative is that Labour caused the crisis by spending too much so that the government now has to cut back, but the accusation of profligacy is misjudged. From 1997 to 2007 the government deficit averaged just 1.3% and by 2008 the debt to GDP ratio stood at 37% compared to 42% in 1997 (Wren-Lewis, 2015b), although this excludes expensive private finance initiatives (PFI) substituting future liabilities for immediate public investment[2], a Conservative idea enthusiastically adopted by Brown. An alternative explanation of the crisis highlights the excesses of global financial institutions in private debt, bank leverage, asset inflation, scale and complexity, international flows and imbalances.[3] There was also large scale misconduct, for which UK banks and building societies have paid out £53bn in penalties since 2000 (Dunkley, 2016). The true criticism of New Labour is that it indulged these excesses. London's central role in global transactions carries high risks, with foreign assets accounting for three-quarters of UK bank losses in the crash (Broadbent, 2012). The banking crisis caused a sharp contraction in UK domestic credit to the private sector from 201% in 2009 to 134% in 2015 (World Bank, 2016a). This demand shock turned a slowdown into the Great Recession.

The impact on public finances can be grasped through a simple closed income-expenditure model, relating government deficit to private sector saving and investment: (G-T) = (S-I), with G government expenditure, T taxation, S saving, I investment. Banks' reluctance to lend as they reduced

---

[2] Owen and Brady (2010) estimated that since 1997 PFI and similar contracts worth £262bn had been signed for programmes with a capital value of £55bn. With 2008 GDP (current prices) of £1.56 trillion (ONS, 2016a), Brown could have kept close to his 40% target by borrowing but including discounted future liabilities adds several percentage points to the debt/GDP ratio.

[3] UK domestic credit to the private sector rose from 110% in 1997 to 200% GDP in 2008 (World Bank, 2016a). The median equity-to-asset ratio for major UK banks fell from just under 5% in 2000 to around 3% in 2008 (Turner, 2009: 19). House prices in England and Wales rose by 268% from Q4 1995 to Q4 2007 (Land Registry, 2016). UK securitised credit issue rose from £20bn in 2000 to £180bn in 2007 (Turner, 2009: 14). From 2000 to 2008, the UK's gross external assets rose from £2,933bn to £10,990bn and liabilities from £3,030bn to £11,074bn (ONS, 2012).

risk and rebuilt capital combined with firm and household deleveraging to raise savings and reduce investment, thereby increasing Public Sector Net Borrowing,[4] as a consequence rather than a cause of the recession, which reduced tax revenues and forced up spending. The international dimension also matters. In an open model (G-T) = (S-I) − (X-M), with X exports, M imports and (X-M) here understood as the current account surplus, including investment income and transfers. Hence a worsening current account and increasing public deficits are directly related. The UK's balance of payments deficit reached a record 5.4% GDP in 2015 (ONS, 2016e), driven not by a deteriorating trade balance but by a sharp fall in investment income (ONS, 2015a). This explains why reducing the government deficit has been arduous even though deleveraging has reversed.[5] Here too, globalised finance has played a central role but the narrative of "Labour spending" is deeply embedded in public consciousness.

Among economists, the crisis shook the complacency of rational expectations and efficient markets, but resurrected Keynesian demand management justifying emergency government expenditure was challenged by claims that fiscal contraction could be expansionary (Alesina and Ardagna, 2009). Yet under austerity the UK recovery has been weak. Total real GDP fell 6.3% from Q1 2008 to Q2 2009 with real GDP per capita only returning to its pre-crisis level by Q3 2015 (ONS, 2016a). An easing of austerity ahead of the 2015 election allowed a slow recuperation but showed that the UK has not lost its habitual imbalances, resting on private debt, consumption and house prices while goods exports are stagnant and growth is regionally skewed.[6] Osborne (2011) had promised a "march of the

---

[4] The household savings ratio rose from 5.4% in 2008 to 11.0% in 2010 (ONS, 2016a); the volume of business investment fell by 17% from 2007 to 2009 (ONS, 2016b); PSNB rose from 2.6% GDP Q1 2008 to 8.7% GDP Q1 2010 (ONS, 2016c).

[5] A fall in net FDI earnings accounted for 79% of the £66 billion decline in the current account primary income balance between 2011 and 2014 (ONS, 2015a); by Q1 2016, PSNB (excluding financial interventions) had fallen to 4.0% (ONS, 2016c) against a projection for 2015-16 of 1.1% (OBR, 2010: 77).

[6] The household savings ratio fell from 11.0% in 2010 to 6.1% in 2015 (ONS, 2016a) while monthly gross consumer credit grew by 12.7 % during 2015 (BoE, 2016: LPMB4TW). From end-2012 to end-2015, average house prices rose across England and Wales rose 22.3% (Land Registry, 2016). The value of UK exports of goods has fallen every year since 2011, although service exports rose by 19.4% (ONS, 2016e). In 2014, London accounted for 22.5% of UK Gross Value Added, up from 21.0% in 2010 (ONS, 2015b).

makers" but by Q1 2016 manufacturing output was no higher than two years earlier (ONS, 2016d) and services remain "the only headline industry in which output has exceeded pre-downturn levels" (ONS, 2016f). Business investment has returned to pre-crisis levels (ONS, 2016b) but Public Sector Net Investment (PSNI) has fallen from 3.0% Q1 2010 to 1.8% Q1 2016 (ONS, 2016c). Prospects looked uncertain even before the Brexit referendum was announced, with Osborne (2016a) himself warning of a "cocktail of threats". Austerity offered an opportunity to shrink the welfare state in the interest of private accumulation, with reduced working age benefits intensifying competition for jobs. Wren-Lewis (2015a) estimates it has cost the UK at least £100 billion, and cuts have hit hardest the disadvantaged and the disabled, with women bearing 86% of the projected burden (Women's Budget Group, 2016).

Managing fiscal balances

Public finance has never been easy ground for Labour from the split of Ramsay MacDonald's cabinet in 1931 over unemployment pay to today's narratives. For McDonnell (2016c) "sound finances are the foundations on which everything else is possible", promising an "absolute commitment to responsible financing". Is this misjudged?

Kalecki (1943) observed that by making employment dependent on confidence the doctrine of 'sound finance' gives indirect control over government policy to owners of capital, and today the financial sector wants reassurance of the state's fiscal capacity to assist again when needed (Obstfeld, 2013). Justifying austerity in his first budget, Osborne (2010) contended credibility in international markets demanded emergency measures to reduce debt, as Kalecki might have predicted. In fact, the UK had no difficulty borrowing long-term at low and stable rates and the "confidence fairy" (Krugman, 2010) would appear only fleetingly[7]. UK experience confirms that fiscal contraction in pursuit of arbitrary targets is

---

[7] End-quarter post-crisis rates on conventional gilts peaked at 3.34% end-Q4 2009 and were 1.37% end-Q1 2016, at which time the average maturity was 17.15 years (DMO, 2016). The OECD (2016c) UK Business Confidence Index rose from early 2009 but then slipped during 2011 and did not recover until 2013, wobbled through 2014 and then fell again during 2015; its consumer confidence index looks similar.

not only damaging but self-defeating. Osborne inherited public sector (excluding banks) net debt equal to 65.2% GDP in May 2010, yet it would reach 83.9% by the time he left office in June 2016 (ONS, 2016c). During a recession, high fiscal multipliers reduce output, as is now widely recognised (Blanchard and Leigh, 2013) so that debt and deficit ratios to GDP remain high while the economy spirals downwards in pursuit of a receding goal.

Challenging the obsession with deficits, Krugman (2015a) argues that "debt is money we owe ourselves", so cannot be stealing from the next generation. But debtors and creditors are different people, most obviously when foreign investors own much of a country's debt, as they do for 27% of UK gilts (DMO, 2016). Even for domestic debt, the inheritors of bonds will be a wealthy subset of the next generation, the rest of whom will be net contributors to repayment and interest, a distinction hidden in an overlapping generations model using representative agent modelling. Debt is not neutral. High dependency on capital markets exposes a country to speculation or conspiracy, either from market participants or through international institutions, and even for sterling loans under English law there could be treaty or other legal perils.[8] A Labour government serious about redistributing wealth will be treated as hostile by plutocratic interests, so averting such hazards is wise. There are good reasons to be wary of excessive debt without succumbing to exaggerated fears. Hence we need a balanced and flexible approach.

Labour promised in its 2015 manifesto to cut the deficit every year but was not believed. In rejecting Osborne's Fiscal Charter, Labour freed itself from the Conservative agenda but then needed to define its own approach. McDonnell's (2016c) Fiscal Credibility Rule would aim for balance on current spending over a target five-year period but allow borrowing for public investment, limited by an objective of lowering the debt/GDP ratio in each Parliament. This can be seen as a promise to restrain spending without starving the economy through austerity. If Labour inherits public sector net debt of 80%, then with nominal GDP growth of 5% the requirement to lower

---

[8] Elliott Management exploited Argentina's vulnerability on dollar-denominated loans but the stance of Judge Griesa in backing Elliott until Macri's election "changed everything" (The *Economist*, 2016b) is a salutary reminder that law is not always above politics. English judges are not immune.

the debt/GDP ratio would permit PSNI borrowing of up to 4%, more than double the current level, but with low NGDP growth this could become constraining.

Monetary policy has long been preferred for managing demand over fiscal policy, with its presumed deficit bias driven by the electoral cycle but the Great Recession has thrown this into question, with low interest rates and quantitative easing boosting asset prices more than stimulating the real economy. McDonnell reserves the right to suspend the targets when monetary policy becomes ineffective around the lower bound for interest rates, so that fiscal measures can also promote recovery and sustain an investment programme, avoiding the trap of rigid targets. Explicitly recognising this distinguishes McDonnell's fiscal rule from that of Gordon Brown.

Restoring growth through increased demand and productive investment would improve fiscal balances through higher tax receipts and reduced benefits but secular upward pressures on spending on health, education, pensions and social insurance require structural increases to the tax base. Reversing tax cuts on capital gains, corporation, inheritance and high incomes will help, as would a financial transaction tax, but retaining revenue lost today through avoidance, evasion and back taxes will be vital. During his campaign Corbyn (2015a) suggested this lost revenue could amount to £120 billion a year, an estimate widely criticised (The *Economist*, 2015a) for implying this sum was recoverable, but McDonnell (2016b) subsequently suggested a target of £30 billion. Radical simplification of what may now be the world's most complex tax code[9] to remove unjustifiable exemptions will be needed, plus assertive collection and international cooperation on accounting rules, multinationals and offshore havens. There are also opportunities to cancel expenditure, such as Trident, with lifetime costs estimated by the Ministry of Defence at £100bn, although the Campaign for Nuclear Disarmament thinks it could be double that (Mills, 2016).

---

[9] Tolley's 2015-16 edition of its handbooks for tax lawyers (Redston, 2015; Cordara, 2015) has 21,062 pages.

People's Quantitative Easing (PQE)?

An alternative to financing government spending through tax or bonds is to use the power of the state to create fiat money as a government with monetary sovereignty can always make any and all payments in its own currency (Mosler, 2010: 13). Exercising that power excessively would be unwise, as government expenditure through money creation adds demand without reducing the claims of the private sector either permanently through taxation or temporarily through loans. Nearing capacity, resource competition would become inflationary and crowd out private demand but when an economy is working well below capacity, with elastic supply, the effect would be felt mainly on output and employment rather than prices. As long as the UK can borrow in its own currency it need never default, unlike Eurozone countries without monetary sovereignty, so there was never any prospect of a Greek-style default (Krugman, 2015b), even if, ultimately, excessive money creation to repay debt would depreciate sterling and undermine the ability to borrow in it. If we recognise the limits, then alongside taxation and debt there could be a useful role for cautious monetary financing.

When Corbyn (2015a) suggested "quantitative easing for people instead of banks" as an option to rebalance the economy away from finance towards high-growth sustainable sectors, mandating the Bank of England to upgrade the economy, he was criticised for the inflation risk with Venezuela a favourite reference (Buttonwood, 2015). Yet the immediate risk is deflation, which Krugman (2015c) advocates fighting with money-financed budget deficits: "When you print money, don't use it to buy assets; use it to buy stuff." The need for fiscal expansion to pull economies out of stagnation (Summers, 2015) is widely recognised, and with conventional monetary policy exhausted, dropping "helicopter money" (Turner, 2015) is just one of many proposals to combat the next recession (The *Economist*, 2016a). Against this background, PQE appears less outlandish, although Labour's leadership now appears to accept the argument of Wren-Lewis (2015c) that the case for long term investment should not depend on a cyclical case for QE. In recession both should come into play.

That loans create deposits, making the money supply endogenous, is now understood by practitioners (McLeay, Radia and Thomas, 2014). Monetary expansion involves both public and private money creation, hence increasing reserves via QE while banks cut loans did not expand broad money supply. By Q1 2016, sterling reserves at the Bank of England were over seven times higher than at end 2008 but sterling liabilities to the private sector of UK monetary financial institutions (M4) had risen by just 10% (BoE 2016: LPMAUYM, LPMBL22). Policy makers assume that raising interest rates will suffice to control monetary expansion but the pre-crisis experience raises doubt. The ability of banks to attract savings then amplify those through derivatives and interbank borrowing sustained rapid increases in the supply of loans, demand for which was encouraged by rising asset prices at the cost of increasing risk.

In 2007, Northern Rock experienced the first run on a British bank since 1866 when deleveraging in credit markets exposed its reliance on institutional investors for short-term funding (Shin, 2008). The lesson here is that more direct control of private money creation will be needed, even if we do not go as far as Wolf (2014) in stopping it entirely. This could also recover for the public sector some of the seigniorage appropriated today by private finance. Osborne is rowing back on restraining finance (Binham and Arnold, 2015) but regulating and dismantling systemically dangerous institutions must be a priority to curb the threat they pose and to rein in the cost of implicit subsidies. By reducing its dependence on the City, the UK could increase the scope for funding public expenditure through judicious fiat money creation.

3. Productivity, labour market, investment and inequality

Does the UK have a productivity problem?

"Supply side economics", emphasising tax cuts and deregulation to stimulate production and claiming the resulting growth would benefit all and even raise government revenues, has been a staple of right-wing views ever since Reagan adopted it, while progressive economists have focused on demand. But this is not territory we should abandon, as McDonnell (2016c) has recognised. Stagnant investment and productivity will not be reversed by yet more neoliberal medicine. Higher productivity would allow us to produce more or better outputs from lower inputs, whether natural resources limited by the environment or labour power constrained by demographic change. Technological advance expands our options without implying unlimited growth or unrestrained consumption.

Calculating productivity is fraught with issues, particularly in finance, but measured labour productivity in the UK dipped sharply after the crash and has yet to return to steady growth. By 2014, UK GDP per hour worked (constant US dollars) was no higher than in 2007, compared with a rise of 5.6% across the G7 (OECD, 2016b). Associated with this prolonged stagnation was a fall in real wages, also unprecedented in the post-war economy. UK median real weekly earnings fell from 2008 to 2014 and by 2015 were 7.4% below their pre-crisis peak (ONS, 2015c). Many reasons have been advanced for this alleged "productivity puzzle" which needs to be considered from both supply and demand sides. Barnett et al. (2014) use a supply focused accounting framework, decomposing labour productivity growth into capital growth, technical efficiency and capacity utilisation, to argue that low productivity is not primarily cyclical because capacity tightened during the recession. Instead, they see impaired resource allocation and low investment as the main factors, with pay following productivity downwards.

Tilly (2015) reverses this, arguing that reduced demand resulting from austerity has lowered total labour income, which in the UK has been experienced as a fall in real wages, with lower rises in unemployment than many other countries. Statistically, output growing less rapidly than employment appears as falling productivity, so there is no puzzle, just the impact of a demand shock on the labour market. The employment rate does not adequately measure capacity when resources are not used to their full potential, although over time skills not updated and plant left unmodernised will constrain supply. Higher demand would put upward pressure on wages, stimulating investment and reallocation to higher quality work, as rising wages squeeze out low productivity, as occurred during the post-war boom (Armstrong, Glyn and Harrison, 1984: 174-75), but without demand pressure there is a risk to jobs from pay rises, such as the increased minimum wage announced by Osborne (2015) as cover for further benefit cuts. Austerity is the immediate barrier to growth.

The market for labour power in the 21st century

The UK labour market remains segmented by gender, ethnicity, education, age and geography, while working patterns have become much more varied, with fewer long-term full-time roles with regular shifts.[10] For some, this has opened opportunities but with the UK having weaker employment protection than any other OECD European country (OECD, 2015) income is often precarious. This trend pre-dated the crash but accelerated as employers facing uncertain demand became less willing to offer secure posts, while technology makes it easier to manage a malleable workforce. The minimum wage provides a floor but does not protect those paid per task or self-employed, nor ensure income to those without guaranteed hours. A benefits squeeze and pension worries have pushed those on the margins into taking whatever work is available and employers have been able to exploit migrant workers. These labour market features explain why real incomes stagnated while employment fell less than in earlier recessions and is now at a historic high.[11]

---

[10] The male-female pay gap for full-time employees has slowly declined by 2015 to 9.4% but 41% of women work part-time compared to 11% of men, giving a gap of 19.2% across all employees (ONS, 2016g). In Q1 2016, 75.6% of white people 16-64 were employed but only 63.6% of those from ethnic minorities (ONS, 2016i). In 2011, 85.3% of graduates 25-64 were in employment but only 48.5% of those without qualifications (ONS, 2014). For the 3 months ending January 2016, overall unemployment was 5.1% but 13.7% for those 16-24 (ONS, 2016h). For year ending September 2015, unemployment varied from 2.0% in Stratford-on-Avon to 11.0% in Middlesbrough, while gross median weekly earnings (April 2015) vary from £389 in North-east Derbyshire to £921 in the City of London (ONS, 2015c). As of Q1 2016, there are 19.6m full-time employees, 7.0m part-time employees and 4.7m self-employed (1.4m of whom are part-time), while 1.1m people have a second job (ONS, 2016h); in Q2 2016, 903,000 people were on zero-hour contracts, up 21% on the year before (ONS, 2016j).

[11] Recorded post-crisis unemployment peaked at 8.4% from August to December 2011 but had reached 11.9% in 1984 and 10.7% in 1993, while 31.4m people were employed Q1 2016 with the employment rate at a record 74.2% (ONS, 2016h). From 2005 to 2015, the proportion of people aged 70-74 in employment rose from 5.5% to 9.9% (DWP, 2015). See section 4 for migrant workers.

Government supporters claim (Nelson, 2014) that the strength of UK employment is evidence of the positive effect of labour market reform, but while variable patterns can sometimes benefit workers, insecure work and irregular income blight millions of lives. Running a high demand economy will assure confidence, while abuses, such as zero-hour contracts, should be curbed. As the population ages, pressure on pension schemes lengthens working lives, with the state pension age rising to 68 by 2048 (DWP, 2015), while radical advances in automation and artificial intelligence threaten up to 15 million UK jobs (Haldane, 2015) across a wide range of professions. Juxtaposing these prognoses of demography and technology obliges us to rethink work: a future in which half the population toils until they drop while the other half is excluded from employment would be untenable. Investment is required to equip people with digital or other skills for future work. A genuinely flexible labour market should enable much more choice over when we work and for how long, so that robots work for people rather than people working for robots' owners.

This entails breaking the tight linkage between work and income endured by everyone without adequate private capital. McDonnell (2016b) is sympathetic to the idea of a universal basic income and its viability should be investigated. Mian (2016) argues this would not optimise the welfare budget, but social insurance as of right, an aspiration of the 1945 government after the degradation of 1930s, would remove the humiliation of means-testing, with taxation retrieving income from the rich. A Job Guarantee (or employer of last resort scheme), as proposed for Australia by Mitchell (2013), is attractive at first sight but running a large scheme offering meaningful work would be daunting in its practical challenges and could veer towards workfare by making other payments harder to justify, although if investment and training restore high employment then a limited programme to smooth irregular income might be feasible. For any of this, active unions and workplace or community organisation are vital. Shrinking the reserve army of the unemployed and loosening the threat to income would shift the balance of power from capital and be resisted. A Labour government will only be able to improve working life with active engagement from workers themselves.

The British Labour Party and the "new economics"

Investment and innovation

Cuts in taxes on capital gains, inheritance and high incomes have not increased investment, which in the UK has fallen from 23.7% in 1979, when Thatcher was elected, to 17.5% in 2015 (World Bank, 2016b). With growth slowing, UK infrastructure lagging (notably in transport which the World Economic Forum (2015) rates as now 13th in the world) and the Treasury able to issue bonds at very low rates, the refusal to borrow looks perverse in the face of calls by both the IMF (2016) and the OECD (2016a) for more public investment. As regards the public balance sheet, investment adds to the asset side as well as to debt. It must be well targeted, planned and managed to contribute to long-term growth, not just provide a short-term boost to demand. With UK public investment having declined from 3.4% GDP in 2009-10 to 1.9% in 2014-15 and still falling (Rhodes, 2016), there are many opportunities in infrastructure or green energy. A forward-looking view would prioritise research and development, new technology and skills enhancement.

Stagnant productivity has encouraged a more positive view of the state as innovative through high-risk projects and market creation, as shown by Mazzucato (2013), who argues that the benefits should be socialised. There should be direct state investment, including equity stakes, but also easier access for small job-creating enterprises to funding and workspaces. Barnett et al. (2014) argue that a high survival rate of firms has hampered resource allocation to more productive enterprises but without adequate demand, finance and policy, Schumpeter's (1942) "creative destruction" leaves industrial deserts like those still visible in Britain's former mining districts. A National Investment Bank (NIB) as proposed by Corbyn (2015a), funded by long-term low interest loans, could finance infrastructure, environment, research and skills to grow the economy. McDonnell's (2016c) Fiscal Credibility Rule should allow public investment to be raised back to the level prior to the crash.

Housing is a major issue, with a significant housing gap, visible in high rents and house prices, further boosted by low interest rates. The shortage has grown since the state abandoned large-scale house building in the 1980s, with the private sector failing to fill the gap in a market where planning rules sustain existing property values, housing law provides little security to tenants and young people find it increasingly unaffordable to buy.[12] With interest rates at historic lows, an opportunity exists for a public building programme through the NIB that could be self-financing in providing homes at well below market rents or mortgage rates.

Towards a more equal society

Income inequality rose sharply during the Thatcher years, with a rise in the Gini coefficient for UK household disposable income from 27.4 in 1979 to 36.8 in 1990, since when it has fluctuated between 32 and 36 (ONS, 2016l). Data on household wealth are less reliable than on income, as tax authorities are only interested in taxable wealth such as property or legacies, which makes identifying trends contentious.[13] Inequality has risen in the UK over the past 40 years, though not to early 20th century levels (Piketty, 2013), with concentration at the very top partly offset by the spread of residential property ownership, although the rise in owner occupation rate from 23% in 1918 to 69% in 2001 has since slipped to 64% in 2011 (ONS, 2013). While variation in outcomes offers incentives, excessive inequality is economically and socially damaging (Pickett and Wilkinson, 2010), especially when derived from unequal access to opportunities, resources or inheritance. The distribution of rewards matters, not just that of chances. In modern economies, financial transactions, intellectual property and network effects create scope for large economic rents that are unacceptable whoever gains them. The labour market is central, as post-war experience shows that sustained high employment boosts wages, reducing inequality.

Progressive taxation addresses inequality as well as public budgets. The 'Panama papers' are just the latest revelation of how the elite avoids tax and

---

[12] The 1974-79 Labour government built on average 156,000 social housing units a year out of a total of 306,000; social housing then fell year after year until the Major government averaged only 36,000 units out of an annual total of 190,000, private housing barely growing; New Labour did no better and with a sharp fall in private housing since the crisis, the coalition averaged only 141,000 total units, of which 32,000 social (DCLG, 2016a). The proportion of 25-34 year olds who are owner occupiers fell from 67% in 1991 to 37% in 2015 (DCLG, 2016b).
[13] Reed (2014) argues that the critique by Giles (2104) of Piketty (2013) fails to allow for data discontinuities.

Corbyn (2016b) has demanded investigation and action against crown tax havens, such as the British Virgin Islands where half the shell companies set up by Mossack Fonseca were registered (The Economist, 2016c). Rising urban land values have amplified inequality (Stiglitz, 2015a), so Labour should restructure and increase property taxes as steps towards a land value tax. We also need to tackle inequalities in pre-tax incomes, including a true living wage plus limits on bonuses and CEO packages. Stiglitz (2015b) argues for rewriting the rules to make markets competitive, fix finance, incentivise growth, rebalance tax and transfers, boost employment, empower workers, and expand economic security and access to labour markets. Miliband (2012) had recognised this but the ugly neologism "predistribution" (Hacker, 2011) blurred the message. Inequality is a big agenda and Labour will need to prioritise issues, develop workable proposals and package them attractively.

4. Democracy and economics

Democratising the economic institutions of the state

A defining characteristic of neoliberalism has been a hollowing-out of the democratic state. We elect our representatives but critical decisions are taken behind sealed doors, nationally and international. McDonnell (2015) has called for reviews of the Treasury, HMRC (the UK's tax collection agency) and the Bank of England. The Treasury has become overwhelmingly powerful, subordinating long-term policy objectives to short-term fiscal management. The independence of the Office of Budget Responsibility would be enhanced by reporting directly to Parliament rather than through the Treasury (Treasury Committee, 2010). The Public Accounts Committee (2015) has raised concerns about HMRC performance on tax evasion, avoidance and collection.

Debate has been most intense around the Bank, with most economists wishing to preserve its perceived independence (Yates, 2015). Arguments for this vary, from a belief that professionals know best, through concerns about institutional separation, to fears monetary powers will be abused by governments, particularly left-wing ones, exploiting short-term trade-offs between growth and stability. A mandate defining an inflationary target that the MPC then manipulates interest rates or money supply to achieve has been seen as best practice, despite its failure to prevent financial implosion or to restore steady growth. The MPC's independence is real within its boundaries but is conditional, as its powers are delegated from Parliament with the Treasury able to issue directions under the reserve powers defined by section 19 of the Bank of England Act 1998 (BoE, 2015: 56). The asset purchases required for QE were authorised by Labour Chancellor Alastair Darling (2009) and subsequent extensions also required political approval. Rescinding the MPC's powers is an option but an alternative could be more frequent adjustments to the mandate, such as raising the inflation target, replacing it with an NGDP objective or targeting employment as well as inflation, with enhanced accountability reinforcing political responsibility for goals if not for operational decisions.

Ownership and management

During his election campaign, Corbyn (2015b) proposed taking rail franchises back into public ownership. This met predictable opposition from those wedded to the superiority of private markets or who recalled the long decline of earlier nationalised industries (Levin et al., 2016). The steel crisis has shown the urgency for state engagement but this should not be posed only as a solution for failing enterprises. As Mazzucato (2014) argues, policy should be directed towards critical missions in areas such as environment or health, with public investment both funding those objectives and providing a portfolio return to society, calculated across the full breadth of public equity, rather than each individual element. There is also the challenge presented by mega-corporations in sectors like pharmaceuticals or technology, often exercising near-monopoly power in their own niche. These are the commanding heights of the modern economy but policy has evolved little beyond concerns about the concentration of wealth, power or data, and a desire to encourage innovation and competition.

McDonnell (2016a) has also argued that employees should have a Right to Own within the companies they work for. This is attractive from the perspectives of both equality and democracy, although it risks leaving workers with both wages and savings dependent on a single firm. Minority ownership can create divided interests while global supply chains and casual work mean that employee equity in a privileged node, such as a technology company with few employees but many sub-contractors,[14] might not ease inequalities across such chains. Value is not always realised where it is created. Nonetheless, widening ownership is important, as are opportunities for workers to run or co-direct private or public organisations. Britain originated the cooperative movement and workers have successfully managed businesses, such as Tower Colliery (Cato, 2004). Labour also recognises the importance of small and micro businesses in a technology-enabled economy and will encourage collaboration through enterprise hubs (Pope, 2016). At stake in all of this is a radical break from the top-down model of managerial dominance in the public as well as the private sphere, encouraging instead bottom-up initiative and decisions.

National and regional policies

The UK state was long highly centralised but this has changed with devolved authorities in Scotland, Wales and Northern Ireland, and tentative moves to decentralise power in England towards some city-regions, such as Manchester. The unacceptability of concentrating decisions in Westminster must be recognised in developing and implementing economic policy, with implications for proposals such as an NIB, which should devolve financing decisions to an appropriate level. Decentralisation also raises questions for existing institutions, such as the Bank of England. During the 2014 Scottish independence referendum, the Scottish National Party, faced with the Eurozone crisis and little support for an independent currency, acknowledged that it would retain sterling (Carrell, 2014), a surrender over monetary policy that weakened its campaign.[15] If the UK holds together, devolved authorities should be represented on major UK-wide bodies, such as the MPC.

Caution is needed over financial decentralisation given large differences in economic output across regions, as poorer areas would be badly exposed

---

[14] Apple is a well-known example of a company reliant on exploitative sub-contracting (Chan, Pun and Selden, 2016) but this is widespread.
[15] The SNP is now reconsidering this stance in the light of the Brexit referendum (Gourtsoyanis, 2016).

without the redistributive effects of managing taxation and benefits at a UK level. This is not a serious issue for Scotland but would be for Wales, Northern Ireland and much of the north of England.[16] We need a balance between autonomy and solidarity that empowers local choices without reinforcing regional inequalities. But permanent dependence on geographic redistribution would be unhealthy, so we must improve productive capacity and diversity in the regions, which continue to rely on industries such as steel that suffer from global over-capacity. This will require active regional and industrial policy, with development banks supporting local businesses.

The European Union and beyond

The June referendum on whether the UK should leave the EU ('Brexit') raised major issues.[17] Attitudes to the EU in the British labour movement vary but the issue has been less divisive than for the Conservatives. Most unions now see the EU as guaranteeing basic rights for workers, pensioners and consumers, and worry about the impact of leaving on jobs dependent on exports or inward investment. Cooperation across Europe is seen as essential on matters from climate change or terrorism to corporate tax. These considerations persuaded Corbyn (2016c) and McDonnell (2016d) to back remaining in the EU despite the reservations they and many on the left still had. The EU's institutions are undemocratic and imbued with neoliberalism, mandating austerity and opposing state aid, except to financial institutions, for which from 2008 to 2014 €4,884bn assistance (including guarantees) was approved, of which €1,935bn has been used (European Commission, 2015). The EU was seen as a potential obstacle for a future left government, even though in retaining sterling the UK has preserved its monetary independence. Hence remain was seen as also requiring reform, working with other progressive parties but "Brexit" will today boost the right in British and European politics.

---

[16] In 2014, London had GVA per head of 173.3% of the UK average with Camden and the City of London at 1212.7%, while Wales had GVA per head of 71.4% of the UK average with the Isle of Anglesey just 53.5%; Scotland's GVA per head is 93.7% of the UK average (ONS, 2015b).
[17] See Afterword for further discussion of this.

Leave campaigners highlighted net migration to the UK from the EU through its free movement of people, the economic impact of which is contentious. Most studies show a small positive fiscal benefit but this result is sensitive to assumptions (Vargas-Silva, 2015) and the macro gains are not evenly distributed, while Nickell and Saleheen (2015) find a small negative correlation between the "immigrant-to-native ratio" and average wages, notably in semi/unskilled wages. Diversity brings vibrancy but population growth adds pressure to stretched services. Cuts intensify competition for jobs, housing, services and benefits, generating resentment often directed at migrants rather than at the policies that heighten contention, while EU disarray over refugees adds to a sense of chaos. The last manifesto offered by Labour (2015) included measures to control labour abuses and commitments on refugees but lacked the courage to challenge the prevailing mood. Faced with a widespread, if nuanced, wish to reduce immigration (Oxford University Migration Observatory, 2016), defining a progressive policy that could gain wide support has so far eluded us.

Migration to the UK is wider than the EU, driven by demography, economic disparities or opportunities, and conflict. ONS (2016k) estimates for 2015 net inward migration of around 170,000 EU citizens and 190,000 non-EU citizens with 40,000 net outward migration of UK citizens. Governments find resisting these pressures difficult, resorting to barbarous methods of exclusion, with barbed wire and insalubrious camps. We should learn to manage the flows of people rather than struggling to block them. That will require measures that spread the benefits, prevent wage-cutting and expand services, while addressing concerns such as integration or security. There is also a challenge for foreign and development policy to address the forces driving migration, not just through aid but more openness to trade with poor or troubled countries, while renouncing military interventions that aggravate political and civil disorder. None of this is easy but it needs serious attention. We need a better world, not higher walls.

225

5. Towards a left Government in the UK?

A coherent and credible programme?

It is alleged (The *Economist*, 2015b) that the new Labour leadership looks backward but neither 1945 nor 1997 offers adequate responses to contemporary problems, such as diverse and flexible labour markets. McDonnell's "New Economics" deliberately explores current and future issues. The main themes of Labour's approach were outlined by Corbyn, (2016a) in his response to Osborne's final Budget: failure, fairness, future. The Chancellor's failures, even against his own declared objectives, are ever more apparent; tax arrangements which only a privileged few can access and cuts to core social insurance are widely seen as unfair; young people face a precarious future. These define a direction for policy. No economic programme will ever be complete but it should indicate clear objectives, tackling major problems with feasible proposals backed by rigorous accounting. Then those must be translated into succinct and repeatable messages that both inspire activists and resonate with a wide public. How well does the emerging programme meet these tests?

Discussion is still embryonic on many topics but the approach on the priority questions of austerity and fiscal policy is now mature enough to assess. Would it work? The focus on investment, with willingness to borrow, addresses both macroeconomic demand and serious shortfalls in infrastructure, housing and environment, while emphasising technology, skills and innovation. As such, it has potential both to raise the quality of employment and to promote future growth and productivity. The challenge will be to implement it effectively, which goes beyond macroeconomic and monetary aggregates into competent planning, managing and delivery. Contention over land use could prove a bigger obstacle to house building than finance. The economic environment might well be difficult but McDonnell's Fiscal Credibility Rule provides space to act.

A radical left government in a major economy would threaten powerful interests and success will ultimately rest on how much active engagement it can win. This is the real question of confidence: can Labour define a narrative convincing enough for its own supporters to back it against the resistance of the global elite?

Campaigning for change

The success of Corbyn's leadership campaign showed that it is possible to win against the animosity of both the political establishment and media. Like Sanders in the US, he attracted many young people aware of their own diminishing life chances, looking for a new politics and organised through social media. He was also able to draw on the experience of older militants formed in the campaign against the Iraq war or earlier industrial and political struggles. But Corbyn's leadership victory does not guarantee future success against an elite determined to preserve its power and privilege. The challenge from some of his own MPs, despite his continuing popularity in the party, illustrates this.

There are serious questions of organisation and culture. Trade unions have shrunk while workplaces and localities are less cohesive, with bodies from choirs to miners' institutes having decayed in working-class districts, although determined groups can sometimes still beat the establishment. The movement that won Corbyn's election needs to be sustained, turning the surge of new party members into activists, linking with campaigns, and spreading into workplaces and communities where years of defeat and the daily grind of survival have left deep residues of apathy and distrust. That is why we are building Momentum (2016), within and beyond the Labour Party.

6. Afterword following the UK's EU referendum

Why did the UK vote to leave the EU?

No single issue explains the close referendum result of 16,141,241 (48.1%) Remain against 17,401,742 (51.9%) Leave, on a turnout 72.2% that exceeded any UK general election since 1992 (Electoral Commission, 2016). Scotland and Northern Ireland voted Remain, but Wales and every English region bar London voted Leave. Across England and Wales, dynamic urban centres and university towns voted to remain but most other districts voted to leave, unconvinced life was better in the EU. Leave leaders objected, with a xenophobic tone, to EU free movement of people, ignoring its benefits to British citizens and making much of its impact on unskilled wages in the UK, yet areas with many foreign-born residents supported the EU although those where immigration is recent wanted out (The *Economist*, 2016e). Many young people saw the EU as an opportunity, unlike most older voters, while social conservatism played a part. In sum, an intricate demographic picture.[18]

Politics also mattered. Leave campaigners were motivated, well-funded and organised. For Remain, Cameron had offered the referendum as a stunt to placate his Eurosceptic party, while the labour movement woke up late to the risk. Corbyn has been blamed (The *Economist*, 2016d) but the problems lay deeper. Cameron must take most of the blame as only 42% of Conservative supporters voted Remain compared to 63% of Labour's (Lord Ashcroft Polls, 2016) but many former Labour voters also wanted out. The fall in Labour's support during the Blair-Brown years has reduced its influence and there were Leave majorities in its traditional strongholds.

The political fallout

Cameron resigned after losing the referendum, which also destroyed the political prospects of Osborne. Having won, the leadership of the Leave campaign imploded, leaving Theresa May as the only credible candidate for Conservative party leader and hence Prime Minister. She had backed Remain with reservations, making her acceptable to both wings of her party, while her alleged competence offered respite from Cameron's recklessness. She has pledged "Brexit means Brexit" but has not yet commenced formal withdrawal, which requires triggering article 50 of the 2007 Lisbon Treaty (EU, 2008), although she is expected to do so in 2017. She has yet to define her bargaining stance but party politics make it unlikely that she will opt for full membership of the European Economic Area, with free access to EU markets but also free movement of people and a contribution to costs, but restricting free movement will have direct costs (The *Economist*, 2016f) and

---

[18] Lord Ashcroft Polls (2016) shows results from polling immediately after the vote; Wren-Lewis (2016) contains several references to initial academic studies.

come at a price in any EU deal. For the EU itself, Brexit adds to what is now acknowledged to be an "existential crisis" (Junker, 2016).

In contrast to the Conservatives' rapid resolution, the Labour Party is engaged in a bitter leadership contest. A cabal of MPs had long plotted to dislodge Corbyn and acted after the EU result. In the feverish post-referendum atmosphere, a no confidence vote was carried by the Parliamentary Labour Party (PLP) but Corbyn refused to resign, resting on his 'one member, one vote' mandate. The PLP majority decided to force a new election, while Labour's National Executive Committee agreed an incumbent leader should automatically be on the ballot (Black, 2016). The PLP settled on Owen Smith as its candidate over the more experienced Angela Eagle, encumbered by having voted for the Iraq War now widely seen as unnecessary (Chilcot, 2016). The stake this year is power, rather than specific policies. As well as most MPs, Smith has the adherence of senior full-time party officials, as well as some left-inclined advisors and journalists, while Corbyn's campaign is driven by community, campaign and workplace activists, for whom he embodies both their own engagement and a guarantee against a return to neoliberalism. Union leaders did not want this contest and most are sticking with Corbyn, who seems to be ahead, (YouGov, 2016). The result will be announced late September.

The economic impact of leaving the EU

Prior to the referendum, there was an unusual degree of agreement among economists that leaving the EU would damage the UK economy. This was backed by several weighty analyses, such as that by HM Treasury (2016a) predicting a central estimated annual loss of £4,300 per household by 2030 from a bilateral negotiated agreement replacing EU membership. The primary reasons were uncertainty, transition costs, market volatility and disruption to trade. As is usual with macroeconomic modelling, the Treasury estimates depend on the assumptions. HM Treasury argued (2016a: 137) that "Overall, with EU trade falling and with a negative impact on non-EU trade, there is a clear reduction in total UK trade under all the alternatives to EU membership." Much of the estimated loss rests on this trade reduction, but its estimated value rests on contentious assumptions, such as the EU's successful completion of trade deals with the US and others (HM Treasury,

2016a: 147), although the Transatlantic Trade and Investment Partnership (TTIP) was in difficulty even before the Brexit vote (Rankin, 2016). Nonetheless, the gravity model (HM Treasury, 2016a: 156), emphasising the importance of distance, income and culture in trade patterns, remains credible in explaining why disruption to trade with the EU will be costly for the UK. But in an atmosphere in which one of the leaders of the Leave campaign, Oxford-educated Michael Gove, could proclaim "people have had enough of experts" (Mance, 2016), the predictions of economists were widely dismissed.

The immediate economic impact of the referendum has been mixed. After the initial shock, the FTSE100 share index quickly recovered but sterling fell sharply from a rate of €1.31 and has since remained below €1.20, pushing import prices up (Douglas and Hodari, 2016). Consumption and manufacturing have so far held up, although there are signs that larger companies are holding back on recruitment and investment (Blitz, 2016). Over the short-term, much will depend on the May government. The Brexit vote has shifted the economic policy terrain, most notably by obliging the new government to defer the targets for fiscal surpluses mandated by Osborne's fiscal charter (HM Treasury, 2015) in the face of the recessionary risk predicted to follow a Brexit vote (HM Treasury, 2016b) but the exact stance will not be known until the Autumn Statement. The Bank of England has reduced its base rate to 0.25% and embarked on £70bn of further QE but some reluctance of institutions to sell long-dated gilts in the absence of re-investment opportunities (FT View, 2016) confirms that monetary policy unsupported by fiscal action is reaching its limits. In the months ahead, the uncertainty over what follows Brexit will take a bigger toll, while the trade and investment effects will work out over years.

Prospects for progressive economic policies

The Labour Party's stance on fiscal deficits was central to last year's leadership election, with Corbyn's record of opposing austerity winning him support. This year, differences on economic policy are playing less of an overt role. With no challenger to his right, Smith is playing into Corbyn's base by adopting an anti-austerity stance while claiming to be a more plausible candidate for prime minister, although many members see little reason to trust a former lobbyist for the pharmaceutical giant Pfizer. Corbyn's election last summer has shifted the policy debate, as seen by the proposal from Smith (2016a) for a £200bn "British New Deal", countered by the post-Brexit plan of McDonnell (2016e) for £500bn investment, of which £350 billion (around 2% GDP) would come from government, supported by regional banks. In other circumstances, such differences could be thrashed out but right now nobody is listening, while MPs who accept austerity are keeping silent. For Smith's champions, Corbyn's pledges cannot be delivered as he will never be elected; for Corbyn's advocates, Smith's promises can never be realised because his backers would not allow it.

Labour's EAC suspended activities after the referendum, citing unhappiness that the leadership had not campaigned more strongly to avoid a Leave result (Elson et al., 2016). Reluctant to excuse Osborne of responsibility for any recession, Corbyn had appeared to cast doubt on Treasury warnings of the costs of leaving (Stone, 2016). It is true that Labour's left found it difficult to summon enthusiasm for EU institutions but uncritical zeal would not have convinced disillusioned voters in deprived areas. Corbyn wanted to keep his distance from the detested Cameron but his nuanced "Remain and Reform" message proved no match for the punchier "Take back control" from the Leave side. He has been criticised for stating on the morning of 24 June that we will now have to invoke article 50 but has since clarified that did not mean rushing into complex negotiations (BBC, 2016).

Perhaps immediate dissolution of Parliament could have created conditions for reconsideration, but refusing to act on the pledge given by Parliament would risk turning animosity towards elites into hatred of democratic institutions. Smith has proposed a second referendum "when the terms are clear" (Asthana and Stewart, 2016) but has not explained how this could work. Following similar comments by other EU leaders, President of the European Council Donald Tusk has clearly stated that "the negotiations cannot begin until the UK activates the process for withdrawal" (European Council, 2016) and once article 50 has been invoked European Commission lawyers see that as an irrevocable legal act (Barker, 2016). The Trades Union Congress (2016) accepts the result, giving priority to protecting jobs and living standards.

Labour's leadership has been criticised by both MPs and commentators (Blanchflower, 2016) for lack of detailed policies, while Corbyn supporters view those offered by Smith (2016b) as watered-down copies with numbers added. Some of this mutual incomprehension reflects differences on policy formation: a top-down view in which proposals are developed by MPs advised by experts versus a bottom-up view emphasising engagement and debate through democratic structures. Corbyn (2015c) promised more involvement in policy, which takes time, particularly as existing party structures inhibit it. This is not about excluding MPs or rejecting expertise but demands an interactive relationship with both members and communities or workplaces. On economic policy, though not on some other areas, there are now enough elements of agreement in stated positions to make searching for consensus worthwhile, even if differences will remain. Most EAC members have declared a willingness to advise Labour in future (Elson et al., 2016) which could help.

The future for Labour

It is hard to see any resolution while both sides view this conflict as existential. For those opposed to Corbyn, without tacking to the centre Labour faces electoral annihilation, while Corbyn's supporters see instead the abyss of neoliberal self-destruction into which several European socialist parties have already fallen. The Momentum organisation is now building a Jeremy for Labour (2016) campaign. Corbyn is predicted to win but many MPs will not be reconciled, while if Smith were to win, activists would feel cheated. A party split is possible, although union backers will resist this. Many members have become weary of internal disputes and wish to return to opposing the government with some degree of unity. Like Brexit, this will play out over time, and will not be easy.

References

Alesina, A., Ardagna, S. (2009). *Large changes in fiscal policy: taxes versus spending.* Available at
http://scholar.harvard.edu/files/alesina/files/largechangesinfiscalpolicy_october_2009.pdf

Armstrong, P., Glyn, A. and Harrison, J. (1984) *Capitalism since World War II*. London: Fontana.

Asthana, A. and Stewart, H. (2016. Owen Smith to offer referendum on Brexit deal if elected Labour leader. *The Guardian*, 13/07. Available at http://www.theguardian.com/politics/2016/jul/13/owen-smith-to-offer-referendum-on-brexit-deal-if-elected-labour-leader

Audickas, L., Hawkins, O, Cracknell, R. (2016) *UK Election Statistics 1918-2016*. London: House of Commons Library. Available at http://researchbriefings.parliament.uk/ResearchBriefing/Summary/CBP-7529#fullreport

Barker, A. (2016) Article 50: The Brexit divorce paper. *Financial Times* 20/07. http://www.ft.com/cms/s/0/2f64f006-4dbd-11e6-88c5-db83e98a590a.html

Barnett, A., Batten, S., Chiu, A., Franklin, J., Sebastiá-Barriel, M. (2014) *The UK productivity puzzle*. Bank of England Quarterly Bulletin 2014 Q2. Available at http://www.bankofengland.co.uk/publications/Documents/quarterlybulletin/2014/qb14q201.pdf

BBC (2016) *Reality check: Has Corbyn changed his mind on Article 50?* Available at http://www.bbc.co.uk/news/uk-politics-uk-leaves-the-eu-36866170

Binham, C., Arnold, M. (2015) A vintage year: 12 gifts for the City in 2015. *Financial Times*, 22/12. Available at https://www.ft.com/content/f0541d44-a57c-11e5-a91e-162b86790c58

Blanchard, O., Leigh, D. (2013) *Growth forecast errors and fiscal multipliers*. IMF working paper. Available at https://www.imf.org/external/pubs/ft/wp/2013/wp1301.pdf

Blanchflower, D. (2016) I advised Corbyn's economics team to learn fast. They didn't. *The Guardian*, 02/08. Available at https://www.theguardian.com/commentisfree/2016/aug/02/i-advised-jeremy-corbyn-economics-team-learn-fast--no-credible-plan-labour-leadership

Blanchflower, D. and 41 others (2015) Letter 'Jeremy Corbyn's opposition to austerity is actually mainstream economics'. *The Guardian,* 23/08. Available at http://www.theguardian.com/politics/2015/aug/23/jeremy-corbyns-opposition-to-austerity-is-actually-mainstream-economics

Black, A. (2016) *Report of Labour's 12 July NEC meeting*. Grassroots Labour. Available at http://grassrootslabour.net/index.php?option=com_content&view=article&id=278:labours-12-july-nec-meeting&catid=36:nec-reports&Itemid=56

Blitz, J. (2016) Brexit Briefing: Whither the UK economy? *Financial Times*, 02/09. Available at https://www.ft.com/content/4cb8e54c-70fc-11e6-9ac1-1055824ca907

BoE (2015) *The Bank of England 1998, the Charters of the Bank and related documents*. London: BoE. Available at http://www.bankofengland.co.uk/about/Documents/legislation/1998act.pdf

BoE (2016) *Bank of England Statistical Interactive database*. http://www.bankofengland.co.uk/boeapps/iadb/ (Accessed on 10/09/2016)

Broadbent, B. (2012) *Deleveraging*, speech to Market News International, 15/03. Available at http://www.bankofengland.co.uk/archive/Documents/historicpubs/speeches/2012/spe ech553.pdf

Brown, G. (1997) *Financial Statement to House of Commons*, 02/07. Available at http://www.publications.parliament.uk/pa/cm199798/cmhansrd/vo970702/debtext/707 02-21.htm

Brown, G. (1998) *Financial Statement to House of Commons*, 17/03. Available at http://hansard.millbanksystems.com/commons/1998/mar/17/public-spending

Brown, G. (1999) *Pre-Budget Statement to House of Commons*, 09/11. Available at http://hansard.millbanksystems.com/commons/1999/nov/09/pre-budget-statement

Buttonwood (2015) The people's QE and central bank independence. *The Economist*, Buttonwood blog, 04/08. Available at http://www.economist.com/blogs/buttonwood/2015/08/economic-policy

Carrell, S. (2014) It's Scotland's pound and we're keeping it, says Alex Salmond. *The Guardian*, 07/08. Available at http://www.theguardian.com/politics/2014/aug/07/scotland-pound-independence-alex-salmond

Cato, M.S. (2004) *The Pit and the Pendulum: A co-operative future for work in the Welsh valleys*. Cardiff: University of Wales Press. Available at http://library.uniteddiversity.coop/Money_and_Economics/Cooperatives/The_Pit_and _the_Pendulum-A_Cooperative_Future_for_Work_in_the_Welsh_Valley.pdf

Chan, J., Pun, N., Selden, M. (2016) Dying for an iPhone: the lives of Chinese workers. *chinadialogue*, 15/04. Available at https://www.chinadialogue.net/article/show/single/en/8826-Dying-for-an-iPhone-the-lives-of-Chinese-workers

Chilcot, J. (2016) *The Report of the Iraq Enquiry*. London: House of Commons. Available at http://www.iraqinquiry.org.uk/media/246416/the-report-of-the-iraq-inquiry_executive-summary.pdf

Chote, R., Emmerson, C., Leicester, A.. Miles D. (2007). *The IFS Green Budget: January 2007*. IFS. Available at https://www.ifs.org.uk/budgets/gb2007/07chap2.pdf

234

Corbyn, J. (2015a) *The Economy in 2020*. Jeremy for Labour campaign. Available at http://www.jeremyforlabour.com/investment_growth_and_tax_justice

Corbyn, J. (2015b) *A People's Railway*. Jeremy for Labour campaign. Available at http://www.jeremyforlabour.com/jeremy_for_public_railways

Corbyn, J. (2015c) Video extract from: *Guardian Live's Labour Leadership Hustings*, 27/08. http://www.theguardian.com/politics/video/2015/aug/28/labour-membership-should-decide-policy-leader-jeremy-corbyn-video

Corbyn, J. (2016a) *Response to Budget Resolutions and Economic Situation amendment to the law*. Hansard,16/03, columns 969-974. Available at http://www.publications.parliament.uk/pa/cm201516/cmhansrd/cm160316/debtext/16 0316-0001.htm

Corbyn, J. (2016b) *Speech launching local elections campaign,* 05/04. Available at http://jeremycorbyn.org.uk/articles/jeremys-corbyns-speech-at-the-local-elections-campaign-launch/

Corbyn, J. (2016c) *Speech to Senate House,* 14/04. Available at http://press.labour.org.uk/post/142784902569/jeremy-corbyn-leader-of-the-labour-party-speech-to

Cordara, R. (2015) *Tolley's Orange Tax Handbook 2015-16*. London: Chartered Institute of Taxation.

Crafts, N. and Toniolo, G. (1995) Post-war growth: an overview. In N. Crafts and G. Toniolo (ed.), *Economic Growth in Europe since 1945*. Cambridge: CUP, 1-37.

Darling, A. (2009) *Statement on Financial Markets*. Hansard, 19/09, columns 483-486. Available at http://www.publications.parliament.uk/pa/cm200809/cmhansrd/cm090119/debtext/90 119-0004.htm

DCLG (2016a) *Live tables on house building* (table 209). Available at https://www.gov.uk/government/statistical-data-sets/live-tables-on-house-building (Accessed on 06/09/2016)

DCLG (2016b) *Statistical data set: Owner occupiers, recent first time buyers and second homes* (table FC2101). Available at https://www.gov.uk/government/statistical-data-sets/owner-occupiers-recent-first-time-buyers-and-second-homes (Accessed on 06/09/2016)

DMO (2016) *Gilt market: Data*. Available at http://www.dmo.gov.uk/index.aspx?page=Gilts/Data (Accessed on 08/09/2016)

Douglas, J., Hodari, D. (2016). UK import prices surge after Brexit vote. *Wall Street Journal*, 16/08. Available at http://www.wsj.com/articles/u-k-import-prices-surge-after-brexit-vote-1471337509

Dunkley, E. (2016) Ten biggest bank scandals have cost £53bn in fines. *Financial Times*, 11/04. Available at https://www.ft.com/content/21099006-fef9-11e5-99cb-83242733f755

DWP (2015) *Employment statistics for workers aged 50 and over, by 5-year age bands and gender.* Available at https://www.gov.uk/government/uploads/system/uploads/attachment_data/file/47382 1/employment-stats-workers-aged-50-and-over-1984-2015.pdf

Electoral Commission (2016) *EU referendum results.* Available at http://www.electoralcommission.org.uk/find-information-by-subject/elections-and-referendums/past-elections-and-referendums/eu-referendum/electorate-and-count-information

Elson, D., Mazzucato, M., Nesvetailova, A., Pettifor, A., Wren-Lewis, S. (2016) 'Statement from members of Labour's Economic Advisory Committee', 23/06. http://www.primeeconomics.org/articles/statement-from-members-of-labours-economic-advisory-commitee

EU (2008) Consolidated version of the Treaty on European Union. *Official Journal of the European Union*, C115, volume 51. Available at http://eur-lex.europa.eu/legal-content/EN/TXT/?qid=1473361316318&uri=CELEX:12008M/TXT

European Commission (2015) *State Aid Scoreboard 2015: Aid in the context of the financial and economic crisis.* Available at http://ec.europa.eu/competition/state_aid/scoreboard/financial_economic_crisis_aid_en.html

European Council (2016) Remarks by President Donald Tusk before his meeting with Latvian Prime Minister Māris Kučinskis. *New Europe*, 08/09. Available at https://www.neweurope.eu/press-release/remarks-by-president-donald-tusk-before-his-meeting-with-latvian-prime-minister-maris-kucinskis/

FT View (2016) The Bank of England sledgehammer hits limits in the gilts market. *Financial Times*, 12/08. Available at https://www.ft.com/content/add92530-5fb8-11e6-b38c-7b39cbb1138a

Giles, C. (2014) Piketty findings undercut by errors. *Financial Times,* 23/05. Available http://www.ft.com/cms/s/2/e1f343ca-e281-11e3-89fd-00144feabdc0.html#axzz3LIE84ypu

Gourtsoyanis, P. (2016) SNP explore options for a separate Scots currency. *The Scotsman*, 18/07. Available at http://www.scotsman.com/news/politics/snp-explore-options-for-a-separate-scots-currency-1-4180084

Hacker, J. (2011) *The institutional foundations of middle class democracy*, Policy Network, 06/05. Available at http://www.policy-network.net/pno_detail.aspx?ID=3998&title=The+institutional+foundations+of+middle-class+democracy

Haldane, A. (2015) *Labour's share*, speech to Trades Union Congress, 12/11. http://www.bankofengland.co.uk/publications/Documents/speeches/2015/speech864.pdf

HM Treasury (2015) *Charter for Budget Responsibility: autumn 2015 update*. http://budgetresponsibility.org.uk/docs/dlm_uploads/OBR_charter_final_web_Oct_2015.pdf

HM Treasury (2016a) *The long-term economic impact of EU membership and the alternatives*. Available at https://www.gov.uk/government/uploads/system/uploads/attachment_data/file/517415/treasury_analysis_economic_impact_of_eu_membership_web.pdf

HM Treasury (2016b) *The immediate economic impact of leaving the EU*. Available https://www.gov.uk/government/uploads/system/uploads/attachment_data/file/524967/hm_treasury_analysis_the_immediate_economic_impact_of_leaving_the_eu_web.pdf

IMF (2016) *United Kingdom 2015 Article IV consultation*, February. Available at http://www.imf.org/external/pubs/ft/scr/2016/cr1657.pdf

Jeremy for Labour (2016) *Jeremy for Labour*. Available at http://www.jeremyforlabour.com/

Junker, J.C. (2016) *State of the Union Address 2016: Towards a better Europe – one that protects, empowers and defends*. European Commission. Available at http://europa.eu/rapid/press-release_SPEECH-16-3043_en.htm

Kalecki, M. (1943) The political economy of full employment. *Political Quarterly*, 1943. Available at http://economie.politique.free.fr/liens/Kalecki_1943.pdf

Krugman, P. (2010) *Myths of austerity*. Conscience of a Liberal blog, 01/07. Available at http://www.nytimes.com/2010/07/02/opinion/02krugman.html

Krugman, P. (2015a) *Debt is money we owe to ourselves*. Conscience of a Liberal blog, 06/02. Available at http://krugman.blogs.nytimes.com/2015/02/06/debt-is-money-we-owe-to-ourselves/

Krugman, P. (2015b) The austerity delusion. *The Guardian*, 29/04. Available at http://www.theguardian.com/business/ng-interactive/2015/apr/29/the-austerity-delusion

Krugman, P. (2015c) *Japan's economy, crippled by caution*. Conscience of a Liberal blog, 11/09. Available at http://www.nytimes.com/2015/09/11/opinion/paul-krugman-japans-economy-crippled-by-caution.html

Labour Party (2015). *Britain can be better: Manifesto 2015*. Available at http://www.labour.org.uk/manifesto

Labour Press (2015) *Labour announces new Economic Advisory Committee*. Available at http://press.labour.org.uk/post/129975218774/labour-announces-new-economic-advisory-committee

Land Registry (2016) *UK House Price Index*: data downloads, April. Available at https://www.gov.uk/government/statistical-data-sets/uk-house-price-index-data-downloads-april-2016

Levine, P. and 55 others (2015) Letter 'Corbynomics has not been thought through seriously', *Financial Times,* 02/09. Available at http://www.ft.com/cms/s/0/23076458-50d2-11e5-8642-453585f2cfcd.html#axzz4J6iN0zsl

Lord Ashcroft Polls (2016) *How the United Kingdom voted on Thursday ... and why*. http://lordashcroftpolls.com/2016/06/how-the-united-kingdom-voted-and-why/

Mance, H. (2016) Britain has had enough of experts, says Gove. *Financial Times*, 03/06. Available at https://www.ft.com/content/3be49734-29cb-11e6-83e4-abc22d5d108c

Mazzucato, M. (2013) *The Entrepreneurial State*. London: Anthem

Mazzucato, M. (2014) Building the entrepreneurial state: a new framework for envisioning and evaluating mission oriented public investments. In: *Mission-Oriented Finance for Innovation Conference* 22-24/07/2014. Available at http://marianamazzucato.com/wp-content/uploads/2014/09/MOFI-2014-PB-01-Mazzucato.pdf

McDonnell, J. (2015) *Speech to Labour Party annual conference,* 28/09. Available at http://press.labour.org.uk/post/130055656854/speech-by-john-mcdonnell-to-labour-party-annual

McDonnell, J. (2016a) *Speech to the Cooperative conference,* 21/01. *Available at* http://press.labour.org.uk/post/137744360189/john-mcdonnell-speech-to-the-co-operative

McDonnell, J. (2016b) *Speech and Q&A at the London School of Economics,* 19/02/2016. Available at https://www.youtube.com/watch?v=FdwAyIyb-58

McDonnell, J. (2016c. *Speech to the RSA*, 11/03/2016. Available at http://press.labour.org.uk/post/140850181484/check-against-delivery-john-mcdonnell-mp

McDonnell, J. (2016d) *Speech at the TUC on the progressive case for the EU*, 17/05/2016. Available at http://press.labour.org.uk/post/144497277949/labours-shadow-chancellor-john-mcdonnell-mp

McDonnell, J. (2016e). *Speech at the National Glass Centre*, 18/07. Available at http://press.labour.org.uk/post/147586365119/john-mcdonnell-labours-shadow-chancellor

McLeay, M., Radia, A., Thomas, R. (2014). Money creation in the modern economy. *Bank of England Quarterly Bulletin*, 2014 Q1. Available at http://www.bankofengland.co.uk/publications/Documents/quarterlybulletin/2014/qb14q1prereleasemoneycreation.pdf

Mian, E. (2016) Don't fall for universal basic income, *Independent* 22/03. Available at don-t-fall-for-universal-basic-income-it-s-a-utopian-fiction-that-wastes-public-money-on-the-rich

Miliband, E. (2012) *Speech to the Stock Exchange*, 06/09. Available at http://www.politics.co.uk/comment-analysis/2012/09/06/ed-miliband-s-redistribution-speech-in-full

Mills, C. (2016) *Replacing the UK's 'Trident' nuclear deterrent*. London: House of Commons Library. Available at http://researchbriefings.parliament.uk/ResearchBriefing/Summary/CBP-7353

Mitchell, B. (2013) *What is a job guarantee?* Billy blog, 04/05/13. Available at http://bilbo.economicoutlook.net/blog/?p=23719

Momentum (2016) *Momentum*. Available at http://www.peoplesmomentum.com/

Mitchell, W. (2010) *Seven deadly innocent frauds of economic policy*. Valance Co. Inc. Available at http://mosiereconomics.com/wp-content/powerpoints/7DIF.pdf

Nelson, F. (2014). 'What's the secret behind our jobs miracle? Welfare reform', *The Telegraph*, 18/07/14. http://www.telegraph.co.uk/news/politics/10973875/Whats-the-secret-behind-our-jobs-miracle-Welfare-reform.html

Nickell, S., Saleheen, J. (2015) *The impact of immigration on occupational wages: evidence from Britain*. Bank of England Staff Working Paper no. 574. Available at http://www.bankofengland.co.uk/research/Documents/workingpapers/2015/swp574.pdf

Obstfeld, M. (2013) On keeping your powder dry: fiscal foundations of financial and price stability. *Monetary and Economic Studies*, vol.31, November. Available at http://www.imes.boj.or.jp/research/abstracts/english/me31-3.html

OECD (2015) *Indicators of Employment Protection*. Available at
http://www.oecd.org/employment/emp/oecdindicatorsofemploymentprotection.htm

OECD (2016a) *Interim Economic Outlook*, 18/02. Available at
https://www.oecd.org/eco/outlook/OECD-Interim-Economic-Outlook-February-2016.pdf

OECD (2016b) *OECD.Stat: Level of GDP per capita and productivity*. *Available at*
http://stats.oecd.org/Index.aspx?DataSetCode=PDB_LV (Accessed on 03/09/2016)

OECD (2016c) *OECD Data: Business Confidence Index (BCI)*. Available at
https://data.oecd.org/leadind/business-confidence-index-bci.htm   (Accessed   on
08/09/2016)

OBR (2010) *Budget forecast,* June. Available at
http://budgetresponsibility.org.uk/docs/junebudget_annexc.pdf

ONS (2012) *The UK's External Balance Sheet – The International Investment Position*. Available at
http://webarchive.nationalarchives.gov.uk/20160105160709/http://www.ons.gov.uk/o
ns/dcp171766_259471.pdf

ONS (2013) *A century of home owning and renting in England and Wales*. Available
http://webarchive.nationalarchives.gov.uk/20160105160709/http://www.ons.gov.uk/o
ns/rel/census/2011-census-analysis/a-century-of-home-ownership-and-renting-in-
england-and-wales/short-story-on-housing.html

ONS (2014) *2011 Census: Qualifications and labour market participation in England and Wales*. Available at
http://www.ons.gov.uk/employmentandlabourmarket/peopleinwork/employmentande
mployeetypes/articles/qualificationsandlabourmarketparticipationinenglandandwales/
2014-06-18

ONS (2015a) *An analysis of Foreign Direct Investment: The key driver in the recent deterioration in the UK's current account*. Available at
https://www.ons.gov.uk/economy/nationalaccounts/balanceofpayments/articles/anan
alysisofforeigndirectinvestment/2015-10-30

ONS (2015b) *Regional Gross Value Added (income approach) dataset*, released 09/11/2015. Available at
https://www.ons.gov.uk/economy/grossvalueaddedgva/datasets/regionalgrossvaluea
ddedincomeapproach

ONS (2015c) *Annual Survey of Hours and Earnings: 2015 Provisional Results*.

ONS (2016a) *United Kingdom Economic Accounts time series dataset*, released 30/06/2016. Available at
https://www.ons.gov.uk/economy/grossdomesticproductgdp/datasets/unitedkingdome conomicaccounts

ONS (2016b) *Business investment time series dataset*, released 26/08. Available at
https://www.ons.gov.uk/economy/grossdomesticproductgdp/datasets/businessinvest ment

ONS (2016c) *Public sector finances time series dataset*, released 19/08. Available at
https://www.ons.gov.uk/economy/governmentpublicsectorandtaxes/publicsectorfinan ce/timeseries/j4dd/pusf

ONS (2016d) *Index of Production time series dataset*, released 07/09. Available at
https://www.ons.gov.uk/economy/economicoutputandproductivity/output/datasets/ind exofproduction

ONS (2016e. *Summary of Balance of Payments, the Pink Book: 2016*. Available at
https://www.ons.gov.uk/economy/nationalaccounts/balanceofpayments/datasets/1su mmaryofbalanceofpaymentsthepinkbook2016

ONS (2016f) *Second estimate of GDP: Quarter 2 (Apr to June) 2016*. Available at
http://www.ons.gov.uk/economy/grossdomesticproductgdp/bulletins/secondestimateo fgdp/quarter2aprtojun2016

ONS (2016g. *What is the gender pay gap?*, 12/02/2016. Available at
http://visual.ons.gov.uk/what-is-the-gender-pay-gap/

ONS (2016h). *Labour Market Statistics time series database*, released 17/08. Available at
http://www.ons.gov.uk/employmentandlabourmarket/peopleinwork/employmentande mployeetypes/datasets/labourmarketstatistics

ONS (2016i) *Labour market status by ethnic group* (dataset A09), released 17/08.
https://www.ons.gov.uk/employmentandlabourmarket/peopleinwork/employmentande mployeetypes/datasets/labourmarketstatusbyethnicgroupa09

ONS (2016j) *Contracts that do not guarantee a minimum number of hours: September 2016*. Available at
https://www.ons.gov.uk/employmentandlabourmarket/peopleinwork/earningsandwork inghours/articles/contractsthatdonotguaranteeaminimumnumberofhours/september20 16

ONS (2016k) *Migration statistics quarterly report: August 2016*. Available at
https://www.ons.gov.uk/peoplepopulationandcommunity/populationandmigration/inter nationalmigration/bulletins/migrationstatisticsquarterlyreport/august2016

ONS (2016l) Household disposable income: financial year ending 2015. Available at http://www.ons.gov.uk/peoplepopulationandcommunity/personalandhouseholdfinanc es/incomeandwealth/bulletins/householddisposableincomeandinequality/financialyear ending2015

Osborne, G. (2010) *Financial Statement*, Hansard 22/06/2010, columns. Available at https://hansard.parliament.uk/commons/2010-06-22/debates/10062245000001/FinancialStatement

Osborne, G. (2011) *Financial Statement*, 23/03. Available at http://www.publications.parliament.uk/pa/cm201011/cmhansrd/cm110323/debtext/11 0323-0001.htm

Osborne (2015) *Financial Statement*, 08/07. Available at http://www.publications.parliament.uk/pa/cm201516/cmhansrd/cm150708/debtext/15 0708-0001.htm

Osborne, G. (2016a) *Speech to Cardiff Business Club*, 07/01. *Available at* https://www.gov.uk/government/speeches/chancellor-on-challenges-facing-uk-economy-in-2016

Osborne, G. (2016b) *Financial Statement*, 16/03. Available at https://hansard.parliament.uk/commons/2016-03-16/debates/16031632000001/FinancialStatement

Owen, J., Brady, B. (2010) 'How government squanders billions', *Independent*, 24/01/2010. Available at http://www.independent.co.uk/news/uk/politics/ios-special-investigation-how-government-squanders-billions-1877276.html

Oxford University Migration Observatory (2016) *Thinking behind the numbers: Understanding public opinion on immigration in Britain*. Available at http://www.migrationobservatory.ox.ac.uk/resources/reports/thinking-behind-the-numbers-understanding-public-opinion-on-immigration-in-britain/

Pickett, K., Wilkinson, R. (2010) *The Spirit Level: why equality is better for everyone*. London : Penguin.

Piketty, T. (2013) *Le capital au XXIe siècle*, Paris : Seuil.

Pope, C. (2016) *McDonnell aims to create 20,000 entrepreneurs a year*. Labour List, 08/04/2016. Available at http://labourlist.org/2016/04/mcdonnell-looks-to-create-20000-entrepreneurs-a-year/

Public Accounts Committee (2015) *HMRC still failing taxpayers*. Available at http://www.parliament.uk/business/committees/committees-a-z/commons-select/public-accounts-committee/news-parliament-2015/hmrc-performance-report-published-15-16/

Rankin, J. (2016) Doubts rise over TTIP as France threatens to block EU-US deal. *The Guardian*, 03/05. Available at https://www.theguardian.com/business/2016/may/03/doubts-rise-over-ttip-as-france-threatens-to-block-eu-us-deal

Redston, A. (2015) *Tolley's Yellow Tax Handbook 2015-16*. London: Chartered Institute of Taxation.

Reed, H. (2014) Piketty, Chris Giles and wealth inequality: it's all about the discontinuities, *The Guardian,* Datablog, 29/05/2014. Available at http://www.theguardian.com/news/datablog/2014/may/29/piketty-chris-giles-and-wealth-inequality-its-all-about-the-discontinuities

Rhodes, C. (2016) *Infrastructure Policy*. London: House of Commons Library. Available at http://www.parliament.uk/briefing-papers/sn06594.pdf

Ridley, N. (1977) *Nationalised Industries Policy Group Report*. London: Conservative Research Department. Available at http://fc95d419f4478b3b6e5f-3f71d0fe2b653c4f00f32175760e96e7.r87.cf1.rackcdn.com/FABEA1F4BFA64CB398 DFA20D8B8B6C98.pdf

Schumpeter, J.A. (1942) *Capitalism, Socialism and Democracy* (2010 edition). Abingdon: Routledge.

Shin, H.S. (2008) *Reflections on Modern Bank Runs: A case study of Northern Rock*. Princeton. Available at https://www.princeton.edu/~hsshin/www/nr.pdf

Smith, O. (2016a) *Speech at Knowledge Transfer Centre Advanced Manufacturing Park,* 17/07. Available at http://labourlist.org/2016/07/the-kind-of-revolution-ill-deliver-owen-smiths-speech-on-industry/

Smith, O. (2016b) *20 policies for our country*. Available at http://www.owen2016.com/20policies

Stiglitz, J. (2015a) The origins of inequality, and policies to contain it. *National Tax Journal*, June, 68 (2), 425–448. Available at http://www8.gsb.columbia.edu/faculty/jstiglitz/sites/jstiglitz/files/2015%20Origins%20o f%20Inequality.pdf

Stiglitz, J. (2015b) *Rewriting the Rules of the American Economy*. New York: Norton.

Stone, J. (2016) Jeremy Corbyn rubbishes George Osborne's claim that Brexit would cause recession. *The Independent*, 02/06/2016. Available at http://www.independent.co.uk/news/uk/politics/jeremy-corbyn-rubbishes-george-osbornes-claim-that-brexit-would-cause-recession-a7061061.html

Stratton, A. (2010) Gordon Brown insists big spending cuts are not inevitable. *The Guardian*, 03/01. Available at http://www.theguardian.com/politics/2010/jan/03/gordon-brown-big-spending-cuts

Summers, L. (2015) Global economy: the case for expansion. *Financial Times*, 07/10/2015. Available at http://www.ft.com/cms/s/0/1e912316-6b88-11e5-8171-ba1968cf791a.html#axzz45aNorslu

The Economist (2015a) Jeremy Corbyn's economic policy: too good to be true. 29/08. Available at http://www.economist.com/news/britain/21662588-what-do-economists-really-think-corbynomics-too-good-be-true

The Economist (2015b). Britain's Labour Party: Backwards, comrades!,19/09. Available at http://www.economist.com/news/leaders/21665024-jeremy-corbyn-leading-britains-left-political-timewarp-some-old-ideological-battles

The Economist (2016a) Fighting the next recession: Unfamiliar ways forward, 20/02. http://www.economist.com/news/briefing/21693205-policymakers-rich-economies-need-consider-some-radical-approaches-tackling-next

The Economist (2016b) Argentina's debt: At last, 05/03. Available at http://www.economist.com/news/americas/21693786-agreement-victory-countrys-new-president-argentina-reaches-deal-its

The Economist (2016c) After the Panama papers: Who next? *The Economist*, 16/04. Available at http://www.economist.com/news/finance-and-economics/21696998-mossack-fonseca-and-its-homeland-are-not-alone-facing-closer-scrutiny-who-next

The Economist (2016d) The Labour Party and Brexit: The culpability of Jeremy Corbyn, 24/06/2016. Available at http://www.economist.com/news/britain/21701333-culpability-jeremy-corbyn

The Economist (2016e) The immigration paradox: Explaining the Brexit vote, 16/07. Available at http://www.economist.com/news/britain/21702228-areas-lots-migrants-voted-mainly-remain-or-did-they-explaining-brexit-vote

The Economist (2016f) Brexit and immigration: Raising the drawbridge, 27/08. Available at http://www.economist.com/news/britain/21705870-hopes-cost-free-cut-european-union-migration-are-illusory-raising-drawbridge

Tilly, G. (2015) *Productivity: no puzzle about it*. London: TUC. Available at https://www.tuc.org.uk/sites/default/files/productivitypuzzle.pdf

Trades Union Congress (2016) *Working people must not pay the price of Brexit*. TUC. Available at https://www.tuc.org.uk/workingpeoplemustnotpaytheprice

Treasury Committee (2010) *Treasury Committee sets out requirements for independent OBR*. 21/09. Available at http://www.parliament.uk/business/committees/committees-a-z/commons-select/treasury-committee/news/treasury-committee-sets-out-requirements-for-independent-obr/

Turner, A. (2009) *The Turner Review: A regulatory response to the global banking crisis*. London: Financial Services Authority. Available at http://www.fsa.gov.uk/pubs/other/turner_review.pdf

Turner, A. (2015) The case for monetary finance - an essentially political issue. *16th Jacques Polack Annual Research Conference*, 5-6/11/2016. Available at https://www.imf.org/external/np/res/seminars/2015/arc/pdf/adair.pdf

Vargas-Silva, C. (2015) *The fiscal impact of immigration in the UK*. Oxford: Oxford University. Available at http://www.migrationobservatory.ox.ac.uk/resources/briefings/election-2015-briefing-fiscal-impacts-of-migration-to-the-uk/

Wintour, P. (2015) Anger after Harriet Harman says Labour will not vote against welfare bill. *The Guardian*, 12/07. Available at http://www.theguardian.com/politics/2015/jul/12/harman-labour-not-vote-against-welfare-bill-limit-child-tax-credits

Wolf, M. (2014) Strip private banks of their power to create money. *Financial Times* 24/04. Available at http://www.ft.com/cms/s/0/7f000b18-ca44-11e3-bb92-00144feabdc0.html#axzz46gMhrxxb

Women's Budget Group (2016). *The impact on women of the 2016 Budget*. http://wbg.org.uk/wp-content/uploads/2016/03/WBG_2016Budget_Response_PDF.pdf

World Bank (2016a) *Dataset: Domestic credit to private sector*. Available at http://data.worldbank.org/indicator/FS.AST.PRVT.GD.ZS?locations=GB (Accessed on 03/09/2016)

World Bank (2016b) *National accounts data: Gross capital formation (% of GDP)*. Available at http://data.worldbank.org/indicator/NE.GDI.TOTL.ZS (Accessed on 14/09/2016)

World Economic Forum (2015) *The Global Competitiveness Report 2015-2016*. Available at http://reports.weforum.org/global-competitiveness-report-2015-2016/

Wren-Lewis, S. (2015a) *The austerity con*, London Review of Books, vol.37 no.4, 19/02. Available at http://www.lrb.co.uk/v37/n04/simon-wren-lewis/the-austerity-con

Wren-Lewis, S. (2015b) *Mediamacro myths: summing up*. MainlyMacro blog, 29/04. Available at http://mainlymacro.blogspot.co.uk/2015/04/mediamacro-myths-summing-up.html

Wren-Lewis, S. (2015c) *People's QE and Corbyn's QE*. MainlyMacro blog, 16/08. Available at http://mainlymacro.blogspot.co.uk/2015/08/peoples-qe-and-corbyns-qe.html

Wren-Lewis, S. (2016) *A divided nation*. MainlyMacro blog, 08/08. Available at https://mainlymacro.blogspot.co.uk/2016/08/a-divided-nation.html

Yates, T. (2015) Corbyn's QE for the People jeopardises the Bank of England's independence. *The Guardian*, Economics blog, 22/09. Available at https://www.theguardian.com/business/economics-blog/2015/sep/22/jeremy-corbyn-qe-for-the-people-jeopardises-bank-of-england-independence

YouGov (2016). *Labour leadership election: Corbyn leads Smith by 24 points*. Available at https://yougov.co.uk/news/2016/08/30/labour-leadership-election-corbyn-leads-smith-24/

Acronyms

BoE: Bank of England
DCLG: UK Department of Communities and Local Government
DMO: UK Treasury Debt Management Office
DWP: UK Department for Work and Pensions
EU: European Union
HMRC: Her Majesty's Revenue and Customs
IMF: International Monetary Fund
OBR: UK Office of Budget Responsibility
OECD: Organisation of Economic Cooperation and Development
ONS: UK Office of National Statistics

Part IV

Economics, justice and democracy

Chapter 6

Employment in a just economy

John Komlos

Introduction

The natural rate of unemployment is a concept minted by Milton Friedman to indicate the "level of unemployment which has the property that it is consistent with equilibrium in the structure of real wage rates" (Friedman, 1968: 8).[1] Thus, the natural rate is the minimum level of unemployment attainable without an accelerating rate of inflation (Friedman, 1976: 458). Its level depends on the characteristics of the labor market and is a function of such factors as "market imperfections, stochastic variability in demands and supplies, the cost of gathering information about job vacancies and labor availabilities, [and] the costs of mobility..." (Pries, 2008). Theoretically, a lower rate of unemployment would be possible temporarily, but it could not be sustained unless at the cost of increasing the rate of inflation, and in the longer run unemployment would return to its "natural" level at a higher inflation rate. In short, it would be futile to use monetary or fiscal policy to try to force the unemployment rate below the natural rate. It would only lead to inflation.

1. The typical rate of unemployment

Although the concept may well be valid as stated above, the goal of this chapter is to argue that the term is nonetheless quite misleading. To be sure,

---

[1] "The 'natural rate of unemployment,'... is the level that would be ground out by the Walrasian system of general equilibrium equations, provided there is imbedded in them the actual structural characteristics of the labor and commodity markets, including market imperfections, stochastic variability in demands and supplies, the cost of gathering information about job vacancies and labor availabilities, the costs of mobility, and so on" (Friedman, 1968: 8).

Friedman had the right to name the concept as he pleased; however, contrary to Shakespeare's belief that "a rose by any other name would smell as sweet," in this particular case we think that another name would have been preferable. The use of the word "natural" seems quite disingenuous, because unemployment does not exist normally in nature. Rather, unemployment depends crucially on how the labor market is constituted. In fact, some economists of the 18th century did not even introduce the concept of unemployment into their theories (Sonnenfels, 1777). Hence, the reference to "nature" is actually a misnomer and is merely a subtle rationalization of the inability of the labor market to provide sufficient number of jobs for all in the economy. It would have been more appropriate to call it a "tolerable" rate, the "expected" rate, or even the "typical" rate.

Moreover, the concept conveys the impression that the labor market imperfections that give rise to the level of underemployment deemed natural are etched in stone; it thereby reinforces the impression that the level of unemployment associated with the "natural rate" is actually inevitable and should be considered normal, as it is inherent to the actual functioning of the economy. It is an equilibrium value that we have to tolerate since it would be futile to try to do anything about it. It is just the way the economy works so we have to accommodate ourselves to it. According to the Federal Reserve it has a range between 5.0% and 6.3%. It is increased slightly when unemployment is high and decreased when unemployment is low (Federal Reserve Bank of St. Louis, 2014).

The extent to which the concept is misleading can be illustrated by the tendency of many economists (including Ben Bernanke) to go a step further and often refer to the "natural rate" as "full employment".[2] The media then takes it over and announces outright in a twist of newspeak that 5% unemployment is "traditional full employment" (Washington Post, 2014). That is invidious, because it encourages policy makers to be complacent about the plight of a substantial segment of the labor force and of course, the confusion among the public is complete. Even at 5% unemployment and an equal amount of underemployment, the cavalier acceptance of the natural

---

[2] "Ben Bernanke Was Wrong", YouTube video, posted by Marcus C. Macellus, July 22, 2009. https://www.youtube.com/watch?v=9QpD64GUoXw . Accessed August 30, 2014.

rate leads us to do nothing about some 15 million people who fall into those categories and are barely scraping by while the economy is supposedly at "full employment". That is precisely why Nobel Laureate William Vickrey referred to the natural rate of unemployment as "one of the most vicious euphemisms ever coined" (1992: 341).

2. Full employment

It should be clear that the standard policy instruments have a limited ability to reduce unemployment. However, we should think creatively about new labor market institutions that would be effective in reducing unemployment to its lowest ever level of 1.2% which was obtained in 1944, even though the labor force expanded by 10% during the war[3] (Carter et al., 2006). Presumably, that level of unemployment was not related to insufficient demand in the labor market but rather to the physical or mental health of those few remaining unemployed. Of course, that was a time of war but the experience does demonstrate clearly the capacity of the economy to create job opportunities and bring unemployment down to negligible levels depending on aggregate demand. All we have to do is to increase effective demand by declaring a war, not in the conventional sense, of course, and not as Paul Krugman suggested – tongue in cheek – by declaring an impending alien invasion (Krugman, 2011), but by declaring other kinds of "wars": on inferior school systems, on slums, on decaying infrastructure, on pollution, on global warming, on poverty, or on energy dependence. There is no shortage of such wars given the backlog of desperately needed investments in the economy. These projects could create enough jobs to create full employment for many years to come (Brenner and Brenner-Golomb 2000; Vickrey 1992; Warner, Forstater, and Rosen, 2000).

3. Binary labor market

The main problem we need to focus on is that the opportunity to work – like wealth and income – is extremely unevenly distributed across the labor

---

[3] Unemployment was also as low in 1918.

force. The problem lies in the way the labor market is organized: the custom is that adjustments in the fluctuations in demand for labor generally occur by reducing the number employed so that their labor time falls abruptly from 40 hours to zero. We might call this system a binary labor market: one is either allowed to work 40 hours or one is not allowed to work at all. Would anyone "behind a veil of ignorance" design such a rigid system from scratch, a system with so much uncertainty and volatility – with working times ranging from 0 to 70 hours per week even in normal times (Rawls, 1971)? If we were to design the framework without knowing if we would end up among the ranks of the overworked or those of the underemployed, surely, risk-averse designers of a labor market would be too apprehensive about ending up among the underemployed to design the labor market as it functions today (Rawls, 1971). It would be much more palatable to have the adjustment occur in the number of hours worked so that instead of dismissing workers, the available work would be divided among those wanting to work. Hence, an institution that distributes work more evenly would be a reasonable solution to this quandary.[4]

4. Institutional change in the labor market

Thus, our aim should be to restructure the labor market in such a way that it would generate full employment. Given that the amount of aggregate demand in the economy at any one moment is a given (Y), the amount of work available (L) derived from that is also a given constant. The capital stock is fixed in the short run (K). Hence, the demand for labor can be approximated as:

$$[L=(\frac{Y}{aK^\beta})^{\frac{1}{1-\beta}}]$$

---

[4] Some tentative steps in this direction were taken in the 2012 "Job Creation Act". Such a program works in Germany where total employment has not decreased at all during the Meltdown (Krugman, 2012). The reduction of the workweek in France from 39 to 35 hrs in large firms in the year 2000 is estimated to have reduced unemployment rate by 1.6% by 2002 (Du, Yin and Zhang, 2013).

and if it falls below full employment (defined here as L < 1.2%) we should reconstitute the institutions of the labor market in such a way as to bring unemployment – including underemployment (U6) down to 1.2%.

Consider that in the Spring of 2012 the average full-time employee worked 41.9 hours per week and the average part-time employee 20.6 hours per week. The total number of hours worked by full time workers (114.5 million people) and those part-time workers who wanted to work full time (7.9 million people) totaled some 5 billion hours per week.[5] Dividing the 5 billion hours of work demanded by 135.9 million supplied (the number of people who work or who would like to work full time) one obtains that the full-employment average number of hours worked would have been about 36.5 per week.[6] Thus, instead of accepting un- and underemployment, one could reduce the number of hours worked for everyone by roughly an hour a day from 8 to 7 hours similarly to what happened when the 10 hour day was reduced to 8 hours. Such a work-sharing system would be a more equitable shock absorber of a decline in the demand for labor than the current system (Baker, 2011).

Other arrangements that would have similar effects include profit sharing wages in which case wages would increase in good times and decrease in recessions so that workers would not have to be fired, keeping the share of total wages in revenue unchanged (Weitzman, 1984). Encouraging cooperatives would also be useful inasmuch as such firms are more likely to adjust pay to fluctuations in demand rather than the number employed (Craig and Pencavel, 1992; Pencavel, 2002; Rosen, Klein and Young 1986). We should also turn to the only other sufficiently powerful institution that has the ability to provide work: the government (Colander, 1981: 204-208). A government agency could become the employer of last resort similar to the government's role as lender of last resort as provider of a backstop to the financial system (Wray, 1997; Colander, 2009: 747ff). The new institution – comparable to the Federal Reserve's role in finance –

---

[5] There are an additional 0.5 billion hours worked per week by part time workers who do not want to work full time and multiple job holders combined. They are not included in this exercise, as they would not have to be provided a full time job.
[6] Full employment = full time workers + unemployed + part time who want to work full time + discouraged workers.

could provide similar stability to the labor market.[7] It would contribute to an inclusive economy in which no one is deprived of the opportunity to work.

Possibly, the earnings of those previously employed would be reduced as well but the government could offset part of their losses through a subsidy (instead of unemployment payments), and everyone would have more leisure time to enjoy. Such a system would increase the quality of life, because it would reduce the psychological burden of unemployment, increase leisure time, and reduce envy by reducing conspicuous consumption. In addition, it would be a much fairer method of distributing the pain of a decline in the demand for labor than the prevailing binary system.

Instead of thinking of a certain amount of underemployment as natural, we should acknowledge that there is a natural right to life. Insofar as exclusion from work threatens one's very existence (except for the few who are independently wealthy) and given that most of us need to work in order to survive, the right to life implies that we need to be guaranteed the right to work. After all, the UN's Universal Declaration of Human Rights states that, "Everyone has the right to work... and to protection against unemployment" (UN, 1948). If the labor market as currently constituted is unable to provide work for everyone then we need to create new institutions that will.

Conclusion

One should introduce different shock absorbers into the labor market instead of the crude binary system we have today. It would be much more reasonable to distribute the burden of shortfall of available work more equitably than concentrating it among 12% of the workforce as the labor market does today. If one were designing a labor market from scratch, one would surely design one that lowered the uncertainty associated with being underemployed and shared the pain rather than concentrating it. Working

---

[7] Moreover, in the age of the information technology (IT) revolution it ought to be possible to match vacancies to willing workers instantaneously, thereby eliminating frictional unemployment. The government could subsidize the cost of relocation and retraining. It is not the case that we have to accept any unemployment as natural.

less would also be progressive. Progress ought not to be measured only by the amount of income generated but the amount of labor time needed to earn that income should also be considered.

A fairer and more utility generating distribution of work would be important not only to provide the means to making a living but also because underemployment has adverse side effects. It has a destabilizing effect on society both politically and socially. The underemployed generate negative externalities such as an increase in criminality and an increase in stress and anxiety about losing one's job. Work is important also from a psychological perspective: unemployment is degrading and makes one feel unwanted. The unemployed do not consider themselves as useful members of the society and suffer from diminished self-esteem. Their skill depreciates during extended spells of unemployment so that it becomes more difficult for them to find a job. In other words, underemployment increases social misery. For instance, the underemployed are twice as likely to be sad or depressed than the employed and 50% more likely to be angry (Marlar, 2010). They are also more likely to be struggling financially (54%) in contrast to 38% of the employed (Manchin, 2012).

To liberate ourselves from the commitment to the concept of the natural rate of unemployment is particularly important in light of the "jobless recovery" in wake of the Great Recession. Given the strains of globalization and technological change that diminished considerably the demand for unskilled labor in the developed world, full employment will otherwise continue to elude us forever (Brynjolfsson and McAfee, 2012). Currently the rate of underemployment at 12% amounts to nearly 19 million workers and if each has just one dependent then we have some 38 million people being directly affected by the scarcity of jobs (Bureau of Labor Statistics, 2014). That is hardly a negligible matter especially since endemic under-employment is likely to be with us for the foreseeable future unless we begin to think creatively about alternative approaches to providing jobs for everyone (Summers, 2014).[8] Thus, the concept of the natural rate of unemployment "is an idea that is past its sell-by-date" (Farmer, 2013: 12). We ought to think seriously about restructuring the labor market to meet the

---

[8] As Farmer suggests, "High involuntary unemployment can persist as an equilibrium of a market economy" (Farmer, 2013: 12).

needs of the 21st century economy and not rely on the current system to allocate work equitably.

References

Baker, Dean (2011) *Work Sharing: The Quick Route Back to Full Employment* (Washington, D.C.: Center for Economic and Policy Research). Available at http://www.cepr.net/documents/publications/work-sharing-2011-06.pdf (Accessed on 21 May 2012)

Brenner, Yehojachin Simon, Brenner-Golomb, Nancy (2000) *A Theory of Full Employment*, 2nd ed, New Brunswick, NJ: Transaction Publishers.

Brynjolfsson, Erik, McAfee, Andrew (2012) *Race Against the Machine: How the Digital Revolution is Accelerating Innovation, Driving Productivity, and Irreversibly Transforming Employment and the Economy,* Digital Frontier Press.

Bureau of Labor Statistics. *Alternative measures of labor underutilization.* Table A-15. Available at http://www.bls.gov/news.release/empsit.t15.htm (Accessed on 16 June 2014)

Carter, Susan B., Gartner, Scott Sigmund, Haines, Michael, Olmstead, R. , Sutch, Alan. L., Gavin Wright, Richard (2006) *Historical Statistics of the United States.* Millennial Edition online. Cambridge: Cambridge University Press, Table Ba470-477 – Labor force, employment, and unemployment: 1890–1990.

Colander, David (1981) A Guaranteed Jobs Proposal, in David Colander (ed.), *Solutions to Unemployment.* New York: Harcourt Brace Jovanovich, Inc.

Colander, David, (2009) *Economics.* New York: McGraw-Hill.

Craig, Ben, Pencavel, John (1992) The Behavior of Worker Cooperatives: The Plywood Companies of the Pacific Northwest. *American Economic Review,* 82 (5), pp. 1083-1105.

Du, Zaichao, Yin, Hua, Zhang, Lin (2013) The macroeconomic effects of the 35-h workweek regulation in France. *B.E. Journal of Macroeconomics* 13 (1), pp. 881-901.

Farmer, Roger E.A. (2013) The Natural Rate Hypothesis: An idea past its sell-by-date. *NBER Working Paper* no 19267.

Federal Reserve Bank of St. Louis. *Economic Research.* Available at http://research.stlouisfed.org/fred2/series/NROU (Acessed on 16 June 16 2014)

Friedman, Milton (1968) The role of monetary policy. *American Economic Review* 58, pp. 1–17.

Friedman, Milton (1977) Nobel Lecture: Inflation and Unemployment. *Journal of Political Economy,* 85 (3), pp. 451-472.

Krugman, Paul (2010) Kurzarbeit. *The New York Times,* September 2. Available at http://krugman.blogs.nytimes.com/2010/09/02/kurzarbeit/ (Accessed 20 May 2014).

Krugman, Paul (2011) Coalmines and Aliens. *The New York Times,* August 24. Available at http://krugman.blogs.nytimes.com/2011/08/24/coalmines-and-aliens/ (Accessed 16 June 2014)

Manchin, Anna (2012) Depression Hits Jobless in UK, U.S. More than in Germany. *Gallup,* November 2. Available at http://www.gallup.com/poll/158879/depression-hits-jobless-germany.aspx (Accessed 21 July 2014)

Marlar, Jenny (2010) The Emotional Cost of Underemployment. *Gallup,* March 9. http://www.gallup.com/poll/126518/Emotional-Cost.-Underemployment.aspx (Accessed 6 May 2014)

Pencavel, John (2002) *Worker Participation. Lessons from the Worker Co-ops of the Pacific Northwest.* New York: Russell Sage Foundation.

Pries, Michael J. (2008) Natural rate of unemployment. *The New Palgrave Dictionary of Economics.* Steven N. Durlauf and Lawrence E. Blume (eds.). Palgrave Macmillan. Second Edition. On line. Available at http://www.dictionaryofeconomics.com/article?id=pde2008_N000024 (Accessed 12 June 2014)

Rawls, John (1971) *A Theory of Justice.* Cambridge, MA: Harvard University Press.

Rosen, Corey M., Klein, Katherine J., Young, Karen M. (1986) *Employee Ownership in America. The Equity Solution.* Lexington, MA: Lexington Books.

Sonnenfels, Josef von (1777) *Grundsätze der Polizey, Handlung und Finanz,* Part 1, Vienna.

Summers, Larry (2014) *Secular stagnation? The Future Challenge for Economic Policy.* Available at http://ineteconomics.org/institute-blog/secular-stagnation-future-challenge-economic-policy (Accessed on 11 September 2014)

United Nations (1948) *The Universal Declaration of Human Rights.* Available at http://www.un.org/en/documents/udhr/index.shtml (Accessed on 13 June 2014)

Vickrey, William (1992) Chock-Full Employment without Increased Inflation. *American Economic Review.* 82 (2), pp. 341-45.

Warner, Aaron W., Forstater, Mathew W., and Rosen, Sumner M. (2000) *Commitment to Full Employment. The Economics and Social Policy of William S. Vickrey* New York: M.E. Sharpe.

Washington Post (2014) *A brief history of U.S. unemployment*. Available at http://www.washingtonpost.com/wp-srv/special/business/us-unemployment-rate-history/ (Accessed on 13 June 13 2014)

Weitzman, Martin (1984) *The Share Economy*. Cambridge: Harvard University Press.

Wray, L. Randall (1997) Government as Employer of Last Resort: Full Employment Without Inflation. *Levy Economics Institute Working Pape*r No. 213.

Chapter 7

Monetary policy, unemployment, inflation and wealth concentration – the US case study

Gerson P. Lima

> The present treatise is an attempt to present a modern version of old doctrines with the aid of the new work, and with reference to the new problems, of our own age (Marshall, 1890, Preface to the First Edition).

Introduction

This chapter is an attempt to present a modern version of an old theory, with the aid of an experiment, aiming to suggest a starting point to the development of a real world economic theory reliable enough to replace the contemporaneous monetarist mainstream doctrine and Bend the Arc of Global Capital Toward Justice.

In all theoretical approaches the economy is moved partially by credit and partially by cost-free money that people get from different sources to spend and satisfy their needs, thus making money to flow around. Money circulates because people, government and companies use it to buy what they need; simple money transfer implies no production and thus does not touch the economy. It follows that money creation is crucial in the study of economics; but, despite the strategic role of money the present mainstream economics blurred its concept to the point that all people and some economists do not know all the means used to create money. "The study of money, above all other fields in economics, is the one in which complexity is used to disguise truth or to evade truth, not to reveal it" (Galbraith, 1975: 5).

Such a disguising attitude may be a matter of politics, for it is up to the few politically empowered individuals the legal right to print money and whoever has the power to print money does it for own sake. The political power in modern democratic countries is, officially, established by their constitutions, supposedly following the Lincoln´s statement "of the people by the people for the people". So, the democratic congress that represents the people should be the monopolist of money emission and should do it only for the sake of the people. Actually, from the standpoint of law and economics a democratic government can print money (Huber and Robertson, 2001; Ryan-Collins, 2015; Werner, 2011; 2012; Blyth and Lonergan, 2014). However, the exclusive power of printing money has been "spontaneously" transferred by some Congresses to some financial capitalists, shareholders of private central bank´s, be it directly (EU, for instance) or "disguisedly" (USA, for instance[1]). The transfer of the power of money emission to the shareholders of private or "privatised" central banks, implies that these shareholders were also given a large share of the political power and the power of commanding the economic policy (Polleit, 2013; Hager, 2013; Page et al., 2013; Hudson, 2015) for their own sake. The power of printing money to himself and deny such power to the people means that such countries and their economic policies are no longer democratic and income and wealth distribution are concentrated. The main goal of this essay is to demonstrate the consequences of the monetary policy on the economy, thus producing such concentration.

Blurring money emission may, not incidentally, serve to publicly disguise the fact that the mainstream economic policy has been marketed by those few to whom it was given the power to print money for their own sake and thus have no reason to adopt an economic policy democratically planned and executed. Consequently, the financial capitalists' interests dominate the economic policy while the real side of the economy just drags behind people´s needs evolution. In contrast to sciences that deal with people, mainstream economics is not concerned with men, but only with money, or

---

[1] The history of the privatisation of the American central bank is well known; an outstanding reference is Brown (2010). Daniel Benham simulates an amazing phone conversation to the FED and gives legal information demonstrating that the FED legal support is questionable (Benham, 2002). The site http://publiccentralbank.com provides huge information on the matter.

perhaps only with men that have huge amounts of money. Therefore, elite's income grows faster than people's income thus causing an ever-lasting income and wealth concentration process.

This chapter assumes that, given its actual ends and the need of being disguised, the contemporaneous monetarist mainstream economics is not qualified to explain what is going on, to tame financial markets, to avoid crises and to provide a concrete solution to the poor and deteriorating situation of the largest portion of the world population. Many people are asking for and expecting a new economics, a real world economic science. These are the reasons for this essay to propose a new approach to economics following one statement by Lars Syll:

> "The Keynes-inspired building-blocks are there. But it is admittedly a long way to go before the whole construction is in place. But the sooner we are intellectually honest and ready to admit that modern neoclassical macroeconomics and its microfoundationalist programme has come to way's end – the sooner we can redirect our aspirations to more fruitful endeavours" (Syll, 2014: 28).

Democratization of the economic policy involves a political action, but this action requires a new economic theory that may replace the present monetarist mainstream autocratic economics. It seems therefore that it is time to look for some dependable real world notions of old times trustworthy economists aiming to create a new theory and test the adherence of its hypotheses to the reality. A promising starting point seems to be one fundamental statement by Keynes to which little attention has been given:

> "But our method of analysing the economic behaviour of the present under the influence of changing ideas about the future is one which depends on the interaction of supply and demand" (Keynes, 1936, Preface: vii).

The lack of connection of the mainstream supply and demand doctrine with reality looks intentional for it induced too many economists to dismiss a reality-backed theory, the theory of supply and demand, and promote assumptions and economic policy ends scientifically unsustainable and socially unjust to the status of mainstream economics. This successful mainstream strategy gave room to the creation of manipulated mathematical models based on irrational assumptions like "rational expectations" which lead to previously established, and convenient, targets. Nowadays "The real macroeconomic challenge is to face and accept uncertainty and still try to explain why economic transactions take place ..." (Syll, 2016).

Accordingly, this essay aims at giving a potential first step in this direction presenting a new version of Marshall[2] and Keynes[3] statements aiming at fixing the real world notion of demand and supply. The test of the hypothesis that the demand and supply theory may adhere to reality was made by the estimate of the United States aggregate demand and supply model, described in details in order to allow real world researchers to replicate the test and confirm or refute its conclusions, especially the demonstration that monetary policy harms society.

The organisation of the paper is as follows: Section 1 presents some evidences of social problems probably created by the monetarist mainstream economic policy. Section 2 brings a critical appreciation of the neoclassical mainstream supply and demand "theory" aiming at the demonstration that it is scientifically unfeasible and that, as *neoclassical* writers say, there is no *neoclassical* real world supply and demand theory. Section 3 presents a new theoretical approach to the real world non-equilibrating supply and demand theory, based on the psychological Hierarchy of Needs and on Book V of Marshall's Principles. Section 4 is dedicated to modelling this new supply and demand theory emphasising that equilibrium is actually unattainable. Section 5 collects some statements about disequilibrium in economics, how to deal with disequilibrium and stresses the straight implication of disequilibrium to econometrics. Section 6 presents the estimate of the US aggregate supply and demand curves detailing the decomposition of the model and the identification of the reduced equations. Finally, Section 7 presents some conclusions.

---

[2] References to Marshall do not imply that the Author or the text is "Marshallian".
[3] References to Keynes do not imply that the Author or the text is "Keynesian".

1. An economy for the 1%

Income falling at the bottom level, income growing at the top level and income and wealth concentration are widespread phenomena that have been reported from many countries. For instance, Credit Suisse Global Wealth Report 2015 reveals that "The top 1% of wealth holders now own half of all household wealth" (Credit Suisse, 2015: 4).

In the report "An economy for the 1% – How privilege and power in the economy drive extreme inequality and how this can be stopped", Oxfam informs that,

> "The gap between rich and poor is reaching new extremes...
> Meanwhile, the wealth owned by the bottom half of humanity
> has fallen by a trillion dollars in the past five years. This is
> just the latest evidence that today we live in a world with
> levels of inequality we may not have seen for over a
> century" (Oxfam, 2016: 2).

The McKinsey Global Institute produced the report "Poorer Than Their Parents? – Flat or Falling Incomes in Advanced Economies". One remarkable finding is that

> "Our research shows that in 2014, between 65 and 70
> percent of households in 25 advanced economies were in
> income segments whose real market incomes – from wages
> and capital – were flat or below where they had been in
> 2005" (McKinsey Global Institute, 2016: 1).

Focusing on the Unites States, for she is the country-case used in the experiment here developed, Figure 1 shows the evolution of the US average income from the Bottom 90% (lower line) to Top 10% and to Top 1% (higher line) levels. One may see that the Top 1% income grew much faster than the others.

Figure 1 US income by level

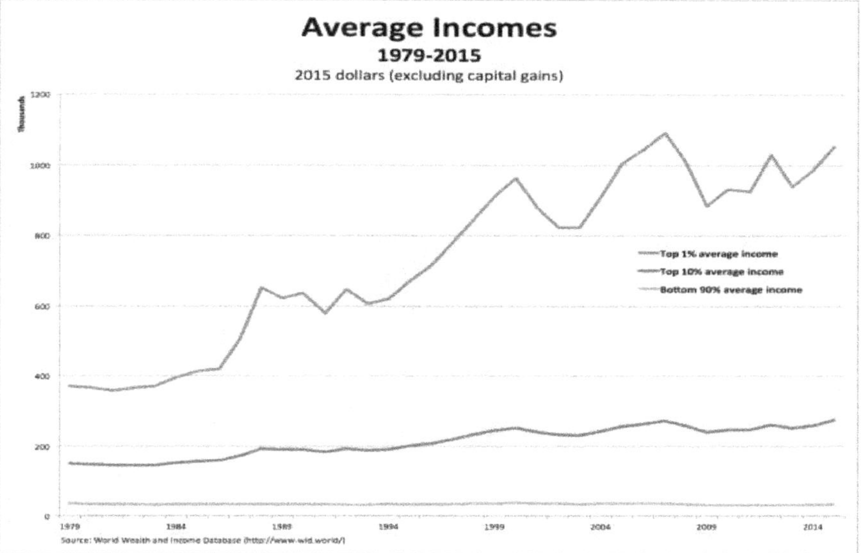

Source: Ruccio (2016b), Data from The World Wealth and Income Database
(http://www.wid.world/)

The Business Insider posted on its website on July 13, 2015 a revealing chart illustrating their study "Since the financial crisis, almost all Americans have seen their wages fall", based on the "Bureau of Labor Statistics study of employment compensation since the financial crisis and Great Recession".

This chart (Figure 2) shows the average change in inflation-adjusted wages for private-sector workers between 2007 and 2014 for each income percentile outside of the very top and very bottom. The conclusion is that "most of the bottom 85% saw a drop in real wages".

Ruccio used "the latest data on inequality in the United States, created and disseminated by Emmanuel Saez and Thomas Piketty" (Ruccio, 2016a), to elaborate the graph in Figure 3 showing that in the period 1979-2015 the Bottom 90% lost share that went to the 90% - 99% intermediary share and to the Top 1%.

Figure 2 Percent change In US real wages by income percentile, 2007-2014

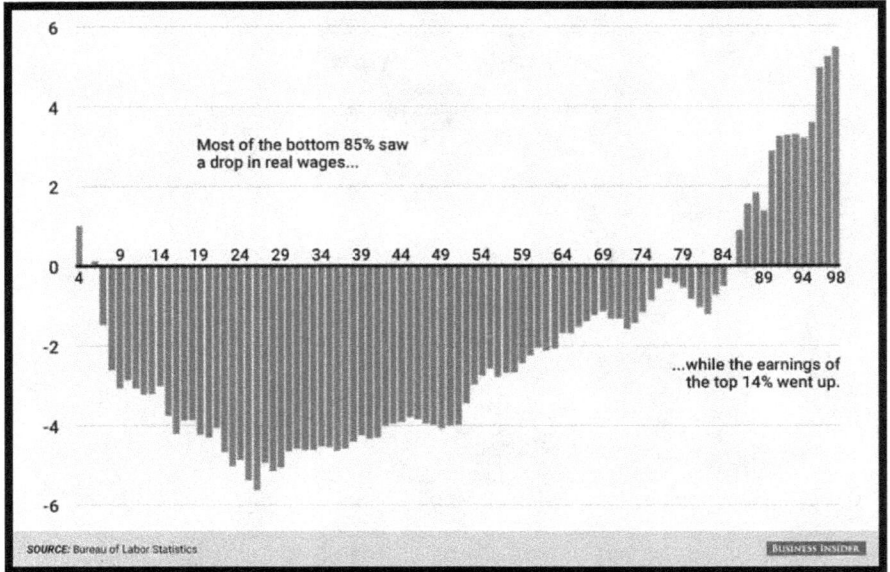

Source: Business Insider (2015), data from US Bureau of Labor Statistics.

Figure 3 US income by share

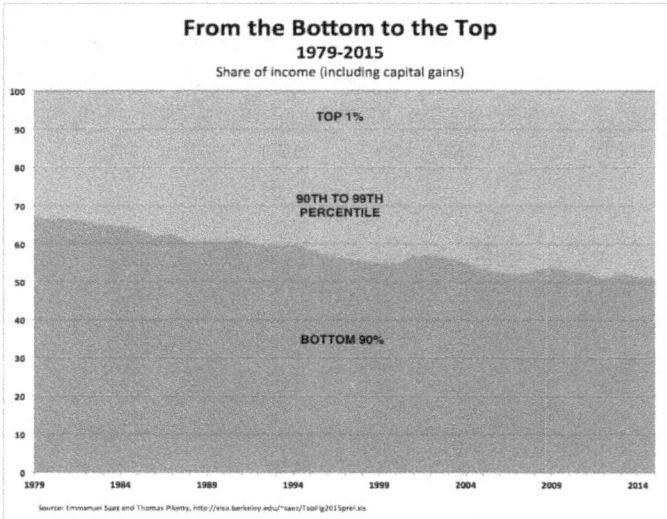

Source: Ruccio (2016a)

These real world facts demonstrate that the economy has actually been directed to please the 1% who commands the economic policy and that its trend points to the final social chaos. It seems that it is time to listen to Keynes and look the economy from the supply and demand standpoint. In fact, Keynes once said: "I regard the price level as a whole as being determined in precisely the same way as individual prices; that is to say, under the influence of supply and demand" (in Kahn, 1984: 59). Of course Keynes was not thinking of the neoclassical fake theory, but probably on Marshall, since both criticized the neoclassical theory.

2. What is wrong with mainstream economics?

At the Top 1% are the financial capitalists who are concerned with money and therefore the main tool of the economic policy created by them shall be money, a strong instrument banks have to influence the economy. Hence, mainstream economics became essentially monetarist; the interest rate has actually been the Maslow's hammer of the monetarist economics. Given that monetary interests prevail, it may be said that the present mainstream economics is the monetarist mainstream economics and its public version is the monetary policy played by the monetarists and founded on the public debt and its interest rent. Despite the fact that any public debt probably follows an explosive trend (Lima, 2015), the economic paradigm, the subject area, method and objects of the economic policy are submitted to a single instrument available, the monetary policy.

Many paradigms have been associated with present mainstream economics but it seems that above all monetarists must necessarily abide by one ultimate commandment: "government should never print money". This statement looks like the true, but covered paradigm of mainstream monetarist economics for there is no monetarist model without it. Complementing, the entire commandment says "government should not print money; they must borrow and therefore collect taxes to pay interest on the public debt". This means that the public debt and the interest expenditure that comes together compose the core of the monetary policy. Academic submission to this paradigm has been closely watched by central banks' staffs (Grim, 2013; Auerbach, 2011). Moreover,

"An adverse aspect of a paradigm is that new ideas outside the paradigm will be difficult to understand by most and, the greater the originality of the ideas, the greater will be resistance to acceptance.

The monopoly-like power of a paradigm exists in many areas of research, where standard rejection (Shepherd, 1995) of original ideas serves to frustrate many who want to publish genuinely new ideas in 'respectable' established journals" (Sy, 2012: 68).

The mainstream research agenda cannot admit the possibility that governments print money to execute the budget democratically discussed and approved by their congresses. The mainstream economics state that government must issue Treasury bonds; only central banks can print money out of nothing – and they do so to buy bonds from the Treasury. Central banks also buy Treasury bonds held by the "public"; but in this case central banks print (unbacked) money also to pay the interest rent to the private holders of the public debt bonds, central banks' shareholders included, send the bill to the Treasury and collect more bonds as payment for such interests. The subject matter of the mainstream economics, since it must be associated with money, is inflation. The purpose of inflation control was not necessarily chosen to please society, but probably to support the value of central bankers' financial capital. The modus operandi of mainstream monetarist economics may be anything, provided that its major claimed object is inflation control by means of the monetary policy.

Moreover, monetarist mainstream economics is a doctrine that absorbed and refined few scientific-looking contributions that were convenient to it. So, it is not necessarily due to its occasional social merits, if any, that neoclassical and monetarist principles were developed and marketed to be the introductory manual of a mainstream economics; mainly, they are convenient to the mainstream monetarist economic policy. "…neoclassical political economy is largely an ideology in the service of the powerful" (Nitzan and Bichler, 2009: 2).

Neoclassical doctrine only exists since it abides by undemocratic political power rules. Neoclassical and monetarist principles do not need to be connected to reality; above all they must be convenient to the mainstream monetarist economics. One of these scientific-looking notions is the idea of utility and profit maximisation, which seems to be compelling for it remains in many research agendas. But since all suggested models of maximisation are not actually different from each other, all of them exhibit the same three basic mistakes.

2.1. Three basic mistakes of the profit maximisation principle

The first neoclassical mistake is about the notion of *competition*. Actually, competition among companies may logically be associated with individual actions intending to expand individual demand curves thus producing individual sales increases, usually taking clients from some competitors. The logical motivation and condition for a company to compete is that for her it is profitable to offer, through marketing strategies, lower prices or higher quality or home delivery or all that and something else.

Sales expansion following a price reduction by only one individual company may be explained by a real world peculiarity of the demand and supply theory. The producer's individual demand's slope may be assumed to be equal to the market demand's slope for consumers' preferences are expected to be strongly attached to the product or service and weakly to the particular supplier. Consequently, at the same market price the individual demand elasticity e_i is equal to the market demand elasticity e divided by the market share (D_i/D) of the individual firm: $e_i = e/(D_i/D)$.

Given that the individual market share is lower than one, it follows that even if the market demand is inelastic, it may be expected that normally companies' individual demands are elastic since the majority of markets is composed of many relatively small firms $(D_i/D<1)$ and a few large ones. High demand elasticity seems to be a good motive for competition since it means that lower prices may lead to individual greater sales and larger profits (Lima, 1992: 54-57; Lima, 1995). This implies that competition exists independently of monetarist mainstream assumptions about market structure. This may be the reason that explains why small businesses are more price-competitive than the great multinational companies. As Marshall said, market prices are ruled by the small firms.

The second mistake is the notion of instantaneous equilibrium between production and sales required by neoclassical maximisation models and provided by the invisible hand, the imaginary auctioneer or the fictional agents' rational expectations.[4] But in the real world production takes time and inventories has normally been inevitable. Thus, in no point of time there is equilibrium between quantities produced and sold. For any time span there is always an immeasurable discrepancy between the actual amount produced and the amount that would be brought about if production were instantaneous.

The third mistake, a consequence of the second one, is the attempt of estimating neoclassical and monetarist models as if production were instantaneous. This assumption requires that all values observed in the real world be the right measure of the equilibrium values of the endogenous variables production and sales. Given that such assumption is never realised, consequently the mainstream notion of equilibrium imposes to mainstream researchers an insoluble problem touching econometric models. Actually, the immeasurable discrepancy between actual and *theoretical* equilibrium values of endogenous variables is an immeasurable exogenous variable whose omission leads to the autocorrelation of residuals that plagues mainstream econometric models. Consequently, long time ago usual econometrics of mainstream models hardly produced statistically acceptable results and then mainstream economists created models and mathematical methods that, for them, dispense with traditional econometrics and provide convenient results. A conclusion about maximisation is that it is not sufficient to allow for the estimate of a supply curve because to mainstream economists it is always necessary to include competition – but maximisation and competition effects cannot be split since there is no independent data on competition. Thus, the neoclassical hypothesis of profit maximisation no longer can be scientifically tested. To scientifically prove that companies abide only by profit maximisation and competition mainstream economists need a kind of "competimeter". Essentially,

---

[4] Syll (2012) presents a comprehensive criticism of the notion and use of rational expectation.

economic science cannot give real world support to the hypothesis of maximisation and does not need to do so. Actually, it is possible to estimate the supply curve without imposing any special behaviour of producers; it is sufficient to assume that they must keep producing and selling to raise money and take profits (Lima, 1992: 164-7).

2.2. Neoclassical economists say there is no neoclassical supply and demand theory

If incidentally neoclassical economics creators had the intention of producing a realistic supply and demand theory, they would have somehow adopted and tried to develop the pioneering Cournot's work on maximization (Cournot, 1838). They would have failed, but actually they never intended to follow Cournot, since they must abide by the monetarist dogma imposing that the general price index is determined by the money supply or the interest rate, both falsely assumed to be under control of the central banks. Mainstream monetarist economists cannot admit that prices and production are determined by demand and supply.

Notwithstanding, at the demand side there is a neoclassical demand model for it is necessary and convenient to the monetarist mainstream paradigm at least twice. First, pretending to support the statement that free (financial) markets may assure social welfare, and second to construct the neoclassical fictional labour market, the cornerstone of the mainstream counterfeit aggregate supply model. Mainstream monetarist economists cannot admit that employment is determined by demand and supply.

Nonetheless, even in the mainstream academic world, it remains applicable the statement that "The (neoclassical) theory of aggregate supply is among the most controversial and the least settled of any in macroeconomics" (Dornbusch and Fischer, 1990: 252). Dornbusch and Fischer offer an alternative but nowadays there are many others, all of them contriving arguments to convince other already convinced monetarists that full employment may be not the rule in the short run but certainly is the normal situation in the long run. Grieve presents a critical analysis of the mainstream AS/AD model stressing its shortcomings and concluding that "As Keynes said long ago, such a doctrine is 'misleading and disastrous' if taken as a guide to macroeconomic policy in the real world" (Grieve, 2014: 59).

On the supply side the mainstream microeconomics statement is that the supply curve may be defined only under the perfect competition condition. Despite that, neoclassical economists are aware of the existence of many kinds of competition that are not perfect. Accordingly, they created a plethora of imperfect competition, game theory and likewise models that do not lead to the supply curve. So, they pretend that outside the perfect competition fantasy world there is no supply curve at all. Therefore *neoclassical* economists state that there is no general *neoclassical* supply curve. The conclusion is thus that in accordance with *neoclassical* economists, there is no *neoclassical* supply and demand theory. Really, monetarist mainstream economics cannot be submitted to the test of reality; so, it is not science and should be dismissed. Monetarist mainstream researchers are not constructing hypotheses to be tested; they are stating how the real world people ought to perform to justify their theorems, support their paradigm and transfer income to the few rich. Mainstream economics is a doctrine that prevents itself from being promoted to the status of science.

The heterodox literature has many works demonstrating that the mainstream notion of supply and demand is flawed and should be dismissed[5]. Unfortunately, such works do not consider the possibility of developing a real world non-equilibrating supply and demand theory. Moreover, the rejection of the neoclassical doctrine of supply and demand does not harm the monetary mainstream paradigm. Central banks will keep supporting neoclassical economists by the traditional means (Grim, 2013) since the neoclassical broken doctrine is very much interesting to the monetarist paradigm dominance. Mainstream followers also developed convenient criticism to many economic theoretical findings that do not support or contradict their doctrine. The most important of these findings mainstream followers must deny seems to be the real world aggregate supply and demand theory, since mainstream economists must convince everybody that there is no involuntary unemployment, the general price level is a monetary concern and monetary policy is a must to fight inflation. A real world supply

---

[5] To mention some works: Lee and Keen, 2004; and Zaman and Saglam, 2012.

and demand theory would prevent monetarist mainstream economists from supporting their denial of the fiscal policy and justifying their monetary policy. Furthermore, the real world aggregate supply and demand theory challenges mainstream economics since it may provide a sound support to the true Keynesian economic theory.

The monetarist mainstream economics is not economic science, perhaps at best a doctrine based on faith, or faith and fraud (Galbraith, 2010; FBI, 2014; Baiman and Rothenberg, 2007). Notwithstanding, what is certainly scientifically unacceptable in the mainstream supply and demand doctrine is not the idea of supply and demand itself, but the mainstream set of assumptions, especially about utility, rationality, maximisation and equilibrium. Perhaps discarding these neoclassical assumptions is the right thing to do if the intention is to design what may someday be accepted as the real world supply and demand theory and the real world economic theory. Meanwhile, non-mainstream works into the real world supply and demand theory are hard to find. We may have been throwing the baby out with the bath water.

3. An analytical method based on a real world supply and demand theory

The theory and method that follow compose an enhanced version of the work developed by Lima (1992). The basic real word phenomenon observed is that people are always buying and selling goods and services, that is, demanding and supplying goods and services in such a way that the ancient notion of demand and supply interaction looks like the smallest economic act, an act without which there would be no flow of money and thus no economics. The assumptions are: first, besides human ontological behaviour, demand and supply interplay depends on many exogenous factors, mainly from politics, economic policy, technology and natural resources. People do not decide autonomously their performance in the demand and supply interactions; their capacity and limits in doing so depend on exogenous non-economic phenomena, especially political decisions. This section presents the assumptions and hypotheses that lead to the real world non-equilibrating supply and demand theory and the economic analytical model that come next.

Joan Robinson once stated that "In the serious sciences, original work is discovery - finding connections that were always there, waiting to be seen" (Robinson, 1965a: 95). For her the construction of a new economic theory should be based on the ever since existing reality. Accordingly, the proposal here is to go back to the real world economist's ideas before the neoclassical doctrine upsurge that provoked the economic science derailment – and restart from there. "To a very great extent the term 'science' is reserved for fields that do progress in obvious ways" (Kuhn, 1962: 159). Alfred Marshall, John Keynes, Joan Robinson and many other old times economists gave contributions that are inconvenient to the contemporaneous monetarist mainstream but important to "the" economic science. Recovering and improving such contributions may be a good starting point in the search for a new real world economic science.

The economic science should not reduce people's motivations to make economic decisions aiming at just one goal that would furthermore be the best possible and always attained. A person is not only *Homo Economicus* but above all *Homo sapiens*; men are the subject matter of other sciences, if not all of them. For instance, Medicine is the science that studies how the human body works and how it is influenced by psychological and external conditions aiming at restoring, preserving and improving individual and social health. Economics could be dedicated to the study of how the economy works and how it is influenced by exogenous tangible conditions and policy decisions, aiming at restoring, preserving and improving individual and, mainly, social material wealth.

The initial economic interaction act is a buying and selling action; there is no money flow and no economics without such action. This act involves at least two persons and determines the values of two economic variables, price and quantity sold/bought. Consequently, the mathematical model that may theoretically explain the values of these two endogenous variables requires two equations, one at the seller's side and the other at the buyer's side. This mathematical model has been the demand and supply two equations system, which in Marshall's words is the fundamental idea of economics.

The supply and demand process is the channel from exogenous causes to economic consequences; it has no life in itself and it is not capable of leading autonomously to some individual and social ideal. Actually, the opposite prevails, since there are more deprived people than welfare state societies; social consequences of economic acts stem from exogenous causes that command supply and demand, not from the supply and demand interplay itself.

The paradigm followed by the theoretical approach here suggested is "none can spend more than one's earnings". This is not an apologia for savings, but a rule of life for everybody and all governments to never be systematically indebted. Saving is thus an individual virtue, but also a social disaster for more savings means less sales and less income to many non-savers; hence, economic policy should also compensate for the social losses caused by personal savings. At the production side the paradigm must be rephrased to mean that "a company must raise more money than it spends". So, the basic duty of professional economists should be to advise companies on production investment decisions. However, the majority of schools of economics dispensed with basic economic disciplines like for instance project elaboration, accounting, law, marketing and management, and are far from preparing for any real world job. As non-mainstream economists know, "we need a revolution in the way we teach economics" (Fullbrook, 2010; Chang and Aldred, 2014).

3.1. Demand

Two initial basic assumptions on supply and demand theory are that demand comes first and that people's motivation to buy is the psychological notion of human needs; money comes next. Previously people must be aware that we cannot produce all we consume and that we have motives to buy what we buy, a human unconscious or conscious need of something that may be satisfied with something that may be bought. Motivations to buy, that is, to act economically, are exogenous to economics. The origin of demand is at the human needs, be it directly (consumption goods and services) or indirectly (production inputs). These human needs whose satisfaction depends on human interaction mainly with money are, like sleeping, breathing and coughing, ontological. They refer to what men need to assure mental and physical health being thus immanent to the human species; their causes are just natural. Accordingly, what Maslow (1943) did was not explaining human needs, but introducing the idea of classifying the human needs. Maslow created the long-lasting Hierarchy of Needs theory which is illustrated by the well-known five stages model of human needs. The chart in Figure 4 is an "economic version" of the five-stages Maslow's model; it follows an order of predominance from the bottom to top.

Figure 4 Maslow's hierarchy of needs

Stages	Category	Sample of Needs	Examples of Products and services	Degrees of satisfaction (by Maslow)	Price and income elasticities
5	Self-Actualization	Self-fulfillment, personal growth, peak experiences.	Post-graduation courses, cultural trips.	10	
4	Esteem	Achievement, mastery, independence, status, prestige.	The same below but with fashion and dearer trademarks.	40	
3	Love	Work group, family, affection, relationships.	Parks, restaurants, tourism.	50	
2	Safety	Security, order, law, income stability.	Medical assistance, insurance.	70	
1	Physiological	Food, drink, shelter, warmth, sex.	Potatoes, water, house, clothes.	85	

Source of original data: Maslow, 1943.

The bottom stage is the first one since it is the more essential to life; from there we go to higher stages after *some* degree of satisfaction is obtained in the preceding levels. In Maslow's words, "As for the concept of emergence of a new need after satisfaction of the prepotent need, this emergence is not a sudden, saltatory phenomenon, but rather a gradual emergence by slow degrees from nothingness" (Maslow, 1943: 14). At each level the degree of satisfaction that Maslow considered reasonable for somebody to "be promoted" to the next level is not scientifically determined, but "arbitrary figures for the sake of illustration" (Maslow, 1943: 14).

Maslow's classification of the human needs naturally follows the notion of essentiality of products and services, starting from the more essential and arriving to the more superfluous at the top level. Of course people are better at a higher than at a lower stage of the Maslow's pyramid, but people need more income to upgrade to higher stages. Thus, people upgrade in the Maslow's pyramid means that they have greater income and can buy better products that are naturally higher priced. The prevailing notion of inflation must be qualified. Accordingly, in the last column it is included a seemingly idea about the evolution of the income and price elasticities from the bottom, plenty of the most essential products and services, to the esteem level, where it is expected that most of the products and services that satisfy this need probably bear the highest elasticities. At the top stage elasticities are expected to be greater than at stage 1 but not necessarily higher than at stage 4. Economists could provide empirical findings giving support to Maslow's statements; demand elasticities are useful real world economic information that businessmen are waiting for. But, once again, until now mainstream economists are not prepared to assume any real world job, but to agree with the leaders.

Any human behaviour is an exogenous variable that may cause some economic consequences; actually, Psychology tells us a realistic reason why people buy, but it is just useful information to economics, like for example human political decisions. Human needs and Maslow's pyramid are not economic facts, but psychological, thus exogenous, facts that support an economic theory susceptible to the test of the real world.

By the way, mainstream economists made efforts to find psychological support to their required hypotheses of selfishness and rationality, but the answer given at the 2003 Annual Meeting of the American Economic Association to them is "...there are no immediate prospects of economics and psychology sharing a common theory of human behaviour" (Kahneman,

2003: 166). This statement by Kahneman made it clear that such mainstream "economic" hypotheses have no psychological backing.

The demand curve, be it exclusive (individual to one specific seller), sectorial, regional, national, etc., is a line connecting the quantity bought (D) to the price (P) of the product or service and to a set of exogenous variables in which income (Y) is certainly the most important:

$$D = f(P^-, Y^+, OV), \quad \text{where OV refers to Other Variables.}$$

To trace this line in the plan (P x D) the income and all other exogenous variables must be fixed and hence the demand curve has a negative slope since higher prices and equal income are associated with less quantity bought. In passing, one strategic exogenous variable among OV is the price of other products for the cross elasticity indicates the degree of competition between producers; the higher the cross elasticity, the more similar the products are and the more intense is the competition among sellers. Intensity of competition may be strategic information to companies in real world markets and economists could estimate the cross elasticity therein to provide a real world proxy measure of the degree of competition companies are dealing with. Normally, for a given set (Y, OV), it may be expected that the line connecting D and P be a straight line, but some odd exogenous variable OV may consistently change the slope dD/dP.

3.2. Supply

This subsection is based mainly on the Book V of the *Principles of Economics* (8th Edition), where Marshall's proposal was to consolidate the supply and demand theory founded "on the pioneering work of his many predecessor economists" (Moss, 2003;[6] Lima, 1992). Marshall was not creating the supply and demand theory, less yet a neoclassical supply and demand theory. He was describing, and obviously improving when he considered appropriate, the state of the arts of his own time. Becattini[7]

---

[6] Moss, L. S. *Marshall's Objective: Making Orthodox Economics Intelligible to Business Leaders*, abstract of the book review by Caldari (2004).
[7] Becattini, G. *The Return of the White Elephant*, abstract of the book review by Caldari (2004).

identified "a turning point in Marshallian studies" and "potential capacities in Marshall's thought", thus stating that Marshall "is now increasingly mentioned and more often in a favourable light" According to Becattini, "Marshall cannot be considered a neoclassical economist, as most interpretations of the past did, because of the presence of important anomalies that make him clearly a sui generis economist", as Walras once put it, calling his English "colleague" a "white elephant" (Caldari, 2004).

About mathematics in Marshall's work, Dardi states that

> "Marshall the mathematical economist and Marshall the methodologist on the use of mathematics in economics should be kept separate. The former was active approximately until the early editions of the Principles of Economics, after which mathematics as a heuristic tool was renounced and remained solely as a forma mentis, in the background. The latter became more and more prominent as the former faded away, but the methodological criteria he elaborated ... do not seem to convey the gist of his previous work as a mathematical economist" (Dardi, 2005: 1).

Marshall's contribution to economics should never be associated with the neoclassical doctrine for "In sections of contemporary non-mainstream economics Alfred Marshall, one of the founding fathers of neoclassical orthodoxy, has been turned into a sort of anti-mainstream champion" (Dardi, 2014: 2). Marshall himself never agreed with being a "founding father of neoclassical orthodoxy" as mainstream creators pretend.

The supply and demand theory directly from Marshall's time, that is, before its de-construction by the creators of the neoclassical doctrine, has four fundamental assumptions: One, demand comes first, implying that Two, supply adjust to demand, through marketing and production; Third, production takes time, and consequently Fourth, there is no real world equilibrium; equilibrium is a just a theoretical idea.

Marshall assumes that it is up to individual sellers to conform their targets to the demand reality, stating that "Production and marketing are parts of the single process of adjustment of supply to demand" (Marshall, 1919: 181). The difference in relation to Cournot and neoclassical creators is that in the process described by Marshall each company adjust its individual supply to its individual demand without following a fixed rule connecting its price and production. Instead, this process may even be split into two "departments" quite independents. One, the marketing department, regularly makes decisions on price considering the production costs and the status of the company's individual demand. The other, the production department, regularly makes estimates of the production to be obtained sometime later considering profits realised and individual demand performance in the near past. Therefore production start-up decisions are made and implemented, but later on the production targeted may actually be obtained or not; market may change in the meantime, thus requiring new decisions that may fix or not occasional problems. Marketing and production departments may work together or not in estimating company's individual demand level variations, and in so doing, they look at the variation of the inventories of finished and in-process products and to the variation of the production and distribution capacities idleness.

Producers do not impose prices; they propose prices (Pb) and, possibly after bargaining, buyers decide how much to buy at the price proposed or the mutually accepted price, and this price may last for months or seconds. For identical products it is expected that competition leads all unknown bid prices Pb to be, on average, statistically not far away from the actual sales price P, the publicly known market price. All the same producers do not impose production levels, they invest with a production level target that sometime later may succeed or not and may be sold or not. Both price (Pb) and production (Q) follow demand shifts in the same direction; lower inventories and less production and distribution capacities idleness (S) mean more demand, more price and, later on, more production. When their individual inventories and production capacity idleness decrease producers realise that their individual demands expanded and hence they, acting in cooperation or huge competition among them, raise their own prices and production target levels. Next, each producer decides whether to accept the amount sold and to keep the selling prices or to change bid prices and observe sales for a while to decide the new price bid and production start-up, endlessly looking for a satisfactory solution that usually never comes about. This satisfactory solution looks like what Keynes defined as producer's expectation (Keynes, 1936, Chapter 5: 46).

Therefore, Marshallian producers have a decision making model that is composed of two decision making functions like for instance the following general model:

the price bidding function: $Pb = P = f(C^+, S^-, OV)$ (1)

the production level start-up function: $Q = f(R^+, S^-, OV)$ (2)

where C is the cost of production, S is the inventory of finished and in-process goods and the idleness of the production and distribution capacities, R is the profit margin which depends on the price P and the production cost C, and OV stands for other variables suited for each particular good or service, company, season, location, and so on. Signs are positive to the cost C and to the profit R, negative to the inventory S and anyone to other variables OV.

The supply curve is the reduced equation of (1) and (2). In fact, replacing the inventory S took from the price function (1) in the production start-up function (2) it comes:

$$Q = f(P^+, R^+, C^-, OV).$$

Next, given that $R = f(P, C)$ we get the supply curve connecting the quantity produced with the actual sales price P with a positive sign:

$$Q = f(P^+, C^-, OV). \tag{3}$$

This function is the supply curve basic formula for it is the common place of the (price x production) points that comes about when, ceteris paribus the cost of production and OV, the individual demand curves shift upwards and downwards (Lima, 1992). If Marshall had observed that, economics would have another history. Moreover, it is expected that all companies follow the same decision model and that parameters are different for each company in a branch. Assuming that all producers' decisions are consistent, it is expected that identical decision making models may be applied to the industry and to the country as a whole.

The supply curve position depends on the exogenous variable cost of production with a negative sign and a set of other exogenous variables OV whose signs may be any; the supply curve is a positive slope line that shifts sideways when the cost components or other specific exogenous variables levels change. The supply curve slope depends on numerous internal and external relatively stable conditions touching companies, like characteristics of the product or service supplied, financial capital availability, perishability of raw materials, finished products and products in process, input's markets, company's organisation and personal abilities, etc., and on the staffs and stockholders idiosyncrasies, among them the propensity to compete or cooperate with other companies in the same branch or outside it, and so on. The theoretical target of obtaining the highest profit possible may at best be one of these conditions; real world restrictions to obtaining it are many others.

3.3. Real world demand and supply

This approach to the supply and demand theory is based upon more two basic assumptions. Firstly, and most importantly, after every exogenous shock some, many or all countless markets have their supply and demand curves moved. Following this, it is the interplay of people supplying and demanding that determine the value of the basic endogenous variables price and production at each market level. The next step sees producers realise revenue and, after deducting the exogenous cost, the profit obtained defines, ceteris paribus, their demands for inputs. Combining then these inputs demands with the respective supplies it comes about the price and production of capital goods, raw materials and intermediary products and services, especially the wage and employment in the labour market, the amount of credit and interest rate in the financial market, the exchange rate, etc., and also the savings by people and companies, the personal and companies' wealth, the level of investment, the national economic growth, the tax revenue, etc., and social consequences on health, education, housing, retirement, peace, and so on. Price and production determined at single markets are at the root of every endogenous value that happens in the economy. This assumption implies that if an exogenous variable variation or the economic policy decisions do not touch supply or demand in some, many or all markets then they have no effect on the economy. In other words, economic policy imposes rules and values of policy instruments; given then these exogenous variables values, people's interactions produce through supply and demand the economic and social consequences we observe.

Second, it is assumed that, independently of personal reasons, every buyer and every seller always keep doing the same they always do, that is, buying and selling products and services to respectively satisfy needs and raise income. This assumption implies that aggregation refers not to quantities, but to people's behaviour consolidation. Consequently, the aggregate supply and demand curves follow the same principles observed at the microeconomic level. Actually, the human collective behaviour exists, but it concerns psychology, sociology, medicine, and other human and social sciences that bring important information to practical applications of the economic theory. But from the economic perspective the collective behaviour is an exogenous variable; it just happens like political decisions and natural resources availability. Therefore, this Marshallian-based model of supply and demand may be submitted to the test of reality, both at microeconomic and macroeconomic levels.

The slopes of the supply and demand curves reflect human behaviour conditioned by some exogenous variables while other exogenous variables shift the curves up and downstairs. Assuming that all buyers and sellers are consistent in their decisions, always buying and selling to satisfy needs and raise money, statistics allow for the estimates of the supply and demand for each and all products and services at the county, state, region, country or union of countries levels. At the macroeconomic level the economic science should guide the search into the real world aggregate supply and aggregate demand interaction that explains the individual and social consequences of economic exogenous phenomena and decisions. Among these exogenous conditioning variables the most important is the economic policy for it depends on political power and on human attitudes and persuasion ability in social environments. The economic science mission should be to discover if and what might be changed in these real-world exogenous conditioning variables in order to inform the political authorities how to intervene, as positively as possible, aiming at improving the human condition like all human sciences ethically intend to do.

4. Modelling supply and demand theory

The proposed model for a real-world demand and supply estimate is based on two more general assumptions. First, both supply and demand curves' slopes are supposed to be rather stable, but their positions are unstable, especially the demand curve position. One may imagine that first some people somehow raise money or credit and demand the product and services they need. Then each producer perceives the level of its individual demand and decides the price to bid and the production amount to launch. Next, buyers decide how much to buy depending on the price asked by sellers. Next, each seller decides to take the quantity sold as a satisfactory production level or to change his price and observe competitors' actions and buyers' decisions on how much to buy at the new price. The human decision process thus started would lead towards some accommodation of players when finally a rather stable market price and production come about. But as a rule what actually happens is that before such accommodation may be observed some new exogenous variables variations both in demand and supply sides create other directions to the players' moves. Players do not complain about continuous reorientation, they keep buying and producing for they need to do so. There are no auctioneer, no invisible hand and no rational expectation; there is a process guided by quite independent but intrinsically consistent human decisions that yields provisional price and production as endogenous variables.

Second, considering that production takes time, the effects of the exogenous variables on the endogenous variables are in general delayed; endogenous variables values in time t result from exogenous variables values distributed in time t, t-1, t-2, t-3... Keynes's idea on the subject is that

> "It is evident from the above that the level of employment at
> any time depends, in a sense, not merely on the existing

state of expectation but on the states of expectation which have existed over a certain past period" (Keynes, 1936: 50).

This does not mean that time must be included as an explanatory variable since "time" is not an exogenous variable germane to economic performance; what is exogenous is not "time" but the dynamic process that, theoretically, directs producers' and consumers' decisions to some realisation. This process obviously takes time, but it is an exogenous phenomenon in itself that most probably has no regular time performance suitable to time series analysis.

This process is complex and unpredictable in essence and duration, for it depends upon consumer's diversified emotional reactions, data availability and quality, financial capital availability, staff and worker's skills, people's ability to analyse the situation, producer's emotional behaviour on decision making, actual producers and consumers alternatives, ability and restrictions to change, competition or cooperation, and so on.[8] The exogenous variable in this context is the continuous process of adjustment of producers' decision which, conditioned by consumers' reaction, *would* in the long run lead to a situation that may ex post be said the best for them or accepted by them just since they would have accepted it. This is what one can do, not the one's dream situation; it is always possible that creative businessman and consumers find still better situations than the majority can do.

This "best" or "acceptable" situation seems to match the Marshall's normal or natural value, defined as the value that "economic forces tend to bring about *in the long run*. It is the average value which economic forces would bring about if the general conditions of life were stationary for a run of time enough to enable them to work out their full effect" (Marshall, 1890: 289). On the matter, Keynes stated that:

"If we suppose a state of expectation to continue for a sufficient length of time for the effect on employment to have worked itself out so completely that there is, broadly

---

[8] This process should not be confounded neither with the mainstream monetarist economics notion of hysteresis nor the classical notion of gravitation which is associated with actual values turning around a stable equilibrium point.

speaking, no piece of employment going on which would not have taken place if the new state of expectation had always existed, the steady level of employment thus attained may be called the long period employment corresponding to that state of expectation. It follows that, although expectation may change so frequently that the actual level of employment has never had time to reach the long-period employment corresponding to the existing state of expectation, nevertheless every state of expectation has its definite corresponding level of long-period employment" (Keynes, 1936: 48).

Accordingly, Joan Robinson wrote that

"The short period is here and now, with concrete stocks of means of production in existence. Incompatibilities in the situation (...) will determine what happens next. Long-period equilibrium is not at some date in the future; it is an imaginary state of affairs in which there are no incompatibilities in the existing situation, here and now" (Robinson, 1965b: 101).

So, Keynes, Robinson and Marshall ideas is that actual values are short run or daily market values, while equilibrium refers to theoretical, natural or long run values or an imaginary state; actually, to them supply and demand never was an equilibrating device, never a self-righting system. It is up to producers to adjust their bid prices and production plans when individually perceived existing demand, costs and other conditions indicate that it is time to change. For each company exogenous variables ups and downs mean opportunity to raise more money or the need of cutting losses. The adjustment process restarts continuously in any point of intersection of demand and supply, at each relevant new information obtained by each producer about own demand, inventories and costs, competitors' strategy, legal regulations, etc., directing thus the adjustment process towards a new point of equilibrium that as ever will be chased but never attained. Economic theory cannot explain the process of adjustment of supply to demand for it is immeasurable; it is a complex exogenous variable that has no central command. Therefore, demand and supply always intersect, but not at a point of equilibrium; disequilibrium prevails. However, a *theoretical* equilibrium point may be calculated for analytical purposes. This approach to theoretical equilibrium and actual disequilibrium delivers an important consequence to econometrics.

5. Equilibrium and econometrics

Producers are assumed to make consistent decisions, but their targets, or expectations, depend on exogenous variables' values that are unpredictable and unstable. Producers are supposed to always be aware about changes in the demand for their individual products and therefore to make decisions on their constantly renewed targets; they are always chasing theoretical targets. From a methodological point of view the process of adjustment of supply to demand imposes an exogenous component to all endogenous variables that would be eliminated only if exogenous variables could stop varying. Being then natural, this exogenous component is not an "error" but a "deviation" or a "lacuna". Recalling Keynes: "For the state of expectation is liable to constant change, a new expectation being super-imposed long before the previous change has fully worked itself out; so that the economic machine is occupied at any given time with a number of over-lapping activities, the existence of which is due to various past states of expectation" (Keynes, 1936: 50). Consequently, before looking for relations among endogenous variables all endogenous variables' series may and should be estimated as lag distributed exogenous variables equations, for instance in the form:

$$Y_t(X) = a + D_i(L) X_{it} + \lceil_t$$

where Y_t is the value of the endogenous variable in time t, $D(L)$ is a lag operator on the exogenous variables set X_t and $\lceil$ is the error term. The endogenous variable cannot be lagged and included as an explanatory variable because this procedure imposes a time component to the equation but time is not an explanatory variable in economics. This equation is also the first stage reduced equation of the two stages ordinary least squares (2SLS) econometric method for the estimate of simultaneous equations models. So, this econometric method is suited to estimate the supply and demand curves both at micro and macroeconomic levels. The first stage of the 2SLS brings about the estimate of the endogenous variables reduced equations which will be transformed into "reduced theoretical equilibrium equations" through a "laboratory experiment". This experiment consists of adding up the coefficients of each significant exogenous variable in the equation above thus creating the expression:

$$Y_{te}(X) = a + (\textcircled{c}b_i) X_{it}$$

where Y_{te} represents the theoretical equilibrium series of an endogenous variable Y and b_i are the coefficients of all significant exogenous variables X_i in the set X. The reduced equilibrium equation simulates a situation in which all exogenous variables stopped varying at the moment t and it is given time enough to the exogenous variables work out their full effect on the endogenous variable, thus producing the "laboratory" or "theoretical equilibrium" values of any endogenous variable at each moment t, that is, the theoretical equilibrium series of each endogenous variable. It may be expected that with some delay the line of theoretical equilibrium values of the endogenous variables somehow follows the line of their actual values, always keeping a lacuna that may statistically be white noise or convergent or constant but never divergent.

These theoretical equilibrium series are used in the second stage of the 2SLS method to estimate the structural relations of the model. This would be a "theoretical equilibrium method" (TEM); it allows for the estimation of the effect of each exogenous variable on all endogenous variables under the theoretical ceteris paribus condition.[9] It is only in a laboratory experiment, or theoretically created equilibrium situation, that economic theory can explain endogenous variables' values and relations, for instance the demand and supply curves. Economic models cannot use actual data directly for economic theory cannot explain disequilibrium values and disequilibrium relations among endogenous variables.

---

[9] A necessary condition to talk "ceteris paribus the variable X" is the presence of the exogenous variable X in the endogenous variable Y reduced equation explanatory set. All variables absent in this explanatory set are varying and possibility influencing Y, other endogenous variables and the relations connecting them.

This method deals with two other econometric issues. First, endogenous variables' disequilibrium values are consequences of exogenous variables' variations effects on the supply and demand interplay. Always that some endogenous variable's value varies at least one exogenous variable's value had changed first. As a corollary, endogenous variables cannot have a kind of "natural" time trend; their trends do not stem from time passing, but from the blending of unpredictable time trends of their exogenous explanatory variables sets. Second, any relation of one endogenous variable to any other endogenous variable is also an endogenous variable and thus short run relations among endogenous variables also assume non-equilibrium values. Hence, all observed values used in estimating one reduced equation must be nominal values since all deflators are endogenous variables.

By the way, mainstream economists are not allowed to see that the actual values of endogenous variables are not equilibrium values since in so doing they deny the mainstream monetarist economics doctrine. It seems thus that the baby was once again thrown out with the bath water; bad econometric results offered by mainstream monetarists have often led to the deduction that econometrics like the 2SLS model serves no purpose and seldom to the quite simple conclusion that monetarist assumptions are scientifically unsustainable.

6. Estimate of the US aggregate supply and demand curves

This section describes an experiment conducted in accordance with the suggested supply and demand theory and econometric method. The successful experiment was the estimate of the aggregate supply and demand curves for the United States in the period 1960-2007.

The aggregate demand curve is just one, but there are two aggregate supply curves, the national aggregate supply curve and the total aggregate supply curve. Their definitions by the National Accounts System are:

National aggregate supply NAS	GDP = CONS + INV + FE + X - IMPORTS	(4)
Total aggregate supply AS	Y = GDP + IMPORTS	(5)
Aggregate demand AD	AD = CONS + INV + FE + X	(6)

The supply side decision making model defined by equations (1) and (2) translated to the macroeconomic level may be described by equations (7) and (8):

Producer's price bid	Pb = g (COST, GAP)	(7)
National production supply	GDP = h (R, GAP, OV)	(8)

Pb is the price asked by producers which is supposed to be not statistically different from the market price **P**; GDP is the US national supply, GAP is a measure of the product inventories and capacity idleness, R is the profit margin given by (P − COST), and COST and OV are exogenous variables to be defined in the sequence.

The endogenous variables to be estimated and transformed in theoretical equilibrium series are thus the Price Index **P**, the National Aggregate Supply **NAS**, the Aggregate Supply **AS** and the Aggregate Demand **AD**.

The first stage of the Two Stages Least Square (2SLS) econometric method is the estimate of the reduced equations of the aggregate demand and supply curves, which are composed exclusively of exogenous variables, including those exogenous variables that explain and replace the explanatory endogenous variables of the model. To start with, taking GAP from the equation (8) and replacing it in equation (7), and replacing profit margin R by its expression (P − COST), it comes the equation (9):

Pb = f (GDP, COST, OV)	(9)

The exogenous variables are defined as follows. The COST is an abstract measure of a theoretical national cost of production defined as a function of:

a) the wage determined in the labour market where the single exogenous variable is the minimum wage **MW**;

b) the cost of financial capital measured by the interest rate determined in the financial capital market where the exogenous variables are the public debt **DP,** which in this case follows an explosive trend (Lima, 2015, p. 94-95) and the money stock **M**; and

c) the exogenous variables exchange rate **ER** and foreign price **PE**.

In the case of the **GDP** there is one immediate exogenous variable, the government expenses on consumption and investment **FE** and four endogenous variables, private consumption CONS, private investment INV, exports X and imports Z. For each of these four endogenous variables the exogenous explanatory variables were defined as follows:

- The endogenous variable private consumption CONS has as explanatory variables the endogenous variables disposable income DI and the price **P**, and the exogenous variable credit, measured by the private credit balance **DEBTS.** In turn, the disposable income DI depends on the endogenous variables **GDP** and on the tax revenue T, which in turn is a function of **GDP**, and on the exogenous variables personal current transfer **TR** and net income received from/send to abroad **NIRFA**.

- The endogenous variable INV is a function of the endogenous variable price **P** as a proxy to investment goods prices and the profit margin R = P -COST, described above.

- Exports of national production X is an endogenous variable defined as a function of the endogenous variable price index **P**, and the exogenous variables exchange rate **ER** and the rest of the world income **YE** and price **PE.**

- Imports are supposedly made by international trade companies intending to sell goods and services internally. "Imports" is thus an endogenous variable defined as a function of the profit margin R and the exogenous variables exchange rate **ER** and foreign price **PE**.

Consequently, the aggregate demand of national products and services has also its exogenous variables properly described. Therefore, replacing the endogenous explanatory variables by their exogenous explanatory variables, the reduced equations for **GDP, Y, AD** and **P** have the same following exogenous variables explanatory set:

GDP, Y, P, AD = f (FE, MW, ER, DP, INT, TR, M, NIRFA, YE, PE, DEBTS)

Four considerations were then made. First, it is assumed that the credit supply **DEBTS** is mostly fed by the interest rent **INT** from the public debt **DP**. This assumption follows the idea that the United States is a rentier-based country while its economy is finance-driven (Baiman and Rothenberg, 2007). The reasoning is that the major part of this rent is added to the financial capital stock, thus fostering the credit supply as suggested by the Figure 5, where **DEBTS** is measured by the total non-financial private sector debts balance and **INTCBACR** is the financial capital resulting from the accumulation since 1946 of the interest expenditure of the US Treasury as informed by the FED and yearly corrected by the yield estimated on the basis of the interest rate over US Treasury bonds. Considering that both variables, interest rent and credit supply, show a quite similar time performance and that they measure the same phenomenon, **INT** was retained and **DEBTS** dismissed.

Second, **TR** was included in **FE,** and third the money stock **M** was dismissed for its measure is not free of controversies and it composes a linear combination with the exogenous variables **FE, ER** and **D** through the exogenous money stock **M's** formation formula:

ΔM = (FE + INT – T) + CAB – ΔD

where **T** is the endogenous variable tax receipts which is a function of the endogenous variables **GDP** while the current account balance **CAB**, in this case a surplus, is tied to the exogenous variable exchange rate **ER**. Given that **INT** is a function of **D**, then one of the exogenous variables in the subset (**FE, ER, D, M**) should be discarded to eliminate the expected effect of a linear combination among the exogenous variables of the reduced equation explanatory variables set.

Figure 5 US federal public debt as a source of credit supply

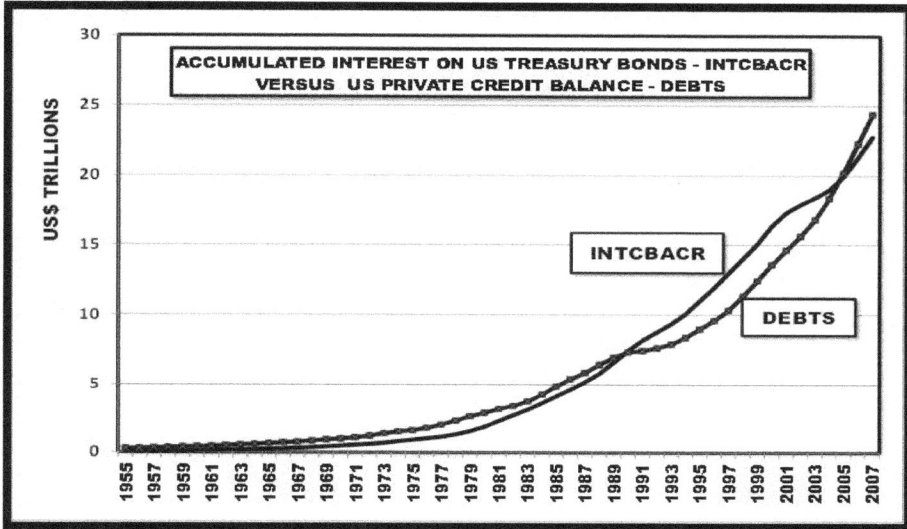

Source: Elaborated by the Author. Data from: Federal Reserve System, Data Download Program.

Fourth, the US Total Federal Debt, shown in Figure 5, is split by the Office of Management and Budget of the White House into two components, **DP** is the Federal Government debt held by the Federal Reserve System and by the public and **DG** is the stock of Treasury bonds held by Federal Government Accounts at some Federal Government agencies. The excess of funds produced by such agencies must legally "be invested in interest-bearing securities backed by the full faith and credit of the United States" (Dave Manuel)[10], that is, Treasury bonds. Clearly, **DG** bonds are "money that the government basically owes to itself, because it borrowed the money from itself" (Dave Manuel). In Figure 6 it is also displayed the truly public held debt DP, named "(Public + FED) Held Federal Debt", and the series "Accounting Total Federal Debt", which is a simulation of the public debt series constructed by accumulating to its actual value in 1945 the annual Federal Government deficits, and the Total Federal Debt line, obtained by adding DG and DP series.

---

[10] http://www.davemanuel.com/investor-dictionary/intragovernmental-holdings/.

Figure 6 US federal public debt held by federal accounts

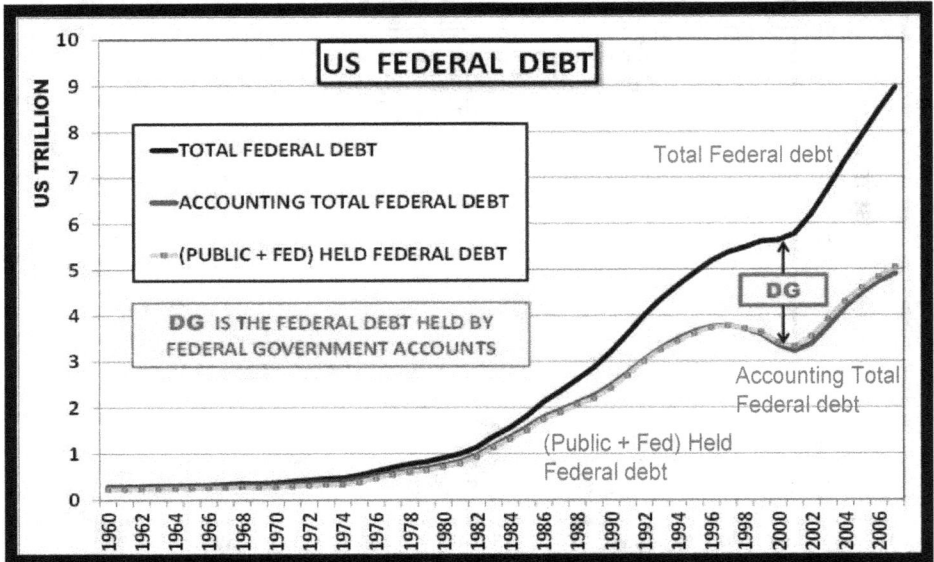

Source: Elaborate by the Author. Data from: White House, Office of Management and Budget, Historical Tables, Fiscal Year 2014.

The coincidence of the actual DP series [(Public + FED) Federal Held Debt] with the simulated Accounting series suggests that the debt held by Federal Government Accounts **DG** implies no cost to the Federal Treasury. Actually, the interest on **DG** could be paid at bonds' maturity with new bonds emissions. **DG** would thus grow continuously with the interest on the previous stock and new Federal Government agencies' excess funds. If this is the case, then **DG** bonds would actually be not debt, but a kind of tax revenue, an endogenous variable with an exogenous component that is not clear and therefore **DG** was dismissed.

This process of refining exogenous variables led to:

GDP, Y, P, AD = f (FE, MW, ER, DP, INT, NIRFA, YE, PE)

The reduced equation to be estimated is thus:

$$\text{GDP}_t, Y_t, P_t, \text{AD}_t = a + D(L)\text{FE}_t + D(L)\text{MW}_t + D(L)\text{ER}_t + D(L)\text{DP}_t + D(L)\text{INT}_t + D(L)\text{NIRFA}_t + D(L)\text{YE}_t + D(L)\text{PE}_t + \int_t$$

293

Capital and Justice

5.1. US National aggregate supply curve

Starting by the **GDP**, after several attempts it was observed that the rest of the world has no significant influence on the US GDP, for **NIRFA, YE** and **PE** were never statistically significant and so they were dismissed. After trying countless lags combinations it was obtained the **GDP** estimate presented in the following Gretl's report.

Collecting the coefficients for each lagged explanatory variable it comes about the theoretical equilibrium equation for the US **GDP**:

GDPe = - 277.807 + 6.36696*FE + 15.5759*ER - 0.40728*DP + 3.92613*INT

US NATIONAL AGGREGATE SUPPLY
Dependent Variable: GDP

Variables	Coefficient	Std. error	t-statistics	p-value	
Const.	-277.807	114.228	-2.4320	0.01984	***
FE_1	6.36696	0.157544	40.4138	<0.00001	***
ER_2	15.5759	4.99176	3.1203	0.00344	***
DP	-2.38844	0.21573	-11.0715	<0.00001	***
DP_1	1.98116	0.226115	8.7618	<0.00001	***
INT_2	-7.76107	1.86308	-4.1657	0.00017	***
INT_3	11.6872	1.79965	6.4942	<0.00001	***

Dependent var. avg.	5283.698		Dep. var. std. error	4128.371
Square residuals sum.	719425.4		Regression std. error	137.5945
R-square	0.999041		Adjusted R-square	0.998889
F (6, 38)	6595.380		F p-value	9.53e-56
Durbin-Watson	1.754499		DW 1% (6,45): 1.065 – 1.643	

It is worth observing that the coefficient of the fiscal expenses **FE** may be identified with the Keynesian multiplier and is very high in this sample: 6.37, thus suggesting that at least in the period 1960-2007 the fiscal policy was the main instrument to expand US GDP and then employment. This is a laboratory research work, a simulated situation in which the **GDP** would be in a state of equilibrium, since at each point in time the exogenous variables have theoretically been kept static supposedly throughout time enough for

294

their full effect to be worked out. Every point is a provisional theoretical equilibrium, but a theoretical equilibrium that, despite never being actually attained, is always quite close to the actual data as the FIGURE 7 shows, demonstrating then that theory here proposed follows the real world.

Figure 7 US GDP estimate

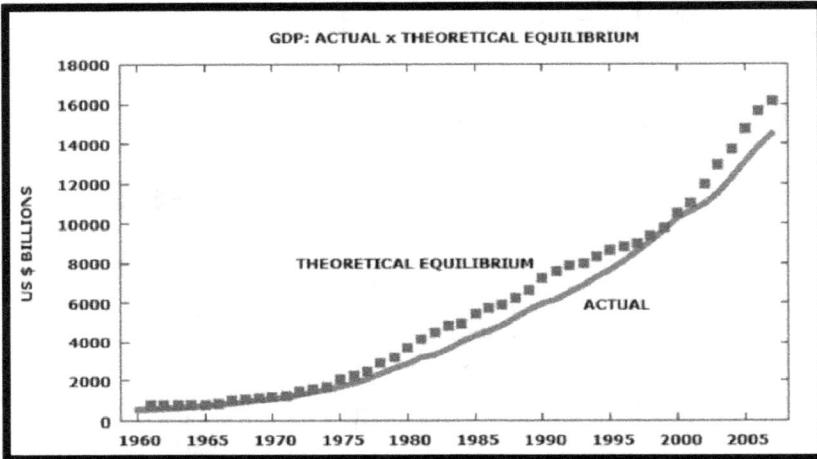

Source: Elaborated by the Author

Next, Figure 8 presents the relative importance of all exogenous explanatory variables to the US GDP composition as measured by their elasticities.

Individual elasticities show that, as expected, the most important variable in the US GDP formation is the fiscal policy for its elasticity (EGDPeFE) is always the greatest one. The exchange rate was for some time also important, but its elasticity (EGDPeER) dropped constantly until becoming almost meaningless. The interest rent has a positive but relatively low effect on the US GDP formation since its elasticity (EGDPeINT) is always below 0.25. In the opposite direction the public debt elasticity (EGDPeDP) suggests that its negative effect on the real side of the economy increased throughout this sample period.

Figure 8 US GDP formation

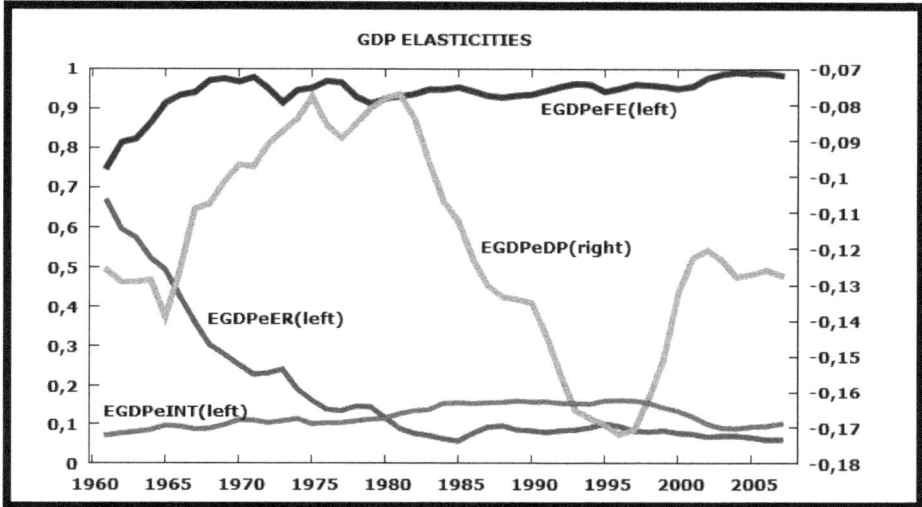

GDP ELASTICITIES

Source: Elaborated by the Author

The next step is the estimate of the price index **P** reduced equation, presented in the Gretl's report below. Therefore, the theoretical equilibrium equation for the US price index **P** is:

Pe = 2.94601 + 0.0352*FE + 12.2312*MW + 0.334376*ER – 0.0085537*DP + 0.178412*INT

US PRICE INDEX
Dependent Variable: P

Variables	Coefficient	Std. error	t-statistics	p-value	
Const.	2.94601	2.17025	1.3575	0.18225	***
FE	0.0667977	0.0116013	5.7578	<0.00001	***
FE_1	-0.0315971	0.0128534	-2.4583	0.01839	**
MW_1	12.2312	0.883105	13.8502	<0.00001	***
ER	0.334376	0.0738559	4.5274	0.00005	***
DP_1	-0.0085537	0.00156301	-5.4727	<0.00001	***
INT	0.178412	0.0100652	17.7256	<0.00001	***

Dependent var. avg.	103.5404	Dep. var. std. error	58.21322
Square residuals sum.	114.7619	Regression std. error	1.693826
R-square	0.999264	Adjusted R-square	0.999153
F (6, 38)	9048.828	F p-value	5.05e-61
Durbin-Watson	1.783228	DW 1% (6,45): 1.065 – 1.643	

Figure 9 shows that the theoretical equilibrium series of the price index Pe is very close to its actual values series P. As expected, Figures 7 and 9 suggest that the theory may adhere to reality. Next, Figure 10 shows the weight of each explanatory exogenous variable in the US Price Index composition.

Figure 9 US price index estimate

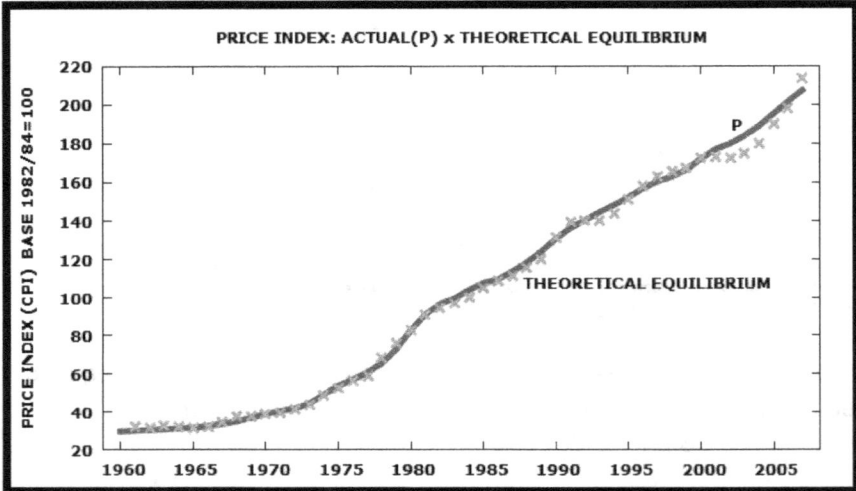

Source: Elaborated by the Author

Figure 10 US price index formation

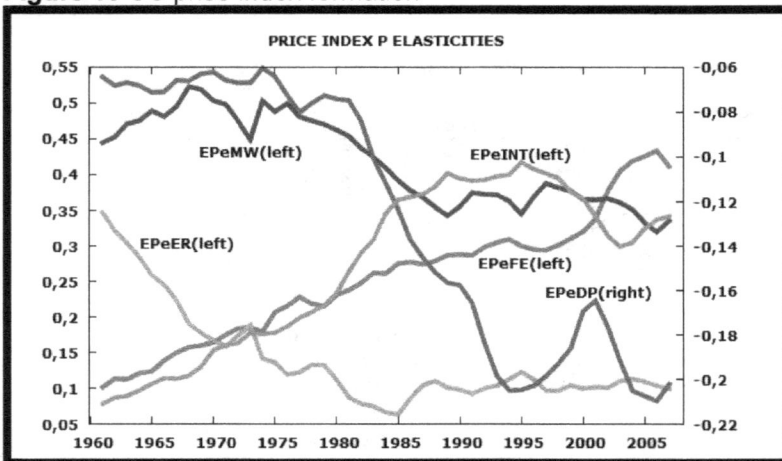

Source: Elaborated by the Author

The fiscal policy, always the most important in GDP formation, for a long period was not the most important in the price index formation; its elasticity EPeFE became the greatest one only in the 21st century. Prices were before pushed upstairs also by the minimum wage (EPeMW), the exchange rate (EPeER) and the interest rent (EPeINT). The exchange rate influence dropped very fast while the minimum wage influence also decayed, but kept relatively high importance. Meanwhile the interest rent effect (EPeINT) grew markedly, being at the end of the sample period almost as important as the minimum wage and the fiscal policy. On the opposite direction there is only the public debt (EPeDP), presenting a negative effect on the price formation that increased significantly. It is not coincidence that the same happened to the elasticity of GDP in relation to the public debt.

Finally, in the second stage of the 2SLS method these two equations are combined to generate the estimate the US national aggregate supply curve. This may be done by taking FE from the price equation Pe as a function of all other variables and replacing FE in the GDPe equation. Alternatively one may say that the supply curve is the common place of the supply and demand intersection points when the aggregate demand curve shifts freely while the supply curve is fixed. This may theoretically be done by estimating GDPe as a function of Pe and all of their explanatory variables but one. In so doing, all variables will follow the ceteris paribus condition while the omitted variable makes the aggregate demand to move constantly. In this case FE is the exogenous variable that must be chosen for it is the sole one that displaces only the aggregate demand and does not influence directly the supply curve. Accordingly, it was run the OLS regression of GDPe as a function of Pe and all exogenous variables but FE, obtaining the result reported below.

Of course the reported statistics are irrelevant; this trick is used to avoid algebraic mistakes. What matters is the theoretical equilibrium **US National Aggregate Supply curve**:

NAS = GDPe = - 810.678 + 180.88*Pe - 2212.37*MW - 44.9059*ER + 1.13991*DP + - 28.345*INT

US NATIONAL AGGREGATE SUPPLY CURVE

Dependent variable: GDPe

Variables	Coefficient	Std. error	t-statistics	p-value	
const	-810.68	1.53249e-011	-5.29E+13	<0.00001	***
Pe	180.88	4.82813e-013	3.746E+14	<0.00001	***
MW	-2212.37	1.18752e-011	-1.86E+14	<0.00001	***
ER	-44.9059	5.46563e-013	-8.22E+13	<0.00001	***
DP	1.13991	0	1.078E+14	<0.00001	***
INT	-28.345	0	-3.59E+14	<0.00001	***

Dependent var. avg.	5782.959	Dependent var. std. error	4516.213
Square residuals sum.	7.81e-21	Regression std. error	1.38e-11
R-square	1.000000	Adjusted R-square	1.000000

All these estimates produce a species of "average" results associated with the sample. For instance, the US national aggregate supply slope (180.88) applies for this sample; other samples will generate different slopes. By the way, this estimate of the US national aggregate supply curve slope suggests that it is quite away from zero. So, this experiment gives no support to the neoclassical vertical aggregate supply curve and full employment ideas. Anyway, it should be interesting to estimate the slope of the aggregate supply curve for many successive samples since it indicates a country's technological development; rotation of the aggregate supply curve toward the horizontal line suggests higher technological development

Accordingly, the constant term also varies and thus the supply curve shifts constantly as time goes by. Companies do not follow an eternal relation between price and production; they make wishful decisions aiming to adapt themselves to all market conditions and hence there is an aggregate supply curve for each point in time, in this case more often or perhaps always shifting to the left. Figure 11 shows the estimate of the US National Aggregate Supply curves for the years 2000 and 2007. The equations are:

$NASc_{2000} = -20648.7524 + 180.88*Pe$, Elasticity : 2.97

$NASc_{2007} = -22411.8767 + 180.88*Pe$, Elasticity : 2.39

Capital and Justice

Figure 11 US national aggregate supply curves

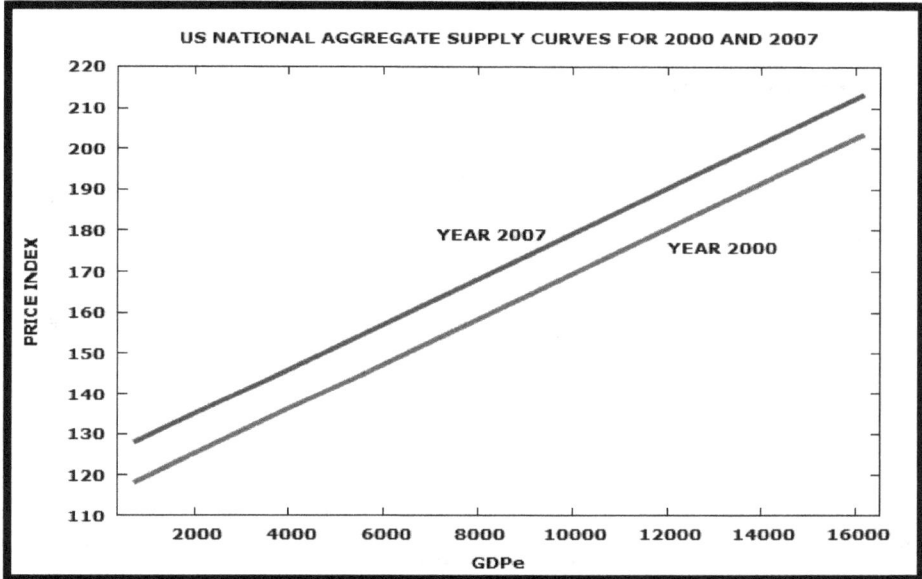

Source: Elaborated by the Author

It also happens that the monetary policy's effects look undefined for the public debt DP expands the aggregate supply while its interest expenditure INT does the opposite. But it is possible to estimate the combined effect of DP and INT by omitting DP in the reduced equations of GDP and P. This omission imposes a bias to INT's coefficient such that INT carries the effect of DP. Alternatively, reminding that INT is a function of DP and thus that makes no sense to talk ceteris paribus one when the other varies, this bias may be introduced without distorting the other coefficients by estimating DP as a function of INT, and in this sample the equation obtained is:

DP = -196.387 + 11.064*INT

Replacing **DP** in the unabridged equations by the expression above the monetary policy is represented by just one exogenous variable, **INT**, in the **ABRIDGED EQUATIONS:**

GDPea = - 197.8225 + 6.36696*FE + 15.5759*ER - 0.580*INT

Pea = 4.6259 + 0.03520*FE + 12.2312*MW + 0.334376*ER + 0.08377*INT

300

Deviations of the new estimates, GDPea and Pea, from the original series are insignificant, as shown in Figures 12 and 13.

Figure 12 Adherence of the abridged reduced GDP equation

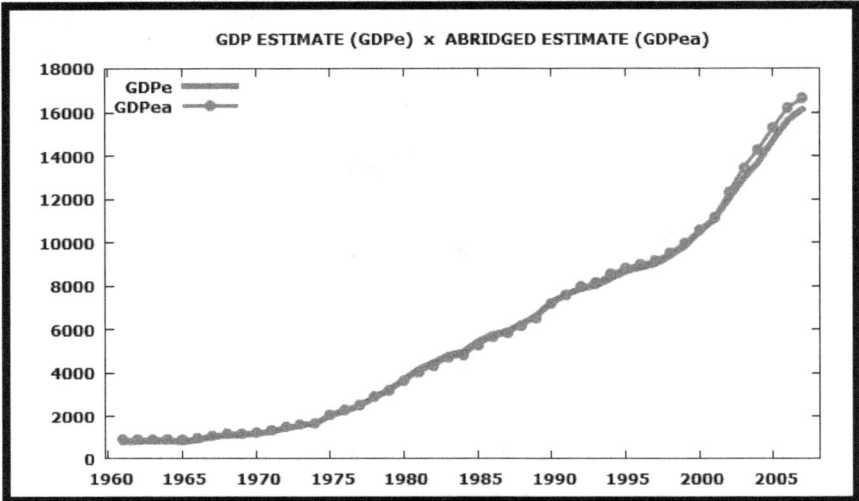

GDP ESTIMATE (GDPe) x ABRIDGED ESTIMATE (GDPea)

Figure 13 Adherence of the abridged reduced price equation

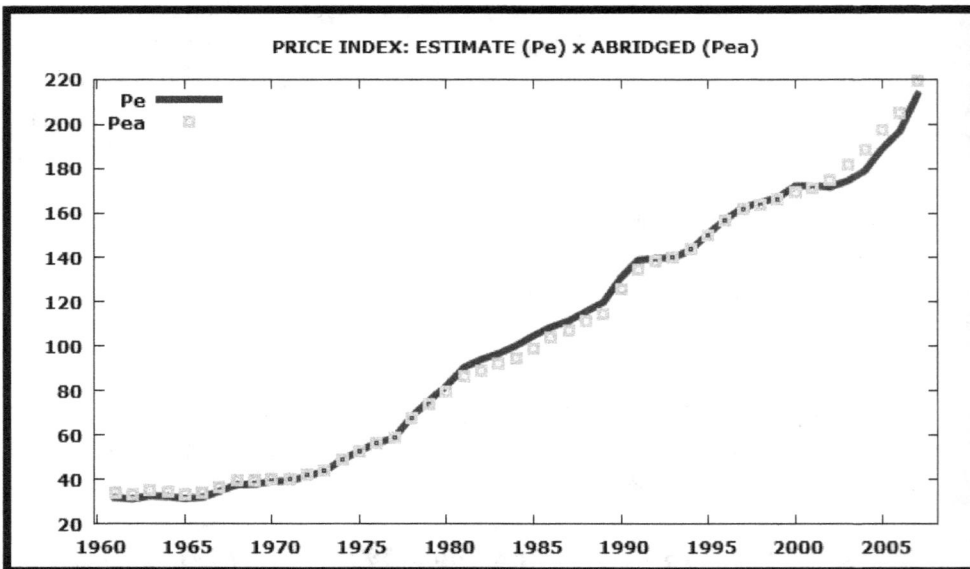

PRICE INDEX: ESTIMATE (Pe) x ABRIDGED (Pea)

Source for Figures 12 and 13: Elaborated by the Author

After abridging it may be seen that signs of **INT**, negative in the **GDPea** equation and positive in the **Pea** equation, allow for the deduction that the monetary policy expanded the aggregate demand, through credit (**DEBTS**), but the shift so attained was less than the expansion required to compensate the simultaneous contraction that the monetary policy imposed to the aggregate supply through public debt **DP**. This means that what prevails is the backward aggregate supply shift as if in a situation of aggregate supply shifting to the left while aggregate demand is stationary. The conclusion is thus that, ceteris paribus, monetary policy caused prices to rise and GDP to fall, and certainly unemployment to grow.

5.3. US aggregate supply curve

The estimate of the US total aggregate supply curve follows the same procedure. First it was obtained the aggregate supply shown in the Gretl's report below.

US AGGREGATE SUPPLY
Dependent variable: Y

Variables	Coefficient	Std. error	t-statistics	p-value	
const	-443.907	134.834	-3.2923	0.00215	***
FE_1	7.6479	0.185963	41.1259	<0.00001	***
ER_2	18.0071	5.89221	3.0561	0.00409	***
DP	-3.12403	0.254645	-12.2682	<0.00001	***
DP_1	2.7259	0.266903	10.2131	<0.00001	***
INT_2	-10.2995	2.19916	-4.6834	0.00004	***
INT_3	12.5255	2.12429	5.8963	<0.00001	***

Dependent var. avg.	5923.867	Dep. var. std. error	4765.919
Square residuals sum.	1002386	Regression std. error	162.4148
R-square	0.998997	Adjusted R-square	0.998839
F- statistic	6308.233	F p-value	2.22e-55
Durbin-Watson	1.889624	DW 1% (6,45): 1.065-1.643	

Collecting coefficients for each lagged explanatory variable it is obtained the estimate of the theoretical equilibrium equation for the US total aggregate supply:

Ye = -443.907 + 7.6479*FE + 18.0071*ER - 0.39813*DP + 2.2260*INT

Monetary policy, unemployment, inflation and wealth concentration

Figure 14 displays the Aggregate Supply elasticities, revealing a performance that, as expected, is quite similar to that of the National Aggregate Supply.

Figure 14 Aggregate supply elasticities

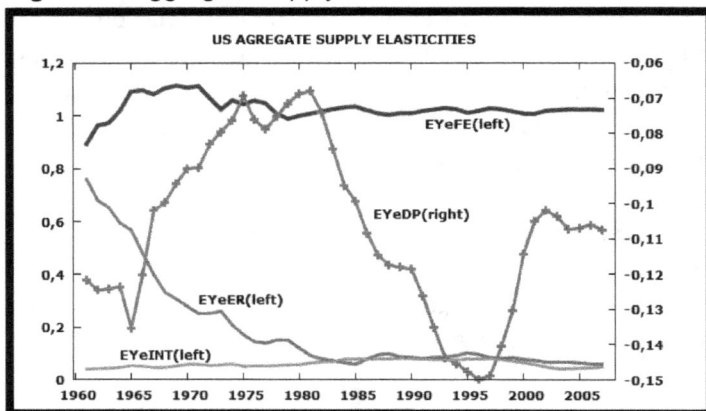

US AGREGATE SUPPLY ELASTICITIES

EYeFE(left)

EYeDP(right)

EYeER(left)

EYeINT(left)

Source: Elaborated by the Author

Next, combining total supply of goods and services with price index under the laboratory condition that only fiscal expenses FE vary freely, the result is the US total aggregate supply curve, presented in the statistical report below.[11]

US AGGREGATE SUPPLY CURVE
Dependent variable: Ye

	Coefficient	Std. error	t-statistics	p-value	
const	-1083.98	5.745E-11	-1.887E+13	<0.00001	***
Pe	217.27	1.810E-12	1.200E+14	<0.00001	***
MW	-2657.47	4.452E-11	-5.969E+13	<0.00001	***
ER	-54.6427	2.049E-12	-2.667E+13	<0.00001	***
DP	1.4604	0	3.685E+13	<0.00001	***
INT	-36.5371	2.961E-13	-1.234E+14	<0.00001	***

Dependent var. avg.	6519.280	Dep. Var. std. error	5239.558
Square residual sum.	1.10e-19	Regression std. error	5.17e-11
R- square	1.000000	Adjusted R-square	1.000000

---

[11] Once again, test statistics are irrelevant; this trick is intended to avoid algebraic mistakes.

Thus, the **US aggregate supply** curve (Figure 15) obtained is:

Ye = - 1083.98 + 217.27*Pe - 2657.47*MW - 54.6427*ER + 1.4604*DP - 36.5371*INT

The US aggregate supply curve for 2000 is:

AS$_{2000}$ = - 25519.2816 + 217.27*Pe

Figure 15 US aggregate supply curves

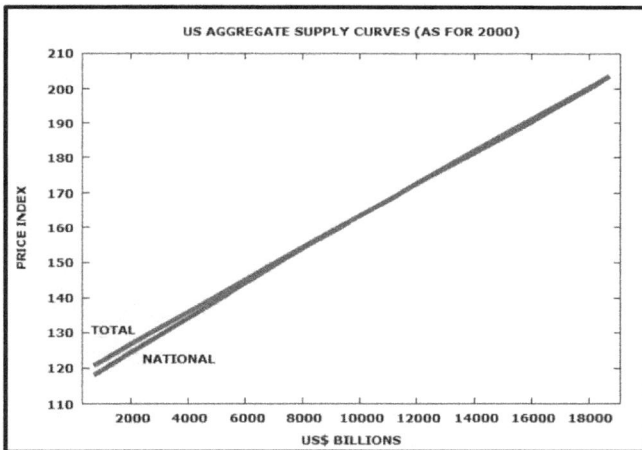

Elasticities for year 2000: National 2.97; Total = 3.15
Source: Elaborated by the Author

5.4. US aggregate demand curve

The demand curve is the common place of the supply and demand intersection points when the supply curve shifts freely while the demand curve rests. This may theoretically be done by estimating the demand "quantity" as a function of the price and all their explanatory variables but one, and one that shifts supply and not demand. In so doing, all explanatory variables will follow the ceteris paribus condition while the omitted variable will make the aggregate supply to move constantly. This condition makes the estimating the aggregate demand curve to normally be a hard work for almost all exogenous macroeconomic variables may displace it. Notwithstanding, in this case it will be shown that it is possible to find out a "proxy" estimate of the US aggregate demand. To start, the Gretl's report below presents the estimate of the US aggregate demand.

US AGGREGATE DEMAND ESTIMATE
Dependent Variable: AD

Variables	Coefficient	Std error	t-statistics	p-value	
Const.	-488.29	131.966	-3.7001	0.00068	***
FE_1	7.55301	0.182008	41.4982	<0.00001	***
ER_2	18.3067	5.7669	3.1744	0.00297	***
DP	-2.96026	0.249229	-11.8777	<0.00001	***
DP_1	2.5789	0.261227	9.8723	<0.00001	***
INT_2	-10.2193	2.15239	-4.7479	0.00003	***
INT_3	12.0638	2.07911	5.8024	<0.00001	***

Dependent var. avg.	5792.963	Dep. var. std. error	4694.226
Square residuals sum.	960203.6	Regression std. error	158.9607
R-square	0.999010	Adjusted R-square	0.998853
F (6,38)	6388.801	F p-value	1.74e-55
Durbin-Watson	1.968257	DW 1% (6,45): 1.065 – 1.643	

Therefore, the US aggregate demand theoretical equilibrium equation is:

ADe = - 488.29 + 7.55301*FE + 18.3067*ER – 0.38136*DP + 1.8445*INT

Figure 16 displays the elasticities of the aggregate demand, showing that the fiscal policy (EADeFE) was always the key variable expanding the US aggregate demand.

Unexpectedly, the minimum wage is not significant to the aggregate demand in this experiment, being then meaningless when compared with the other explanatory variables. This suggests that the economic policy despised minimum wage as an income distribution instrument thus contributing to increase income concentration. The same neglect applies to the exchange rate since its potential to push aggregate demand (EADeER) dropped from 0.8 to near 0.1. But maybe it is not neglect that explains why the monetary policy demand-push multiplier (EADeINT) is so low; probably, compared to FE it is always irrelevant. In the opposite direction the negative burden of the public debt (EADeDP) seems sufficiently low to do not allow for a conclusion about the consequence of the monetary policy over the aggregate demand.

Figure 16 US aggregate demand elasticities

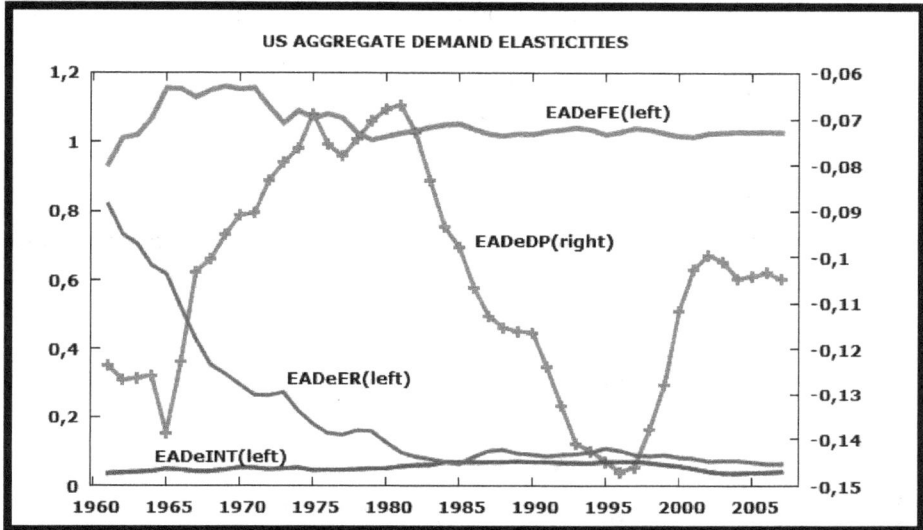

Source: Elaborated by the Author

Notwithstanding, it was previously shown that abridging the monetary policy it may be seen that what happens is the same as an aggregate supply drop while aggregate demand is stationary. Therefore, in abridged versions of the aggregate demand and price index the exogenous variable **INT** may play the role of shifting the aggregate supply curve without touching the aggregate demand curve. Consequently, the abridged versions of the theoretical equilibrium equations of the aggregate demand ADe and price index Pea allow for the estimate of the US aggregate demand curve, or at least a "proxy" or "surrogate" aggregate demand curve. Reminding thus the abridged equation of the price index P and replacing DP in ADe equation by the function:

DP = -196.387 + 11.064*INT

It comes the US aggregate demand abridged reduced equations:

ADea = - 560.809 + 7.55301*FE + 18.3067*ER - 2.3749*INT

Pea = 4.6259 + 0.03520*FE + 12.2312*MW + 0.334376*ER + 0.08377*INT

Figure 17 shows that, coherently with previous results, fiscal policy is the main instrument to expand the aggregate demand while the exchange rate effect almost vanished and that the monetary policy measured by the combination of the public debt and its interest rent caused a contraction of the aggregate demand that may be said low.

Figure 17 Aggregate demand (ADea) abridged elasticities

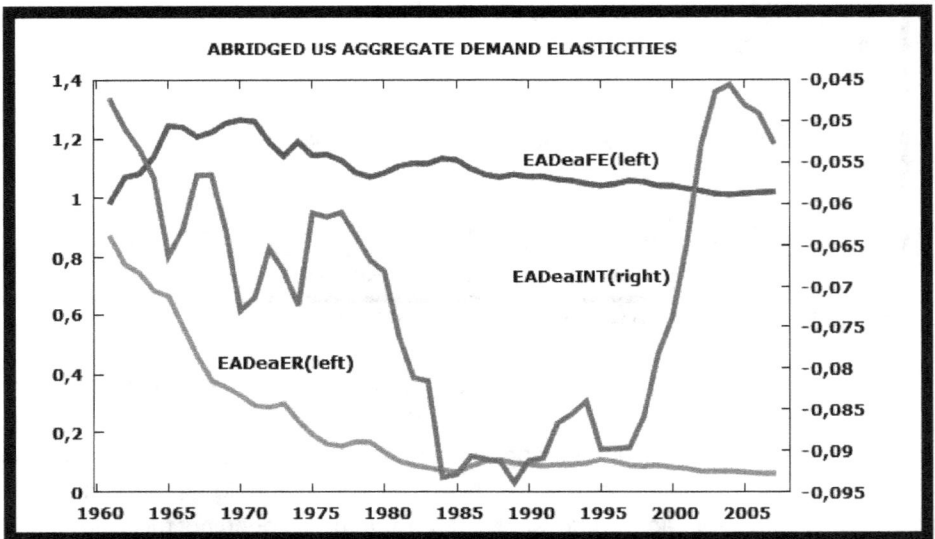

Source: Elaborated by the Author

Therefore, the Gretl's report below displays the estimate of the "proxy" or "surrogate" US aggregate demand curve.

The "proxy" or "surrogate" theoretical equilibrium US aggregate demand curve equation is thus:

ADc = - 429.664 – 28.3502*Pea + 8.55094*FE + 346.758*MW + 27.78963*ER

US AGGREGATE DEMAND CURVE Dependent variable: ADea					
Variables	Coefficient	Std. error	t-statistics	p-value	
const	-429.664	7.68158e-012	-5.593E+17	<0.00001	***
Pea	-28.3502	4.60277e-013	-6.159E+17	<0.00001	***
FE	8.55094	0	5.153E+18	<0.00001	***
MW	346.758	9.52144e-012	3.642E+17	<0.00001	***
ER	27.7863	3.31824e-013	8.374E+17	<0.00001	***

Dependent var. avg.	6215.828		Dependent var. std. error	5210.907
Square residuals sum.	3.35e-21		Regression std. error	8.92e-12
R-square	1.000000		Adjusted R-square	1.000000

The estimation of an aggregate demand curve does not mean that consumers behave as Maslow described and less yet that they assure that their needs are 100% satisfied. To Economics it is irrelevant to "prove" that consumers buy stuffs to satisfy needs or that they have another target than that. Like the aggregate supply curves, the aggregate demand also changes at each explanatory variables change. Figure 18 below shows the US aggregate demand curve for the 2000 data, when explanatory variables values lead to the equation:

$ADea_{2000}$ = 16173.236 – 28.3502*Pea

Finally, Figure 19 presents the traditional image of the supply and demand curves for the year 2000 data, and their shifters.

Figure 18 US aggregate demand curve

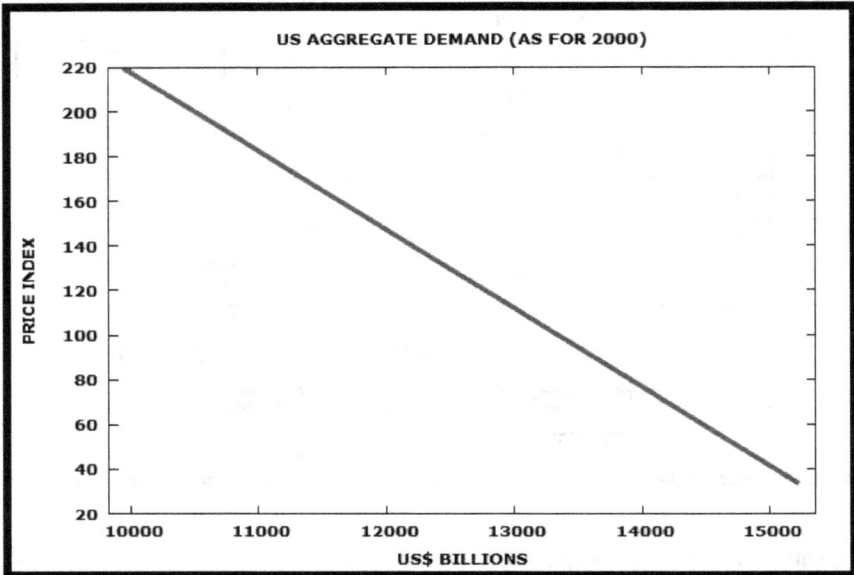

Elasticity for the year 2000 = − 0.43
Source: Elaborated by the Author

Figure 19 The traditional aggregate demand and supply graph

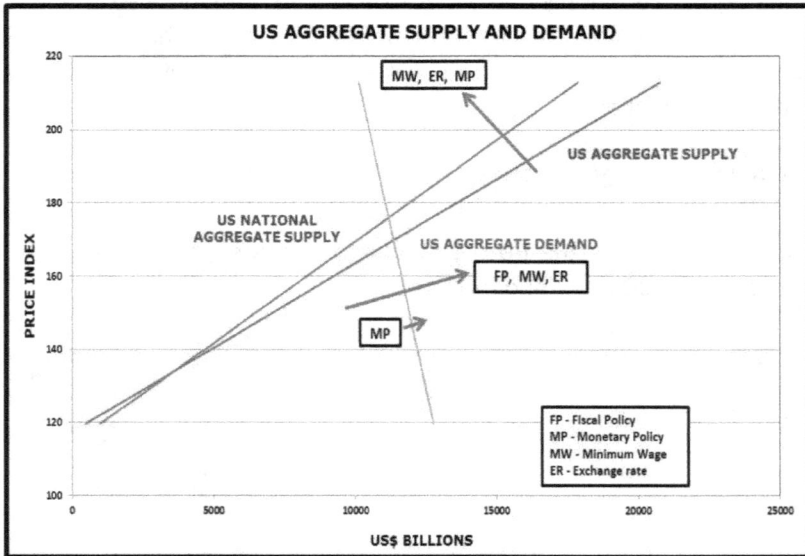

Source: Elaborated by the Author

7. Conclusions

Results obtained by the experiment on the US economy suggests that the supply and demand theory proposed looks promising as a starting point to the development of a modern supply and demand theory and a real world economic theory that may replace the monetarist mainstream theory and economic policy.

Generalizing the estimated effects in the period 1960-2007 of the mainstream monetarist economic policy of the United States, the world leading country, it may be said that the dominance of the mainstream monetarist ends and tools in the economic policy mix of many countries may explain the evidences of the widespread undemocratic social problems we highlighted in this chapter. *Ceteris paribus*, the public debt reduces the aggregate supply, while the interest rent from the public debt expands the aggregate demand. However, the former effect is stronger than the latter in such a way that the monetary policy core: public debt and interest rent donation to the few rich, causes prices to inflate and GDP to drop, and certainly real wages and employment to stagnate or fall.

The situation created by the monetary policy is not worse due to the other three economic policy instruments. Firstly, fiscal expenses shift the aggregate demand curve to the right while the aggregate supply curve rests, thus providing more production, more jobs and more income to workers, especially the newcomers. Of course prices also rise, but then workers may probably be better than before, since they have more income that allow them to climb the Maslow pyramid and buy more expensive products and services. The notion of inflation calls for a revision.

Secondly, dollar undervaluation shifts the aggregate supply curve to the left, but displaces the aggregate demand curve to the right more than offsetting its negative effect on GDP. Currency devaluation works like the fiscal policy. Thirdly, higher minimum wage means aggregate demand expansion and aggregate supply reduction such that greater minimum wage leads to more income to workers, despite possibly not increasing GDP, and to a less concentrated distribution of income without causing production contraction or unemployment. Minimum wage is essentially an economic policy instrument of income (re)distribution.

Combining all these mainstream economic policy instruments it becomes clear that what democratically create and distribute income and wealth are the fiscal policy and national currency devaluation, both criticized by the mainstream monetarist bodyguards claiming that they are inflationary. What mainstream followers do not say is that inflation, partially caused by them, must be avoided in order to do not devaluate the capital of the financial capitalists that actually rule the economic policy. The mainstream economic monetary policy does not serve the society democratically; it serves the few economic policy rulers, especially and intentionally transferring income from the workers to them.

The main conclusion is that what must necessarily be dismissed is the neoclassical demand and supply indoctrination based on unsustainable assumptions chosen to lead to results that are never observed but convenient to the monetary mainstream economic policy. Persistence in maintaining the mainstream monetarist economic policy points to more social injustice. Replacing the monetarist mainstream economics looks essential to "Bend the Arc of Global Capital Toward Justice".

References

Auerbach Robert (2011) When Five Hundred Economists Are Not Enough. *The Huffington Post Business*, May 25. Available at http://www.huffingtonpost.com/robert-auerbach/when-five-hundred-economi_b_278418.html. (Accessed 23 May 2016)

Baiman, R., Rothenberg, M. (2007) Rentier-Based Finance-Led Macroeconomies: Keynesian or Classical in the Short-run, but Unsustainably Debt Dependent and Minskyan in the Long-run. *Chicago Political Economy Group Working* Paper 2007-1. Available at http://www.cpegonline.org/workingpapers/CPEGWP2007-1.pdf. (Accessed 14 June 2016)

Benham, D. D. (2002) A Phone Call To The Fed. *Rense.com*, September, 8. Available at http://www.rense.com/general29/ringring.htm. (Accessed 12 October 2015)

Blyth, M.,Lonergan, E. (2014) Why Central Banks Should Give Money Directly to the People. *Foreign Affairs*, September/October. Available at https://www.foreignaffairs.com/articles/united-states/2014-08-11/print-less-transfer-more (Accessed 28 July 2016).

Brown, E. H. (2010) *The Web of Debt*. Third Millenium Press, 4th Edition, USA: Baton Rouge.

Business Insider (2015) *Since the financial crisis, almost all Americans have seen their wages fall.* Jul. 13. Available at http://www.businessinsider.com/change-in-real-wages-by-income-percentile-2015-7. (Accessed 20 July 2016)

Caldari, K. (2004) *Book Review: Arena, R. and Quéré, M. (eds). The Economics of Alfred Marshall - Revisiting Marshall's Legacy* (New York: Palgrave MacMillan, 2003). EH.NET, September. Available at https://eh.net/book_reviews/the-economics-of-alfred-marshall-revisiting-marshalls-legacy/. (Accessed on 15 May 2016)

Chang, H., Aldred, J. (2014) After the crash, we need a revolution in the way we teach economics. *The Guardian,* May 11. Available at http://www.theguardian.com/business/2014/may/11/after-crash-need-revolution-in-economics-teaching-chang-aldred. (Accessed 11 October 2014).

Cournot, A. A. (1838) *Principes Mathématiques de la Théorie des Richesses*. Paris: Marcel Rivière & Companie, 1938 Edition.

Credit Suisse (2015) *Global Wealth Report 2015*. Credit Suisse Research Institute, October 2015. Available at https://www.google.com.br/webhp?sourceid=chrome-instant&ion=1&espv=2&ie=UTF-8#q=Credit+Suisse+Research+Institute+Global+Wealth+Report+2015. (Accessed 15 August 2016)

Dardi, M. (2005) Alfred Marshall and Mathematics. *9th European Society for the History of Economic Thought Conference*. Stirling, Scotland, June 9-12, 2005. Available at http://www.lib.hit-u.ac.jp/service/tenji/amjas/Dardi.pdf. (Accessed 18 January 2008).

Dardi, M. (2014) Philosophy and psychology of mathematics according to Alfred Marshall. *The Cambridge Journal of Economics*. December 22. Available at http://cje.oxfordjournals.org/content/early/2014/12/22/cje.beu078. (Accessed 3 April 2016).

Dornbusch, R., Fischer, S. (1990) *Macroeconomics*. 5th edition, USA: McGraw-Hill.

Fullbrook, E. (2010) How to bring economics into the 3rd millennium by 2020. *Real-World Economics Review,* 54, September 27, pp. 89-102. Available at http://www.paecon.net/PAEReview/issue54/Kessler54.pdf. (Accessed 15 Dec. 2010)

Galbraith, J. K. (1975) *Money: Whence It Came, Where It Went*. Boston, USA: Houghton Mifflin Publishers.

Galbraith, J. K. (2010) *Statement.* Judiciary Committee, Subcommittee on Crime, US Senate, Washington D.C., May 4. Available at http://utip.gov.utexas.edu/Flyers/GalbraithMay4SubCommCrimeRV.pdf.   (Accessed 25 April 2010).

Grieve, R. H. (2014) Right back where we started from: from the Classics to Keynes, and back again. *Real-World Economics Review*, 68, August 21, pp. 41-61. Available at http://rwer.wordpress.com/comments-on-rwer-issue-no-68/. (Accessed 31 August 2014)

Grim, R. (2013) Priceless: How The Federal Reserve Bought The Economics Profession. *The Huffington Post.* May 13. Available at http://www.huffingtonpost.com/2009/09/07/priceless-how-the-federal_n_278805.html. (Accessed 25 April 2010)

Hager, S. B. (2013) What Happened to the Bondholding Class? Public Debt, Power and the Top One Per Cent. *New Political Economy*, April, pp. 1-28. Available at http://bnarchives.yorku.ca/356/ (Accessed 28 November 2014)

Huber, J., Robertson, J. (2001) Creating New Money. *New Economics Foundation.* Available at http://www.jamesrobertson.com/book/creatingnewmoney.pdf. (Accessed 5 July 2016)

Hudson, M. (2015) Financial avoidance of public taxes and duties. *Real-World Economics Review Blog*, August 3, Available at https://rwer.wordpress.com/2015/08/03/financial-avoidance-of-public-taxes-and-duties/. (Accessed 3 August 2015)

Kahn, R. F. (1984) *The Making of Keynes' General Theory.* New York, USA: Cambridge University Press.

Kahneman, D. (2003) A psychological perspective on economics. *The American Economic Review, Papers and Proceedings of the One Hundred Fifteenth Annual Meeting of the American Economic Association.*, 93 (2), May, pp. 162-168.

Keynes, J. M. (1936) The General Theory of Employment, Interest and Money. Orlando, USA: First Harvest Harcourt Brace Edition, 1964.

Kuhn, T. S. (1962) *The Structure of Scientific Revolutions.* Chicago, USA: University of Chicago Press.

Lee, F. S., Keen, S. (2004) The Incoherent Emperor: A Heterodox Critique of Neoclassical Microeconomic Theory. *Review Of Social Economy*, LXII (2), June. Available at http://heterodox-economics.org/archive/micro/ROSE-2004-Lee-Keen-incoherentemperor.pdf. (Accessed 11 May 2008)

Lima, G. P. (2015) Public debt is economic nonsense. In O. Ugarteche, A. Puyana, A and M. A. Madi (eds.), *Ideas towards a new international financial architecture?*, World Economics Association Book Series, pp. 74-97. Available at http://www.worldeconomicsassociation.org/ (Accessed 15 July 2016)

Lima, G. P. (1995). Cartels, Cooperation and Rivalry. *XXIII Annual Meeting of the Brazilian National Association of Post-graduate Courses in Economics*, December, 1995. Available at http://www.macroambiente.com.br/downloads/newdown/eng/cartels_cooperation_riv alry.pdf (Accessed 15 July 2016)

Lima, G. P. (1992) *Une Analyse Critique des Fondements Théoriques et Empiriques de la Courbe d'Offre*. PhD dissertation, University of Paris X, February, Unpublished.

McKinsey Global Institute (2016) Poorer Than Their Parents? Flat or Falling Incomes in Advanced Economies. McKinsey Global Institute, July. Available at http://www.mckinsey.com/global-themes/employment-and-growth/poorer-than-their-parents-a-new-perspective-on-income-inequality (Accessed 18 August 2016)

Marshall, A. (1890) *Principles of Economics*. London: The MacMillan Press. 8th edition, printing of 1986.

Marshall, A. (1919) *Industry and Trade*. New York, USA: Augustus M. Kelley. First edition, printing of 1970.

Maslow, A. H. (1943) *A Theory of Human Motivation*. Classics in the History of Psychology. August 2000. Available at http://psychclassics.yorku.ca/Maslow/motivation.htm. (Accessed 12 July 2016)

Nitzan, J., Bichler, S. (2009) *Capital as Power - A study of order and creorder*. The Bichler & Nitzan Archives. Available at http://bnarchives.yorku.ca/259/ (Accessed 1 April 2015)

OXFAM (2016) An economy for the 1%. *Oxfam Briefing Paper*, 210, 18 January. Available at https://www.oxfam.org/files/file_attachments/bp210-economy-one-percent-tax-havens-180116-en_0.pdf (Accessed 28 March 2016)

Page, B. I., Bartels, L. M., Seawright, J. (2013) Democracy and the Policy Preferences of Wealthy Americans. *Perspectives on Politics*, 11 (01), March, pp. 51-73. Available at http://journals.cambridge.org/action/displayAbstract?fromPage=online&aid=8864478&fileId=S153759271200360X (Accessed 12 March 2015)

Polleit, T. (2013) Central Banks: The True Centers of Political Power. *Mises Daily,* November 07. Available at http://mises.org/daily/6578/Central-Banks-The-True-Centers-of-Political-Power (Accessed 25 July 2015)

Robinson, J. (1965a) *Kalecki and Keynes. Collected Economic Papers*, vol. IV. Oxford: Brackwell, pp. 92-99.

Robinson, J. (1965b) *The General Theory after Twenty-Five Years.* Collected Economic Papers, vol. III. Oxford: Brackwell, pp. 100-102.

Ruccio, D. (2016a) *Chart of the day.* Occasional links and bits of commentary blog. *July 6. Available at https://anticap.wordpress.com/2016/07/06/chart-of-the-day-525/ (Accessed 8 July 2016)*

Ruccio, D. (2016b) Average incomes in the US 1979-2015. *Real-World Economics Review Blog,* July 14. Available at https://rwer.wordpress.com/2016/07/14/average-incomes-in-the-us-1979-2015/ (Accessed 11 July 2016)

Ryan-Collins, J. (2015) Is Monetary Financing Inflationary? A Case Study of the Canadian Economy, 1935–75. *Levy Economics Institute Working Paper* No. 848, October. Available at http://www.levyinstitute.org/publications/is-monetary-financing-inflationary-a-case-study-of-the-canadian-economy-1935-75 (Accessed 15 June 2016).

Shepherd, G. (1995) *Rejected: leading economists ponder the publication process.* Available at http://www.chichilnisky.com/pdfs/papers/187.pdf. (Accessed 1 April 2008).

Sy, W. (2012) Endogenous crisis and the economic paradigm. *Real-world economics review,* 59, March. Available at http://www.paecon.net/PAEReview/issue59/Sy59.pdf (Accessed 13 March 2012)

Syll, L. P. (2012) Rational expectations – a fallacious foundation for macroeconomics in a non-ergodic world. *Real-World Economics Review,* 62, December, pp. 34-50, http://www.paecon.net/PAEReview/issue62/Syll62.pdf (Accessed 15 February 2014)

Syll, L. P. (2014) Micro vs. macro. *Real-World Economics Review,* 66, January, pp. 12-29. Available at http://www.paecon.net/PAEReview/issue66/Syll66.pdf (Accessed 15 February 2014)

Syll, L. P. (2016) Macroeconomic models – beautiful but irrelevant. *Real-World Economics Review Blog,* April 12. Available at https://rwer.wordpress.com/2016/04/12/macroeconomic-models-beautiful-but-irrelevant/ (Accessed April 12 2016)

United States, Federal Bureau of Investigation (2014) *Financial Crimes Report 2010-2011,* August 5. Available at http://www.fbi.gov/stats-services/publications/financial-crimes-report-2010-2011 (Accessed 12 December 2014)

Werner, R. (2011) Debt Free & Interest Free Money. Video, 26 May. Available at https://www.youtube.com/watch?v=zIkk7AfYymg (Accessed 12 April 2015)

Werner, R. (2012) The case for localised banking. The *Just Banking Conference*. Video, April 20. Available at https://www.youtube.com/watch?v=O0wA6SbsHg8 (Accessed on 12 April 12 2015)

Zaman, A., Saglam, I (2012) The Conflict Between General Equilibrium and the Marshallian Cross. *Koç University-Tüsiad Economic Research Forum*, Working Paper Series, July. Available at https://ideas.repec.org/p/koc/wpaper/1219.html. (Accessed 15 July 2015).

Appendix: Variables definitions and sources. Data are current values.

GDP - Gross Domestic Product, US$ billion, US Bureau of Economic Analysis. http://www.bea.gov/national/index.htm.

P - US Bureau of Labor Statistics, CPI Detailed Report. http://www.bls.gov/cpi/cpid1405.pdf.

AD - Aggregate demand, US$ billion, US Bureau of Economic Analysis and White House, Office of Management and Budget, Historical Tables. http://www.bea.gov/national/index.htm . and http://www.whitehouse.gov/omb/budget/Historicals.

FE - Federal Government, Fiscal Expenditure, estimated by subtracting Net interest expenditure from Total outlays, US$ billion, White House, Office of Management and Budget, Historical Tables, Fiscal Year 2014, Tables 3. http://www.whitehouse.gov/omb/budget/Historicals.

MW - Federal minimum wage, US$ per hour, U.S. Department of Labor. http://www.dol.gov/esa/whd/flsa/.

ER - Exchange rate, average exchange rate in US dollars needed to buy a foreign currencies basket weighted by the corresponding US exports. Original data: OECD. Sample: Austria, Belgium, Canada, China, France, Germany, Ireland, Italy, Japan, Mexico, Netherlands, Switzerland and United Kingdom. http://stats.oecd.org/Index.aspx?DataSetCode=SNA_TABLE4.

DG - Federal Government debt held by Federal Government Accounts, US$ billion, White House, Office of Management and Budget, Historical Tables, Fiscal Year 2014, Tables 7.1. http://www.whitehouse.gov/omb/budget/Historicals.

DP - Federal Government debt held by the central bank system and the public, US$ billion, White House, Office of Management and Budget, Historical Tables, Fiscal Year 2014,Tables 7.1. http://www.whitehouse.gov/omb/budget/Historicals.

INT - Federal Government interest expenditure, US$ billion, Federal Reserve System, Data Download Program. http://www.federalreserve.gov/datadownload/Choose.aspx?rel=Z1.

Monetary policy, unemployment, inflation and wealth concentration

DEBTS - Private credit balance, Nonfinancial business, Households and Non-profit organizations, credit market instruments, liability, Series D.3, annual, US$ billion, Federal Reserve System.
http://www.federalreserve.gov/datadownload/Choose.aspx?rel=Z1.

NIRFA - Net unilateral current transfers, U.S. International Transactions Accounts Data, US$ billion, US Bureau of Economic Analysis.
http://www.bea.gov/national/index.htm.

YE - Foreign income measured by the GDP of the OECD area except US, US$ billions, OECD Statistics. http://www.oecd.org/statistics.

PE - Foreign consumers price index measured by the average Consumer Prices Index, weighted by the GDP, base 2005 = 100, original data: OECD, consumer prices, sample: Australia, Austria, Belgium, Canada, Denmark, France, Germany, Greece, Italy, Japan, Netherlands, New Zealand, Portugal, Spain, Sweden and United Kingdom. http://www.oecd.org/statistics.

Chapter 8

Capital, nationality and state sovereignty: new links for the 21st century

Marc Morgan-Milá

Introduction

This chapter seeks to explore the connection between capital and nation-states in our current globalized world. It is motivated from three premises. First, conventional belief upholds the view that capital is without borders, increasingly without tax jurisdiction, often linked to transnational corporations (TNCs), more and more mobile due to progress in information technology and thus cannot possess a legal nationality. Second, the findings of Zucman (2013a) corroborate this view somewhat, by showing that a non-negligible portion of the global financial wealth of households is held offshore, escaping national jurisdictions. This is specifically damaging to the sovereignty of states with respect to their fiscal and developmental policies. Moreover, the stock of unrecorded assets is double the recorded net debt of rich countries, which is sufficient to make the U.S. and Europe net creditors, rather than net debtors to the rest of the world as is officially held. Third, these first two premises reflect an asymmetry in knowledge regarding the respective identity of sovereign debtors and private creditors. While the national identity of the former is easily known in financial contracts, that of the latter is much more difficult to verify. This matters because without effectively knowing the nationality of private capital, national tax systems are undermined and states are increasingly dependent on international capital markets for financing their domestic needs.

This chapter challenges the first premise by arguing that, while capital does not fully possess a nationality *de jure,* it can be said to have a nationality *de facto.*[1] This is essentially because the nationality of capital mirrors the

---

[1] For the remainder of this essay I use the terms de *jure* (or quasi-*de jure*) and de

nationality of the capitalist, although the economic and political environments within which this nationality is manifested have changed over time, as this essay shall explain. Within the current environment of increasingly unregistered capital located in tax havens and opaque information regarding ownership (premises two and three), this essay shall highlight some guidelines as to how capital can fully come to have a quasi-*de jure* nationality. The immediate effect will be to eliminate the existing knowledge asymmetry between public debt and private assets, by ensuring that the latter follows a similar international recording system as the former, given that they are two sides of the same coin.

The remainder of the chapter is structured as follows. Section 1 will define the key terms of the essay – capital and nationality – and their relationship from a present perspective; Section 2 will examine how capital came to have a *de facto* nationality, from a historical perspective, while Section 3 offers proposals to effectively "naturalize" capital from a practical viewpoint before concluding.

1. The meaning of capital and nationality in a globalized world

To begin with it will be useful to properly define "capital" and to offer a more concrete understanding of what is meant by "nationality". For the purposes of this essay, the concept of "capital" is understood in broad economic terms. Thus, it is the productive and monetary value of all material and non-material wealth, encompassing all national assets, domestic and foreign, financial (equity, bonds, deposits, cash, pension funds, etc.) and non-financial (real estate, machinery, patents, etc.) held by private entities.[2] The concept of "debt" is anchored in that of capital, given that all financial (domestic and foreign) liabilities are somebody else's assets, as defined through double-entry bookkeeping. Indeed, the common definition of

facto for illustrative purposes to distinguish nationality in law from nationality as revealed through action or habit.
[2] This definition does not intend to diminish the notion of capital as embodying underlying social relations of production, as emphasized by Marx. Rather, it is judged to be relevant because it concerns material distributional conditions. It is partly due to prevailing distributional conditions that capital and nationality (mediated by the concept of power), have a link as is argued below.

"capital" between the 13th and late 18th centuries was "the capital assets of a trading firm", including "funds, stock of merchandise, cash and money bearing interest" (Braudel, 1979: 201). The fact that capital was often referred to as the "principal of a loan" and later as the "sums of money or their equivalents brought by partners into a partnership of company" (Schumpeter, 1954: 322), reveals how capital is linked to the capitalist system of debt.[3] Not only is capital advanced to form or expand an enterprise, but capital assets also need to be used as collateral to obtain such money loans in the first place. "Sovereign debt" works in similar ways. When the government creates more money it automatically creates a debt for itself and a corresponding asset (bond) for the investor. The government does not need to formally put up collateral for the loan, since it has a monopoly over legal tender, through the central bank, and over the collection of taxes.

A particular emphasis is placed in this essay on financial capital, for obvious reasons, namely, it's almost instantaneous mobility from one side of the world to the other and its intangible nature, which make it difficult to track and regulate. The treatment of non-financial capital (i.e. the physical means of production) is placed mostly in the context of transnational corporations (TNCs), given their multi-country location and production. These two forms of capital capture the essence of economic globalization in the present age. They also provide the premises to the argument that capital has no nationality. In this respect, they are worth examining a little closer.

It is plain to see that we no longer live in the post-war paradigm of national governments limiting the movement of capital across borders, but in one that vigorously defends the free capital movements and the end of national regulatory and supervisory power. Paradoxically, the capital market liberalization we are so familiar with today in developed countries can be

---

[3] This is firmly embedded in the system of money creation. Modern money is created by crediting and debiting money values on balance sheets, such that an asset and a corresponding liability of equal size are brought into being with a keystroke. When a debt is repaid both the asset and the liability are extinguished from the balance sheet. Hence, according to Hyman Minsky, "A capitalist economy can be described by a set of interrelated balance sheets and income statements" (Minsky, 1992: 12). Thus, all references to "capital" made in this essay should be understood as also encompassing debt, both private and public.

traced from the post-war period. Already in the 1950s, the creation of Eurocurrency markets allowed for easier and quicker conversions between major currencies (Tobin, 1978; Eatwell and Taylor, 2000). The 1960s and 1970s saw the definitive breakdown of the Bretton Woods system and the effective privatization of foreign exchange risk, as governments abandoned all intervention in exchange markets. Financial liberalization was given a more fertile ground on which to work during the 1980s, with the creation of global bond markets, and further during the 1990s, with the creation of global equity markets and the complete removal of the remaining capital controls left over from the Bretton Woods era (Eatwell and Taylor, 2000). These sequential events *appear* to have had the consequence of removing the national character of financial capital. No longer does capital have any obligations to anybody other than its private owners, so the argument goes.[4]

Unlike financial globalization, the phenomenon of TNCs, as we know it today, does not have a historical antecedent. While, it is true that the globalization of trade during the 1870-1914 period pre-dates our current wave, the nature of the traditional manufacturing firm has drastically changed. In the world of yesterday, "U.S. companies employed U.S. workers in the United States to manufacture tangible goods, which U.S. citizen-salesmen abroad sold in foreign markets" (Kirsch, 2007: 464). In today's world, U.S.-based TNCs operate using segmented production structures in which manufacturing is produced at multiple worldwide locations using subsidiaries or subcontractors. The answer then, to whether capital has a nationality should be in the name "transnational" corporation (or 'multinational' corporation). With the capital used in production being spread across many countries, it cannot pledge allegiance to any particular nation-state, but only to a unifying transnational motive – profit maximization. Arguments like these reveal that the only thing that is truly 'free' in a *free market* – a political economy structure of one dollar one vote, where everything is commodified – is capital. Individuals are free insofar as they

---

[4] It is noteworthy that our current age of financial globalization is not a historical anomaly. The period between 1870 and 1914, often described as the "first globalization" of finance and trade, was as integrated as our "second globalization" – it took until the early 21st century for developed countries to regain the same level of stock-market capitalization relative to GDP than had existed in the 1870-1914 period (Piketty, 2013). Similar to what we are used to, individuals back then could avail of sophisticated capital markets that served diversified portfolios of assets, both domestic and foreign, albeit not as complex as those existing today (ibid).

own capital (and insofar as they own their labour power). But this argument should not be confounded with the argument that capital has no nationality. This would erroneously equate freedom of movement with having no nationality when, in fact, it is proof of nationality that gives license to move.

The concept of "nationality" can be generally defined within the domain of international law, by which legal status is given to the attachment of an individual to a nation-state, via passports or national IDs (Weil, 2011). But being a national of a certain legally defined territory is also connected to two further features. It can be argued that having a nationality gives one the right to participate, up to further legally defined boundaries, in the political and civic life of the society one is a national of, for example by voting in elections and referenda or by volunteering in different kinds of social activities. It can also be argued that having a nationality affords one the psychological comfort of having a "home", or a sense of belonging. These features all come under the definition of "citizenship" (ibid). Yet given that they usually (but not strictly) require nationality, it is plausible to make use of them when exploring the concept of nationality.

Bridging the concepts of capital and nationality, it is not clear, *prima facie,* how they can be connected. Nationality, legally defined, pre-supposes that the link is between individual *persons* and nation-states. Capital, on the other hand, is an abstract concept – it is an aggregation of many different tangible and nontangible saleable assets. Yet it derives its meaning from a specific context of property relationships. It is in these relationships that capital can come to possess (indirectly if you will) a nationality – by following the nationality of its owner(s). Capital's aggregate abstract nature, however, should not detract us from the asymmetry concerning private assets and sovereign debts when it comes to identifying their respective nationalities. Government debt, issued in the form of bonds, has a *de jure* and *de facto* nationality – in practice, when investors and credit rating agencies have to assess the security of a government's debt, they are very aware of *where* that debt comes from, since countries can differ with respect to their policies and thus risk profiles. Moreover, when a government defaults on its debt, it is the nation-state, and its taxpayers, that can be brought to court and it is they who bear the burden of the ruling. On the other hand, private entities and individuals, who are largely the bondholders of a state's sovereign debts, are less easily associated to a nationality by law or by standard practice. One can notice this asymmetry in the Greek government debt debacle, where the identity of its counterpart, namely the nationality of the investors in Greek bonds, remained opaque. This is by no apparent means a media-driven conspiracy. It simply reflects the lack of an integrated cross-national accounting system that would effectively determine who owns what. Despite these limits, capital can be legally connected to national persons through enforced property rights or contract laws, at least in Capitalist societies.[5] By default, this means that capital is someway under the dictates of nationhood and its correlates, as defined above. By being under the mandate of its owner, capital usually finds its movements and ends directed towards the interests of this owner, which are usually defined in close proximity to the 'home' of the capitalist. And these interests are ruled by what capital affords. Ownership of economic capital is a statement of personal wealth. Wealth is both a stock of individual purchasing power and, when taken in the aggregate, an accounting variable for economic stability (its swift removal from the balance sheet of a country can be a cause of great economic instability). In increasingly commodified societies like ours, where almost everything can be put up on the market for sale, economic capital is thus a means to social, cultural and political power. And this power is more acute the more concentrated the ownership of capital is. Exercising the power that capital affords, whether it is in the form of purchasing goods and services for domestic use, for maintaining a certain social status or for influencing the direction of national economic and cultural policymaking, requires the capitalist to be connected to a 'home' or a place of residence. This logic renders the globalization argument irrelevant, as open borders increase the speed and movements of capital, but do not alter its ultimate objective or destination. And it is an inherent aspect of human nature – dependency on a "home" (where power and prestige can have meaning) – that determines this destination.

In the case of TNCs, the "nationality" of capital can be derived from the separate legal protection that incorporated businesses receive under most jurisdictions. In this exceptional case, one could interpret capital as having a

---

[5] On the other hand, capital in centrally planned Communist countries is, by definition, easier to connect to a nationality, since all capital is the property of the state.

quasi-*de jure* nationality. This protection, however, also reveals one side of capital's double standards upon exercising its nationality. When seeking protection under the law, for whatever reason, U.S.-based corporations are quick to be "American". They too like to display their nationality, when voluntarily contributing to social expenditures of any kind (infrastructure, donations for education, etc.) in the form of corporate philanthropy. Yet, they often forgo their nationality in as much as it is possible when made to contribute mandatorily, often towards the same ends, but through different means, namely public taxation. These trends are characteristic of TNCs in developed countries in general; examples of this strategy of tax minimization are plentiful today. Therefore, TNCs may have a quasi-*de jure* nationality but they only exercise it *de facto* when it is of their own private interest.

In general, therefore, capital's nationality is derived from the country where its owners permanently reside. Where nationality does not overlap with place of residence, it is the passport of the capitalist that overrides the place of residence in determining the nationality of capital, given that protection of property rights is of a more foundational interest to the capitalist than the economic, political or cultural ends this capital can facilitate (you cannot have the latter without the former). And as with financial capital, the nationality of corporate capital can be derived from the place of residence of its owners or top decision makers, which is usually the country where the corporation is registered.[6] Here the globalization argument for capital having no nationality is again redundant, and at most used as an excuse.

2. The origins of capital's *de facto* nationality

From the above logic we may conclude that capital is endowed *de facto* with a nationality (only in exceptional cases it can rely on some sort of quasi-*de jure* nationality). The roots of this relationship can be sourced from specific periods in the history of capitalism. Over time the relationship has evolved

---

[6] Similarly to the case of financial capital, if the owners change residence without applying for a new nationality, the capital of the corporation remains the nationality of the country where the corporation is registered, which is usually the original place of residence of the owners, as shall be argued below. The exceptions are cases where companies are registered *offshore* in tax havens (more on this below).

into new forms, but the organic link between capital and the nation continues to be maintained. According to the globalization argument, we have no reason to think so. Capital's interest is allied solely to profit, independently of where it must travel to achieve maximum return. In conjunction, it is mal-practice to regulate the foreign ownership of capital in a country, as used to be done by governments, since governments should only care about corporations creating jobs and domestic wealth, not whether they are owned by its citizens or by foreigners (Chang, 2011). Arguments like these are prone to portray that things have always been like this. History, however, tells us otherwise. In particular, there are two features linked to capitalism's history that are rarely emphasized, but which explain how capital came to acquire a *de facto* nationality. These are, the 'emulation principle' of national economic policy and the "home bias" in capital investment.

2.1 The "emulation principle"

The history of economic policy from roughly the seventeenth century onwards is marked by a simple heuristic that held sway among national policy makers of different emerging nations. This heuristic is best described as the "emulation principle" – "the endeavor to equal or surpass others in any achievement or quality" (Reinert, 2009). In essence, the principle is about emulating "the best in the class", and then relying on a comparative advantage at a higher stage of development than would have otherwise been possible without emulation. This simple strategy has been applied by all of the presently developed countries, with few exceptions. It starts off with the protection, nurture and promotion of those economic activities with the highest value-added for the domestic economy that can be attained at a given level of development.[7] This has commonly taken the path of upgrading economic capabilities from labor-intensive agricultural production and raw commodity extraction (sugar, coffee, fish, cotton, rubber, primary metals, etc.) to "light" manufacturing industry (clothing, shoes, textiles) and subsequently to capital-intensive "heavy" manufacturing industry (steel, washing machines, cars, ships, airplanes, computer technology, industrial machinery, medical equipment, etc.). The emulation that occurred on the production side was in a way satisfying a demand for emulation in

---

[7] This strategy is sometimes referred to as the "infant industry strategy" in the literature.

consumption between individuals of different countries – what can be interpreted as a "keeping up with the Joneses" mentality. An infant industry strategy thus bred specific state-managed policies, which were most successful when they were both import substituting and export promoting.[8]

The principle of emulation experienced vast popularity among policymakers, and can be seen in action in Britain's attempt to protect and nurture its industry to emulate the Dutch in the seventeenth century; with German and U.S. efforts to emulate the British in the eighteenth and nineteenth centuries; to East Asian countries like Japan and eventually South Korea to catch up the developed West in the 20th century, to all active industrializers in between not wanting to be left behind, including France, Italy, Scandinavia and evidently the Soviet Union. Only when their economies had sufficiently developed, were trade barriers, capital controls and financial regulations gradually abandoned from the strategy (Chang, 2007; Reinert, 2009). State sovereignty was thus closely managed and better preserved. Also, in this historical period, public debt was much more locally managed, depending largely on the capital of national individuals and companies. A prime example is the U.K from the late 17th century onwards, when the government granted royal charters to national companies that bought public debt, while various forms of bond and annuities (e.g. "consols") were offered to the affluent classes of the country (Venture and Voth, 2015).

The ideology defining this early history of capitalism was rooted in mercantilist nationalism, whereby it was the wealth of the nation through its trade that was desired. This united national policymakers and domestic merchants towards the same cause (providing glory to the former and wealth to the latter). War remained (until the mid-20th century) a useful outlet through which the productive wealth of a nation could be enhanced, but as Albert Hirschman insightfully points out in his book the *Passions and the Interests* (1977), the birth of capitalism channeled human competitive instincts away from purely violent pursuits and into commercial activities of

---

[8] This strategy had its most visible origins in Britain and the United States. British Prime Minister William Walpole is credited with being the first policy-maker to have implemented a comprehensive infant industry program in 1721, which influenced Alexander Hamilton, the first Treasury Secretary of the U.S. to be the first to present the theory of infant industry protection in his *Report on Manufactures* in 1791 (Chang, 2007).

greater social use. For much of the emulation period of the developed West, capital was devoted to "working" for the glory and power of the state. This thinking is nowhere more visible than from the minds of the *German Historical School* of economic thought, which influenced thinkers on both sides of the Atlantic. Political economists like Friedrich List (1789-1846) and Gustav Von Schmoller (1838-1917) promoted mercantilist policies and the infant industry strategy as means to promote "national economy-making – a national economic program for modernization and power" – very much in the spirit of the emulation principle (Magnusson, 1994).[9]

Not only does the early history of capitalism provide us with instances of patriotic emulation policies, but the extent of the competitive drive between nations also bred "anti-emulation" policies, especially in Europe. For example, the Venetian city-state prohibited the outward migration of her skilled glass workers with the death penalty, while England forebode the export of her industrial machinery for many years during her early industrialization period (Reinert, 2009). The English case is a perfect illustration of the *de facto* nationality that capital came to have upon the birth of capitalism and the Industrial Revolution. And characteristic of the economic strategy of the time, "England only gave up her export prohibition of machinery, when the English machine producers themselves successfully argued that if they were restricted from competing in world markets they would lose ground to foreign machine producers" (Reinert, 2009: 21). There have been yet other, more explicit, cases where capital has carried a nationality. These have usually revolved around war. One of the clearest examples is The European Recovery Program of 1947, commonly known as the Marshall Plan, through which a destroyed post-war Europe received large inflows of U.S.-sourced capital so as to help rebuild the continent's economy, which was of vital importance to the developing U.S. economy.

---

[9] The opposing school of thought was the "Neoclassical" or "Marginalist" School, whose economic maxim was *laissez-faire*, thus leaving the state out of economic affairs and promoting voluntary exchange between 'profit-maximizing' entrepreneurs and "utility-maximizing" consumers. While over time this latter school has come out as the intellectual victor, history remains on the side of the Historical School, which viewed man as a historical creature molded by evolving institutions and social conditions, rather than as a hedonistically motivated rational economic agent (Magnusson, 1994). It is still debated into which school Adam Smith best fit in, but careful reading of his *Wealth of Nations* suggests that he thought there was a time and a place for each view to be put into practice.

The Plan was probably the most successful economic development assistance program in human history, and it carried the U.S. seal on it (Reinert, 2009). Moreover, this episode also reveals how capital can be directed by national economic and political interest – the Plan not only helped to rebuild an important market for U.S. production, but it also successfully contained the spread of Soviet influence in Western Europe (ibid).

A further example relates to the reparation payments that the German state was forced under by the Allies in the aftermath of World War I. The Peace Treaty crafted by the Allies included numerous provisions of German capital expropriation – the ceding of her mercantile marine (vessels, trawlers, fishing boats); her colonies; the retention and liquidation of her foreign investments (properties, rights and interests) therein; a payment of up to $5,000,000,000 to be given in-kind "whether in gold, commodities, ships, securities or otherwise" (Art, 235); and the appropriation and exploitation of her coal-mines and iron-ore fields (Keynes, 2011 [1919]: 28-41). These provisions were explicitly geared at the destruction of Germany's oversees commerce and wealth, and her domestic industrial production (ibid). It effectively imposed a large sovereign debt on Germany that significantly curtailed her sovereignty. The Treaty can also be rightly interpreted as the most venomous form of emulation, given that Germany was at the time the Continent's first industrial power, to which her neighbors were playing catch up.[10] The Treaty essentially gave countries like France and Italy the time and supplies to emulate the industrial prowess that Germany had developed over the previous decades, apart from laying the ideological foundations for the Second World War. This historical excerpt portrays how capital can be understood to possess a nationality in practical affairs and how, when deemed appropriate, this nationality can be legally confiscated and replaced.[11]

---

[10] France was one of the three principal parties involved in the drafting of the Treaty, alongside Britain and the United States (Keynes, 2011 [1919], chapters III and IV).

[11] Concerning Germany's overseas possessions, Keynes writes: "…not only are German sovereignty and German influence extirpated from the whole of her former overseas possessions, but the persons and property of her nationals resident or owning property in those parts are deprived of *legal status* and *legal security*" (2011 [1919]: 29, emphasis added).

2.2 The "home bias"

The emulation principle offers one important link between capital and the nation, which is mediated by the *state,* as policymaker and national economic coordinator. The second feature of capital's rooted nationality moves us from the state to the individual capitalist and private corporation. It is represented through the "home bias" of capital investment.

This home bias is most easily seen in the behavior of private corporations, for whom "home" is defined as the countries where ownership of the corporation resides – that is, in the countries their top decision makers are nationals of. Therefore, one of the most visible examples of the home bias is in the appointment of top executives to the corporation. Even when companies are acquired by or merge with foreign firms, it is the nationality composition of the board of directors and principal shareholders that matters for determining the *de facto* nationality of a firm. For developed country corporations, the nationality of top decision makers then becomes important for determining the location of key productive activities, such as high-end research and development and high-skilled manufacturing. The home bias is strong for the former in shielding it from foreigners, while the latter answers to a home bias in a more political sense – when having to close down production units or lay-off workers, corporations are prone to it last at "home". The fact that still only around a third of the output of U.S.-based manufacturing firms is done abroad or that the figure is close to ten percent for Japanese firms, speaks for itself (Chang, 2011).

Some of these decisions may be more political (avoiding a backlash from unions, domestic citizens or governments) than economic, but this does not conceal the corporate drive to maximize global profits. Indeed, this motive is present in decisions to separate the legal domicile of a company from its operations headquarters, through "holding companies" registered in low tax jurisdictions like Amsterdam, Dublin or Luxembourg. Despite the confusion that this adds to the calculation of a corporation's "home", the bias can be tracked from following the income flows in national accounts. To take illustrative examples, the value of Ireland's national income is only about 80 percent of the value of its domestic production, while in Luxembourg the figure is roughly 66 percent (Zucman, 2013b). This means that approximately one fifth of Irish GDP and one third of Luxembourg's GDP leave the countries in repatriated income each year. This is income going to foreign expatriate workers, owners of foreign banks, foreign corporations, domestically registered holding companies of foreign corporations and foreign clients of domestically registered hedge funds, in other words capital flows that, instead of staying in these countries, return to *the home* of their owners.

The existence of a home-country bias is not a coincidence. It is likely to have deep moral, economic and historical motives. It is quite normal for capitalists to have moral sentiments towards the society that has allowed them to build their individual wealth or corporate enterprises. There is thus a temporal reciprocity, which is a proximate idea to that developed by Adam Smith in his lesser referred to book, *The Theory of Moral Sentiments* (1759). At the level of the TNC, there is also an economic motive to the home bias, in that there is a certain category of capabilities and productive networks that require 'a conducive institutional environment', and thus "tend to stay at home" (Chang, 2011: 82). For most TNCs these usually relate to skilled workers, networks of suppliers, financial intermediaries, business networks, organizational routine and legal practice. For individual, risk-averse investors it is knowledge asymmetries related to legal practice, taxation, and institutional risk that seem to explain the observed home bias in the asset portfolios of developed country citizens, even when a foreign bias has been estimated to be more profitable (Coeurdacier and Rey, 2013). This is reflected by the popular investments in government bonds and U.S. Treasury bills by own nationals or nationals of similar countries. Here, the "home bias" can the understood as a portfolio bias towards the debt of "safe" countries, which are usually those whose laws and economic climate one is familiar with. For citizens of the rich world, this is usually their home country or countries from similar geopolitical regions.

These type of arguments were well understood back in the 18th century, when merchants preferred a home market to employ their capital because they had greater oversight of their investment, they were more acquainted with business networks of their home country and ultimately with its laws. This was especially true in cases when merchants needed to seek redress for damages or malpractice of any kind. It was Adam Smith, writing in the

18th century, who understood this best. In his highly cited (but seldom read) book, *The Wealth of Nations*, Smith highlights how capital is drawn towards its equilibrium, which he defines to be the home of the capitalist:

> "Home is in this manner the center, if I may say so, round which the capitals of the inhabitants of every country are continually circulating, and towards which they are always tending (...)" (1976 [1776], IV ii: 455).

It is primarily in the context of capitalists favoring domestic industry that Smith uses his now famous metaphor of the "invisible hand". And it is by relying on the institutional safety and geographic proximity of the home market that produces the greatest gain for the capitalist and the national economy:

> "By preferring the support of domestic to that of foreign industry, he intends only his own security; and by directing that industry in such a manner as its produce may be of the greatest value, he intends only his own gain, and he is in this, as in many other eases, led by an invisible hand to promote an end which was no part of his intention" (ibidem: 456).

Smith was well aware of the economic benefits of patriotism in production and commerce. Indeed, a plausible interpretation of the context in which Smith uses the term "invisible hand" is to validate the emulation principle discussed above (Reinert, 2009). The only time the term is employed for illustrative purposes in his book is to acknowledge a form of import substitution, characteristic of the mercantilist strategy. It could only have been possible for an English capitalist to derive the greatest value from supporting domestic industry if English consumers preferred domestically produced goods to foreign goods. And this could only be the case if domestic industry was adequately protected and developed so as to serve these local demands[12]. This evidences how the home bias and the emulation

---

[12] Reinert (2009) argues that this logic may explain why Smith, deep down, regarded the Navigation Acts – a body of laws designed to protect the English shipping industry and foreign trade – as "perhaps, the wisest of all the commercial regulations

principle are intrinsically linked in uncovering the effective nationality of capital.

The home bias of individual capitalists and private corporations has its own history and motives. However, we should not forget the particular history of a state involved in institutionalizing the home bias of capital through citizenship-based taxation. This is the case of the government of the United States, which in principle taxes its citizens, whether they are residents or not, on their global income sourced from their financial/real estate capital and their labour (Kirsch, 2007). The history of this legislation provides an example of a national constitution recognizing the claim that a sovereign state has on the capital of its nationals, living at home or abroad. This was historically defended on the grounds that U.S. nationality continues to afford its beneficiaries protection over their person and property by the U.S. government, whether or not they reside in the country (ibidem). It could be argued that all sovereign governments tax their citizens' capital income (through property taxes, capital acquisition taxes, capital gains taxes, wealth taxes, etc.), albeit not of nonresidents like the U.S. These governments thus legislate a national claim on the capital of private individuals residing in the country and thus grant capital a quasi-*de jure* nationality. Capitalists may change their place of residence, but their capital, as long as it is declared, retains the nationality of where they are living. But here, skeptics may still point to an auxiliary feature of the globalization argument, which is that there is a substantial and increasing portion of the world's financial wealth that is not declared by being registered in offshore accounts in tax havens.

3. Naturalizing capital

Despite attempts to legislate the nationality of capital through the tax law or through property law, these are exceptions that largely prove that nationality remains *de facto* (whatever the arguments made by globalization enthusiasts). Once we recognize this, two questions then arise: should we care about giving capital a quasi- *de jure* nationality, and, if so, how should we go about it?

---

of England" (Smith, 1976, IV ii: 465).

The above analysis revealed the motives, both historical and current, that have tended capital towards a nationality in practice. But in some instances, where these motives were once strong they are now weak. For example, the emulation principle is more a relic of history than a key pillar in current economic policymaking. Among the current advanced economies, it is evident that emulation saturation has kicked in some time ago. Tax competitiveness is now the strategy of the period, which is fuelled by the emergence of tax havens, and ultimately leads to a "race-to-the-bottom" mentality. Moreover, international organizations such as the IMF, the World Bank or the World Trade Organization – which are principally governed by the advanced economies – have been anti-emulation for much of their existence (see Chang 2007).[13] The policy advice thus imparted by these organizations to the developing world has been that the state should not seek to build up its claims on national capital through nationalizations or high taxation of any kind.

The strength of the home bias argument today is also compromised by the fact, already alluded to, that an increasing amount of national capital is unrecorded in tax havens. Currently, this hidden capital has been estimated to represent approximately 8 percent of the global financial wealth of households (Zucman, 2013a, see Figure 1 in the Appendix below). The estimated order of magnitude for Europe is 10 percent (see Figure 2, in the Appendix). This implies that national authorities cannot determine who owns the 5 to 8 trillion euros worth of wealth that is managed by hedge funds and investment societies in places like Switzerland, the Cayman Islands, Luxembourg, Singapore, etc. These are substantial sums of money. For example, Zucman's estimates equate to roughly twice the value of French GDP in 2013. This hidden wealth of nations has two direct implications.

The first relates to a puzzle in international macroeconomics. In the official data, the rich world seems to be a large net debtor to the rest of the world, determined in large part by the negative net positions of Europe and the U.S, as depicted in Figure 1.[14] Yet the explanations for this imbalance remain

---

[13] The psychology is self-evident: the idea that developing countries should be fostered to emulate the advanced economies does not sit well with the latter, for competitive reasons, given that they are at the technological frontier.

[14] This means that foreigners own more assets in Europe and the U.S. than what

obscure, despite efforts linking U.S. net debt with Chinese exports and savings. The emerging view is that external debts are in rich countries (with the exception of Japan) and that developing countries like China are increasingly "owning the world" (Zucman, 2013a). However, accounting for the unrecorded wealth in tax havens, and making plausible assumptions of regarding the origins of this wealth, turns the Eurozone from the world's second largest net debtor into a net creditor, and significantly improves the U.S. net position. Given worries about the sustainability of global imbalances, these results would suggest that the necessary adjustment is not as large as the official data state (ibid).

The second implication relates to the annual cost of bank secrecy from a public finance perspective, and is in many ways more pertinent. The estimated annual loss in fiscal receipts to the world's governments is around 190 billion dollars, which represents the sum of the non-declared portion of the capital located in tax havens that avoids paying an income tax (on interests and dividends), an inheritance tax or a wealth tax (see Figure 3, in the Appendix). Again, to put this cost into perspective, without the tax evasion that such bank secrecy permits, in the case of France, its public debt in 2013 would not have been 94 percent of GDP, but 70 percent of GDP, the level observed before the recent financial crisis (Zucman, 2013b).[15] Here the issue of sovereign debt sustainability in Europe is turned on its head when the hidden wealth of European countries is made public.

In the face of the threat that tax evasion and bank secrecy pose for welfare states in the developed world as well as for the development strategies of currently developing countries (constrained by tax havens and policy conditionality by the international economic organizations), it would seem wise to consider proposals that seek to give capital a legally recognized and binding attachment to its country of origin. Naturalizing capital in this way must go beyond considerations to legislate corporate personhood, or capital

---

Europeans and North Americans own in foreign countries. Thus the net foreign asset position (foreign assets minus foreign liabilities) is negative.
[15] These figures should be treated as a lower bound, given that they exclude the indirect fiscal cost of the substantial reduction in rates that top income, capital and inheritance taxes have experienced over the previous decades in order to precisely ease the flight of national capital to tax havens (Zucman, 2013b). This is exemplary of the "race-to-the-bottom" economic strategy highlighted above.

personhood. The U.S. has been one of the few countries to have legally interpreted "corporate personhood" from its constitution (Bloch and Lamoreaux, 2014), yet it has apparently not prevented a continuous increase in the share of tax havens in U.S. total corporate profits and corporate profits made abroad, since the 1980s (see Figures 4 and 5 in the Appendix). States should instead pursue a plan that ultimately places a nationality on all capital, wherever it is located. This would help countries combat tax evasion as well as giving their development strategies more flexibility and sovereignty.

Although he does not phrase it thus, Gabriel Zucman's proposal for the automatic exchange of bank information – that is, the end of bank secrecy – to be encouraged through commercial sanctions by regional coalitions on non-cooperating countries and verified by a "world financial registry" under the supervision of an international public organization has all the ingredients of a binding naturalization of financial capital. The proposal is realistic and adequate for its intended purpose of combating tax evasion (but also for its indirect consequence of naturalizing capital). A world financial registry would in effect identify the owners and jurisdiction (i.e. nationality) of all global financial assets in circulation, allowing national fiscal administrations to verify that their contributors have honestly declared all their financial assets inscribed in the registry.[16]

Legislating the nationality of capital through this registry would be facilitated by the creation of a global tax on capital, withheld at source by say the IMF on behalf of the individual countries. The rate of this tax could be around the 2 percent mark, or at least over and above the highest national rate observed. It would act as a sufficient constraint against financial opacity, since the tax would only be reimbursed to the proprietaries of the assets once they declare these assets on their tax form in their home countries, thus allowing states to preserve their fiscal sovereignty.[17]

---

[16] Such a proposal is not necessarily "utopian", as similar types of registries are already in existence, though managed by different private entities, such as the Depository Trust Corporation in the U.S., Clearstream in Luxembourg, Euroclear France, etc. The aim would be to unite the dispersed registries that exist into a global registry supervised by an international public body like the IMF (Zucman, 2013b).

[17] This reimbursement clause would also be a constraint against the use of trusts, foundations and "sociétés-écrans" by individuals in order to conceal their identity.

For countries that already have a wealth tax, as is the case of France, their taxpayers would be reimbursed the difference between what is withheld at source by the IMF and what is due to the fiscal authorities in their home countries[18] – in the case of France, for example, the wealthiest contributors subject to the highest rate of the national wealth tax (ISF) at 1,5 percent, would be reimbursed 0,5 percent, assuming that the global rate is 2 percent. The citizens not subject to any rate under the ISF would be reimbursed the entirety of the 2 percent (Zucman, 2013b: 103-104).

A global tax on capital may also facilitate or motivate countries that currently do not have a progressive wealth tax to create one, without fearing capital flight. Thus the complementary tools of a world financial registry and a global tax on capital have the opportunity to return to states the national sovereignty that they have increasingly lost to the financial industry. However, this would not prevent individuals, outside of U.S. citizens, from changing their place of residence to tax havens, so as to escape their national country tax burdens. In this case, countries could follow the U.S. by implementing citizenship taxation, whereby tax liability would follow the passport and not the place of residence. Under this legal framework, individuals would be taxed on their global income according to the rates and schedules applied in their home country, but would be compensated, via tax credits, the amount of personal tax paid to foreign governments in whose country they reside (Kirsch, 2007).[19]

Beyond proposals to naturalize financial capital, there are also proposals to naturalize nonfinancial (or corporate) capital. The present design of the corporate tax system among countries is such that corporations are able to

---

[18] Hence the importance of setting a global rate higher than the highest rate observed at any national level, so as to detract as far as possible individuals that desire to conceal their financial wealth.

[19] In effect, the tax due by the individual would be the difference between the tax liability of the country of nationality and the tax liability of the country of residence. This would also work for individuals with multiple legally recognized nationalities. The tax due would be the difference between the tax liability of the country of residence and the liability of the country with the highest rates the individual is a nationality of, in the case that they are different to the country of residence. These rules would reverse the downward pressure on fiscal regimes, as it would provide guarantees and incentives for countries to apply higher tax burdens on their more affluent citizens without fearing their relocation.

optimize where they want their profits to appear by taking advantage of "judicial subtleties", in an operation known as "transfer pricing" (Zucman, 2013b: 107). This operation brings tax havens once more into the foreground, as they are often the preferred locations where corporations set up subsidiaries so as to overprice other subsidiaries located in high tax countries for products or services bought by the latter. In this way profits may appear on the books of the subsidiaries located in the Cayman Islands, in Bermuda, Luxembourg or in Ireland, instead of in France, Japan or the United States (Figure 5 illustrates this for the U.S.). As is evident, such a price manipulation can have substantial fiscal costs.[20]

All this quasi-legal optimization is facilitated by the very design of a corporate tax system that seeks to tax each company's profits country by country. A more effective design would be to tax the *global* profits of corporations and distribute the receipts to the countries according to the proportion of sales they represent in the total sales of the corporation, or either according to each countries' weight in the payroll of the corporation or the capital used in production, which are plausible proxies for where most of the value-added is created. Each country would then be free to tax these profits at the rate they wish (Zucman, 2013b: 109).

A world registry, similar to the one described for financial assets, could even be formed for the activity of TNCs, which would detail the global profits of corporations and the geographical distribution of their sales, payroll and value of productive capital. An international public body like the United Nations could also manage this registry. With such a formula, a naturalization of corporate capital could effectively be achieved, whereby most of the tax revenues would likely flow to the countries whose corporate capital (i.e. corporation) is headquartered in, as was argued in section 2.2 above.

The proposals just described are clear indications of an implicit desire to give financial and corporate capital a quasi-*de jure* nationality in a world where financial opacity has threatened much of the viability of welfare state

---

[20] Estimates on U.S. data suggest that transfer pricing reduce corporate tax receipts by 30 percent (Clausing, 2011).

politics in developed countries and development strategies in developing countries.

Conclusion

This chapter sought to scrutinize the question of whether capital really has a nationality and thus whether states really have sovereignty. It can be concluded from the preceding analysis that despite the best efforts by globalization enthusiasts to claim that capital operates with disregard to nations, and despite the growing relevance of tax havens, economic and financial capital (both assets and debts) has always been, and continues to be, deeply attached to nations – hence its *de facto* nationality. This nationality is filtered through the nationality of the owners and managers of capital. The history of capitalism, as portrayed in the acts and writings of its associated policymakers and scholars, provides illuminating examples of this logic at work – from the state-led development process of industrializing nations encapsulated in the principle of emulation, to the private capitalist's preference for the safety of and familiarity with his home country's laws and networks.

Therefore, capital has always come with a symbolic stamp of nationality attached to it, much in the same way as minted coins have always come with the mark of their home country on them. Even in our age of increased financialization and dissimulation, capitalists are still keen to hold a large bulk of their capital within the confines of their national jurisdiction – after all the share of tax havens in global financial wealth barely reaches double digits. Nevertheless, their increasing trends motivated this essay to suggest proposals to combat the harm that they pose to global balance sheet accounting and to the public finances. In their very nature, these proposals also end up "naturalizing" capital. This is founded on the basis that capital currently has no binding obligation to fully disclose its *de facto* nationality, whose organic roots have a long history but remain visible and relevant nonetheless.

References

Bloch, R. H., Lamoreaux, N. R. (2014) Corporations and the Fourteenth Amendment. *Yale Working Papers*. USA.

Braudel, F. (1979) *Civilisation matérielle, Economie et Capitalisme, XVᵉ-XVIIIᵉ Siècle, Tome 2: Les Jeux de l'Echange*. Paris: Armand Colin.

Chang, H. J. (2007) *Bad Samaritans*. London: Random House Press.

Chang, H. J. (2011) *23 Things They Don't Tell You About Capitalism*. London: Penguin Books.

Clausing, K. A. (2011) The Revenue Effects of Multinational Income Shifting. *Tax Notes*, March 28.

Coeurdacier, N., Rey, H. (2013) Home Bias in Open Economy Financial Macroeconomics, *Journal of Economic Literature*, 51 (1), pp. 63-115.

Eatwell, J., Taylor L. (2000). *Global Finance at Risk*. Cambridge: Polity Press.

Hirschman, A. (1977) *The Passions and the Interests: Political Arguments for Capitalism before Its Triumph*. Princeton: Princeton University Press.

Keynes, J. M. (2011) *The Economic Consequences of the Peace* [1919]. New York: Digireads Publishing.

Kirsch, S. M. (2007) Taxing Citizens in a Global Economy. *Scholarly Works. Paper* 547.

Magnusson, L. (1994) *Mercantilism: The Shaping of an Economic Language*. London and New York: Routledge.

Minksy, H. (1992) Reconstituting the United States' Financial Structure: Some fundamental issues. *Working Paper* 69. Annandale-on-Hudson, NY: Levy Economics Institute of Bard College.

Piketty, T. (2013) *Le capital au XXIe siècle*, Paris: Ed. du Seuil.

Reinert, S. E. (2009) Emulation versus Comparative Advantage: Competing and Complementary Principles in the History of Economic Policy. *Working Papers in Technology Governance and Economic Dynamics,* No. 25.

Schumpeter, J. A. (1954) *History of Economic Analysis*. Oxford, Oxford University Press.

Smith, A. (2010) [1759] *The Theory of Moral Sentiments*. London: Penguin Classics.

Smith, A. (1976) [1776] *An Inquiry into the Nature and Causes of the Wealth of Nations*. Oxford University Press.

Tobin, J. (1978) A Proposal for International Monetary Reform. *Eastern Economic Journal*, 4 (3-4), Jul. - Oct., pp. 153-159.

Ventura, J., Voth, H-J. (2015) Debt into Growth: How Sovereign Debt Accelerated the First Industrial Revolution, *Barcelona GSE Working Paper Series*, No. 830, Spain.

Weil, P. (2011) From conditional to secured and sovereign: The new strategic link between the citizen and the nation-state in a globalized world. *International Journal of Constitutional Law*, 9 (3–4), pp. 615–635.

Zucman, G. (2013a) The Missing Wealth of Nations: Are Europe and the U.S. Net Debtors or Net Creditors?, *The Quarterly Journal of Economics* (2013), pp. 1321–1364.

Zucman, G. (2013b) *La Richesse Cachée des Nations*, Paris: Le Seuil.

Zucman, G. (2014) Taxing Across Borders: Tracking Personal Wealth and Corporate Profits. *Journal of Economic Perspectives*, 28 (4), pp. 121-148.

Zucman, G. (2015) *The Hidden Wealth of Nations: The Scourge of Tax Havens*, Chicago: University of Chicago Press.

Appendix

Figure 1 Recorded net assets of the rich world and estimated unrecorded assets held in tax havens

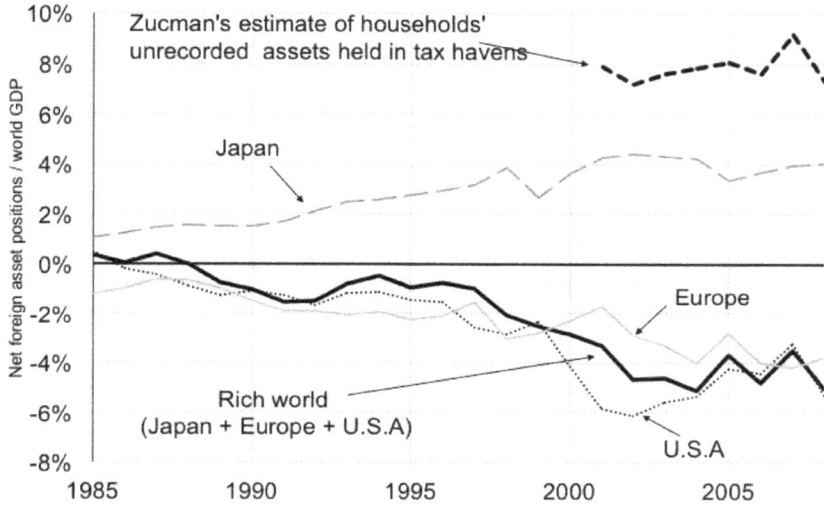

Source: Zucman (2013a).

Figure 2 The wealth of Europeans held in tax havens (% European financial wealth)

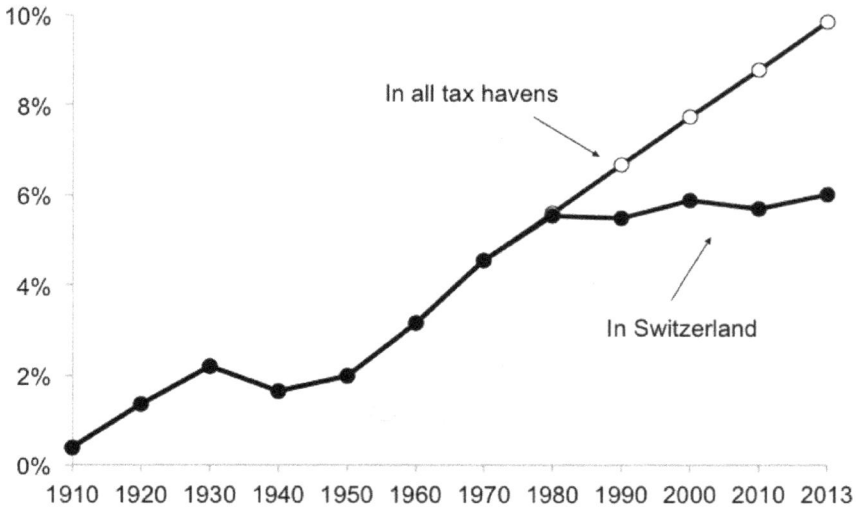

Source: Zucman (2015)

Figure 3 The global cost of offshore evasion (2014)

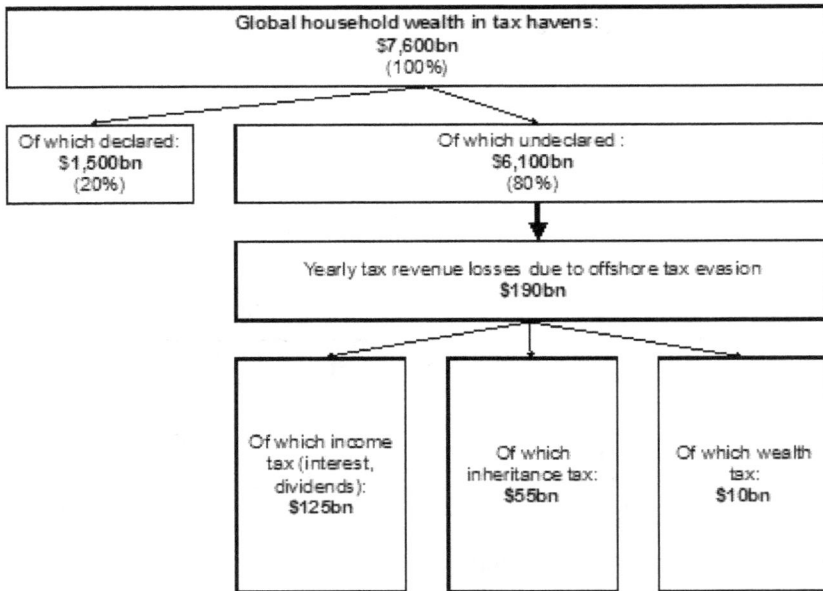

Source: Zucman (2015)

Figure 4. The share of tax havens in US Corporate profits.

Source: Zucman (2014)

Figure 5 The Share of tax haven in US corporate profits made abroad.

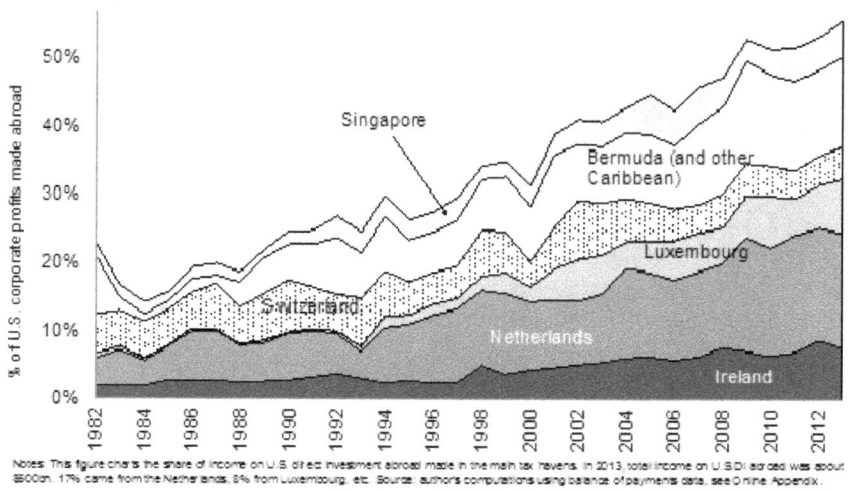

Source: Zucman (2014)

Part V
Conclusion

Moving forward

Gerson P. Lima and Maria Alejandra Madi

Main conclusions

The contributions presented in this book focus on the theoretical analysis and empirical discussions about the contemporary relations among the inflated financial markets, the low investment trends and the changes in the patterns of production and employment.

In Part II, Richard Koo, Arthur Hermann and Maria Alejandra Madi call for more realism in economic analysis in order to cope with the economic and social challenges of our times.

Richard Koo closes his chapter warning that, in current Western societies, the economic profession must realize the following problems: i) the existence of investment opportunities and willing borrowers should never be taken for granted; ii) shortages of borrowers have always been a bigger problem for growth; iii) it was no longer the case that everybody in society was benefiting from growth. Indeed, he calls for a rethinking of macroeconomics since, at the most fundamental level, the economics profession needs to confront the problems head-on instead of making facile assumptions (such as those of mainstream economics) about "trend growth rates". In Koo's view, this is true especially in countries that are in balance sheet recessions or are being pursued from behind, a group that includes every advanced country in the world today.

Reinforcing the challenges to achieve full employment, and economic and social progress, Arthur Hermann addresses the relevance of theories inspired in John Maynard Keynes' theoretical contribution that provide important elements for a more realistic account of the actual working of economic systems and a more effective policy action. In his view, a more far-reaching theoretical background would foster a better coordination of

347

many relevant dimensions of policy action. Among others, Hermann mentions macroeconomic policies targeted at driving effective demand to the level of full employment mainly by means of a balanced public spending; in addition to progressive taxation, a permanent low level of interest rate and a reform of the banking system. In following these policies, structural transformations of the system towards individual and social progress should also be considered.

Complementing the analysis of the current macroeconomic challenges, mainly related to short-termism in investment trends, with a microeconomic approach of business strategies and working conditions, the contribution by Maria Alejandra Madi concludes that in the current global investment scenario, the apprehension of the meaning and dynamics of the recent spread of private equity finance is crucial to the understanding of the social impacts of the evolution of contemporary capitalism. The practices of the private equity firms have revealed increasing social vulnerability favoured by institutionalized short-termism in the workplace and in society. Indeed, under the euphemism of "rationalization strategies", the private equity business model aims to increase short-term profits. The financial practices of the private equity funds are, in truth, mechanisms that promote the expansion of the global financial markets with decisive effects on wealth, income growth and working conditions. As a result, the effects of the financial strategies at the core of workplace have added deep pressures on workers and trade unions. In fact, changing working conditions have become a constant feature of today's global business restructuring. Considering the current investment and technological scenario and its outcomes in terms of labour challenges, Madi concludes that, in the near future, workers will be increasingly polarized into two forces: on one side, an elite that controls and manages the high-tech and financial global economy; and on the other side, a growing number of displaced workers who have few prospects for meaningful job opportunities.

The author's conclusions, in Part III, highlight the need to rethink practical actions toward changes in the policy agenda in order to achieve realistic programs that could promote progressive economic policies.

C.R. Yadu and B. Satheesha's main conclusion is that financialization of land is the channel through which neo-liberalism and remittance inflows affected the wealth distribution in Kerala. Indeed, the concentration of wealth in the hands of the richest is associated with an increase in the share of land in their asset portfolio and the decline in the share of the poorest class. The authors call for changes in the economic policy agenda in order to bring back the relevance of "redistribution policies". If not, the current regime of accumulation will spell doom for Kerala's economically and socially marginalized. Apart from Piketty's (2014) suggestion of a global wealth tax, Yadu and Satheesha highlight the need for a second set of land reforms in Kerala, filling the gaps of the land reform of 1970.

Taking into account the British experience, Lyn Eynon recognizes the influence of the few super-rich on the economic policy. However, he states that the main issue at stake is the practical problem of defining a realistic program offering genuine progress in contemporary Britain. This program should have both sufficient credibility to attract both electoral backing and active support against hostility from global elites. Indeed, Eynon reveals the political tensions inherent to economic policy decisions that reflect differences in policy formation: a top-down view in which proposals are developed by politicians advised by experts versus a bottom-up view emphasizing engagement and debate through democratic structures. After a deep and detailed analysis of the British experience, Eynon concludes that the main issue at stake is not about excluding politicians or rejecting expertise, but demands an interactive relationship with both members and communities or workplaces. And the author adds that, on economic policy there is the need to search for consensus, even if differences will remain.

Part IV calls for rethinking the theoretical background in economics in order to effectively move towards progressive economic policies that could enhance social justice.

John Komlos proposes a rethinking of the theoretical concepts in labor economics and, as a result, of the policy actions toward unemployment that has a destabilizing effect on society both politically and socially. In his view, a realistic economic theory should liberate itself from the commitment to the concept of the natural rate of unemployment as particularly important in light of the "jobless recovery" in the wake of the Great Recession. Besides, given the trends of globalization and technological change that diminished considerably the demand for unskilled labor in the developed world, full employment will otherwise continue to elude us forever. Indeed, Komlos call for a theoretical and empirical reflection on the current challenges of work, unemployment and progress in order to build alternative economic thinking. According to Komlos, work is important also from a psychological perspective: unemployment is degrading and diminishes self-esteem. As a result, the main problem to focus on is that the opportunity to work is extremely unevenly distributed across the labour force. As a result, in the attempt to face unemployment, it would be important to introduce different shock absorbers into the labour market to distribute the available work in a more equitable fashion instead of the crude binary system we have today. Komlos's proposal aims to create an inclusive labor market and envisions a just economy.

Gerson P. Lima also stresses the mistaken mainstream economic policy and calls for a rethinking of the foundations of the dynamics of macroeconomics. In his view, the economic policy has been commanded by the central banks' shareholders, since the supposed core of the democratic political power, the Congress, transferred to them the exclusive political power of printing money. In this scenario, it may be expected that whoever has the power of printing money do it for the own sake and who has sufficient money has the power to buy everything one desires, like a powerful army, a communication vehicles worldwide system, the pharmaceutical industry, universities, economic think tanks, man's conscience, convenient laws and everything else needed to create and sustain a convenient economic policy to be used to assure whatever the one's ends may be. So, the contribution of economics to a democratic economic policy should be a sound real world economic theory. Therefore, Lima's theoretical and empirical attempt to present a modern version of an old theory inspired in statements by Marshall and Keynes, shows that, in reality, uncontrolled exogenous variables move the crossing point continuously. Therefore, supply and demand is a non-equilibrating system and the method used to estimate the curves takes this condition into account, thus providing a theoretical equilibrium solution that allows for a scientific analysis, and not a pretending real world solution. Lima's main conclusion is that the neoclassical demand and supply indoctrination based on unsustainable assumptions are convenient to the monetary mainstream economic policy dominance. Based on the result of the experiment on the US Economy described in his chapter, Lima adds that the main features of the mainstream economic policy agenda in terms of monetary policy and public debt reveal that the persistence in maintaining the mainstream monetarist economic policy may foster more social injustice. In short, Lima warns that the replacement of the monetarist mainstream economics looks indispensable to "Bend the Arc of Global Capital Toward Justice".

Finally, at the core of the discussions about the current theoretical challenges in Economics are the interactions between capital, nationality and state sovereignty. In this respect, Morgan-Milá shows that the challenging conventional viewpoint that capital has no nationality implies limited state sovereignty with regards to fiscal policy and developmental strategies. The author concludes that despite the best efforts by globalization enthusiasts to claim that capital operates with disregard to nations, and despite the growing relevance of tax havens, economic and financial capital (both assets and debts) has always been, and continues to be, deeply attached to nations – hence its *de facto* nationality. In short, this nationality is filtered through the nationality of the owners and managers of capital. As a result, capital has always come with a symbolic stamp of nationality. Even in our age of increased financialization, capitalists are still keen to hold a large bulk of their capital within the confines of their national jurisdiction – after all the share of tax havens in global financial wealth barely reaches double digits. After evaluating various proposals to "quasi-naturalize" capital for the benefit of state sovereignty in the 21st century, Morgan-Milá proposes a world financial registry that would in effect identify the owners and jurisdiction (i.e. nationality) of all global financial assets in circulation, allowing national fiscal administrations to preserve their sovereignty.

Steps forward

The attempt of economists to rethink the relations between Economics and Democracy is not new. For instance, Edward Fullbrook, one of the founders of the World Economics Association, once stated that:

> "So long as the country's university economics departments are allowed to be operated as political propaganda centres and one-paradigm closed-shops, successive generations of citizens, including journalists and politicians, will be indoctrinated in the Neoclassical-Neoliberal creed. This situation is not compatible with normal ideas of democracy" (Fullbrook, 2007).

More recently, a proposal to deal with this challenge has been launched in the book *The Econocracy - The perils of leaving economics to the experts*, by Joe Earle, Cahal Moran and Zach Ward-Perkins (2016). The authors are three founding members of the Post-Crash Economics Society at the University of Manchester. In the Introduction of their book, they define Econocracy explaining that

> "An econocracy has all the formal institutions of a representative democracy – like political parties and regular elections– but the goals politics seeks to achieve are defined in narrow economic terms and conducted without significant public oversight. Of course, some areas of politics, like war and national security, aren't justified in terms of their effect on the economy, but the overall trend of reducing politics to economics is clear... Such a democratic deficit leads to a system where some people have economic authority without public oversight" (Earle, Moran and Ward-Perkins, 2016, Introduction).

Indeed, this book *Capital and Justice* is a contribution to the current debate. It has been organized with some questions in mind: Which are the main topics to be addressed in the understanding of the current economic, social and political challenges to build a just society? If all of our desired reforms toward justice are actually implemented what will capitalism look like? Will be really achieved social justice? In spite of the progressive attempts, will there be vestiges of the old regime? How can we bend the arc of global capital toward justice?

Although many difficult questions still surround the reflection about a just economy, the book provides a framework for addressing relevant topics. The current global economic scenario leads to slow growth and a quite concentrated income and wealth distribution. As a result, one of the main topics at stake is the manifest conflict between capitalism and democracy.

Besides, other topic underlined throughout the book is that the economics profession in the 21st century requires a radical change in thinking Economics. New theoretical approaches and policies are needed in order to improve the understanding of the deep interactions between economics and the political forces in order to build social justice.

Nowadays, the absence or deficit of democracy also depends on the economic policy decision making process- mainly based on mainstream economic proposals. Indeed, the outcomes of monetary policy in the Western World have been an efficient instrument of income transfer from the bottom that works to the top where some people "have economic authority". Although public oversight is not sufficient to eliminate the democratic deficit, at best it may reduce the negative social consequences of the economic policy decisions that have favored people at the top.

This book is certainly an attempt to deepen the critique of mainstream economic theory and policy proposals and to illuminate the path in rethinking and reconceptualizing real-world economics. We hope the book will stimulate further debate among students, professional economists and social scientists – whether academics or not – on how to progress towards rethinking the relations between economics, justice and democracy, that is, between economics and politics.

Therefore, closing this book is a call for action for real world economists to join efforts in order for further developing "the" **real world economic theory** that leads to a **democratic and progressive economic policy**. As Lyn

Eynon notes, we need a new economic agenda "with sufficient credibility to attract both electoral backing and active support to resist the hostility from global elite's selfishness".

References

Earle, J., Moran, C. and Ward-Perkins, Z. (2016) *The econocracy - The perils of leaving economics to the experts*. Manchester, UK: Manchester University Press.

Fullbrook, E. (2007). "Economics and Neoliberalism" In: G. Hassan, ed., *After Blair: Politics After the New Labour Decade*. 1st ed., London: Lawrence & Wishart, pp. 160-72.

About the editors and authors

Gerson P. Lima is PhD in Economic Theory by the University of Paris X (1992). Before assuming academic positions, he was a leading real world economist at some private companies and public institutions. After getting the PhD degree, he became professor of macroeconomics (graduate and post-graduate courses) at the Federal University of Paraná, while he also served the Economics Teaching Committee of the Federal Government, the National Association of Post-graduate Courses in Economics, and the Regional Professional Economists Council as vice-President. Currently, retired from the Federal University of Paraná, he develops consultancy activies and also publishes papers and book chapters as a result of his reseach interests. His major contribution to economic theory and teaching, the textbook *Economics, Money and Political Power* (in Portuguese) has been successfully used to teach real world Economics to non-economics students at private colleges.

Maria Alejandra Madi holds a PhD in Economics, UNICAMP, Brazil. Former professor and researcher at the State University of Campinas in Brazil (1983-2012), her career includes visiting professorships at the University of Manitoba (2008) and the University of Kassel (2010) and a position of Avocational Lecturer at Steinbes University Berlin (2014-2015). Currently, she is Chair of the World Economics Association (WEA) Conferences and Assistant Editor of the *International Journal of Pluralism and Economics Education*. She co-edited some of the Green Economic Institute books, including *The Greening of Global Finance* and *The Greening of Latin America*. More recently, she has co-edited the WEA book *The Economics Curriculum: towards a radical reformulation* and *Ideas towards a new international financial architecture?* Her latest books include *Global Finance and Development* and *Small Business in Brazil: competitive global challenges*. She blogs at WEA Pedagogy Blog and at Real-World Economics Review Blog.

Richard C. Koo is the Chief Economist of Nomura Research Institute. Best known for developing the concept of balance sheet recession, which is now widely used around the world to explain post-1990 Japanese and post-2007 Western economies, he has also advised successive prime ministers on how best to deal with Japan's economic and banking problems. Before joining Nomura, he was an economist with the Federal Reserve Bank of New York (1981-84) and a Doctoral Fellow of the Board of Governors of the Federal Reserve System (1979-81). Author of many books on Japanese economy and economics in general, he holds BAs in Political Science and Economics from the University of California at Berkeley (1976), and MA in Economics from the Johns Hopkins University (1979). From 1998 to 2010, he was a visiting professor at Waseda University in Tokyo.

Arturo Hermann is a Senior Research Fellow in Economics at the Italian National Institute of Statistics (Istat), Rome, Italy, in his main research fields: Institutional Economics, especially in its "original" tradition, Keynesian and other "non-orthodox" macroeconomic theories, Sustainable Economy and Social Justice, Political Economy. He develops interdisciplinary studies, considering the relations between Economics, Psychology and Psychoanalysis. He has authored five books and numerous articles in scholarly Journals. He is a member of many economics' associations — in particular, AFIT, AHE, AISPE, ASE, EAEPE, ICAPE, STOREP, URPE, WEA, Green Economics Institute — and regularly participates in their Conferences and activities.

C.R. Yadu is a Ph.D student at Centre for Development Studies (CDS), Trivandrum, India. His principal research interests are inequality, agrarian change, and labour relations. His research approaches the economic issues from a political economy perspective. Currently, he works on his Ph.D thesis titled "Agrarian Question and Transition of Rural Labour in India".

B. Satheesha is a Ph.D student at Indian Institute of Technology (IIT), New Delhi, India. His principal research interests are inequality, regional development, and labour migration. His research focuses on using large scale secondary data sets. He is currently working on his Ph.D thesis on rural labour markets in India.

About the editors and authors

Lyn Eynon studied Philosophy, Politics and Economics at Oxford, and then worked for 35 years in IT, most of that time in the telecommunications sector, where he was a union representative at local and national levels. Like many others, he rejoined the Labour Party in 2015 when the Jeremy Corbyn's leadership campaign reopened the possibility of pursuing socialist policies thereafter many years when that seemed excluded. He is now an independent economist, secretary of his local Labour Party branch and secretary of the Welsh Labour Grassroots / Momentum group in Cardiff, South Wales.

John Komlos is Professor Emeritus of Economics and of Economic History at the University of Munich and is currently visiting professor at Duke University as well as at UNC-Chapel Hill. He has also taught at Harvard University and the University of Vienna. Born in Budapest, he became a refugee and grew up in Chicago, where he received PhDs in both history and in economics from the University of Chicago. His mentor was the Nobel-Prize winning economic historian Robert Fogel. He has written critically of recent economic policies and advocated a humanistic economics in his articles for the PBS blog (http://www.pbs.org). He also teaches a course on the "Economics of Poverty and Inequality" for the African American Studies Department and Duke University.

Marc Morgan-Milá is a Ph.D. candidate at the Paris School of Economics and at L'Ecole des Hautes Etudes en Sciences Sociales (EHESS). He studies economic distribution, considering the personal and functional income distribution, besides the accumulation, composition and distribution of wealth and sectoral balances from historical, political economy, and macroeconomic perspectives. This feeds into his interest on topics related to the distribution of the means of production, such as corporate ownership and property rights over capital. His other research interests include public finance (taxation, public debt, redistributive policies, the European economy), long run development (investment, structural change, political economy of ideas and institutions, macroeconomic theories of development), economic history and the history of economic thought. He holds a B.A. (Hons.) in Economics and Philosophy from Trinity College Dublin and a M.Sc. in Public Policies and Development from the Paris School of Economics and EHESS.